Praise for *Racing Ahead with Reading*

"*Racing Ahead with Reading* is a great textbook that uses a thematic approach to teaching reading skills. These authors should be commended for their hard work and focus on our students of today."

—Dr. Billy Jones, Miami Dade College

"*Racing Ahead with Reading* is an excellent text for a beginning reading class. I would highly recommend it."

—Nancy Wood, University of Arkansas at Little Rock

"It is the kind of book that stimulates enthusiasm and gratitude for our profession and eagerness to share the literature with our students."

—Jordan Fabish, Long Beach City College

"*Racing Ahead with Reading* is a lively and interesting text which readers should enjoy using. It has ample coverage of components and skills, a wide variety of intriguing reading selections, and effective exercises, graphics, and organization. Execution of instructional pedagogy is first rate. I congratulate the authors on a job well done."

—Bob Akin, Houston Community College System

"The book is student-friendly and not as intimidating or imposing as some textbooks. . . . There are appropriate stories, cartoons, poems, graphs, charts, comprehension, and vocabulary exercises, along with written assignments, which would give the instructor more than enough choices to use both in and out of the classroom."

—Jerolynn Roberson, Miami Dade College

"Clear explanations; variety of exercises; conciseness . . . I have not seen another book on the market with as much information as this one."

—Kathleen A. Carlson, Brevard Community College

"I appreciate the inclusion of so many readings that would appeal to various audiences. Instructors have many choices according to the levels and interests of their students."

—Linda Brown, Bainbridge College

"I really like the text for the selections and variety of activities. It is well-organized and definitely would be interesting to the student because of the relevant themes."

—Mary Welborn, Rose State College

McGraw-Hill Companies, Inc.

Racing Ahead with Reading

Racing Ahead with Reading

Peter Mather ◆ **Rita McCarthy**

Retired, Glendale Community College
Glendale, Arizona

Glendale Community College
Glendale, Arizona

McGraw-Hill
Higher Education

Boston   Burr Ridge, IL   Dubuque, IA   New York   San Francisco   St. Louis
Bangkok   Bogotá   Caracas   Kuala Lumpur   Lisbon   London   Madrid   Mexico City
Milan   Montreal   New Delhi   Santiago   Seoul   Singapore   Sydney   Taipei   Toronto

**McGraw-Hill
Higher Education**

Published by McGraw-Hill, an imprint of The McGraw-Hill Companies, Inc., 1221 Avenue
of the Americas, New York, NY 10020. Copyright © 2009. All rights reserved. No part of
this publication may be reproduced or distributed in any form or by any means, or stored
in a database or retrieval system, without the prior written consent of The McGraw-Hill
Companies, Inc., including, but not limited to, in any network or other electronic storage
or transmission, or broadcast for distance learning.

This book is printed on acid-free paper.

1 2 3 4 5 6 7 8 9 0 WCK/WCK 0 9 8

SE ISBN: 978-0-07-304767-6   AIE ISBN: 978-0-07-304769-0
SE MHID: 0-07-304767-8   AIE MHID: 0-07-304769-4

Editor in Chief: *Michael Ryan*
Sponsoring Editor: *John Kindler*
Marketing Manager: *Tamara Wederbrand*
Developmental Editor: *Gillian Cook*
Editorial Coordinator: *Jesse Hassenger*
Production Editor: *Chanda Feldman*
Manuscript Editor: *Jennifer Gordon*
Design Manager: *Preston Thomas*
Text and Cover Designer: *Glenda King*
Art Editor: *Ayelet Arbel*
Photo Research: *Natalia Peschiera, Romy Charlesworth*
Text Permissions Coordinator: *Marty Moga*
Production Supervisor: *Tandra Jorgensen*
Composition: *11/13 Palatino by Newgen*
Printing: *45# New Era Matte Plus, Quebecor-World*

Cover: © Bernardo Bucci/Corbis, Digital Vision/Getty Images

Credits: The credits section for this book begins on page C-1 and is considered an
extension of the copyright page.

Library of Congress Cataloging-in-Publication Data

Mather, Peter.
   Racing ahead with reading / Peter Mather, Rita McCarthy.—1st ed.
      p.   cm.
   Includes index and references.
   ISBN-13: 978-0-07-304767-6; ISBN-10: 0-07-304767-8 (alk. paper)
   ISBN-13: 978-0-07-304769-0; ISBN-10: 0-07-304769-4 (AIE : alk. paper)
   1. Reading (Higher education)—United States.   2. English Language—Rhetoric.
3. Critical thinking—Study and teaching (Higher)—United States.   4. Study skills—
United States.   I. McCarthy, Rita.   II. Title.
   LB2395.3.M80 2008
   428.07′1—dc22   2007051473

The Internet addresses listed in the text were accurate at the time of publication. The
inclusion of a Web site does not indicate an endorsement by the authors or McGraw-Hill,
and McGraw-Hill does not guarantee the accuracy of the information presented at these
sites.

Peter dedicates this book to his late parents,
Carl and Dorothy Mather; and his brother and sister-in-law,
John and Peggy.

Rita dedicates this book to her parents,
Adolph and Bertha; her sons, Ryan and Steve;
her grandchildren, Zachary and Kate,
and especially to her husband, Greg.

About the Authors

Peter Mather—earned a B.A. in government from the University of Redlands; his first M.A., in African studies, from the University of California, Los Angeles; his second M.A., in reading, from California State University, Los Angeles; and his Ed.D. in curriculum and instruction from the University of Southern California. Before retiring from Glendale Community College, he taught at the secondary, adult-education, and community-college levels for over 30 years. While at Glendale Community College, he taught both developmental reading and critical and evaluative reading. He also taught American government and was the college director of the America Reads/ Counts Program. In addition to this textbook, he has been the co-author of three editions of *Reading and All That Jazz* and two editions of *The Art of Critical Reading*.

Rita Romero McCarthy—earned her B.A. in sociology and history from the University of California, Berkeley, and her M.A. in education from Arizona State University. She has taught at the elementary, secondary, adult-education, and community-college levels. For the past 20 years she has taught developmental reading and E.S.L. at Glendale Community College. Ms. McCarthy has published articles in professional journals and other media on the use of bibliotherapy. She has also published reading lists for beginning and remedial readers and is a reading specialist. In addition, she has been the co-author of three editions of *Reading and All That Jazz* and two editions of *The Art of Critical Reading*.

Brief Contents

Contents

Contents xi

Preface to the Instructor

Racing Ahead with Reading is the third book in our series of reading textbooks that include *Reading and All That Jazz* and *The Art of Critical Reading*. While *Jazz* and *Art* are aimed at intermediate and advanced reading students, *Racing* is intended for introductory reading classes.

We feel that students at all levels need to be drawn into the reading process so that they become motivated to read, and this is especially true for college students who are reading at a basic introductory level. The intention of this book is not only to teach students basic reading skills but also to stimulate them to read because "those who don't read are no smarter than those who can't read"—Anonymous. It is for this reason that we include a wide range of stimulating textbook selections, relevant articles from newspapers and magazines, and even some poetry and cartoons. Many of our selections are written by award-winning authors, and our textbook includes readings from both classical and contemporary literature.

Theme and Title

We have chosen the general theme of sports because of the similarities between sports and reading. First, playing any sport requires a knowledge of the basics. Great coaches and managers constantly stress the basics in their particular sport. Basketball coaches often go back to teaching basic dribbling exercises while football coaches may reteach basic tackling techniques even to their college or professional players. Learning to read is similar. Readers need to know such basics as phonics, how to use a dictionary, how to find the main idea in a paragraph or article, the patterns of organization writers use, and the difference between fact and opinion. Because these basic reading skills are so important, we have included separate chapters on each.

Second, any sport requires repetition. It is important not only to learn basic skills but to practice them as well. A shortstop's throw to first base may look easy, but that shortstop has practiced that throw over and over again. Reading is the same. The more you practice a specific skill, the easier that skill becomes. After we introduce each skill, we provide ample exercises for students to practice and master that skill.

Third, all sports require athletes to apply their skills in game situations. A tennis player in a tournament has to know immediately whether to hit a baseline shot or just tap the ball over the net. Because readers need to be able to use all their skills together at one time, we have included readings on which students can practice their new skills. Although we have a loose theme of sports that runs throughout the text, we have also included articles on a variety of other interesting and engaging topics such as bats, memory, and the polygraph machine, as well as humorous articles by Dave Barry and the late Art Buchwald.

Reading Selections

Each chapter includes one or more readings. There are also supplementary readings in the last chapter. Readings were chosen for their broad appeal to students. They have all been successfully field-tested in our classes or in those of our colleagues. The full-color design and color photos add to the attractiveness and appeal of the readings.

We introduce each reading with short sections titled "Getting Focused," "Bio-Sketch," and "Tackling Vocabulary." "Getting Focused" gives students a short introduction to the reading so they have some preliminary background about the topic of the reading. The "Bio-Sketch" gives students information about the author to provide them some insight into the author's point of view. "Tackling Vocabulary" discusses important words and phrases used in the selection with which students might not be familiar.

Various types of follow-up activities appear after each reading. Every reading has a "Comprehension Checkup" section. This includes objective questions such as multiple-choice, true-false, or fill in the blank. "Comprehension Checkup" is usually followed by a vocabulary review section. These vocabulary sections include an assortment of activities including vocabulary in context exercises and crossword puzzles. Sections titled "In Your Own Words" and "Written Assignment" require students to synthesize information, while the "Internet Activity" allows students to further pursue information related to the reading. Margin quotes also encourage students to reflect on what they have read.

Organization of the Text

The text is organized into five parts and eleven chapters.

Part I: Tackling the Basics (Introduction and Warm-Ups 1–4)

Part I introduces students to basic reading skills. It includes a review of phonics, an introduction to word parts, a chapter on using the dictionary, and a chapter on the study skills necessary to be successful in regular college classes. The Introduction is meant to be completed during the first week of class. The questions in it are designed to allow instructors to quickly assess the skills of individual students and the class as a whole.

Part I is designed to be completed in a variety of ways. Some instructors will have students complete only a part of each warm-up, while others will have students complete the material in its entirety. Instructors who feel that their students are already proficient in the basics should feel free to proceed directly to Part II. Some instructors may choose to complete a portion of the warm-ups in conjunction with other chapters in the textbook. In Part I, as with the other parts, instructors should pick and choose the material appropriate for their students and classes.

- The Introduction is meant to present basic reading skills. The two readings are motivational in nature.
- For some students the chapter on phonics will be a review, and for other students, especially students learning English as a second language, this chapter can be an introduction to the sounds of the English language.
- The chapter on study skills introduces students to time management skills, skimming, scanning, and SQ3R, skills necessary for all successful college students.

Part II: Discovering Meaning Through Structure (Chapters 1–4)

This part is directed at helping students learn about the basic structures that authors use in their writing. Two chapters are included to teach students how to identify topics, stated and unstated main ideas, and details. Other chapters in this part deal with the important subjects of identifying an author's purpose and tone and how to recognize transition words and different patterns of organization.

- The chapter on the implied main idea begins with introducing students to paraphrasing.
- The chapter on author's tone and purpose not only introduces students to the three different purposes of writing but also teaches them how to identify an author's tone.

Part III: Interpreting What We Read (Chapters 5–8)

This part emphasizes the interpretive process and introduces students to reading critically. Topics discussed in this part include inference, figurative language, fact and opinion, and bias. It is important that students not only learn to read literally but also learn to read critically.

- The chapter on figurative language includes discussion not only of similes, metaphors, and personification, but also of extended metaphors, symbols, and imagery.
- Chapter 8 on bias includes coverage of bias in advertising as well as in writing.
- Also included are textbook selections that discuss problems with using polygraph machines and the mistakes that eyewitnesses can make in a courtroom.

Part IV: Understanding Textbook Material (Chapters 9–10)

The first chapter of this part teaches students how to read and interpret visual aids while the second chapter introduces students to various study techniques. Students need to learn about the different types of visual aids that are found both in their textbooks and in other media as well. They also need to learn such study skills as highlighting and underlining, annotating, outlining, mapping, and summarizing.

- Each exercise in the visual aid chapter is tied to a reading in the book. Instructors can either teach this chapter as a separate unit or integrate the visual aid exercises into the readings.
- The textbook selection chapter is intended to prepare students for studying for their other classes.

Part V: Supplementary Readings (Chapter 11)

Readings in this part are considered supplementary selections. They can be used in any order if and when the instructor feels it is appropriate to do so. The two themes that organize the readings are "World of Work" and "Relationships and Behavior."

Chapter Organization

Each chapter begins with an overview of the chapter topic and a concise discussion of key terms needed for understanding the topic. This material is followed by clear examples, numerous creative short exercises designed to help students understand and master the topic, and engaging longer reading selections. The exercises in each chapter are sequential, progressing from relatively easy to more difficult. They use many different formats in order to maintain student interest and are designed so that the instructor can have students work on them individually or in groups.

Teaching and Learning Aids Accompanying the Book

Supplements for Instructors

- **Annotated Instructor's Edition**—The AIE includes the full text of the student edition plus answers to objective questions and some suggested answers to open-ended questions.
- **Instructor's Manual and Test Bank**—The Instructor's Manual is available online, is password protected, and can be downloaded to an instructor's personal computer. This resource is written by the authors of the textbook and is a robust resource that provides innovative teaching tips, unit tests, supplementary activities, and useful connections to other resources, such as poems, movies, and political and cultural events.
- **PowerPoint Slides**—Also available on the instructor's site are PowerPoint slides on which the instructional content of each chapter is summarized for overhead projection.

Supplements for Students

- **Online Learning Center**—Our companion website offers journal prompts for each chapter and links to direct students to reliable web sources, as well as many other resources.

Acknowledgments

No textbook can be created without the assistance of many people. First, we relied on the thoughtful reactions and suggestions of our colleagues across the country, who reviewed this project at various stages:

Bob Akin, *Houston Community College System*

Susan Bowling, *University of Arkansas at Little Rock*

Linda Brown, *Bainbridge College*

Sally Cain, *Angelina College*

Kathleen A. Carlson, *Brevard Community College*

Jordan Fabish, *Long Beach City College*

Christine Flax, *Villa Julie College*

Sandra Griffin, *Western New Mexico University*

Nikka Harris, *University Center of Rochester*

Susie Johnston, *Tyler Junior College*

Billy Jones, *Miami Dade College*

Kimberly Jones, *College of Southern Idaho*

Barbara Migden, *Georgia Court College*

Rose Monroe, *Baltimore City Community College*

Stephen Monti, *Lawson State College*

Betty Raper, *Pulaski Technical College*

Jerolynn Roberson, *Miami Dade College*

Alan Shuttleworth, *Sierra College*

Susan Simpson, *Montgomery College*

Tonya Strickland, *Bainbridge College*

Mirian Torain, *Prince George's College*

William Turner, *De Anza College*

Mary Welborn, *Rose State College*

Nancy Wood, *University of Arkansas at Little Rock*

We owe special thanks to the honest and valuable criticism from our collegues at Glendale Community College. In particular, we would like to thank Roberta Delaney, Frederica Johnson, Viva Henley, and David Rodriguez. Others who helped us with the first edition of this book include Marilyn Brophy, Nancy Edwards, Cindy Gilbert, Mary Holden, Bob Jenson, Virg Lass, Arlene Lurie, Glenda Mead, Lynda Svendsen, and Gwen Worthington.

We'd like to thank all those at McGraw-Hill who have helped us in the production of this book. We are especially grateful to our senior sponsoring editor, John Kindler, who always kept us on track and provided necessary feedback. We owe a huge debt to our developmental editor, Gillian Cook, who was very helpful in the production of the manuscript. Writing the first edition of any book is always stressful, but Gillian's unfailing good humor, sound advice, and pleasant criticism made the production of *Racing* as stress-free as possible. We also want to especially thank our copy editor Jennifer Gordon. She was a pleasure to work with and was extremely helpful in helping the project go forward so smoothly. Others we want to thank are our permissions coordinators Romy Charlesworth and Marty Moga, editorial coordinator Jesse Hassenger, and our production editor Chanda Feldman. We would also like to give special thanks to our McGraw-Hill sales representative, Sheree D'Amico, who not only was supportive of our efforts with this first edition, but also obtained books for us at a moment's notice.

Finally, we wish to thank our students, who in addition to reading the selections and completing the exercises, made countless helpful suggestions.

Peter Mather
Rita McCarthy

Preface to the Student

When we began to write this book, our goal was an ambitious one—to help you become a better reader and to make reading a significant part of your life. The title *Racing Ahead with Reading* was chosen because it reflects how the theme of sports connects to the reading process. Becoming a better reader requires the same kind of dedication as becoming a better athlete. In both sports and reading, practice makes perfect. The great sports stars make things look easy because of the amount of hard work they have put into perfecting their game. The great readers are the same. They work on their reading skills until they are so good that reading is effortless.

A person learning a new sport always starts with the basics. And so should a person trying to perfect the reading process. To that end, we are providing you with exercises that, with lots of practice, will make you a better reader.

Racing Ahead with Reading is divided into five parts. Part I is devoted to mastering the fundamentals—phonics, dictionary skills, and word parts. Part II deals with the structure of reading, in particular, deciphering an author's main ideas. Part III focuses on interpretation and introduces critical reading. Part IV emphasizes understanding textbook materials such as visual aids. *Racing* concludes with the supplementary readings in Part V. High-interest readings from a variety of sources on many different topics were chosen to stimulate discussion.

Each reading follows a basic format. We begin with "Getting Focused," a section designed to create a connection between you and the reading selection. This is followed by a brief "Bio-Sketch" of the author, and then "Tackling Vocabulary," a section that provides definitions for key vocabulary words. After the reading selection, you will find the "Comprehension Checkup," which includes a variety of questions in many different formats. The "In Your Own Words" section allows you to respond orally or in writing. Two other sections, "Written Assignment" "Internet Activity," are also provided.

There are many who believe that sport is a metaphor for life. Even though some do better than others, people who try hard and do their best can't be counted out. Instead, how well you play the game matters. It's our hope that our textbook will provide you with the tools to play the game of "reading" well. When you complete your coursework, you will have become so good at reading that you can "race ahead" in life.

Walkthrough: A Guided Tour

Contents

x

Chapter titles

Main topics

Longer reading selections

Welcome! The following pages illustrate how this book works. Spending a few minutes getting to know the features and organization of the text will help you get the most out of *Racing Ahead with Reading*.

The text begins with a **table of contents** to give you an overview of what you will find in the book.

Each chapter opens with a **cartoon, picture, poem, quiz, or other feature with text** that ties it to and illustrates chapter content in a way that is interesting and meaningful.

CHAPTER

8   Bias

1. What bias is being expressed in the cartoon?

_____

2. What clues led you to your answer?

_____

In this cartoon, the Native Americans are expressing a desire to close the borders and keep the new immigrants, the Pilgrims, out. The author's point of view is that we should probably be more tolerant of immigration. An author's point of view can be favorable, unfavorable, or neutral. In this case, the author is biased in favor of immigration.

356

21. What pattern of organization is paragraph 5?

_____

22. What year was the safety razor patented? _____

23. When was the electric razor invented? _____

READING

"All Ralston had in mind was a weekend break from his job at an Aspen mountaineering store."

GETTING FOCUSED

Many of us have faced problems that offered no easy solutions. In this excerpt from *Between a Rock and a Hard Place*, mountaineer Aron Ralston, facing near-certain death, saves his own life by amputating his right hand and wrist.

BIO-SKETCH

Thomas Fields-Meyer is a writer and associate editor for *People* magazine. In addition to writing for *People* magazine, Vicki Bane is the author of *Dr. Laura: The Unauthorized Biography*. Jason Bane has written for the *St. Louis Post-Dispatch* and *Inside Education* magazine.

TACKLING VOCABULARY

ingenuity   the quality of being clever or resourceful

AWOL   an acronym meaning "absent without official leave." An acronym is a word formed from the first letters of two or more words. The military applies the acronym AWOL to soldiers who leave their military duties without permission

trailhead   the beginning point of a hiking trail

cronies   close friends or associates

Aspen   a ski resort in Colorado

adrenaline   a hormone the body often secretes when a person is under extreme stress. Adrenaline often causes increased heart rate, blood pressure, and cardiac output

gumption   courage

dude   a slang term meaning "person"

Each chapter also includes a number of longer **reading selections.** These reading selections start with an introductory section that aims to spark your interest and provide background information.

A **quotation** from the reading engages your interest.

Getting Focused provides background information.

The **Bio-Sketch** provides information about the author's life and writing experience.

The **Tackling Vocabulary** helps you understand the more difficult words in the reading selection.

READING   *continued*

BIO-SKETCH

James Kirby Martin is a distinguished professor of history at the University of Houston. His areas of special interest include early American history and social and cultural issues in America.

TACKLING VOCABULARY

fidgeted   moved about in a nervous or restless way

prohibited   forbidden

barnstormed   played in small towns

balk   an illegal motion by a pitcher

virtuoso   showing special knowledge or skill in a field

INTEGRATION IN SPORTS

James Kirby Martin

On April 18, 1946, the sports world focused on a baseball field in Jersey City, an industrial wasteland on the banks of the Passaic River. It was the opening day for the Jersey City Giants of the International League. Their opponents were the Montreal Royals, the Brooklyn Dodgers' farm team. Playing second base for the Royals was Jackie Roosevelt Robinson, a pigeon-toed, highly competitive, marvelously talented African-American athlete. The stadium was filled

---

The reading selections are taken from **magazine articles, news stories, textbooks, fiction, and poems.** This will help you prepare for the wide range of reading you will be asked to do in college.

Many of the reading selections include **illustrations** that reinforce topics and provide context.

8 Integration in sports preceded integration in society at large. But in both sports and the civil rights movement, racial gains were paid for by individuals willing to risk serious hardships. Change seldom came easily and the struggle never ended quickly.

Excerpts from *America and Its Peoples*, Vol. 2, 5th ed. by James Kirby Martin et al. Copyright © 2004 by James Kirby Martin, Randy Roberts, Steven Mintz, Linda O. McMurry and James H. Jones. Reprinted by permission of Pearson Education, Inc.

COMPREHENSION CHECKUP

Fact and Opinion

Directions: Identify statements of fact with an **F** and statements of opinion with an **O**.

_____ 1. Their opponents were the Montreal Royals, the Brooklyn Dodgers' farm team.

_____ 2. It was not just another season-opening game.

_____ 3. Jackie Robinson came to bat in the first inning.

_____ 4. He didn't even swing at the first five pitches.

_____ 5. Professional football then became the next to be integrated.

_____ 6. In 1950 the Boston Celtics of the National Basketball Association signed Chuck Cooper of Duquesne to a professional contract.

_____ 7. Opposition runners spiked him, and pitchers threw at him.

_____ 8. Patient, witty, and quick to forgive, he endured extraordinary humiliation.

_____ 9. Robinson's teammate Roy Campanella said, "nothing compared to what Jackie was going through."

_____ 10. Change seldom came easily, and the struggle never ended quickly.

Directions: Identify each numbered sentence in the following paragraphs as either a fact (**F**) or an opinion (**O**).

(1) In the third inning, Robinson took his second turn at bat. (2) With runners on first and second, he swung at the first pitch and hit it over the left-field fence 330 feet away. (3) In the press box sat Wendell Smith and Joe

Objective questions test your understanding and provide practice for standardized tests.

After the longer reading selections, you will find a **Comprehension Checkup,** with a variety of exercises to test your understanding and provide practice for other college tests.

Main Ideas and Details   **157**

Column A	Column B
_____ 1. misunderstood	a. full of
_____ 2. interview	b. between; among
_____ 3. supernatural	c. before
_____ 4. reaction	d. apart; away
_____ 5. investigated	e. badly
_____ 6. distinction	f. above; over
_____ 7. information	g. see
_____ 8. visualizing	h. condition or result
_____ 9. previous	i. again; back
_____ 10. helpful	j. in; into

Vocabulary in Context exercises help you expand your vocabulary.

In Your Own Words

1. Do you think James Randi's $1,000,000 prize will ever be claimed? Why or why not?

2. Why do you think people continue to believe in psychic phenomena when confronted with contradictory evidence produced by Randi and others?

Written Assignment

1. You have probably driven down a street and seen a sign in front of a store window or small house advertising palm readings or fortune telling. Do you believe that palm readers and fortune tellers have psychic powers?

2. What kind of research would be necessary to establish that a particular psychic phenomenon is genuine?

In Your Own Words and **Written Assignments** give you a chance to express your own thoughts.

Internet Activity

Read more about the Amazing Randi's skeptical approach to supernatural phenomena at his website:

www.randi.org

Watch one of his videos at

www.randi.org/images/081304-ForkBend.mpg

Can you tell whether you are watching a psychic phenomenon or magic? Write a paragraph describing your reaction.

Internet Activities send you to the World Wide Web to find out more about the topic and/or author of the reading.

Vocabulary in Context

Directions: Using the vocabulary words below, fill in the crossword puzzle.

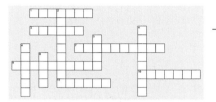

chaotic	insight	overwhelm	task
cope	manageable	priority	urgent
enable	modify	productive	

Crossword puzzles enhance learning.

The Vocabulary in Context sections also contain **crossword puzzles** to add some fun to your vocabulary studies.

ACROSS CLUES
1. confused or disordered
3. requiring immediate action; pressing
7. fruitful
9. capable of being controlled
10. intuitive understanding
11. amend; change somewhat

DOWN CLUES
2. burden excessively
4. something given special attention
5. to face and deal with problems
6. make possible or easy
8. chore

USING YOUR COMPUTER AND THE INTERNET

To do well in college today, you need to have a basic proficiency with computers and the Internet. The Internet is a powerful tool for communicating with others, doing research for papers, and completing other classroom projects. As one expert has said, "Don't let that little glowing screen become an adversary. If you plan correctly, the computer can become your most useful tool at college—next to your brain." And of course your computer and Internet skills also will serve you well when you leave college and enter the workforce. More and more jobs require at least minimal computer skills, and many jobs are going to require higher levels of computer skills. Your mastery of basic computer skills is important for achieving college—and ultimately occupational—success.

---

tion. Then look at the units of measure on the left-hand vertical axis and the areas of the world that are named along the bottom or horizontal axis.

Directions: After looking at the graph and becoming familiar with its information, answer the questions that follow.

1. Over what years was the information collected? _____

2. What organization put the information in this graph together? _____ Those letters stand for the United Nations Education, Social, and Cultural Organization, a major part of the United Nations.

3. The percentage numbers for illiteracy rates on the left-hand vertical axis give percentages in _____ percent intervals.

4. What region has the lowest illiteracy rates for both men and women?

   _____

5. What region has the highest illiteracy rates for women? _____

   _____

6. In the Arab states and in South and West Asia, the percentage of illiteracy for women is roughly _____ percent higher than for men.

Because much of your college work requires you to read **visual aids**, *Racing Ahead with Reading*, includes an entire chapter (Chapter 9) on how to do so successfully. The chapter includes numerous **examples** of graphic aids, **explanations** of how to use them, and **exercises** for practice in reading them.

FIGURE 9.3 **World Illiteracy Rates by Region and Sex, 2000–2004.** From UNESCO website: www.uis.unesco.org/ev.php?ID=5020_201&ID2=DO_TOPIC - 25k

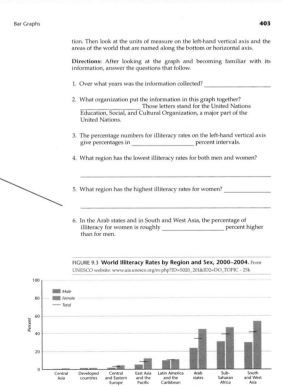

questions you might have about it. Now look at the reading on pages 425–426 and note the annotations in the margin of the text.

The following is a list of techniques you can use for making annotations. They are suggestions: You can adapt them and add your own abbreviations and symbols to make your own system of annotation.

- Underline important terms and concepts.
- Write MI next to main ideas.
- Circle definitions and meanings or write Def. (definition) in the margin.
- Write key words and definitions in the margin or write KV (key vocabulary) beside important words.
- Use EX to indicate an example.
- Signal where important information can be found with (IMP) or a symbol like an asterisk (*) in the margin.
- Signal summaries with SUM or write your own short summaries in the margin.
- Use a question mark (?) in the margin to indicate a point that needs further explanation.
- Indicate where the answers to particular questions in the text can be found by writing ANS (answer).

Exercise 1: Underlining, Highlighting, and Annotating

Directions: The following excerpt titled "Three Types of Memory" has been underlined and annotated for you. Use this as a model to annotate paragraphs 1–14 of the reading titled "Memorization" on page 487.

THREE TYPES OF MEMORY

MI   There are three different memory storage systems or stages through which information must travel if it is to be remembered: sensory, short-term, and long-term. The first stage, **sensory memory**, refers to the initial, momentary
DEF   storage of information, lasting only an instant. A momentary flash of lightning, the sound of a twig snapping, and the sting of a pinprick all represent stimulation of exceedingly brief duration. Such stimuli are initially—and briefly—stored
Stage I Sensory—   in sensory memory, the first repository of the information the world presents to
initial memory stage   us. Sensory memory in general is able to store information for only a very short time. If information does not pass to short-term memory it is lost for good. Sensory memory employs a "file or forget it" approach to its job. It operates as a kind of snapshot that stores information for a brief moment in time. But it is as if each snapshot, immediately after being taken, is destroyed and replaced with a new one. Unless the information in the snapshot is transferred to some other type of memory, it is lost.

Much of your college work requires you to read and study college texts. Chapter 10 includes information on **annotating, outlining, mapping,** and **summarizing,** as well as **two longer textbook selections** for you to practice these skills on.

IS CHOCOLATE A VEGETABLE?

- Chocolate is derived from cacao beans. Bean = vegetable. Sugar is derived from either sugar CANE or sugar BEETS. Both are plants, which places them in the vegetable category. Thus, chocolate is a vegetable.
- To go one step further, chocolate candy bars also contain milk, which is a dairy product. So candy bars are a health food.
- Chocolate-covered raisins, cherries, orange slices, strawberries, and cranberries all count as fruit; so eat as many as you want.

Diet tip: Eat a chocolate bar before each meal. It'll take the edge off your appetite, and you'll eat less.

- If calories are an issue, store your chocolate on top of the fridge. Calories are afraid of heights, and they will jump out of the chocolate to protect themselves. (We're testing this with other snack foods as well.)

NEWS FLASH: "Stressed" spelled backward is "desserts." So, to reverse being "stressed" . . . CHOCOLATE!!!

Author Unknown—from Thomas S. Ellsworth—Ed:anon.

Internet Activity

1. Go to the Hershey's website, www.hersheys.com, and find a Hershey's product you are not familiar with. Write a description of the product and three things you learned about it. The website is obviously written to get you to buy Hershey's products. What information might have been left out in the description of this product that could discourage you from buying it?

2. Do some chocolate research. Who gave chocolate its name and what does *theobroma cacao* mean? What did the Olmec, Mayan, and Aztec civilizations have to do with chocolate? What dishes are popular in Mexico that combine chocolate and chili?

RELATIONSHIPS AND BEHAVIOR

READING

"But the other person is obviously in pain. What should you
do? Should you keep giving shocks or should you stop?"

GETTING FOCUSED
After World War II, the major excuse that Nazi officers gave for their participation in atrocities during the war was that they were "only following orders."
(continued)

To read well, you need to read all the time. Chapter 11 of *Racing Ahead with Reading* includes **eight additional practice readings** related to the **themes of work and relationships and behavior,** each with the same pre- and post-reading features as the longer selections in the text.

GETTING STARTED

Most of us have a goal, something we'd like to accomplish in life. The easy part is seeing the goal; the hard part is making it happen. This section introduces you to a reading selection written by Walter Cunningham in which he describes techniques for becoming a better student. We then give you an opportunity to become better acquainted with your textbook, which is often the first step in doing well in class. The section concludes with an excerpt from Christine Brennan's autobiography. Christine's goal was to be a sportswriter, and through hard work and sacrifice, she was able to realize it.

Our hope is that when you finish the Introduction, you will know a bit more about how to attain your own specific goal. Good students are not born; they are made. And once you master the basics, in the words of Dr. Seuss, "Oh, the places you'll go."

READING

"Practice active, purposeful learning. It isn't enough to passively absorb knowledge provided by your instructor."

GETTING FOCUSED

You have made the decision to attend college. In addition to helping you prepare for a career, a college education is likely to pay off monetarily. Did you know that the average person with a college degree earns about 50 percent more each year than the average person with only a high school diploma? Because college is a huge investment of your time, energy, and money, it is important to be successful. Developing good study habits can go a long way to helping you succeed. The following selection provides tips to help you become a better student.

BIO-SKETCH

William P. Cunningham is an emeritus professor at the University of Minnesota.

TACKLING VOCABULARY

prophecy   a foretelling or prediction of what is to come

inflation   a general increase

carrel   a cubicle or desk partitioned off for private study in a library

adage   a traditional saying expressing a common experience or observation

HOW CAN I GET AN A IN THIS CLASS?

William P. Cunningham

"What have I gotten myself into?" you are probably wondering as you begin to read this book. Do I have a chance to get a good grade? The answers to these questions depend, to a large extent, on you and how you decide to apply yourself. Expecting to be interested and to do either well or poorly in your classes often turns out to be a self-fulfilling prophecy. As Henry Ford once said, "If you think you can do a thing, or think you can't do a thing, you're right."

Develop Good Study Habits

2 Many students find themselves unprepared for studying in college. In a survey released in 2003 by the Higher Education Research Institute, more than two-thirds of high school seniors nationwide reported studying outside of class less than one hour per day. Nevertheless, because of grade inflation, nearly half of those students claim to have an A average. It comes as a rude shock to many to discover that the study habits they developed in high school won't allow them to do as well—or perhaps even to pass their classes—in college. Many will have to triple or even quadruple their study time. In addition, many need to learn to study more efficiently or effectively.

3 How good are your current study skills and habits? Making a frank and honest assessment of your strengths and weaknesses will help you set goals and make plans for achieving them. Answer the questions in **Table 1** below as a way of assessing where you are now and what you need to work on to improve your study habits.

TABLE 1: Assess Your Study Skills

Rate yourself on each of the following study skills and habits on a scale of 1 (excellent) to 5 (needs improvement). If you rate yourself below 3 on any item, think about an action plan to improve that behavior.

_____ How strong is your commitment to be successful in this class?

_____ How well do you manage your time? For example, do you always run late or do you complete assignments on time?

_____ Do you have a regular study environment that reduces distraction and encourages concentration?

_____ How effective are you at reading and note-taking? For example, do you remember what you've read? Can you decipher your notes after you've made them?

_____ Do you attend class regularly and listen for instructions and important ideas? Do you participate actively in class discussions and ask meaningful questions?

_____ Do you generally read assigned chapters in the textbook before attending class or do you wait until the night before the exam?

_____ Are you usually prepared before class with questions about material that needs clarification or that expresses your own interest in the subject matter?

_____ How well do you handle test anxiety? For example, do you usually feel prepared for exams and quizzes or are you terrified of them? Do you have techniques to reduce anxiety or turn it into positive energy?

_____ Do you actively evaluate how you're doing in a course based on feedback from your instructor, and then make corrections to improve your effectiveness?

_____ Do you seek out advice and assistance outside of class from your instructors or teaching assistants?

4   One of the first requirements for success is to set clear, honest, attainable goals for yourself. Are you willing to commit the time and effort necessary to do well? Make goals for yourself in terms that you can measure and in time frames within which you can see progress and adjust your approach if it isn't taking you where you want to go. Be positive but realistic. It's more effective to try to accomplish a positive action than to avoid a negative one. When you set your goals, use proactive language that states what you want rather than negative language about what you're trying to avoid. It's good to be optimistic, but setting impossibly high standards will only lead to disappointment. Be objective about the obstacles you face and be willing to modify your goals if necessary. As you gain more experience and information, you may need to adjust your expectations either up or down. Take stock from time to time to see whether you are on track to accomplish what you expect from your studies.

"We are what we repeatedly do. Excellence, therefore, is not an act but a habit."

—Aristotle

5   One of the most common mistakes many of us make is to procrastinate and waste time. Be honest, are you habitually late for meetings or in getting assignments done? Do you routinely leave your studying until the last minute and then frantically cram the night before your exams? If so, you need to organize your schedule so that you can get your work done and still have a life. Make a study schedule for yourself and stick to it. Allow enough time for sleep, regular meals, exercise, and recreation so that you will be rested, healthy, and efficient when you do study. Schedule regular study times between your classes and work. Plan some study times during the day when you are fresh; don't leave all your work until late night hours when you won't get much done. Divide your work into reasonable sized segments that you can accomplish on a daily basis. Plan to have all your reading and assignments completed several days before your exams so you will have adequate time to review and process information. Carry a calendar so you will remember appointments and assignments.

6   Establish a regular study space in which you can be effective and productive. It might be a desk in your room, a carrel in the library, or some other quiet, private environment. Find a place that works for you and be disciplined about sticking to what you need to do. If you get in the habit of studying in a particular place

and time, you will find it easier to get started and to stick to your tasks. Many students make the mistake of thinking that they can study while talking to their friends or watching TV. They may put in many hours but not really accomplish much.

7   How you behave in class and interact with your instructor can have a big impact on how much you learn and what grade you get. Make an effort to get to know your instructor. Sit near the front of the room where you can see and be seen. Pay attention and ask questions that show your interest in the subject matter. Attend every class and arrive on time. Don't fold up your papers and prepare to leave until after the class period is over. Arriving late and leaving early says to your instructor that you don't care much about either the class or your grade.

From *Environmental Science: A Global Concern,* 9th ed., by William P. Cunningham et al. Copyright © 2007 The McGraw-Hill Companies, Inc. Reprinted by permission of The McGraw-Hill Companies, Inc.

Think about the A, B, Cs of doing well in college.

    A. **A**lways go to class.

    B. **B**e at your class on time and don't leave early.

    C. **C**omplete all of your work on time.

◢ COMPREHENSION CHECKUP

Directions: Answer the following questions using information from the selection.

1. What is the selection about? developing good study habits _____

2. Of all of the tips presented by William Cunningham, list the four that you find most helpful. Answers will vary.

    a. _____

    b. _____

    c. _____

    d. _____

3. Give two examples of positive goals and explain how you're going to accomplish them.

    Example: The biology chapter is 30 pages. I will read six pages a day to complete the chapter in five days.

    a. _____

    b. _____

Multiple Choice

Directions: Write the letter of the correct answer in the blank provided.

___a___ 1. According to Cunningham, students should study
  a. in a quiet area free from distractions.
  b. while talking to friends or watching TV.
  c. only at the library.
  d. as little as possible.

___c___ 2. It is best to study
  a. late in the evening.
  b. at the last minute.
  c. at regular times between your classes and work.
  d. both a and b.

___d___ 3. According to the author, college students
  a. want to take only classes in which they can achieve an A.
  b. might have to study more than they did as high school students.
  c. often need to learn how to study more efficiently.
  d. both b and c.

True or False

Directions: Indicate whether each statement is true or false by writing **T** or **F** in the blank provided.

___T___ 1. Many students are unprepared for doing well in college.

___T___ 2. A student should have one specific place to study.

___F___ 3. The author recommends waiting until right before a test to study.

___F___ 4. The author suggests sitting in the back of the classroom so that you can more easily converse with your friends without being noticed.

___F___ 5. If you're trying to achieve an A in a class, it's best to arrive late and leave early.

___T___ 6. A procrastinator is likely to put off work until the last minute.

___T___ 7. The author suggests having a formal study schedule that allows time for study, sleep, meals, and leisure activities.

___F___ 8. A good way to accomplish a goal is to set the bar really high.

___T___ 9. The author recommends attending class regularly.

Crossword Puzzle

Directions: Using the vocabulary words below, fill in the crossword puzzle.

absorb	decipher	objective	perspective
anonymity	generate	optimistic	proactive
comprehend	habitually	passively	procrastinate

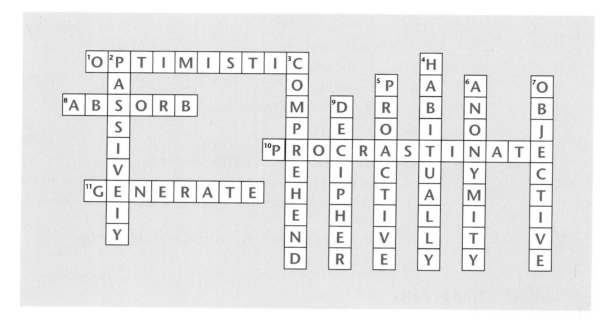

ACROSS CLUES

1. looking at the more favorable set of future events
8. to take in; assimilate
10. to put off doing something
11. to bring into existence; originate; produce

DOWN CLUES

2. receiving or subjected to an action without responding in return
3. understand the meaning of something
4. acting in a customary manner or practice

5. acting in advance to deal with an expected difficulty
6. quality of being unknown
7. uninfluenced by emotions or personal prejudices
9. make out the meaning of something that is difficult to read or understand

Written Assignment

What do you think are going to be your biggest challenges as you work toward your goal of achieving success in college? Is it going to be balancing school and work? Or school and family obligations? Write a short paragraph discussing potential pitfalls in your quest for higher education.

Internet Activity

Are you curious about how many college students actually graduate? For up-to-date information, type in the key words "U.S. college dropout rate" into any search engine. Write a short paragraph discussing your findings.

GETTING ACQUAINTED WITH YOUR TEXTBOOK

To get off to a good start in a class, you need to become familiar with your textbook and understand how it is structured. Below you will find an introduction to the key features of textbooks in general. Then you will practice locating specific pieces of information from this textbook.

A. Preface

The Preface usually includes the author's explanation of why the book was written, the approach taken, the scope of the book, and how the book differs from other books. The author's goal is to give a clear picture of what he or she is trying to accomplish in the textbook. When the author includes a "To the Student" section, it is especially important that you read this material. This special message to you may affect your attitude toward the textbook.

Read the Preface to the Student for this text carefully and then sum up what it says in your own words.

Answers will vary.

_____

_____

_____

_____

B. Walkthrough

The Walkthrough is included to illustrate how the book works. It is important to familiarize yourself with this material so you get to know the features and organization of the text. List four special features contained in this textbook that are mentioned in the Walkthrough.

1. Answers will vary. _____

2. _____

3. _____

4. _____

C. Table of Contents

The Table of Contents lists the chapters in the book and the page numbers. It provides a survey of the contents and organization of the book. Find the answers to the following questions about this textbook by looking at the Table of Contents.

1. Does this textbook have an introduction? _____yes_____

2. How many parts does this textbook have? ____5_____

3. How many chapters does this textbook have? _____II_____

4. Does this textbook have an appendix? _____yes_____

5. List the title of one reading selection in Chapter 3. _____Heroes, Stand Up

   ____for Yourself; Between a Rock and a Hard Place_____

D. Appendices

The Appendices, which are located at the end of the book, contain supplementary information. List below examples of information you find in the appendices.

____Answers to Two-Minute Mysteries in Warm-Up 2_____

E. Index

The Index is a detailed, alphabetical listing of topics, concepts, and authors presented in the textbook. Because it gives page numbers for each item included, it is very useful for quickly locating material. The index is found at the back of the textbook. Locate the page numbers for the following items in this textbook:

1. Where can you find material by Dr. Seuss? _____p. 2_____

2. Where can you find material by Abraham Lincoln? _____p. 452_____

3. Where can you find material by Lance Armstrong? _____p. 259_____

4. Where can you find material on imagery? _____p. 323_____

F. Additional Material

Most textbooks include other special features such as cartoons, illustrations, charts, diagrams, marginal notes, footnotes, maps, and graphs. List a page number where you can find one of the following in this textbook: Answers will vary.

1. Cartoon: _____

2. Chart: _____

3. Marginal notes: _____

4. Illustration: _____

5. Graph: _____

The following selection discusses a person who accomplished her goal by working hard and maintaining a positive realistic attitude.

READING

"Some children rebel against fathers like mine, against all the detail, the minutiae, the rules. I drew closer."

GETTING FOCUSED

Many people attribute their success in life to their parents. It's commonplace today when an athlete receives an award to hear him or her say, "Thanks Mom" or "Thanks Dad." If you happened to be watching TV when Tiger Woods won his first Masters, his heartfelt embrace of his father Earl Woods is probably etched in your memory. In the following selection, Christine Brennan, a sportswriter who broke barriers her whole life, pays tribute to the lessons she learned from her father.

BIO-SKETCH

Christine Brennan has twice been named one of the nation's top ten sports columnists. She is currently a *USA Today* columnist and commentator for ABC News and NPR. Her book, *Inside Edge*, was named one of the top 100 sports books of all time. In gratitude to *both* of her parents for encouraging her in her trailblazing career, Brennan said, "At a time when most girls were not

(continued)

R E A D I N G   *continued*

being encouraged to play or follow sports, Dad, and Mom too, never said no to me, even if the rest of the world was thinking that we were rather strange."

TACKLING VOCABULARY

Arizona Memorial   During the attack on Pearl Harbor on December 7, 1941, the battleship *USS Arizona* was the most seriously damaged. The explosion that rocked it was so fierce that over a thousand men died on board. President Eisenhower later approved the creation of a memorial for all those who died during the attack. Ultimately, a decision was made to build a memorial over the midsection of the sunken *Arizona*.

serendipitous   fortunate; lucky

BEST SEAT IN THE HOUSE

Christine Brennan

"Son, learn what I teach you and never forget what I tell you to do. Listen to what is wise and try to understand it."

—Proverbs 2:1–2

Looking back on it, I was comfortable being so different because of the simple lessons Mom and Dad were teaching me. Dad gave all of us some demanding ground rules for life. We played by his rules, not society's. His were much tougher. He never quite said this, but I knew he was thinking it: You play by my rules and you'll find life's rules to be a piece of cake.

2   It started with school. We are not allowed to get a grade in junior high or high school lower than the first letter of our last name. If it happened, and it did once or twice for me, we had a meeting with Dad to discuss it. My freshman year of high school, I could not figure out how to break the news to him that I was about to receive a horrifying D for the quarter in geometry. I didn't tell him for several days until I nearly burst—then it came out in a flood of tears in our kitchen.

3   Dad immediately took me into the den, closed the door, told me he was very disappointed, and then came up with a plan. He would call my teacher. He would arrange for me to meet with the teacher as well. He told me he would stay on top of the situation, go to the school if necessary. "I'm going to help you make sure this doesn't happen again," he said. He never yelled, never raised his voice. For a moment I thought that I detected just a touch of sympathy in his bright blue eyes. I received the grade associated with our last name in that class the next quarter.

4   Almost every day, Dad reminded us how lucky we were to be born in the United States. The two times we moved as a family, the first thing Dad did was have a flagpole installed so he could fly the U.S. flag every day of the year. And we did have to use that term: the U.S. flag. It was not the American flag. The Americas included Canada and Mexico, and the nations of Central and South

America as well. How presumptuous of us, Dad said, to appropriate the hemisphere as all ours and take the name for our own.

5   Patriotism was serious business to Dad. On a family vacation to Hawaii in 1974, when I was sixteen, we took a day to visit Pearl Harbor. After spending some time on the *Arizona* memorial, we were ready to catch the boat back to shore—all of us, that is, except Dad.

6   We found him standing ramrod straight, hands clasped behind his back, staring at the wall of names of those who were killed on December 7, 1941.

7   "Dad," I said, agitated and ready to leave, "what are you doing?"

8   "I'm reading every name and saying thank you."

9   We didn't leave until he reached the last one.

10   If patriotism was part and parcel of being a Brennan, precision was too. No one worked *for* Dad at his company. Everyone worked *with* him. If I ever got it wrong, he'd correct me.

11   We had to learn and recite all the U.S. presidents in order. Next came the books of the Bible and the Gettysburg Address. Gettysburg was special to Dad. We walked the battlefields with him for the first time on spring break in 1969. It wasn't the last time. Before that trip, Dad assigned my sister Kate and me to write a report on the battle.

12   There was detail in every phase of our lives. Dad was a stickler for everything, but most of all dates. He remembered everyone's birthday and anniversary.

13   Dad often called our attention to the obituaries in the *Blade*.

14   "Look at this," he would say. "This man was born in 1906, yet they say he was a veteran of World War I. He was twelve when the First World War ended."

15   We also had to date every piece of paper we used, preferably in the upper-right-hand corner.

16   One day in the kitchen, having become a teenager who was getting slightly exasperated with her father, I told Dad I didn't need to put a date on a piece of paper because I was only going to write down a phone number, call it, then throw the paper away.

17   "I don't care," he replied. "Put a date on it."

18   I furiously scribbled the date, dialed the number, then balled up the paper and dramatically threw it in the wastebasket, scowling at my father. Dad didn't say a word. He didn't have to. I've dated every piece of paper since. Dad's obsession has become mine, with the most serendipitous of results. Whenever I reach for one of the old notebooks I have stashed in a cabinet and wonder when I conducted an interview—sometimes a very important piece of information as I'm researching a story or column—I simply open the notebook and there is the date at the top of the page.

19   The discipline to put a date on everything followed hand in hand with my interest in keeping a diary. Mom and Dad gave me a new one every Christmas, and they encouraged me to write in it every day, which I did. Throughout high school, into college, and all the way into the mid-1980s, I didn't miss a day. It was like a game to me, to see if I could keep it up and not break the streak. I became the Cal Ripken Jr. of diary writers.

20   Dad used our everyday games to teach us his life lessons. Monopoly was his favorite. He never was too easy on us and let us win; he believed playing fair and square as an adult was a far better lesson for his children. As we played, his advice to us was simple: "If you land on it, buy it." Sometimes he mortgaged

property just so he could buy more. This was a metaphor for the way he lived: Make a decision and never look back. Never second-guess. Be confident and bold. "There will be no shrinking violets in this family," he said.

21 Some children rebel against fathers like mine, against all the detail, the minutiae, the rules. I drew closer. I wanted him to quiz me on my homework or about what happened one hundred years ago today. I wasn't afraid not to know the answer; if I didn't, I knew I would learn it from him right away. I was my father's willing disciple. He encouraged me to ask questions of anyone about anything, and he did so early on.

22 Sometimes Dad would grab one of our green and white volumes of the World Book Encyclopedia and start reading it just for fun; soon I would be reading the encyclopedia too, "just for fun."

23 I quickly became as caught up in precision as Dad was. In the days leading to my tenth birthday, I asked Mom exactly what time I was born. She told me 7:58 P.M.

24 On May 14, 1968, as the minute drew near, I camped out in front of the clock in the kitchen until the second hand reached twelve at exactly two minutes to eight.

25 "I'm officially ten," I announced.

26 Mom gave me a look that said only one thing: Oh no, not another one.

27 As I grew older, Dad's sayings popped up when we spoke on the phone, during my numerous visits to Toledo, even during an argument. "To whom much is given, much is expected. . . . How are you going to make a difference? . . . Get up early and get going. . . . You're lucky to have this day. . . . You're tough enough to handle anything. . . . Your name is Brennan. You are different. Do more."

28 And one that I try to remember at press conferences, "Put your brain in gear before you put your mouth in motion."

29 But the one saying that continued to ring in my ears was his all-time best: "This ain't no dress rehearsal."

 COMPREHENSION CHECKUP

True or False

Directions: Indicate whether each statement is true or false by writing **T** or **F** in the blank provided.

____T____ 1. A soldier on guard duty might stand ramrod straight.

____F____ 2. Christine Brennan's initial grade in geometry was a C.

____F____ 3. This selection is primarily about rules made by Christine's mother.

____F____ 4. Christine spent her entire childhood in the same house.

_____F_____ 5. Mr. Brennan left the *Arizona* memorial quickly because it was too painful for him.

_____T_____ 6. According to Christine, her father's rules were tougher than society's rules.

Multiple Choice

Directions: Write the letter of the correct answer in the blank provided.

_____c_____ 1. The best title for this selection would be

    a. "Make a Decision and Never Look Back."

    b. "Teach the Lessons of Life with Monopoly."

    c. "What My Father Taught Me."

    d. "Making Decisions."

_____b_____ 2. According to the selection, Christine was taught all of the following lessons *except*

    a. the importance of dating every piece of paper.

    b. the importance of never spending more money than you have.

    c. the importance of getting no grade lower than a B.

    d. the importance of making a decision and never looking back.

_____d_____ 3. Mr. Brennan was

    a. a stickler for dates.

    b. patriotic.

    c. interested in precision.

    d. all of the above.

_____c_____ 4. Mr. Brennan was

    a. physically abusive to Christine.

    b. verbally abusive to Christine.

    c. none of the above.

    d. both of the above.

Details

Directions: Fill in the word or words that correctly complete each statement.

1. Mr. Brennan pointed out obituaries from the ___newspaper – *Blade*___ .

2. Christine and her Dad read the ___encyclopedia___ just for fun.

3. Christine was born at exactly ___7:58 P.M.___ on May 14, 1958.

4. Christine was the _____Cal Ripken Jr._____ of diary writers.

5. Mr. Brennan used the game of _____Monopoly_____ to illustrate life's lessons.

6. It was important to Christine and her father to _____date_____ every piece of paper.

7. Mr. Brennan demonstrated his _____patriotism_____ on a trip to Hawaii.

8. The battlefield at _____Gettysburg_____ was especially important to Mr. Brennan.

9. Christine often visited her father in _____Toledo_____.

10. Christine was required to learn the names of the _____U.S. presidents_____ in order.

Vocabulary

Directions: Match each word in column A with its antonym (opposite) in column B. Write the letter of the antonym in the space provided.

Column A		Column B
1.	g	straight	a. withholding
2.	i	serious	b. unfortunate
3.	j	agitated	c. leader; master
4.	h	bold	d. imprecision; inaccuracy
5.	f	rebel	e. reluctantly; indifferently
6.	e	expectantly	f. conform
7.	a	donating	g. bent
8.	d	precision	h. meek
9.	b	lucky	i. light-hearted
10.	c	disciple	j. calm

Directions: Match each of the following expressions to its correct definition.

_e_   1. ground rules

_h_   2. piece of cake

_i_   3. on top of the situation

_c_   4. stickler

_b_   5. second guess

_d_   6. hand in hand

_a_   7. dress rehearsal

_f_   8. shrinking violet

_g_   9. fair and square

a. practice session in preparation for the real event

b. to criticize a decision after its outcome is known

c. perfectionist; one who insists on something unyieldingly

d. in cooperation; jointly

e. common set of agreed standards

f. shy and retiring person

g. just and honest

h. something easily accomplished

i. in control

Directions: Using a dictionary, define the following words. Then use each of the words in a sentence. You may change or add endings. The paragraph number in parentheses tells you where the word is located in the reading selection.

1. sympathy (paragraph 3)   the ability to share the feelings of another

_____

2. hemisphere (paragraph 4)   half of the terrestrial globe

_____

3. phase (paragraph 12)   a stage in the process of change

_____

4. obsession (paragraph 18)   the domination of one's thoughts by a

persistent idea

5. minutiae (paragraph 21) small or trifling matters

In Your Own Words

1. What sort of child was Christine Brennan? What was her personality like? What kind of person do you think she is today?

2. What did Mr. Brennan mean when he said, "This ain't no dress rehearsal"?

3. How did Mr. Brennan's advice and example contribute to his daughter's ultimate success as a journalist?

4. Given Christine Brennan's examples, what kind of man do you think Mr. Brennan was?

5. How would you characterize the way Mr. Brennan raised Christine?

6. What do you think of Mr. Brennan's reaction to the U.S. flag referred to as the American flag? What does he mean when he says it's "presumptuous"?

7. How did Mr. Brennan treat his employees? Do you think people would like to work for him? Why or why not?

Written Assignment

Directions: Choose one of the following and write a short paragraph.

1. Mr. Brennan made an indelible impression on Christine. Is there someone in your life who has made that kind of impression on you? Describe a person for whom you have a great deal of respect. Give reasons for your choice.

2. What is your definition of a good parent?

3. Most of the excerpt consists of Christine Brennan's reminiscences of her childhood. Write a few paragraphs describing your own childhood.

4. What picture do you get of Christine Brennan's father? Of the relationship between Christine and her father? Try describing the relationship between yourself and another person making use of specific examples as Christine does.

5. What kind of boss would you like to work for? Write a few paragraphs comparing a good boss to a bad boss.

6. Write a paragraph explaining and evaluating one of the following statements:

   "Make a decision and never look back."

   "To whom much is given, much is expected."

   "You're tough enough to handle anything."

   "Put your brain in gear before you put your mouth in motion."

Internet Activity

1. Christine Brennan is the most widely read woman sports columnist in the United States. Locate one of her columns in *USA Today* and write a paragraph telling what you learned.

   www.usatoday.com

2. Find out more about Title IX, the first comprehensive federal law to prohibit discrimination against students and employees of education institutions. Write a few paragraphs describing the implications of the amendment.

Phonics: Consonants, Vowels, and Syllabication

There are 26 letters in the English alphabet. But, these letters make more than 26 sounds. Some languages have a direct correspondence between sounds and symbols so that every symbol or letter has its own distinctive sound. This is not so with English, which is one reason English is a difficult language to learn. As an example of how complex English pronunciation can be, study the cartoon below and determine what G H O T I really spells.

In order to determine what G H O T I spells, pronounce

GH as in "tou*gh*"

O as in "w*o*men"

TI as in "emo*ti*on"

Solution: When you pronounce GH as "ff," O as "ih," and TI as "sh," G H O T I really spells FISH!

PHONICS: A REVIEW

Phonics is the study of speech sounds and ways to represent them in writing. Most languages have two types of letters: vowels and consonants. **Consonants** are sounds that are pronounced when a speaker's voice is blocked by lips, teeth, or tongue. **Vowels** are sounds that are pronounced when the speaker's voice is open or not blocked by lips, teeth, or tongue.

Although English has much in common with the Romance languages such as Spanish, Italian, and French, it also has been influenced by many other languages. Even today, English continues to change as people from all over the world move to English-speaking countries and bring their own languages with them. In addition, as with other languages, people in different parts of the world, or even in different parts of the same country, speak English in different ways in varying dialects.

Because of these many influences, phonics helps us only to a certain point. Still, knowledge of phonics provides a valuable tool for sounding out unfamiliar words. By pronouncing the separate speech sounds and then blending them you can approximate the sound of the word and make a good guess as to its meaning.

Consonants

Single Consonants with One Sound

Most consonant letters have just one sound. Say the following words and listen to the sound of the initial consonant.

bat lamp take pipe violin move ride honey keep

Single Consonants with More Than One Sound

Listen to the difference between the sounds for the consonants C and G.

C Followed by e, i, or y (usually soft sound like the "s" in *sun*):
  cent, city, bicycle

C Followed by a, o, or u (usually hard sound like the "k" in *kind*):
  cat, come, curb

G Followed by e, i, or y (usually soft sound like the "j" in *jet*):
  germ, giant, gymnast

G Followed by other letters (usually hard sound like the "g" in *go*):
  good, glad, goat

Exercise 1: Single Consonant Sounds for C and G

Directions: Give two of your own examples for each of the following sounds.
Answers will vary.

soft c _____   hard c _____

soft g _____   hard g _____

Consonant Digraphs

Sometimes two letters that are next to each other form a single sound. These are called *consonant digraphs*. Some languages even have separate symbols or letters for such sounds. Say the following words to yourself and hear the single sound of the underlined letters.

then   church   what   sharp   phone

Consonant Blends

Consonant blends occur when side-by-side consonants keep their own sounds but are pronounced together. Say the following words and listen to the sound of each of the consonants in the underlined blend.

black   flower   spider   glass   brown   scan   smoke   creep
plate   slow   train   clean   slice   steep   winter   cold

Exercise 2: Consonant Digraphs and Blends

Directions: Pronounce the following words and then write on the line whether the first two letters of each word contain a consonant digraph (**D**) or consonant blend (**B**).

1. shell _____D_____

2. creek _____B_____

3. smile _____B_____

4. ship _____D_____

5. flu _____B_____

6. think _____D_____

7. brown _____B_____

8. phonics _____D_____

9. study _____B_____

10. chef _____D_____

Silent Consonants

When two of the same consonant letters come one after the other, the second one is silent, as in the following words.

ball   purr   odd   miss   hitting   egg   well

Silent consonants can also occur when the side-by-side consonants differ. Pronounce each of the words below and underline the silent consonant.

knife   pneumonia   sign   calf   island   sight   duck
psalm   wrap   debt

Exercise 3: Words with Silent Consonants

1. **Directions:** Sometimes the letters l, k, w, h, t, b, and gh are silent. Add the silent letters to the words below.

   a.   _w_ rite   _w_ rist   _w_ rong

   b.   ni_gh_ t   hi_gh_   fi_gh_ t

   c.   dum_b_   thum_b_

   d.   ca_t_ ch   wi_t_ ch   ki_t_ chen

   e.   _k_ nee   _k_ nob   _k_ nock

   f.   wa_l_ k   ta_l_ k

   g.   _h_ onest   _h_ our   g_h_ ost

2. **Directions:** On the line below, give three of your own examples of words with silent consonants.

   Answers will vary.

Vowels

Rule 1: Long Vowels with Silent E

The vowels in English are a, e, i, o, u, and sometimes y. Vowels have two basic sounds—long and short. Long vowels say their own names and in the dictionary are marked with a line over the letter as in $\bar{e}$. The following words have long vowels in them. Make a long mark over each long vowel.

   $\bar{a}$te $\bar{u}$se   n$\bar{o}$te   r$\bar{o}$pe   pl$\bar{a}$ce   b$\bar{i}$te $\bar{i}$ce   sm$\bar{o}$ke

As you can see, all of these words have an e at the end of the word. The final e is often silent and makes the previous vowel long. Notice the difference in how *not* and *note* are pronounced.

Rule 2: Double Vowels

It is sometimes said about double vowels that "the first one does the talking, and the second one does the walking." In other words, the first vowel says its own name (a long sound) while the second vowel is silent. Make a long mark over each long vowel.

   r$\bar{a}$in   w$\bar{e}$ed   s$\bar{e}$a   m$\bar{e}$at   l$\bar{o}$an   p$\bar{i}$e   l$\bar{e}$af   sw$\bar{e}$et

Rule 3: Single Vowel at the End of a Short Word or Syllable

Vowels are usually long when there is only one vowel at the end of a short word or syllable, as in *no*. Mark the following vowels long.

   g$\bar{o}$ s$\bar{o}$l$\bar{o}$ h$\bar{e}$ w$\bar{e}$ sh$\bar{e}$ h$\bar{i}$

Rule 4: Short Vowels

All the vowels discussed above also have short sounds. Short vowels are usually marked by a breve over the letter as in ă. A vowel is usually short if it is the only vowel at the beginning of a short word, as in the word *it*. A vowel is also usually short if it is the only vowel between two consonants, as in *bet*. In each of the following words, place a breve over the short vowel.

hĭt nŏt ăt jăm ĭn măp mĕn Tĭm rĕd wĭn

Rule 5: Other Combination Vowel Sounds

In the following words, the two side-by-side vowels combine to form a new sound.

r<u>ou</u>nd s<u>ou</u>p c<u>ou</u>sin f<u>oo</u>t c<u>oo</u>l c<u>au</u>se l<u>au</u>ndry br<u>ea</u>d c<u>oi</u>n b<u>oy</u>

Exercise 4: Vowel Sounds

Directions: Read the following words and decide whether the vowels are short, long with a silent e, double vowel with one vowel silent, or a combination vowel sound. Write your answers on the lines below.

1. ship ___short___
2. size ___long/silent e___
3. aid ___double vowel___
4. pet ___short___
5. coal ___double vowel___

6. pound ___combination___
7. fat ___short___
8. cause ___combination___
9. king ___short___
10. soup ___combination___

NOTE: Here is a reminder for the rules for short and long vowels:

NŌ ĪCE CRĒAM ĬN BĔD!

no—rule 3   ice—rule 1   cream—rule 2   in bed—rule 4

The Letter Y as a Consonant and as a Vowel

1. The letter y is sometimes a consonant and sometimes a vowel. At the beginning of a word, it is a consonant, as in the following words:

   yellow   yes   yet   yank   you   yell

2. In the middle of a word, y is a vowel and usually has the short sound of i (ĭ), as in *gym*.

3. At the end of words with one syllable, the y is pronounced as a long i (ī), as in

   by   dry   my   fly

4. At the end of words with two or more syllables, y is usually pronounced like a long e (ē), as in the following words:

many   partly   happy   baby

Exercise 5: Words with Y

Directions: Create your own words with Y. Answers will vary.

1. Y at the beginning of a word as a consonant _____

2. Y in the middle of a word with a short vowel sound _____

3. Y at the end of a word with a long vowel sound _____

Frank and Ernest

© 2003 Thaves / Reprinted with permission. Newspaper dist. by NEA, Inc.

R Control

The consonant letter r changes the sound of a vowel. Vowels before r do not have a short sound. For example,

car   for   her   dirt   nurse

Give an example of your own for each of the sounds indicated. Answers will vary.

ar _____   or _____

er _____   ir _____   ur _____

The Schwa

The schwa is not a letter of the alphabet. It can, however, stand for all five vowels and even for a vowel that is followed by an r. The schwa when pronounced sounds like "uh." In the dictionary it is represented by an upside-down e.

about (ə bout)   clemency (kleman sē)   positive (paz ə tiv)
tomorrow (tə mar ō)   industry (in dəs tre)

Exercise 6: Letter-Changing Games

Long Vowels

Directions: Change the word *hold* below by adding or subtracting letters, but you must keep the vowel o long. See how many words you can make. Answers will vary.

hold _____

_____

Short Vowels

Directions: Change the word *sat* by adding or subtracting letters, but you must keep the vowel "a" short. Answers will vary.

sat _____

_____

Phonic Irregularities

As mentioned in the Introduction, English is not completely phonetic. Sometimes a word is pronounced differently depending upon how it is being used or according to the context. Read the following sentences aloud and notice how the same sequence of letters can have different sounds and meanings.

1. The bandage was *wound* around the *wound*.
2. We must *polish* the *Polish* furniture.
3. He could *lead* if he could get the *lead* out.
4. The insurance was *invalid* for the *invalid*.
5. I did not *object* to the *object*.
6. Upon seeing the *tear* in the painting I shed a *tear*.
7. I had to *subject* the *subject* to a series of tests.
8. Since there was no time like the *present*, he thought it was time to *present* the *present*.
9. When shot at, the *dove dove* into the bushes.
10. I should have *read* the assignment that the teacher told me to *read*.

How many ways can the combination of the letters o-u-g-h be pronounced? List all the ways you know on the line below. (The answer appears at the bottom of p. 28) Answers will vary.

PHONICS: PRACTICE

Exercise 7: Phonics

A. **Directions:** If the c has a soft sound (*cent*), write **S** next to the word. If the c has a hard sound (*can*), write **K** next to the word.

1. once ___s___
2. decide ___s___
3. spruce ___s___
4. cool ___k___
5. college ___k___
6. common ___k___
7. fence ___s___
8. course ___k___
9. peace ___s___

B. **Directions:** If the sound of g is the soft sound (*germ*), write **j** next to the word. If the sound of g is the hard sound (*good*), write **g** next to the word.

1. hinge ___j___
2. stage ___j___
3. gain ___g___
4. gold ___g___
5. God ___g___
6. large ___j___
7. gift ___g___
8. rage ___j___
9. forge ___j___

C. **Directions:** Each of the following words has a consonant blend, consonant digraph, or both. Underline the blends and circle the digraphs.

1. swish
2. plush
3. flush
4. inspect
5. chest
6. drench
7. brisk
8. squash
9. thick

D. **Directions:** Write the correct blends in the blank.

1. Too many _sw_eets will give you cavities.
2. _Pl_ease whisper! _Sl_eeping baby!
3. I like to _dr_ink lots of _fr_esh lemonade on a hot day.
4. The _gr_ound in our backyard is too _dr_y for any _fl_owers to _gr_ow.
5. I _br_ought some food and _pl_enty of iced tea for our picnic.

E. **Directions:** Read the paragraph below and write the long or short vowel sound you hear in the numbered words.

Not so[1] many years in the past[2], when I was a kid[3], I could hardly wait[4] for snow. It was fun[5] to play in clean[6], white[7] snow. Today I think[8] snow is wet[9], and cold, and messy[10].

1. ō   2. ă   3. ĭ   4. ā   5. ŭ

6. ē   7. ī   8. ĭ   9. ĕ   10. ĕ, ē

F. Directions: Mark the vowels long or short: hăt, hāte.

1. līke   2. trŭck   3. tūbe   4. hōme

5. wĭll   6. păss   7. slŏt   8. gāme

G. Directions: Use what you know about phonics to write the correct English spellings of these words.

1. sope ____soap____   3. cou ____cow____   5. kwik ____quick____

2. doun ____down____   4. shigh ____shy____   6. klok ____clock____

Exercise 8: Phonics

Directions: For each of the vowel sounds listed below, write the key words that contain that sound.

Key Words

bang	dive	knew	smile
beach	drown	noisy	tank
blew	Ed	note	toy
bone	face	rain	truck
caution	feet	rob	under
check	fix	round	
chop	jaw	sin	

1. Short a ____bang____   ____tank____

2. Short o ____chop____   ____rob____

3. Short u ____truck____   ____under____

4. Long e ____beach____   ____feet____

_____

Answer to Question 10 on p. 28: In the English language, the letters o-u-g-h can be pronounced in the following different ways: *Coughing* and *hiccoughing*, a *dough*-faced man strode *through* the streets.

5.	Long i	smile	dive
6.	aw/au	caution	jaw
7.	ew/ue	knew	blew
8.	oi/oy	toy	noisy
9.	ou/ow	round	drown
10.	Long a	rain	face
11.	Short e	Ed	check
12.	Short i	fix	sin
13.	Long o	bone	note

Exercise 9: Phonics

Directions: Read the following paragraph and then place each word in the correct category. Use each word only once. Omit *of, to, a, the.*

Dave has a very hard job. Dave gets out of bed at dawn to clean his large yard. A boy named Paul joins him. First, Dave cuts the weeds and chops down a tree. Paul hauls the wood to the dump in his car. Next, Dave cuts the lawn. Soon his yard looks neat and nice.

Long Vowels with Silent E

1. Dave

2. named

3. nice

Double Vowels

1. clean

2. weeds

3. tree

4. near

R Control

1. very

2. hard

3. large

4. yard

5. first

6. car

Combination Vowels

1. out

2. dawn

3. boy

Short Vowels

1. has

2. job

3. gets

4.	Paul	4.	bed
5.	joins	5.	at
6.	down	6.	his
7.	hauls	7.	him
8.	wood	8.	cuts
9.	lawn	9.	and
10.	soon	10.	chops
11.	looks	11.	dump
		12.	in
		13.	next

Exercise 10: Phonetic Spelling

Directions: Use your knowledge of phonics to identify the answers to the following jokes. Write the correct answer on the line provided.

1. When does school usually begin?

   to͝o so͝on

   Answer: _____ too soon _____

2. What's the difference between a pen and a pencil?

   yoo poosh ā pən bət ā pen-səl məst bē led

   Answer: _____ you push a pen but a pencil must be led _____

3. What's a synonym?

   ā wurd yoo yooz hwen yoo kant spel thə uther wurd

   Answer: _____ a word you use when you can't spell the other word _____

4. When is attendance at school like a gift?

   hwen yoor̄ prezənt

   Answer: _____ when you're present _____

5. Why did the failing student apply for a charge card?

    hē nēd-ed ĕk-struh krĕ-dĭt

    Answer: ___he needed extra credit_____

6. Why did he miss reading class?

    hē g̃ŏt hookt ŏn fŏn ĭks

    Answer: ___he got hooked on phonics_____

7. Why do old school teachers never die?

    thā just grāde ə-wā

    Answer: ___they just grade away_____

8. When is a teacher like a bird of prey?

    hwen shē woches yoo līk ā hok

    Answer: ___when she watches you like a hawk_____

9. What happened when the English teacher's dictionary was stolen?

    shē wuz ăt ā lŏs for wurdz

    Answer: ___she was at a loss for words_____

10. Why was the library so crowded?

    ĭt wuz ol bookt ŭp

    Answer: ___it was all booked up_____

11. Who does everyone in college confide in?

    thə dēn əv ăd-mĭsh əns

    Answer: ___the dean of admissions_____

    Keller, Charles, *The Little Giant Book of School Jokes*, New York: Sterling Publishing
    Co., 2000

Internet Activity

For more practice with phonics, go to the following two websites, which feature word games.

http://www.surfnetkids.com/quiz/phonics/

http://www.surfnetkids.com/games/phonics-mm.htm

SYLLABLES

Breaking words down into syllables can help you read and pronounce unfamiliar words. A word may have one or more syllables. Each syllable has only one vowel sound that is heard. Look at the following words:

knob   hunter   silly   cheeseburger

The word *knob* has only one syllable because it has only one vowel sound that is heard:

short o

The word *hunter* has two syllables because it has two vowel sounds that are heard:

hun   ter

The word *silly* has two syllables because it has two vowel sounds that are heard:

sil   ly

The word *cheeseburger* has three syllables because it has three vowel sounds that are heard:

cheese   burg   er

Exercise 11: Syllables

A. **Directions:** Count the number of syllables you hear in the words below. Write the number for each on the lines provided.

1. __3__ family   5. __2__ paper

2. __2__ yellow   6. __1__ take

3. __1__ deep   7. __2__ sorry

4. __2__ worker   8. __2__ dancing

B. **Directions:** Write your own name and the names of five other people you know. Write the number of syllables that you hear in each name. Answers will vary.

1. _____   4. _____

2. _____   5. _____

3. _____   6. _____

Rules for Dividing Words into Syllables

Rule 1: VC/CV

mis/ter   con/duct   can/cel   cur/rent

If two vowels in a word are separated by two consonants, divide between the two consonants. Consonant blends may or may not be separated. In **mister**, the word is divided between the *st* blend. In the word **impress**, the division is made before the blend as in *im/press*. Digraphs are usually not separated. For example, **mother** is divided after the *th* as in *moth/er*.

Rule 2: V/CV

vi/rus   fu/ture

If the first vowel in a word is long, divide after the long vowel sound. In this pattern, a vowel is often followed by a single consonant.

Rule 3: VC/V

di/vide   rig/or

If the first vowel in a word is a short vowel, divide after the short vowel and the consonant.

Rule 4: Compound Word

home/work   sun/shine

Divide a compound word between the two smaller words it contains.

Rule 5

rent/ed   deed/ed

When a t or d is at the end of a word (usually a verb) and it is followed by ed, the ed forms a separate syllable.

Exercise 12: Syllables

Directions: Divide the following words into syllables and write the rule number you used.

1. hun|ted   Rule ___5___   6. se|cond   Rule ___3___

2. can|not   Rule ___4___   7. e|vil   Rule ___2___

3. stom|ach   Rule ___3___   8. bed|room   Rule ___4___

4. num|ber   Rule ___I___   9. sal|ad   Rule ___3___

5. be|low   Rule ___2___   10. be|lief   Rule ___2___

Exercise 13: Syllables

Directions: Use only two-syllable words to complete each sentence.

1. Many young people have trouble deciding whether to go to
   ____college____ .
   (work, college, university)

2. During summer vacation, many families like to travel across the country
   to ___visit___ old friends.
   (visit, join, see)

3. Every four years, the American voters ___select___ a new president.
   choose, select, pick

4. Many students need work schedules that are ___stable___ in order to
   attend class.   (flexible, stable, short)

5. It takes the average student many years to ___exit___ from college.
   (graduate, separate, exit)

READING

"'But the best part of (a book) is the story
that it tells,' said their mother."

GETTING FOCUSED

The short selection below describes an incident in the life of King Alfred (849–899) of England. Alfred is best known for his strong defense of England against the Danes. He is considered to be the "Father of the English Navy."

A well-read man, Alfred established schools and encouraged education throughout his kingdom. He was a scholar who translated works of Latin into the Anglo-Saxon tongue. He also founded a university at Oxford. He was buried in Winchester, and is the only English monarch to carry the title "the Great."

BIO-SKETCH

James Baldwin was a well-known author of the twentieth century. His most famous novel is *Go Tell It on the Mountain*.

TACKLING VOCABULARY

leaves   sheets of paper or other writing material

monk   a person who lives in a monastery as a member of a religious order
Most monks take vows of poverty, chastity, and obedience

HOW A PRINCE LEARNED TO READ

James Baldwin

A thousand years ago boys and girls did not learn to read. Books were very scarce and very precious, and only a few men could read them.

2   Each book was written with a pen or a brush. The pictures were painted by hand, and some of them were very beautiful. A good book would sometimes cost as much as a good house.

3   In those times there were even some kings who could not read. They thought more of hunting and fighting than of learning.

4   There was one such king who had four sons, Ethelbald, Ethelbert, Ethelred, and Alfred. The three older boys were sturdy, half-grown lads; the youngest, Alfred, was a slender, fair-haired child.

5   One day when they were with their mother, she showed them a wonderful book that some rich friend had given her. She turned the leaves and showed them the strange letters. She showed them the beautiful pictures, and told them how they had been drawn and painted.

6   They admired the book very much, for they had never seen anything like it.

7   "But the best part of it is the story that it tells," said their mother. "If you could only read, you might learn that story and enjoy it. Now I have a mind to give this book to one of you."

8   "Will you give it to me, mother?" asked little Alfred.

9   "I will give it to the one who first learns to read in it," she answered.

10   "I am sure I would rather have a good bow with arrows," said Ethelred.

11   "And I would rather have a young hawk that has been trained to hunt," said Ethelbert.

12   "If I were a priest or a monk," said Ethelbald, "I would learn to read. But I am a prince, and it is foolish for princes to waste their time with such things."

13   "But I should like to know the story this book tells," said Alfred.

14   A few weeks passed by. Then one morning Alfred went into his mother's room with a smiling, joyous face.

15   "Mother," he said, "will you let me see that beautiful book again?"

16   His mother unlocked her cabinet and took the precious volume from its place of safe-keeping.

17   Alfred opened it with careful fingers. Then he began with the first word on the first page and read the first story aloud without making one mistake.

18   "O my child, how did you learn to do that?" cried his mother.

19   "I asked the monk, Brother Felix, to teach me," said Alfred. "And every day since you showed me the book, he has given me a lesson. It was no easy thing to learn these letters and how they are put together to make words. Now Brother Felix says I can read almost as well as he."

"The fact of knowing how to read is nothing. The whole point is knowing what to read."

—Jacques Ellul

20   "How wonderful!" said his mother.

21   "How foolish!" said Ethelbald.

22   "You will be a good monk when you grow up," said Ethelred with a sneer.

23   But his mother kissed him and gave him the beautiful book. "The prize is yours, Alfred," she said. "I am sure that whether you grow up to be a monk or a king, you will be a wise and noble man."

24   And Alfred did grow up to become the wisest and noblest king that England ever had. In history, he is called Alfred the Great.

"How a Prince Learned to Read" by James Baldwin is from The Baldwin Online Children's Literature Project at 222.mainlesson.com. Reprinted with permission.

✔ COMPREHENSION CHECKUP

True or False

_____ T   1. King Alfred's father could not read.

_____ T   2. Alfred was the youngest of his father's sons.

_____ F   3. Alfred's mother thought the book had little value.

_____ T   4. Alfred's mother knew how to read.

_____ T   5. Alfred took reading lessons from Brother Felix.

___F___ 6. Alfred's brothers were equally interested in learning to read.

___F___ 7. Ethelbald won the book prize.

___F___ 8. It was easy for Alfred to learn how to read.

___F___ 9. Alfred became a monk.

___T___ 10. Alfred's mother was surprised by Alfred's ability to read.

Vocabulary

Directions: Look through the selection and find the word that matches each of the following definitions.

1. insufficient to satisfy need or demand _____scarce_____

2. of great value _____precious_____

3. strongly built _____sturdy_____

4. thin or slight _____slender_____

5. happy; jubilant _____joyous_____

6. protection; care; custody _____safe-keeping_____

7. a look or expression of scorn _____sneer_____

8. of a high quality; distinguished; imposing _____noble_____

Phonics and Syllable Practice

___b___ 1. All of the following words from the reading contain digraphs *except*

    a. thousand.

    b. scarce.

    c. child.

    d. brush.

___d___ 2. All of the following words from the selection contain blends *except*

    a. sturdy.

    b. friend.

    c. drawn.

    d. read.

___b___ 3. All of the following words from the reading are two syllables *except*

    a. pictures

    b. beautiful

    c. mother

    d. morning

___a___ 4. All of the following words from the selection have a long *a* sound *except*

    a. scarce.

    b. painted.

    c. strange.

    d. waste.

___d___ 5. All of the following words from the selection have a short vowel sound *except*

    a. hunt.

    b. much.

    c. hand.

    d. me.

In Your Own Words

The following quotes are both attributed to King Alfred.

> "My will was to live worthily as long as I lived,
> and after my life to leave to them that should
> come after, my memory in good works."

Does this quote tell you anything about how King Alfred tried to live his life?

> "Therefore he seems to me a very foolish man,
> and truly wretched, who will not increase his
> understanding while he is in the world."

Do you think that King Alfred believed this when he was a boy learning to read?

Written Assignment

In a short paragraph, explain what the following quote by King Alfred means to you.

> "The just man builds on a modest foundation and
> gradually proceeds to greater things."

Internet Activity

1. Do a Google search using the following key words: "illuminated manuscripts" or "monastic scribes." Look for information explaining how the illuminated manuscripts were created. What techniques were used?

2. Go online to view the *Book of Kells* (the four gospels of Christian scripture). It was produced by Celtic monks around A.D. 800 and is on permanent display at Trinity College Library in Dublin, Ireland.

   http://www.tcd.ie/Library/heritage/Kells

2 WORD STRUCTURE

Look at the following poem by Pulitzer Prize–winning poet Richard Wilbur. In it, Wilbur uses the word *penniless*, which contains the suffix *less*, meaning "without." He also refers to the phrase "heads or tails," which contains a pair of antonyms, words that mean the opposite of each other.

What is the opposite of penny?

I'm sorry, but there isn't any—

Unless you count the change, I guess,

Of someone who is penniless.

When people flip a penny, its

Two sides, of course, are opposites.

I'll flip one now. Go on and choose:

Which is it, heads or tails? You lose.

_____

Can you try to write an antonym poem of your own?

This warm-up focuses on word parts, synonyms, and antonyms. Studying word parts—prefixes, roots, and suffixes—is important because it helps you learn how to "dissect" a word in order to determine its meaning.

The English language contains many words that are similar or dissimilar in meaning. Words that are similar in meaning to each other are called **synonyms.** Words that have the opposite meaning to each other are called **antonyms.**

WORD PARTS: A REVIEW

One way of determining what a word means is to examine its word parts. Many words in English are based on Latin and Greek word parts. The Greeks and Romans devised a system of word parts, which we still use today. If you know the meaning of enough of these word parts, you can discover a word's meaning without referring to a dictionary. Let's examine the word *predicted.* Read the following sentence:

I heard that Miguel **predicted** the winner of this year's Super Bowl.

After reading this sentence, you know that Miguel stated ahead of time who was going to win the game. Now let's look at the word parts in *predicted. Pre* means "before"; *dict,* as in *dictator* or *dictionary,* means "to say." Thus the word *predicted* means "to say what the outcome of an event will be before the event actually takes place."

Let's try another word: **subtract.**

Marie was asked to *subtract* the hours she spent talking with her boyfriend from her timesheet.

You know the meaning of this word and probably know that *sub* means "under." But what about *tract? Tract,* as in *tractor,* means "to pull." So, when you *subtract* one number from another, you are literally pulling the number below from the number above.

The Greeks used three types of word parts—prefixes, suffixes, and root words. **Prefixes** come at the beginning of words, **suffixes** at the end of words, and **root words** are the basic core of the word. In our example of *predicted, pre* is the prefix, *ed* is the suffix, and *dict* is the root word. In *subtract, sub* is the prefix, and *tract* is the root word.

Prefixes

Prefixes are a syllable or syllables placed at the beginning of a word to change its meaning. For example, *uncomfortable* means the opposite of *comfortable* because the prefix *un* means "not."

The following is a list of common prefixes.

Prefix	Meaning	Example
ad	toward	advance
anti	against	antifreeze
auto	self	automobile
bene	well	beneficial

Prefix	Meaning	Example
bene	well	beneficial
co, com, con	with	coordinate, committee, continue
de	opposite, down, away	depart
dis	apart, away	disagree
in, im , ir, il	not or opposite	incorrect, impossible, irresponsible, illegal
in, im	in, into	increase, import
inter	between, among	interstate
intra	within	intramural
mal	bad	malnutrition
mis	bad(ly)	miscalculate
non	not	nonreturnable
over	too; too much	overcrowded
pre	before	prescribe
post	after	postnatal
re	again, back	refresh, recede
sub	under, below	submarine
super	above, over	supervisor
trans	across	transport
un	not	unable

The following is a list of common prefixes that indicate a number.

Prefix	Meaning	Example
uni	one	unicycle
bi	two	bicycle
tri	three	tricycle
quad	four	quadriceps
oct	eight	octopus
dec	ten	decade
cent	hundred	century

Suffixes

Suffixes consist of a syllable or syllables placed at the end of a word to form a different part of speech. Suffixes can change words into adjectives, adverbs, nouns, or verbs. For example, by adding different suffixes to the root word *agree*, the part of speech and meaning of the word are changed as you can see in this example.

agreeable   He was *agreeable* to our plan.
(adjective)

agreeably   He worked *agreeably* with the other people on the project.
(adverb)

agreement   The two countries finally managed to forge an *agreement*.
(noun)

Here is a list of common suffixes.

Suffix	Meaning	Example
able, ible	able to	movable, eligible
ance, ence	a quality or state of action	assistance, preference
ant, ent	act or cause	automate
ate	marked by having	assistant, attendent
er, or, ist	one who	teacher, counselor, biologist
ful	full of	careful
ic, al	to make	quantify, realize
ify, ize	relating to, characterized	patriotic, maternal
ion, tion	likely to	instructive
ive	condition or result	permission, position
less	without	meatless
ly	like something	brotherly
ment	state of being	amendment
ness	quality of, condition	sadness
ology	study of	sociology

Roots

A **root** is the main part of a word to which prefixes or suffixes are attached. The root gives a word its basic meaning. Knowing roots can help you recognize unfamiliar words.

The following is a list of common root words.

Root	Meaning	Example
ann, enn	year	annual, centennial
audio	hear	audience
biblio	book	bibliography
bio	life	biology
cap	head	capital
capt	take, seize	capture
dic, dict	say, tell	dictate
duct	lead	conduct
gam	marriage	polygamy
graph	write	graphite
man	hand	manual
mit, mis	send	remit, mission

Root	Meaning	Example
ped, pod	foot	pedestrian, podiatrist
phobia	fear	claustrophobia
phono	sound	phonics
port	carry	report
scope	instrument for seeing	microscope
scribe, script	write	inscribe, description
spect	see	inspect
ven	come	invent
vert, verse	turn	invert, reverse
vis	see	vision
voc	call	vocation

The following exercises will give you practice in working with word parts. Most of the word parts can be found in the lists above, but you may have to consult your dictionary to look up the word parts for a few words.

WORD PARTS: PRACTICE

Exercise 1: Prefixes, Roots, and Suffixes

A. **Directions:** Separate the following words into prefixes, roots, and suffixes. Then write a definition for each word.

Word	Prefix	Root	Suffix	Definition
1. unfaithful	un	faith	ful	not faithful
2. immeasurable	im	measure	able	too large to measure
3. reusable	re	use	able	able to be used again
4. disagreement	dis	agree	ment	state of failing to agree
5. unfairness	un	fair	ness	condition of not being fair
6. distasteful	dis	taste	ful	not of good taste
7. unlovable	un	love	able	cannot be loved
8. repayment	re	pay	ment	the state of paying back
9. replaceable	re	place	able	able to be replaced
10. predictable	pre	dict	able	easily predicted

B. **Directions:** Each of the following words contains a root and either a prefix or a suffix. Using your knowledge of word parts, determine the meaning of each word and write a definition. Then check your definition with a dictionary.

Word	Prefix	Root	Suffix	Definition
1. fearless		fear	less	without fear
2. sculptor		sculpt	or	person who sculpts
3. predict	pre	dict		to tell what will happen in the future
4. darkness		dark	ness	state of being dark
5. uncertain	un	certain		not certain
6. substandard	sub	standard		below standard
7. antiwar	anti	war		against war
8. insecure	in	secure		not secure
9. improper	im	proper		not proper
10. agreeable		agree	able	willing to agree

Exercise 2: Prefixes, Suffixes, and Root Words

A. **Directions:** For each of the following words, write the prefix, the root, and a definition.

	Prefix	Root	Word Definition
1. unknown	un	known	not known
2. disagree	dis	agree	not agree
3. insane	in	sane	not sane
4. misbehave	mis	behave	behave badly
5. misunderstand	mis	understand	understand badly, wrong
6. imperfect	im	perfect	not perfect
7. nonalcoholic	non	alcoholic	not alcoholic

8. refinance	re	finance	finance again
9. preheat	pre	heat	heat before, ahead
10. antisocial	anti	social	not liking to be with people

B. **Directions:** For each of the following words, write the root, the suffix, and a definition.

	Root	**Suffix**	**Word Definition**
1. nervousness	nervous	ness	condition of being nervous
2. sugarless	sugar	less	without sugar
3. fearful	fear	ful	full of fear
4. inventor	invent	or	person who invents
5. perishable	perish	able	able to perish
6. appointment	appoint	ment	someone chosen for job, or a meeting
7. meatless	meat	less	without meat
8. leader	lead	er	person who leads
9. creation	create	ion	the act of creativity
10. breakable	break	able	able to be broken

C. **Directions:** Add one of the following prefixes to each of the words listed below: **un, dis, re,** or **pre.** Then write a sentence using the word. Answers will vary.

1. __re__ test _____

2. __dis__ count _____

3. __pre__ view _____

4. __dis__ agree _____

5. __dis__ cover _____

Exercise 3: Prefixes, Roots, and Suffixes

Directions: In the following list, combine each root with a prefix or suffix to make a common word. You may use prefixes and suffixes more than once. Then use your dictionary to write a definition for each word. Answers will vary.

Prefixes	Roots	Suffixes
un	break	ful
re	read	ed
non	law	ive
in	pay	able
over	sight	ment
pre	take	less
mis	grace	ness
de	part	en
dis	know	er
im	remark	s/ion
	measure	t/ion
	prove	

1. _____ Definition: _____

2. _____ Definition: _____

3. _____ Definition: _____

4. _____ Definition: _____

5. _____ Definition: _____

6. _____ Definition: _____

7. _____ Definition: _____

8. _____ Definition: _____

9. _____ Definition: _____

10. _____ Definition: _____

11. _____ Definition: _____

12. _____ Definition: _____

Extras

13. _____ Definition: _____

14. _____ Definition: _____

15. _____ Definition: _____

16. _____ Definition: _____

Exercise 4: Prefixes and Suffixes

Directions: Read each sentence and fill in the missing prefix or prefixes using the following list: **dis, pre, mis, un,** or **re.**

1. Rafael ____dis____ likes any person who is ____dis____ honest with him.

2. Please ____re____ place the broken window. It's very ____un____ wise to leave it like that.

3. Can you ____re____ call if we paid the utility bill?

4. It was a big ____mis____ take to leave the back door ____un____ locked because a burglar got in.

5. She has an eating ____dis____ order. She leaves most of the food on her plate ____un____ touched.

6. Elvia is going to ____re____ heat what's left of the pizza.

7. It's not ____un____ common to find bottles for ____re____ cycling alongside highways.

8. Please ____re____ fill my glass of lemonade. I was so thirsty that it ____dis____ appeared quickly.

Directions: Read the sentence and fill in the correct prefix or suffix.

1. I love to feel the soft ____ness____ of the kitten's fur.   full   less   ness

2. We saw a beauti ____ful____ sunset over the lake.   ish   ful   able

3. She hopes to be a professional danc ____er____ .   ly   er   ish

4. I ___dis___ like waiting for a bus.   dis   un   re

5. He has a rare blood ___dis___ order.   dis   re   pre

6. Please ___re___ mind me to pay the fine on time.   un   re   dis

7. It was a big ___mis___ take not to finish college. un   pre   mis

8. That is the pretti ___est___ picture she's ever painted.   er   est

C. **Directions:** For each word, write the letter for the correct definition in the blank provided.

___b___ 1. unable   a. to cry out

___c___ 2. exchange   b. not able

___f___ 3. inhuman   c. to give in place of something else

___h___ 4. unsafe   d. not fit

___g___ 5. refill   e. to loosen; take off; separate

___a___ 6. exclaim   f. not human

___e___ 7. detach   g. to fill again

___d___ 8. unfit   h. not safe

SYNONYMS AND ANTONYMS: A REVIEW

A **synonym** is a word or phrase that is close in meaning to another word. Learning synonyms is a good way to expand your vocabulary. Knowing synonyms allows you to be precise and choose the most suitable word to express what you want to say. Notice the synonyms in the following sentences.

Frantically, Marla tried to finish her English paper before the *due date.*

In a *frenzy,* Marla tried to finish her paper before the *deadline.*

An **antonym** is any word or phrase that has an opposite or contrasting meaning. Notice the antonyms in the following sentence.

Unlike her *panicky* classmates, Marla *calmly* worked on her paper.

(Wizard of ID) Reprinted by permission of John L. Hart FLP and Creators Syndicate, Inc.

SYNONYMS AND ANTONYMS: PRACTICE

The following exercises will give you practice in working with synonyms and antonyms.

Exercise 5: Synonyms and Antonyms

Directions: Study the **underlined** words. Put an **S** on the line next to the synonyms for each word and an **A** on the line next to the antonyms.

1. <u>able</u>   S capable   A ineffective   S competent   S skillful

2. <u>perfect</u>   S flawless   A faulty   S unblemished   A defective

3. <u>gentle</u>   S docile   S mild   A rough   S tender

4. <u>abolish</u> S void   S destroy   A enact   S revoke

5. <u>rational</u> A silly   A absurd   S reasonable   S logical

B. **Directions:** Write the words below on the appropriate lines.

advance	cheerful	exhibit	protect	tender
alteration	coarse	individual	rapid	withdraw
amuse	discordant	modern		

1. synonym for display   exhibit

2. synonym for defend   protect

3. synonym for hasty   rapid

4. antonym for tough   tender

5. synonym for retreat   withdraw

6. antonym for harmonious   discordant

7. synonym for move   advance

8. antonym for fine   coarse

9. antonym for group   individual

10. synonym for entertain   amuse

11. antonym for antique   modern

12. synonym for bright   cheerful

13. synonym for change   alteration

Exercise 6: Synonyms and Antonyms

A. **Directions:** Write the correct synonym for each word on the lines below.

attorney	outlaw
disagreement	practice
dismiss	sadistic
duty	scream
menial	tart
neat	weep
normal	

1. shout _____scream_____

2. cry _____weep_____

3. cruel _____sadistic_____

4. obligation _____duty_____

5. criminal _____outlaw_____

6. dispute _____disagreement_____

7. average _____normal_____

8. sour _____tart_____

9. tidy _____neat_____

10. lawyer _____attorney_____

11. discharge _____dismiss_____

12. rehearse _____practice_____

13. low _____menial_____

B. **Directions:** Write the correct antonym for each word on the lines below.

applaud	dirty	guilty	many	popular	save	sober
careful	dull	healthy	neat	punish	selfish	sorrow
cheerful	fact	honest	nothing	reject	servant	sorry
cowardly	friend	light	odd	relaxed		

1. few _____many_____

2. adversary _____friend_____

3. heavy _____light_____

4. altruistic _____selfish_____

5. innocent _____guilty_____

6. clean _____dirty_____

7. joy _____sorrow_____

8. untidy _____neat_____

9. unpopular _____popular_____

10. ailing _____healthy_____

11. inebriated _____sober_____

12. fiction _____fact_____

13. everything _____nothing_____

14. dishonest _____honest_____

15. master _____servant_____

16. boo _____applaud_____

17. approve _____reject_____

18. sharp _____dull_____

19. usual _____odd_____

20. sorrowful _____cheerful_____

21. careless _____careful_____   24. unrepentant _____sorry_____

22. spend _____save_____   25. courageous _____cowardly_____

23. praise _____punish_____   26. uptight _____relaxed_____

Exercise 7: Synonyms

THE CASE OF THE BOTTLE OF CYANIDE

Arthur maxim *sagged* in an easy chair. His right hand lay in his lap, *clutched* about a bottle of cyanide.

"He's been dead about 15 minutes," Dr. Haledjian told Carter. "Have you *called* the police?"

"Yes, but I *called* you first. I knew you were at the hotel. Arthur was depressed but I never *dreamed* he'd kill himself!"

"You knew him well?" asked Haledjian.

"We were kids together," *retorted* Carter.

"Since his wife divorced him, he's been *despondent*. I *proposed* this vacation. He *seemed* better yesterday. We played golf and fished. But, half an hour ago I went down to the *vestibule* for a newspaper. Just as I returned, he drank that bottle in his hand."

Inspector Winters arrived. Haledjian summed up his findings.

"You'll notice how *lax* the body is," said the detective. "Cyanide kills *instantaneously* and the muscles go limp."

Two days later the Inspector told Haledjian: "The lab substantiates that Maxim's death was due to cyanide."

"That *clinches* it!" was the reply. "Arrest Carter on suspicion of *homicide*!"

WHY? (See Answer Key on page A-1.)

Sobol, Donald J., *More Two-Minute Mysteries,* New York: Scholastic, 1971, pp. 11–12

Directions: Find the synonym for each italicized word in the reading in the word list below and write it on the appropriate line.

appeared	grasped	lobby	replied	suggested
confirms	imagined	murder	slack	
dejected	immediately	phoned	slumped	

1. sagged _____slumped_____

2. clutched _____grasped_____

3. called _____phoned_____

4. dreamed   ____imagined_____

5. retorted   ____replied_____

6. despondent   ____dejected_____

7. proposed   ____suggested_____

8. seemed   ____appeared_____

9. vestibule   ____lobby_____

10. lax   ____slack_____

11. instantaneously ____immediately_____

12. clinches   ____confirms_____

13. homicide   ____murder_____

Exercise 8: Synonyms

THE CASE OF THE BLACKMAILER

I don't mind telling you, Dr. Haledjian," said Thomas Hunt, "that *inheriting* the Hunt millions has had its nerve-wracking moments. Do you remember Martin, the gardener?"

"A smiling little chap," said Haledjian, pouring his young friend a brandy.

"That's the fellow. I *dismissed* him upon inheriting the house in East Hampton. Well, three days ago he came to my office *smirking,* and demanded one hundred thousand dollars.

He claimed to have been tending the spruce trees outside my father's study when Dad drew up another will, naming his brother in New Zealand *sole heir.*"

"You believed him?"

"I *confess* the news hit me like a thunderbolt. Dad and I had *quarreled* over Veronica sometime during the last week in November. Dad opposed the marriage and it seemed *plausible* that he had cut me off."

"Martin *asserted* he possessed this second will, which he felt sure would be worth a good deal more to me than he was asking. As it was dated November 31—the day after the executed will—it would be legally recognized, he claimed."

"I refused to be blackmailed. He tried to *bargain*, asking fifty thousand and then twenty-five thousand."

"You paid nothing, I hope?" asked Haledjian.

"I paid—with my foot firm on the seat of his pants."

"Quite right," answered Haledjian."Imagine trying to peddle a *tale* like that!"

What was Martin's *blunder*? (See Answer Key on page A-1.)

Sobol, Donald J., *Two-Minute Mysteries*, New York: Scholastic, 1967, pp. 17–18

Directions: Find the synonym for each italicized word in the reading in the word list below and write it on the appropriate line.

acquiring	beneficiary	error	only
admit	declared	grinning	squabbled
believable	discharged	negotiate	story

1. inheriting   _acquiring_

2. dismissed   _discharged_

3. smirking   _grinning_

4. sole   _only_

5. heir   _beneficiary_

6. confess   _admit_

7. quarreled   _squabbled_

8. plausible   _believable_

9. asserted   _declared_

10. bargain   _negotiate_

11. tale   _story_

12. blunder   _error_

Exercise 9: Antonyms

THE CASE OF THE SECOND WILL

"Young Mark Rall insists he *found* this in an Old Testament in his uncle's library," said Evans the attorney. He handed Dr. Haledjian a document as both men *sat* in the criminologist's library. Haledjian *released* a low whistle. The document was a last will and testament. It bequeathed the bulk of Arthur Colby's millions to his 22-year-old nephew, Mark Rall.

"This will is either *genuine* or a clever forgery," said Haledjian. "When did Colby die?"

"Last April—April 21, to be exact," answered Evans. "If this will is genuine, it will mean Colby's two *elderly* sisters, my clients, will be out a fortune."

"I assume this new will is dated *after* the one leaving the fortune to your clients?"

"Yes, twelve days later," said Evans.

"When did young Rall find it?"

"Last week," said Evans. "He says he had *opened* a copy of the Old Testament and there between pages 157 and 158 was this will."

"He's willing to settle out of court—for half his uncle's estate! But I must give him an answer in two hours. Can you spot anything *wrong* with the will he claims to have found?"

"I'm no *expert* in the field," concluded the sleuth. "Nevertheless, I should tell young Rall to put this will back where he found it!"

HOW COME? (See Answer Key on page A-1.)

Sobol, Donald J., *More Two-Minute Mysteries*, New York: Scholastic, 1971, pp. 87–88

Directions: Find the antonym for each italicized word in the word list below and write it on the appropriate line.

before	correct	held	stood
beginner	counterfeit	lost	youthful
closed	elderly		

1. young   elderly

2. found   lost

3. sat   stood

4. released   held

5. genuine   counterfeit

6. elderly   youthful

7. after   before

8. opened   closed

9. wrong   _____correct_____

10. expert   _____beginner_____

Exercise 10: Synonyms

THE CASE OF THE THEFT AT THE CIRCUS

Willie the clown, still *attired* in his comic knight suit of pots and pans, clanked and clattered to the pile of folded chairs and sat down *disconsolately*.

"It's true I passed Princess Minerva's trailer five minutes ago. But I didn't steal her money!"

"I saw him slip out of the trailer," insisted Kathy Winslow, an aerial ballerina. "He looked around, stuck a bag under his arm, and hurried off. I couldn't mistake him in that *get-up!*"

"Come now, Kathy. You're *overwrought,*" said Princess Minerva, the circus' trapeze star. "Everyone knows where I keep my cash. Why would Willie rob me? We've been together with the circus for twenty years!"

"Calm down yourself," *cautioned* Dr. Haledjian as he finished bandaging Princess Minerva's head. "You're going to be out of action a couple of days."

"Never mind me," said Princess. "Find the thief. I was sitting with my back to the door reading. I never heard the *louse* sneak in. What did he hit me with?"

"This," answered Haledjian, holding up a battered pot.

"It's not mine!" *protested* the clown.

"Don't believe him," said Kathy.

Haledjian studied Willie. His eyes narrowed.

"Your attempt to *frame* Willie is *contemptible,*" he said to Kathy.

How did Haledjian know? (See Answer Key on page A-1.)

Sobol, Donald J., *More Two-Minute Mysteries,* New York: Scholastic, 1971, pp. 105–106

Directions: Find the synonym for each italicized word in the reading in the word list below and write it on the appropriate line.

costume	dressed	hysterical	objected	smashed
despicable	forlornly	incriminate	rascal	warned

1. attired   _____dressed_____

2. disconsolately   _____forlornly_____

3. get-up   _____costume_____

4. overwrought   _____ hysterical _____

5. cautioned   _____ warned _____

6. louse   _____ rascal _____

7. battered   _____ smashed _____

8. protested   _____ objected _____

9. frame   _____ incriminate _____

10. contemptible   _____ despicable _____

READING

*"Scholars would speculate on the lost meanings
of the figures for nearly 1,500 years."*

GETTING FOCUSED

Scholars have long been fascinated with the decorative writings covering Egyptian tombs and monuments. The breakthrough in deciphering these written inscriptions didn't come until the discovery of the Rosetta Stone, a decree in honor of Ptolemy V. After that, scholars made rapid progress in deciphering the hieroglyphic language.

TACKLING VOCABULARY

Egyptologists   people who study Egyptian antiquities

Jean Francois Champollion   compiled a dictionary of the ancient Egyptian language

HOW TO READ EGYPTIAN HIEROGLYPHICS

Carol Donoughue

The Rosetta Stone

Nearly 5,000 years ago, the ancient Egyptians developed one of the earliest written languages known: hieroglyphics. For the next 3,000 years, this writing system evolved into a tool for recording commerce and government policy, for praising gods and guiding the dead in the afterlife, and even for writing romantic poetry. Then around 400 A.D., after the kingdoms of ancient Egypt had fallen as a result of numerous invasions, the writing system was forgotten.

2   Scholars would speculate on the lost meanings of the figures for nearly 1,500 years. Finally, in 1799, soldiers of Napoleon's army in Egypt excavated the Rosetta Stone. The key inscriptions on the stone were translated by Jean Francois Champollion in 1822. He discovered that the same words were written in three different scripts on the large, dark gray basalt stone.The first section was written in hieroglyphics, the second section in demotic script (cursive), and the third section in ancient Greek. The stone's hieroglyphs matched the ancient Greek text next to them. Because ancient Greek had survived, the Rosetta Stone was easily translated into French and English. From this starting point, Egyptologists were able to reconstruct the huge hieroglyphic system within 30 years.

Newsprint, 3000 B.C.

3Hieroglyphics, a Greek word meaning "sacred carvings," were often carved into limestone by a sculptor or painted on papyrus sheets. Papyrus, the earliest known type of paper, was uniquely Egyptian. Made from overlapping layers of the husk of the papyrus plant that grows along the Nile River, papyrus "paper" was lightweight, durable, and easy to write upon. However, while the plant was common, limestone was actually less expensive due to the labor involved in making the paper. Writing brushes were made from reeds, and ink from soot and other natural materials.

Differences Between English Writing and Hieroglyphics

4To see more clearly the differences between ancient Egyptian and modern-day English, let's write the word "hieroglyphics" in ancient Egyptian. The first step is translating the word phonetically.

HIEROGLYPHICS = HIROGLIFIKS

Next, eliminate the vowels (a, e, i, o, u, and y), leaving only the consonants. Unlike English, the Egyptians did not use vowels in writing.

HRGLFKS

Finally, refer to the symbol key on page 60 to find the hieroglyph that best matches each of these sounds.

H   R   G   L   F   K   S

Grouping and Direction of the Signs

5Hieroglyphs are arranged in what might seem like a haphazard, illogical manner from an English perspective. They can be written left to right like the writing you are reading here, or from right to left like Arabic and Hebrew, or in columns from top to bottom like Chinese. You can tell which way hieroglyphs are supposed to be read by looking at the animals. If they face left, start reading from the left. If they face right, begin on the right.

6   The following line of hieroglyphs was inscribed on a temple.

7   You can see that all of the animals and birds are facing the same way. They are facing towards the beginning of the line, and so the reader needs to read the line from left to right as in English.

8   When the ancient Egyptians wrote words in hieroglyphs, they arranged them carefully, making them look attractive. For example, if an ancient Egyptian wrote the name "Frank" in hieroglyphs, he probably would have arranged the symbols like this:

9   If you look closely at the Rosetta Stone, you'll notice another problem with hieroglyphic script. In the Egyptian writing, there are no spaces between the words, so it is very hard to tell where one word ends and another begins, whichmakesitverydifficulttoread. There are also no commas, periods, or paragraphs.

Hieroglyph Key

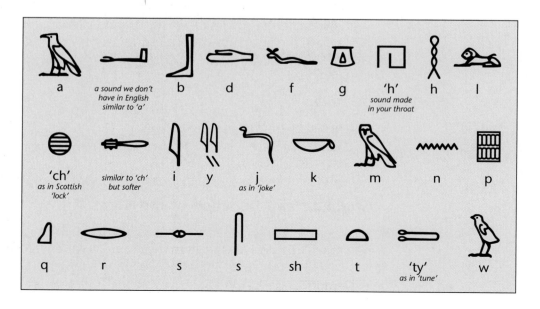

The Rosetta Stone
Hieroglyphic Script

Demotic Script

Greek

Excerpts about Ancient Egyptian Writing are from *The Mystery of the Hieroglyphs: The Story of the Rosetta Stone and the Race to Decipher Egyptian Hieroglyphs* by Carol Donoughue. Illustrations by Claire Thorne. Copyright © 1999 by Carol Donoughue. Reprinted by permission of Oxford University Press.

COMPREHENSION CHECKUP

Fill in the Blanks

1. The ancient Egyptians developed a form of language that is now called ___hieroglyphics___ .

2. At approximately ___400 A.D.___ , the writing system was forgotten.

3. In 1799, soldiers in Napoleon's army discovered the ___Rosetta Stone___ .

4. A translation of the stone's inscriptions was provided by ___Champollion___ .

5. Demotic script is similar to ___cursive___ writing.

6. The word "hieroglyphics" means <u>sacred carvings</u> .

7. <u>Papyrus</u> is a type of paper that is associated with the Egyptians.

8. Hieroglyphics are typically written using only <u>consonants</u> and no vowels.

9. You can tell which way hieroglyphs are supposed to be read by looking at the direction the <u>animals</u> are facing.

10. In Egyptian writing, no <u>spaces</u> are left between words.

11. In hieroglyphic script, there are no <u>periods</u> at the ends of sentences.

True or False

<u>T</u>   1. The Rosetta Stone became the key to deciphering Egyptian hieroglyphs.

<u>F</u>   2. The Egyptian hieroglyphs were accompanied by a Latin translation that could be read.

<u>T</u>   3. The Rosetta Stone displays text in three different scripts.

<u>F</u>   4. Hieroglyphs were often carved into sandstone or marble.

<u>T</u>   5. Brushes were frequently made from reeds.

<u>T</u>   6. Papyrus is an early type of paper.

<u>F</u>   7. The hieroglyphic system of writing remained a mystery until 1922.

<u>F</u>   8. In hieroglyphics, typically only the vowels are written.

Vocabulary in Context

Directions: Select one of the following words to complete each of the sentences. Use each word only once.

evolved	inscription	reconstruct
excavated	natural	speculate
haphazardly	overlapping	
illogical	perspective	

1. Over the years as he matured, his thinking ___evolved___ .

2. I can only ___speculate___ about what she's going to do after she graduates; I certainly don't know for sure.

3. The FBI ___excavated___ a large area on a Michigan farm trying to see if Union boss Jimmy Hoffa was buried there.

4. The ___inscription___ on her headstone read: "Beloved, wife, mother, grandmother."

5. The detective tried to understand the evidence at the scene of the crime to ___reconstruct___ the events leading to the murder.

6. Their ___overlapping___ duties were going to cause problems since they were both responsible for some of the same things.

7. The pizza, considered the best in the United States, was made with only the freshest ___natural___ ingredients.

8. It's no wonder he's doing poorly in school since his papers are strewn about ___haphazardly___ all over the floor of his room.

9. When we disagree with what someone is arguing, we might think the argument is ___illogical___ .

10. Living and working in Africa gave her a new ___perspective___ on world issues.

Practice with Word Parts

Directions: Referring to the lists of common prefixes, suffixes, and roots on pages 41–44, write a definition of the following words from the reading. Use a dictionary to check your definitions. Answers will vary.

1. reconstruct _____

2. illogical _____

3. perspective _____

4. inscribed _____

5. translated _____

6. carefully _____

7. sculptor _____

8. scripts _____

In Your Own Words

1. There are two basic forms of writing: sign writing, in which the symbols represent pictures as in Egyptian hieroglyphics and Chinese pictographs, and phonetic writing, which involves the use of an alphabet as in English. Do you see any difficulties with the pictograph system? What are some problems the Chinese might face in trying to adapt a pictograph system to the modern computer?

2. What kinds of changes do you think come to a society with the development of writing? What could people do then that they couldn't easily do before? How did people preserve knowledge before writing?

3. What do you think happened to those people who failed to learn to write, or were denied the opportunity to write, in past civilizations?

Written Assignment

1. Do you think that Egyptian antiquities that were orginally looted or stolen from Egypt should be returned to Egypt? Why or why not?

2. Try writing your name in hieroglyphics. An example is given.

   First, write your name normally: _____Susan_____

   Second, rewrite your name phonetically (exactly as it sounds). _____Soowsin_____

   There can often be several correct phonetic spellings of a name.

   Third, remove all vowels from your phonetic name. _____Swsn_____

   Fourth, match each sound to a symbol in the hieroglyph key._____

Internet Activity

1. To learn more about recent archaeological discoveries in Egypt, you can visit the following websites:

   www.egyptologyonline.com

   www.virtual-egypt.com

   www.crystalinks.com

   Choose one of the new discoveries and write a brief paragraph about your findings.

2. The following site examines Egyptian hieroglyphs:

   www.logos.uoregon.edu/explore/orthography/Egypt.html

3. The Rosetta Stone is kept in the British Museum. To view it, go to either of the following two websites:

   www.thebritishmuseum.ac.uk

   www.ancientegypt.co.uk

   The latter site provides information on Egyptian life.

3 DICTIONARY

Frank and Ernest

IT'S A CORDLESS SPELL CHECKER!

DICTIONARY

THAVES

© 2004 Thaves. Reprinted with permission. Newspaper dist. by NEA, Inc.

Dictionaries are valuable resources. The cartoon above illustrates one use of a dictionary—to show how words are spelled. In addition, dictionaries define words, show how they are pronounced, give their parts of speech, and give the etymologies, or histories of words. Some include examples showing the correct usage of words in phrases or sentences.

Can you think of any problems associated with computer spell checkers?

_____

_____

_____

Do you think your computer spell checker can tell the difference between words that sound alike such as "way" and "weigh"? Why or why not?

_____

_____

_____

Don't allow yourself to become dependent on your computer spell checker to find mistakes. That's what a dictionary is for.

DICTIONARIES

There are two important requirements for a good dictionary—being up-to-date and being complete.

An Up-to-Date Dictionary

English is constantly changing with new words being added constantly. Think of all the new computer terminology (bit, bytes, CD-ROM, download, hard drive) added over the last few years. There are also new definitions for words that have been around for centuries. Take the word *mouse*. Look at the following definitions from the 1960 *Webster's New Collegiate Dictionary*. What current definition of the word is missing?

> **mouse** (mous), *n.; pl.* MICE (mīs). [AS. *mūs*, pl. *mȳs.*] **1.** Any of numerous species of small rodents, esp. the *house mouse* (*Mus musculus*), now found in human habitations throughout most of the world. Cf. VOLE. **2.** A person, as a woman, so called by way of endearment. **3.** *Slang.* **a** A dark-colored swelling caused by a blow. **b** A person without spirit or courage. **4.** *Naut.* **a** A knob made on a rope with spun yarn parceling, or the like, as to prevent a running eye from slipping. **b** = MOUSING.
>
> **mouse** (mouz), *v. i.;* MOUSED (mouzd); MOUS'ING (mouz'ĭng). **1.** To hunt for and catch mice. **2.** To watch for or pursue anything in a sly manner. — *v. t.* **1.** *Obs.* To handle as a cat does a mouse; hence, to pull about roughly in sport; to toy or play with wantonly. **2.** To hunt as a cat hunts a mouse.

Now look at the definitions for *mouse* from the 2004 edition of the same dictionary. You will notice the addition of definition 4 that relates to a computer mouse.

> ¹**mouse** \'maus\ *n, pl* **mice** \'mīs\ [ME, fr. OE *mūs;* akin to OHG *mūs* mouse, L *mus,* Gk *mys* mouse, muscle] (bef. 12c) **1** : any of numerous small rodents (as of the genus *Mus*) with pointed snout, rather small ears, elongated body, and slender tail **2** : a timid person **3** : a dark-colored swelling caused by a blow; *specif* : BLACK EYE **4** *pl also* **mous·es** : a small mobile manual device that controls movement of the cursor and selection of functions on a computer display
>
> ²**mouse** \'mauz\ *vb* **moused; mous·ing** *vi* (13c) **1** : to hunt for mice **2** : to search or move stealthily or slowly ∼ *vt* **1** *obs* **a** : BITE, GNAW **b** : to toy with roughly **2** : to search for carefully — usu. used with *out*

Completeness of the Dictionary

Dictionaries vary in how complete they are. The most complete dictionaries, the unabridged dictionaries, are found in most libraries. The goal of these dictionaries is to show all of the definitions for all of the words in the English language. The best type of dictionary to keep at home is a good hardbound dictionary such as the *Merriam-Webster's Collegiate Dictionary, American Heritage College Dictionary, Random House Webster's College Dictionary,* or *Webster's New World College Dictionary*. Many of these dictionaries come with CDs that you can install on your computer.

Most of the large dictionary companies also sell smaller paperback dictionaries that you can carry with you to your classes. These are good for quick reference while at school, but remember they are not as complete as hard-

THE FAMILY CIRCUS   By Bil Keane

"You have to be strong to use an unabridged dictionary."

bound dictionaries. For example, look at how the *Merriam-Webster's Dictionary* (the paperback version of the *Merriam-Webster's Collegiate Dictionary*) defines the word *mouse*.

> **mouse** \'maús\ *n, pl* **mice** \'mīs\ **1** : any of numerous small rodents with pointed snout, long body, and slender tail **2** : a small manual device that controls cursor movement on a computer display

This paperback dictionary does not even define the word *mouse* as a verb. Notice also that the paperback dictionary does not give the etymology of the word and that the definition for a computer mouse is much less complete.

No dictionary is perfect—each has its own strengths and weaknesses. Go to your college bookstore or a large local bookstore and look at the selection. It's a good idea to own a hardbound dictionary written by one company and a paperback dictionary written by another. Dictionary companies hire experts in different fields of study to write word definitions, so the definitions in each dictionary are not quite the same. One way to find the best dictionary for your needs is to take some sample words from a field of study that you're familiar with and see which dictionaries do the best job of defining those words.

Using a Dictionary

There are a number of features that are common to most dictionaries, and they will be described in this section. A sample page from the *Random House Webster's College Dictionary* on page 69 is used to illustrate these features.

Guide Words

Dictionaries, like telephone books, list the first and last entries on each page at the top of the page.

What are the guide words for the sample dictionary page?

_____ rabbit-racket _____

Entry Words

All dictionaries list words in alphabetical order, and the entries are usually in bold-faced type. Many dictionaries list biographical and geographical names in the main part of the dictionaries along with regular words, but some dictionaries such as *Merriam-Webster's* have separate sections at the end for these two categories.

In the sample dictionary page, what word comes after *racecourse*?

_____ racehorse _____

rab•bit (rab′it), *n.*, *pl.* **-bits**, (*esp. collectively*) **-bit. 1.** any of several large-eared, hopping lagomorphs of the family Leporidae, usu. smaller than the hares and characterized by bearing blind and furless young in nests. **2.** the fur of a rabbit or hare. [1375-1425; prob. < ONF; cf. Walloon *robett*, dial. D *robbe*]

rab′bit ears′, *n.pl.* an indoor television antenna consisting of two telescoping, swivel-based aerials. [1965-70]

rab′bit fe′ver, *n.* TULAREMIA. [1920-25]

rab′bit punch′, *n.* a short, sharp blow to the nape of the neck or the lower part of the skull. [1910-15]

rab•ble¹ (rab′əl), *n.*, *v.*, **-bled, -bling. —n. 1.** a disorderly crowd; mob. **2.** **the rabble,** the lower classes; the common people. **—v.t. 3.** to beset as a rabble does; mob. [1350-1400; ME *rabel* (n.)]

rab•ble² (rab′əl), *n.*, *v.*, **-bled, -bling.** *Metall.* **—n. 1.** a tool or mechanically operated device used for stirring or mixing a charge in a roasting furnace. **—v.t. 2.** to stir (a charge) in a roasting furnace. [1655-65; < F *râble* fire-shovel, tool, MF *raable* < L *rutābulum* implement for shifting hot coals] **—rab′bler,** *n.*

rab′ble-rous′er, *n.* a person who stirs up the passions or prejudices of the public. [1835-45] **—rab′ble-rous′ing,** *n.*, *adj.*

Rab•e•lais (rab′ə lā′, rab′ə lā′), *n.* **François,** c1490-1553, French satirist and humorist.

Rab•e•lai•si•an (rab′ə lā′zē ən, -zhən), *adj.* of, pertaining to, or suggesting Rabelais or his broad, coarse humor. [1855-60]

Ra•bi¹ (rä′bē), *n.* **Isidor Isaac,** 1898-1988, U.S. physicist.

Ra•bi² (rub′ē), *n.* **1.** Rabi I, the third month of the Islamic calendar. **2.** Rabi II, the fourth month of the Islamic calendar.

rab•id (rab′id), *adj.* **1.** irrationally extreme in opinion or practice. **2.** furious or raging; violently intense. **3.** affected with or pertaining to rabies: *a rabid dog.* [1605-15; < L *rabidus* raging, rabid < *rabere* to rave] **—rab•id•i•ty** (rə bid′i tē, ra-), **rab′id•ness,** *n.* **—rab′id•ly,** *adv.*

ra•bies (rā′bēz), *n.* an infectious, usu. fatal disease of dogs, cats, and other warm-blooded animals, caused by a rhabdovirus and transmitted to humans by the bite of a rabid animal. [1655-65; < L *rabiēs* ferocity, frenzy, rabies, akin to *rabere* to be mad, rave]

Ra•bin (rä bēn′), *n.* **Yitzhak,** 1922-95, Israeli military and political leader: prime minister 1974-77 and 1992-95; Nobel peace prize 1994.

Ra•bi•no•witz (rə bin′ə vits, -wits), *n.* **Solomon,** ALEICHEM, Sholom.

rac•coon (ra kōōn′), *n.*, *pl.* **-coons,** (*esp. collectively*) **-coon. 1.** any small, nocturnal carnivore of the genus *Procyon,* esp. *P. lotor,* having a masklike black stripe across the eyes and a bushy, ringed tail, native to North and Central America. **2.** the thick, brownish gray fur of this animal. [1608, Amer.; < Virginia Algonquian *aroughcun*]

race¹ (rās), *n.*, *v.*, **raced, rac•ing. —n. 1.** a contest of speed, as in running, riding, driving, or sailing. **2. races,** a series of races, run at a set time over a regular course. **3.** any contest or competition, esp. to achieve superiority: *an arms race.* **4.** an urgent effort, as when a solution is imperative: *a race to find a vaccine.* **5.** onward movement; an onward or regular course. **6.** the course of time or life. **7. a.** a strong or rapid current of water, as in the sea or a river. **b.** the channel or bed of such a current or of any stream. **8.** an artificial channel leading water to or from a place where its energy is utilized. **9.** a channel, groove, or the like, for sliding or rolling a part or parts, as the balls of a ball bearing. **—v.i. 10.** to engage in a contest of speed; run a race. **11.** to run horses or dogs in races. **12.** to run, move, or go swiftly. **13.** (of an engine, wheel, etc.) to run with undue or uncontrolled speed when the load is diminished without corresponding diminution of fuel, force, etc. **—v.t. 14.** to run a race against. **15.** to enter (a horse, car, etc.) in a race. **16.** to cause to run, move, or go at high speed: *to race a motor.* [1250-1300; < ON *rās* a running, race]

race² (rās), *n.* **1.** a group of persons related by common descent or heredity. **2.** *Anthropol.* **a.** a classification of modern humans, sometimes, esp. formerly, based on an arbitrary selection of physical characteristics, as skin color, facial form, eye shape, and now frequently based on such genetic markers as blood groups. **b.** a human population partially isolated reproductively from other populations, whose members share a greater degree of physical and genetic similarity with one another than with other humans. **3.** any people united by common history, language, cultural traits, etc.: *the Dutch race.* **4.** the human race or family; humankind. **5.** *Zool.* a variety; subspecies. **6.** any group, class, or kind, esp. of persons. **7.** the characteristic taste or flavor of wine. [1490-1500; < F < It *razza,* of uncert. orig.]

Race (rās), *n.* **Cape,** a cape at the SE extremity of Newfoundland.

race•course (rās′kôrs′, -kōrs′), *n.* **1.** RACETRACK. **2.** a current of water, as a millrace. [1755-65]

race•horse (rās′hôrs′), *n.* a horse bred or kept for racing, esp. in flat races or steeplechases. [1620-30]

ra•ce•mate (rā sē′māt, rə-), *n.* a racemic compound.

rac•e•mose (ras′ə mōs′), *adj.* **1.** *Bot.* bearing or arranged in the form of a raceme. **2.** *Anat.* resembling a bunch of grapes. [1690-1700; < L *racēmōsus* full of clusters, clustering. See RACEME, -OSE¹]

rac•er (rā′sər), *n.* **1.** a person, animal, or thing that races or takes part in a race. **2.** anything having great speed. **3.** any of several slender, active snakes of the genera *Coluber* and *Masticophis.* [1640-50]

race•run•ner (rās′run′ər), *n.* a whiptail lizard, *Cnemidophorus sexlineatus,* common in the eastern and central U.S., that runs with great speed. [1640-50]

race•track (rās′trak′), *n.* **1.** a plot of ground, usu. oval, laid out for horse racing. **2.** the course for any race. [1855-60]

race′ walk′ing, *n.* the sport of rapid walking, in which one foot must be in contact with the ground at all times. **—race′ walk′er,** *n.*

race•way (rās′wā′), *n.* **1.** a track on which harness races are held. **2.** a channel for protecting and holding electrical wires. [1820-30]

Ra•chel (rā′chəl), *n.* Jacob's favorite wife, the mother of Joseph and Benjamin. Gen. 29-35.

ra•chis (rā′kis), *n.*, *pl.* **ra•chis•es, rach•i•des** (rak′i dēz′, rā′ki-). **1.** any of various axial structures of a plant, as the stem of a leaflet. **2.** the part of the shaft of a feather bearing the web. **3.** SPINAL COLUMN. [1775-85; < NL < Gk *rháchis* spine]

ra•chi•tis (rə kī′tis), *n.* RICKETS. [1720-30; < NL < Gk *rhachîtis* inflammation of the spine. See RACHIS, -ITIS] **—ra•chit′ic** (-kit′ik), *adj.*

Rach•ma•ni•noff or **Rach•ma•ni•nov** (räкн mä′nə nôf′, -nof′, räk-), *n.* **Sergei Wassilievitch,** 1873-1943, Russian pianist and composer.

ra•cial (rā′shəl), *adj.* **1.** of, pertaining to, or characteristic of one race or the races of humankind. **2.** between races: *racial harmony; racial relations.* [1860-65] **—ra′cial•ly,** *adv.*

ra•cial•ism (rā′shə liz′əm), *n.* RACISM. [1905-10] **—ra′cial•ist,** *n.*

Ra•cine (rə sēn′, ra- *for 1;* rə sēn′, rā- *for 2*), *n.* **1. Jean Baptiste** (zhän), 1639-99, French playwright. **2.** a city in SE Wisconsin. 82,510.

rac′ing form′, *n.* a sheet that provides detailed information about horse races, including data on the horses, jockeys, etc. [1945-50]

rac•ism (rā′siz əm), *n.* **1.** a belief or doctrine that inherent differences among the various human races determine cultural or individual achievement, usu. involving the idea that one's own race is superior. **2.** a policy, system of government, etc., based on such a doctrine. **3.** hatred or intolerance of another race or other races. [1865-70; < F *racisme.* See RACE², -ISM] **—rac′ist,** *n.*, *adj.*

rack¹ (rak), *n.* **1.** a framework of bars, pegs, etc., on which articles are arranged or deposited: *a clothes rack.* **2.** a fixture containing tiered shelves, often affixed to a wall: *a spice rack.* **3.** a framework set up on a vehicle to carry loads. **4. a.** a triangular wooden frame in which balls are arranged before a game of pool. **b.** the balls so arranged. **5.** *Mach.* **a.** a bar, with teeth on one of its sides, adapted to engage with the teeth of a pinion **(rack and pinion)** or the like, as for converting circular into rectilinear motion or vice versa. **b.** a bar having a series of notches engaging with a pawl or the like. **6.** a former instrument of torture on which a victim was slowly stretched. **7.** a cause or state of intense suffering of body or mind. **8.** violent strain. **9.** a pair of antlers. **—v.t. 10.** to torture; distress acutely; torment. **11.** to strain in mental effort: *to rack one's brains.* **12.** to strain by physical force or violence. **13.** to stretch the body of (a person) on a rack. **14. rack up, a.** *Pool.* to put (the balls) in a rack. **b.** to gain, achieve, or score: *The new store is racking up profits.* [1250-1300; ME *rakke, rekke* (n.) < MD *rac, rec, recke*]

rack² (rak), *n.* wreckage or destruction; wrack: *to go to rack and ruin.* [1590-1600; var. of WRACK¹]

rack³ (rak), *n.* **1.** the fast pace of a horse in which the legs move in lateral pairs but not simultaneously. **—v.i. 2.** (of horses) to move in a rack. [1570-80; perh. alter. of ROCK²]

rack⁴ (rak), *n.* **1.** a group of drifting clouds. **—v.i. 2.** to drive or move, esp. before the wind. [1350-1400; ME *rak*]

rack⁵ (rak), *v.t.* to draw off (wine, cider, etc.) from the lees. [1425-75; < OF]

rack⁶ (rak), *n.* **1.** the neck portion of mutton, pork, or veal. **2.** the rib section of a foresaddle of lamb, veal, etc. [1560-70; orig. uncert.]

rack′ and pin′ion, *n.* See under RACK¹ (def. 5a).

rack•et¹ (rak′it), *n.* **1.** a loud noise or clamor, esp. of a disturbing or confusing kind; din; uproar. **2.** social excitement, gaiety, or dissipation. **3.** an organized illegal activity, such as the extortion of money by threat or violence. **4.** a dishonest scheme, business, activity, etc. **5.** *Slang.* **a.** an occupation, livelihood, or business. **b.** an easy or profitable source of livelihood. **—v.i. 6.** to make a racket or noise. **7.** to take part in social gaiety or dissipation. [1555-65; metathetic var. of dial. *rattick;* see RATTLE] **—Syn.** See NOISE.

rack•et² (rak′it), *n.* **1.** a light bat having a netting of catgut or nylon stretched in a more or less oval frame and used in tennis, badminton, etc. **2.** the short-handled paddle used to strike the ball in table tennis and paddle tennis. **3. rackets,** (*used with a sing. v.*) RACQUET (def. 1). **4.** a snowshoe made in the form of a tennis racket. Also, **racquet** (for defs. 1, 2, 4). [1490-1500; < MF *raquette, rachette,* perh. < Ar *rāhet,* var. of *rāhah* palm of the hand]

From *Random House Webster's College Dictionary,* New York: Random House, 2001, pp. 1088–1089.

Word and Pronunciation Divisions

Words of more than one syllable are divided into syllables by small black dots, slashes, or blank spaces. Words of one syllable like *race* are not divided.

How many syllables are there in the word *racetrack*?   __2__

Word Pronunciations

Directly following each entry word is the same word with the pronunciation symbols added. You must study these symbols in order to learn how to pronounce the entry word correctly. If two pronunciations are given, the first pronunciation is the more commonly accepted one. Notice the alternate pronunciation for the plural of *rachis* in the sample dictionary page.

Write out the pronunciations for the following words using the sample dictionary page:

racket   ___rak' it_____

raccoon   ___ra koon'_____

English has 26 letters, which can be arranged to produce approximately 75 different sounds. Although most dictionaries use standard symbols, there are variations. Since there is no universal format, each dictionary has a pronunciation key that is usually located toward the front of the dictionary. It contains a listing of the different pronunciation symbols used with representative words that indicate how a specific letter or letter combination is pronounced. In addition, most **dictionaries** provide a brief summary of key sounds at the bottom or side of each double-page spread. On the facing page is the pronunciation key for *Random House Webster's College Dictionary*.

Using the pronunciation key, answer the following questions.

1. What words in the pronunciation key show how t is pronounced?

    ___ten, matter, bit_____

2. The first i in *crisis* is pronounced like the i in the key word ___ice___ .

3. The second i in *crisis* is pronounced like the i in the key word ___if___ .

4. The y in *crispy* is pronounced like the e in the key word ___equal___ .

5. The pronunciation guide for the word *critic* uses the letter k to represent

    the letter c. Which key word represents that sound? ___keep___ .

6. The first a in the word *Croatia* is pronounced like the a in the word

    ___age___ .

Etymology

The etymology of a word tells you its history. Most hardbound dictionaries give etymologies for important entries. For example, the word *rabid* on the

Pronunciation Key

English Sounds

a	act, bat, marry	l	low, mellow, bottle (bot′l)	t͟h	that, either, smooth
ā	age, paid, say	m	my, summer, him	u	up, sun
â(r)	air, Mary, dare	n	now, sinner, button (but′n)	ûr	urge, burn, cur
ä	ah, balm, star	ng	sing, Washington	v	voice, river, live
b	back, cabin, cab	o	ox, bomb, wasp	w	witch, away
ch	child, pitcher, beach	ō	over, boat, no	y	yes, onion
d	do, madder, bed	ô	order, ball, raw	z	zoo, lazy, those
e	edge, set, merry	oi	oil, joint, joy	zh	treasure, mirage
ē	equal, bee, pretty	o͝o	oomph, book, tour	ə	used in unaccented syllables to indicate the sound of the reduced vowel in alone, system, easily, gallop, circus
ēr	earring, cheerful, appear	o͞o	ooze, fool, too		
f	fit, differ, puff	ou	out, loud, cow	ᵊ	used between i and r and between ou and r to show triphthongal quality, as in fire (ī ᵊr), hour (ou ᵊr)
g	give, trigger, beg	p	pot, supper, stop		
h	hit, behave	r	read, hurry, near		
hw	which, nowhere	s	see, passing, miss		
i	if, big, mirror	sh	shoe, fashion, push		
ī	ice, bite, deny	t	ten, matter, bit		
j	just, tragic, fudge	th	thin, ether, path		
k	keep, token, make				

Stress

Pronunciations are marked for stress to reveal the relative differences in emphasis between syllables. In words of two or more syllables, a primary stress mark (′) follows the syllable having greatest stress, as the first syllable of **rabbit** (rab′it). A secondary stress mark (′) follows a syllable having slightly less stress than primary but more stress than an unmarked syllable, as the second syllable of **jackrabbit** (jak′rab′it).

From Random House Webster's College Dictionary, New York: Random House, 2001, p. xxvi

sample dictionary page comes from the Latin (L) word *rabidus.* You will usually find a list of abbreviations, including those for languages of origin, at the beginning of a dictionary.

Many words in the English language come from Latin or Greek word parts. You learned more about Latin and Greek word parts later in this warm-up.

What is the etymology of the word *rachis*? _____ Greek (spine)

Synonyms

Synonyms are words that have similar meanings. The words *lawyer* and *attorney* are synonyms because they have similar meanings. Dictionaries often give synonyms as definitions for the main entry word.

What is a synonym for the first entry of the word *racket*? _____ noise

Example of Word in a Sentence or Phrase

Dictionaries often give examples of the use of entry words in sentences or phrases. Notice that the second dictionary definition for the first *rack* entry (rack[1]) uses a phrase—*spice rack.*

What is an example of a phrase using the word *rabid*?   a rabid dog

Suffixes

New words can be formed by adding endings to existing words. A common noun suffix is *ness*. A common adverb suffix is *ly*. Notice that the entry word *rabid* has an adverb suffix added to make *rabidly* and a noun suffix added to make *rabidness.*

What additional noun suffix is given for *rabid*?   ity (rabidity)

Parts of Speech

Each entry will give the part or parts of speech for the word. For example, *n* for noun, *vb* for verb, *adj* for adjective, *adv* for adverb, *conj* for conjunction. According to the dictionary page, the word *race* can be both a noun and a verb. Sometimes the entry will give *vt* for a transitive verb (a verb requiring a direct object) and *vi* for an intransitive verb (a verb that does not have a direct object).

What is the part of speech for *raccoon*?   noun

The following is a quick review of parts of speech.

PARTS OF SPEECH

NOUN (N)

A noun is a word that names something—either a person, place, thing, or idea.

> Abraham Lincoln
> Harvard University
> psychology book
> democracy

PRONOUN (PRON.)

A pronoun is a word that takes the place of a noun.

> Juanita wants to go to the store. She wants to go to the store.
>
> Mark and Carol are going to class. They are going to class.

VERB (V.)

A verb is a word that expresses action or state of being.

> David Beckham scored a free kick.
> I am happy.

ADJECTIVE (ADJ.)

An adjective describes or modifies a noun or pronoun.

> The elderly worker wanted to retire soon.
> She is beautiful.

ADVERB (ADV.)

An adverb describes or modifies a verb, an adjective, or another adverb. An adverb may answer questions such as where, how often, or how much.

He is absent <u>frequently</u>.

He is <u>greatly</u> missed by his family.

PREPOSITION (PREP.)

A preposition shows the relation of a noun or pronoun to another word in a sentence.

Next year she will work <u>for</u> the magazine.

He isn't <u>in</u> the house right now.

CONJUNCTION (CONJ.)

A conjunction joins words or groups of words.

Juan <u>and</u> Maria took turns driving to California.

Rachel <u>or</u> Susan will cook dinner tonight.

Exercise 1: Dictionary Usage

Directions: Refer to the sample dictionary page on page 69 to answer the following questions.

1. Write the guide words for the sample dictionary page. <u>rabbit-racket</u>

2. Write the origin (etymology) of each of the following words.

    rabble¹ <u>ME Middle English</u>

    rabies <u>Latin</u>

    racemose <u>Latin</u>

    racket² <u>MF Middle French</u>

3. Write the Latin meaning for *racemose*.

    <u>full of clusters, clustering</u>

4. Write the part or parts of speech for each of the following entry words.

    rabble¹ <u>noun, verb</u>

    racer <u>noun</u>

    racial <u>adjective</u>

    racism <u>noun</u>

5. Write the plural forms of the following entry words.

   rabbit rabbits
   _____

   raccoon raccoons
   _____

   rachis rachises, rachides
   _____

6. What are some sample phrases for rack[1]?

   a clothes rack, a spice rack, to rack one's brains, racking up profits
   _____

   _____

7. What suffixes are added to change race[1] to different parts of speech?

   raced (ed), racing (ing)
   _____

8. Who are the following people?

   a. Racine a French playwright
   _____

   b. Rabelais a French satirist and humorist
   _____

   c. Rachel Jacob's favorite wife, mother of Joseph and Benjamin
   _____

9. Pronounce the following words. Then write each word using the correct spelling.

   rās race
   _____

   rāsər racer
   _____

10. Answer the following questions. Use **T** for true and **F** for false.

   _____T_____   The raccoon is native to North America.

   _____F_____   A raccoon is active during the day.

   _____T_____   A racer is a kind of snake.

   _____F_____   A racerunner is a small bird.

   _____T_____   Yitzhak Rabin won a Nobel peace prize in 1994.

Exercise 2: Phonetic Spelling

Directions: Use the dictionary pronunciation key on page 71 to identify the answers to the following riddles. Write the correct answers on the lines provided.

1. Which is right, "Six and five *are* thirteen?" or "Six and five *is* thirteen?"

    Answer: nēthər iz kə-rekt. siks and fīiv är i-lev- ən.

    Neither is correct. Six and five are eleven.

2. Your grandmother has four daughters. Three of them are your aunts. Who is the fourth one?

    Answer: yoor muth-ər

    your mother

3. How do you talk to an elephant?

    Answer: yooz ver-ē big wûrdz

    use very big words

4. Of all the things in the world, I am the shortest and the longest, the swiftest and the slowest. I am the thing people waste the most. Yet they need me more than anything else, for without me nothing can be done. What am I?

    Answer: tīm

    time

5. What is the end of everything?

    Answer: thə let-ər "g"

    the letter g

6. You throw away the outside and cook the inside. Then you eat the outside and throw away the inside. What is it?

    Answer: ən ēr uv kôrn

    an ear of corn

7. What is it that belongs to you, yet is used by others more than by you?

Answer: <u>yoor nām</u>

<u>your name</u>

From *Unriddling* by Alvin Schwartz

Definitions of Words

People look in dictionaries to find the meaning of words. In some languages, each word has a separate and distinct meaning. Not so in English. Take the word *mouse* used on page 67. Today *mouse* not only means "a small rodent," but also means "a device to move the cursor on the computer screen." When you are looking up the definition of a word in a dictionary, you are often looking for a particular definition— the one that fits the way the word is being used in a sentence or phrase. Read the following sentence and then decide which of the definitions is the most appropriate for the italicized word *virus*.

> Even though Nancy took appropriate precautions, her new computer still caught the Sasser *virus*.

> **vi•rus** (vī′rəs), *n.*, *pl.* **-rus•es. 1.** an ultramicroscopic (20 to 300 nm in diameter), metabolically inert, infectious agent that replicates only within the cells of living hosts, mainly bacteria, plants, and animals: composed of an RNA or DNA core, a protein coat, and, in more complex types, a surrounding envelope. **2.** a disease caused by a virus. **3.** a corrupting influence on morals or the intellect; poison. **4.** a segment of self-replicating code planted illegally in a computer program, often to damage or shut down a system or network. [1590–1600; < L *vīrus* slime, poison; akin to ooze²] —**vi′rus•like′,** *adj.*

Definition 4 is the correct answer because that's the only definition related to computers.

Try another example. What's the best dictionary definition for *coddled* as used in the following sentence?

> The bicycle rider was *coddled* by his friends after he broke his hand in a bike accident.

> **cod•dle** (kod′l), *v.t.*, **-dled, -dling. 1.** to treat tenderly or indulgently; pamper. **2.** to cook (eggs, fruit, etc.) in water just below the boiling point. [1590–1600; var. of *caudle* CAUDLE] —**cod′dler,** *n.*

Coddling eggs obviously has nothing to do with how *coddled* is used in this sentence, so definition 1 is the correct meaning for *coddled* as used in this context.

Exercise 3: Dictionary Usage

Directions: Find the correct dictionary definition for the italicized word in each sentence below. Then write in the letter of the correct definition.

_____c_____   1. The airline pilot kept the *attitude* of her commercial aircraft 5 degrees above the horizon.

at·ti·tude (at′i tōōd′, -tyōōd′), *n.* **1.** manner, disposition, feeling, position: *a cheerful attitude.* **2.** position or posture of the body appropriate to or expressive of an action, emotion, etc.: *a threatening attitude.* **3.** the inclination of the three principal axes of an aircraft relative to the wind, to the ground, etc. **4.** *Slang.* a testy, uncooperative disposition. [1660–70; < F < It *attitudine* < LL *aptitūdō* APTITUDE] —**at′ti·tu′di·nal,** *adj.* —**Syn.** See POSITION.

a. definition 1
b. definition 2
c. definition 3
d. definition 4

_____c_____ 2. Many countries such as Great Britain call their head of state a prime *minister* instead of a president.

min·is·ter (min′ə stər), *n.* **1.** a person authorized to conduct religious worship; member of the clergy; pastor. **2.** a person authorized to administer sacraments, as at mass. **3.** a person appointed to some high office of state, esp. to that of head of an administrative department. **4.** a diplomatic representative, usu. ranking below an ambassador. **5.** a person acting as the agent or instrument of another. —*v.i.* **6.** to perform the functions of a religious minister. **7.** to give service, care, or aid: *to minister to the hungry.* [1250–1300; (n.) ME (< OF *menistre*) < L *minister* servant = *minis-*, var. of *minus* a lesser

a. definition 1
b. definition 2
c. definition 3
d. definition 7

_____c_____ 3. Who is the *star* of the latest James Bond movie?

star (stär), *n., adj., v.,* **starred, star·ring.** —*n.* **1.** any of the various types of hot, gaseous, self-luminous celestial bodies, as the sun or Polaris, whose energy is derived from nuclear-fusion reactions. **2.** any celestial body, except the moon, that appears as a fixed point of light in the night sky: *the evening star.* **3.** Usu., **stars.** a heavenly body, esp. a planet, regarded as an astrological influence on human affairs. **4.** one's fortune or success in relation to advancement or decline: *Your star will rise someday.* **5.** a conventionalized figure usu. having five or six points radiating from or disposed about a center. **6.** this figure used as an ornament, badge, mark of excellence, etc. **7. a.** a prominent actor, singer, or the like, esp. one who plays the leading role in a production. **b.** a gifted or highly celebrated person in some art, profession, or field. **8.** an asterisk. **9. a.** the asterism in a crystal or a gemstone, as in a star sapphire. **b.** a crystal or a gemstone having such asterism. **c.** STAR FACET. **10. a.** a gold or bronze star worn on the ribbon of a naval decoration to represent an additional award of the same decoration. **b.** a silver star worn in place of five gold or bronze stars. **11.** a white spot on the forehead of a horse. —*adj.* **12.** celebrated, prominent, or distinguished; preeminent: *a star reporter.* **13.** of or pertaining to a star or stars. —*v.t.* **14.** to set with or as if with stars; spangle. **15.** to feature as a star: *an old movie starring Rudolph Valentino.* **16.** to mark with a star or asterisk, as for special notice. —*v.i.* **17.** to shine as a star; be brilliant or prominent. **18.** (of a performer) to appear as a star. —*Idiom.* **19. see stars,** to appear to see brilliant streaks of light before the eyes, as from a severe blow to the head. [bef. 900; ME *sterre,* OE *steorra,* c. OFris *stēr,* OHG, OS *sterra;* akin to OHG *sterno,* ON *stjarna,* Go *stairno,* L *stella,* Gk *astér*] —**star′less,** *adj.* —**star′like′,** *adj.*

a. definition 2
b. definition 5
c. definition 7a
d. definition 10a

_____d_____ 4. Pictures taken with digital cameras have now almost completely replaced *slides* and prints.

> **slide** (slīd), *v.*, **slid** (slid), **slid•ing**, *n.* —*v.i.* **1.** to move along in continuous contact with a smooth or slippery surface. **2.** to slip or skid. **3.** to glide or pass smoothly. **4.** to slip easily or unobtrusively on or as if on a track (usu. fol. by *in, out,* etc.). **5.** to pass or fall gradually into a specified state, character, practice, etc. **6.** to decline or decrease. **7.** to pursue a natural course without intervention: *to let a matter slide.* **8.** *Baseball.* (of a base runner) to cast oneself forward along the ground towards a base. —*v.t.* **9.** to cause to slide or coast, as over a surface or with a smooth, gliding motion. **10.** to hand, pass along, or slip (something) easily or quietly (usu. fol. by *in, into,* etc.). —*n.* **11.** an act or instance of sliding. **12.** a smooth surface for sliding on, esp. a type of chute in a playground. **13.** an object intended to slide. **14. a.** a landslide or the like. **b.** the mass of matter sliding down. **15.** a transparency, as a frame of positive film, mounted for projection on a screen or magnification through a viewer. **16.** a usu. rectangular plate of glass on which objects are placed for microscopic examination. **17.** a shelf sliding into the body of a piece of furniture when not in use. **18.** a U-shaped section of the tube of an instrument of the trumpet class, as the trombone, that can be pushed in or out to alter the length of the air column and change the pitch. **19.** (of a machine, mechanism, or device) **a.** a moving part working on a track or channel. **b.** the surface, track, or channel on which the part moves. [bef. 950; ME (v.), OE *slīdan,* c. MLG *slīden,* MHG *slīten*] —**slid′a•ble,** *adj.*

a. definition 1
b. definition 4
c. definition 8
d. definition 15

Exercise 4: Shades of Meaning

Directions: Use your dictionary to determine the meaning of the italicized word in each of the following sentences and then write in the letter of the correct answer.

_____d_____ 1. Please don't *act* like a fool in class.
a. a thing done; deed
b. a law or decree
c. one of the main divisions of a play
d. to behave like

_____b_____ 2. Steve was very *attached* to his two dogs, Cookie and Bandit.
a. to fasten or join together as by sticking
b. to bring close together by feelings of love or affection
c. to add at the end; affix
d. to take property from a person by order of a court of law

_____c_____ 3. Because of an inner ear infection, Marla lost her *balance* frequently.
a. person's normal steady state of mind
b. the amount of money held in a bank account
c. the ability to keep the body steady without falling
d. equality in amount, weight, value, or importance between two things

_____d_____ 4. Corinné was in a *bind* because she had promised to be in two
places at the exact same time.
a. to tie together with rope or other material
b. to hinder free or comfortable movement
c. to put a bandage on
d. to be in a difficult position

_____a_____ 5. Greg has bought the same *brand* of jeans for the last three
years.
a. a particular kind or make
b. a mark of shame
c. a mark burned on the skin with a hot iron
d. to make a lasting impression

_____b_____ 6. When she goes on her trip to Ireland, she will travel first
class.
a. a group of students who graduate together
b. a division or grouping according to grade or quality
c. a number of things thought of as a group because they are
alike in certain ways
d. fine style or appearance; excellence

_____b_____ 7. Early missionaries tried to *convert* the natives to Christianity.
a. change from one form or use to another
b. change from one belief or religion to another
c. to exchange for something of equal value
d. to score an extra point or points after a touchdown

_____d_____ 8. For her main *course*, Marilyn decided to serve a leg of lamb.
a. a way or path along which something moves
b. an area of land or water used for certain sports or games
c. the direction taken
d. a part of a meal served at one time

_____a_____ 9. Karla's English instructor told her that the introduction to
her essay was fine, but the *body* and conclusion needed to be
rewritten.
a. the main part of a piece of writing
b. a group of people or things thought of as a single unit
c. the whole physical person or animal with all its parts, alive
or dead
d. any of the natural objects visible in the sky

_____c_____ 10. In an emergency it is his *habit* to remain calm.
a. a religious costume
b. clothing for a certain occasion
c. a usual or typical way of doing or being
d. something done so often that it becomes hard to stop

CONTEXT CLUES

When you encounter a word that you are unfamiliar with, your job is made much easier if you can use the context of the sentence or paragraph to help you determine its meaning. By examining the surrounding words, it is possible in many instances to find clues that help you come up with a fairly accurate understanding of the unfamiliar word. Following are some of the types of context clues you can use.

Definition Clues

A **definition** directly defines a word. Definitions are often set off in a sentence by commas, parentheses, or brackets. They also follow verbs such as "means," "refers to," or "is." Here are some examples:

> The colon is subject to the development of *polyps*, small growths arising from the lining.
>
> Mader, *Human Biology,* 9th, p. 123

In this example, a comma precedes the definition.

> People today generally find *in vitro fertilization* (fertilization in laboratory glassware) an acceptable way for couples to reproduce.
>
> Mader, 9th, p. 10

In this example, the definition is stated in parentheses.

> The term *disaster* refers to a sudden or disruptive event or set of events that overtaxes a community's resources, so that outside aid is necessary.
>
> Schaeffer, *Sociology,* 10th, p. 45

In this example the phrase *refers to* introduces a definition.

Synonym Clues

A **synonym,** or a word with a similar meaning, may be included in the same sentence as the unfamiliar word or in a nearby sentence. Here are some examples:

> Until recently, *monetary sanctions* were not used much in the American legal system, but today the use of fines is increasing.
>
> Adler, *Criminal Justice,* 4th, p. 389

In this example, a synonym for *monetary sanctions* is *fines*.

> When trying to detect a lie, the polygraph operator begins by asking *irrelevant* questions such as, "Did you eat lunch today?" However, even starting with unimportant questions is not enough to put some people at ease.

In this example, a synonym for *irrelevant* is *unimportant*.

> *Hoaxes* have long been used to sell newspapers. In fact, these personal deceptions were so commonplace that when the telegraph was invented in 1848, many readers thought it was just another media prank.
>
> Rodman, *Mass Media in a Changing World,* p. 510

In this example, a synonym for *hoax* is *deception*.

Explanation Clues

An **explanation** provides details that explain the meaning of a word. Explanations usually include more than one sentence. Here are some examples:

> *Socialization* occurs through human interactions. It is a lifelong process in which people learn the attitudes, values, and behaviors appropriate for members off a particular culture. *Socialization* helps us learn how to behave properly and what to expect from others.
>
> Schaefer, 10th, p. 74

> If you claim that an innocent person is guilty of criminal or unethical behavior, that would be *defamation*. If you engage in any type of false communication that injures the reputation of an individual, you are *defaming* them.
>
> Rodman, p. 489

> *Fair use* allows the copying of a work for a noncommercial use, as long as that copying does not interfere with sales by the copyright holder.
>
> Rodman, p. 493

Example Clues

An author may give an **example** or examples to illustrate a word's meaning. This method is based on the reader drawing on his or her personal experience to understand the example given. Here are some examples:

> A *trademark* identifies one seller's goods and distinguishes them from goods sold by others. Names like Jell-O and XEROX and symbols such as McDonald's golden arches and the Energizer bunny are registered *trademarks*.
>
> Rodman, p. 494

> *Conflict of interest* occurs when some outside activity of a media professional—be it business, social, or personal activity—influences the reality that is presented to the public. Critics objected, for example, when Larry King called the play *Jekyll and Hyde* the best musical he had ever seen. The critics didn't mind his plugging the show, but he failed to mention that his nephew was the producer.
>
> Rodman, p. 530

"Punch $200 into the machine or I'll blow you away." With these words Curtis K. Taylor would approach customers at automated teller machines throughout California. Taylor was *prolific*, perhaps the most *prolific* of all teller-machine bandits in the United States. When apprehended in 1988, he pleaded guilty to 37 robbery and attempted robbery charges.

Adler, 4th, p. 283

Antonym Clues

An **antonym** is a word with an opposite or contrasting meaning to the unfamiliar word. An author may include an antonym in the same sentence or a nearby sentence. Transition words like *but, instead,* or *however* may signal an antonym is being used. Here are some examples:

> Victims of white-collar crime range from the *savvy* investor to the unsuspecting consumer.
>
> Adler, 4th, p. 58

In this example, the antonym of *savvy* is *unsuspecting.* A *savvy* person is someone who is shrewd.

> Not all telemarketing is *genuine.* The New York State Attorney General estimates that approximately 10 percent of the over 140,000 New York businesses using telemarketing to sell their products are frauds.
>
> Adler, 4th, p. 62

In this example, the antonym of *genuine* is *frauds.*

> Consumers are easy prey for land swindlers. Instead of a *lucrative* investment, they end up with a purchase of overvalued or worthless land.
>
> Adler, 4th, p. 62

In this example, *lucrative* means "profitable" or "money-making." The antonym of *lucrative* is *worthless.*

Exercise 5: Context Clue Practice

Directions: Write the letter of the definition that best fits the way the italicized word or phrase is used in each of the following sentences.

___b___ 1. It is *crucial* that you take your medicine or the infection could get worse.
   a. helpful
   b. vital
   c. unimportant

___c___ 2. He is very *vocal* about supporting legislation for health care reform, talking constantly about the subject.
   a. inarticulate
   b. quiet
   c. outspoken

____a____ 3. Gabriella has the *motivation* to be a great musician; she plays the piano and violin, takes a music class, and listens to classical music.
a. desire
b. speed
c. grace

____a____ 4. My mother was *ambivalent* about my attending college. On the one hand, she thought I might get a better job after graduation, and on the other she thought college cost too much money.
a. conflicted
b. enthusiastic
c. disgusted

____b____ 5. Many people consider the flag *sacrosanct* and don't like to see anyone spit on it or burn it.
a. trivial
b. sacred
c. colorful

____a____ 6. I *eavesdrop on* my children's telephone conversations because they never tell me what's going on in their lives.
a. listen in on
b. ignore
c. question

____a____ 7. After wandering in the desert for hours, Irene became *disoriented*.
a. confused
b. clear-minded
c. organized

____c____ 8. Everyone at work is fond of Carmen because she is *considerate of* everyone.
a. hostile to
b. neutral about
c. respectful of

____a____ 9. The victim's family was ready to *retaliate* when the judge gave their daughter's killer a light sentence.
a. seek revenge
b. forgive
c. accept

____b____ 10. I was greeted *amicably* by the president of the company and welcomed to my new job.
a. in a hostile way
b. in a friendly way
c. in an uncaring way

_____a_____ 11. The thief was filled with *remorse* after stealing from an
                  elderly lady with no means of support.
                  a. sorrow
                  b. satisfaction
                  c. callousness

_____b_____ 12. After losing a considerable sum of money in Las Vegas, Tyler
                  concluded that gambling might not be a *lucrative* occupation.
                  a. boring
                  b. profitable
                  c. costly

_____c_____ 13. He is such a *pariah* that no one wants to be around him.
                  a. favorite
                  b. hero
                  c. social outcast

_____a_____ 14. The bank robber drove the getaway car fast, trying to *elude* the
                  police.
                  a. escape from
                  b. attract
                  c. contact

READING

*"I'm the American Idol, which seems like a fairy tale, but
I can't even read a fairy tale to my four-year old daughter."*

GETTING FOCUSED

In the excerpt below, Fantasia Barrino discusses her difficulty with reading. In
the United States, 21 to 23 percent of the population read at only a basic level
of literacy—approximately a fifth-grade reading level.

BIO-SKETCH

Fantasia Barrino was raised by her mother and grandmother, both ministers.
At age 5, she began singing. At age 17, she became pregnant and dropped
out of school. She became a household name at 19 when she became the
third winner of *American Idol*. A made-for-TV movie based on her best-selling
book (and starring Fantasia) was released in 2006.

TACKLING VOCABULARY

illiterate   unable to read and write

ashamed   distressed by feelings of guilt, foolishness, or disgrace

R E A D I N G   *continued*

gossip   idle talk or rumor, especially about the private affairs of others

esteem   favorable opinion or judgment

shame   the painful feeling of having done or experienced something dishonorable, improper, or foolish

fairy tale   a story, usually for children, about magical creatures

LIFE IS NOT A FAIRY TALE

Fantasia Barrino

"The limits of my language mean the limits of my world. All I know is what I have words for."

—Ludwig Wittgenstein

My biggest mistake ever was dropping out of school, and I pay for it every day. You see, I'm what I would call a functioning illiterate. That means that I "get by" in life but my rea ding isn't what it should be. *I am workin' on it.* I am still not confident with words or letters. If I see a word that I'm not familiar with, I still get *scared.* Sometimes I don't even know how to begin to pronounce words or even how to sound the letters out. Not a day goes by that I'm not ashamed about my situation. If you hand me a newspaper, I just look at the pictures and try to figure out what happened. I do recognize the common words like "death," "money," "taxes," "president," "baby," "marriage," and "rich," but most big words or too many words together just scare me. When people ask me to write a special message, I have trouble forming words right on the spot, so I write something short like "Be Blessed," something that I already know how to write. Whatever I write, I mean it from my heart.

2   Although I made it to the ninth grade, I have forgotten a lot of things. I never made good grades except for that one time in Charlotte when I actually sat and listened to what the teachers were saying, but that was a long time ago. It was the only time that I wasn't distracted with dreams clouding my brain. I know that I'm smart. I'm just not *educated.* I used to say that I was never blessed with "smarts." But I feel differently now. I'm blessed with "smarts" because I haven't given up and I will learn to read all of the words there are to read someday soon. That is my promise to myself.

3   You must think I'm crazy to put my business out here like this, but the reason I'm doing this is to go behind the gossip and let you know that this is *one* mistake that *no one* should ever make. *Ever.* In those days, when I was thinking I was being cool by not going to school, I didn't realize that the coolest part of my life should have been spending my days at Montlieu Elementary School, A. Laurin Welborn Middle School, and T. Wingate Andrews High School. The coolest part of my nights should have been struggling with math homework and writing papers. Most of my friends were actually going to school and learning something, and I was at home looking stupid—watching TV, not being able to read, not being able to count. In those days I didn't even feel comfortable counting.

4   Truthfully, I never applied for many jobs, because I couldn't fill out the application. Whenever I tried, I left so many questions blank because I couldn't read

them that the applications always ended up in the garbage. That is dumb. *Plain out dumb.* This is how you see that one big mistake just creates another one. It's a chain reaction.

5   I was embarrassed and ashamed and I still am, despite the *Idol* competition, despite the pictures in magazines, despite my improved self-esteem. I was stupid for not staying in school. And the private part of my shame is that I want to be as smart as everyone else. I want to be wise about my own money, I want to be able to understand a contract that's presented to me and not have to ask someone else what it means. I want to be able to read a script and take it home and think about it on my own time instead of needing someone to go through it with me. I want to be able to think for myself and not have to walk around with people all the time, helping me get through the simplest things.

6   My public mistake is that I didn't finish school. My private mistake is that, although I'm talking about it now for the first time, I'm ashamed and hating myself for my choices. I'm angry that my life brought me to this place. I'm angry that my parents couldn't control me better. I'm angry that I have already missed opportunities in my life. Although my reading thing makes a good story, the real story is how I have managed to fool the world into thinking that I could read. The real story is how Hollywood and show business wouldn't want the world to know that illiteracy is a real thing that affects a lot of young people, like me. It is one of those ugly things that no one wants to talk about, yet keeping a secret just makes a new generation of illiterates. This is why so many young kids don't have jobs—they can't read a job application. Instead of getting a free car, what I could have used was a tutor.

7   I don't want anyone to lose faith in me, but I decided to be honest so that all of the other young people like me will know in advance what dropping out of school really turns into. My life looks like a fairy tale in many ways, but you have to remember that life is not a fairy tale. I'm the American Idol, which seems like a fairy tale, but I can't even read a fairy tale to my four-year-old daughter.

> Excerpt reprinted with permission of Simon & Schuster Adult Publishing Group from *Life Is Not a Fairy Tale* by Fantasia. Copyright © 2005 19 Merchandising Ltd.

 COMPREHENSION CHECKUP

Multiple Choice

Directions: Write in the letter for the correct answer to each question.

____b____   1. The best title for this selection would be

   a. "Not Being Able to Fill Out a Job Application."

   b. "Regrets About Being Illiterate."

   c. "The Importance of Singing on *American Idol*."

   d. "Problems in Elementary School."

____b____   2. This selection discusses all of the following *except*

   a. Fantasia's goals for the future.

   b. the songs Fantasia sings.

   c. Fantasia's dropping out of school.

   d. Hollywood's lack of concern for illiteracy.

True or False

Directions: Decide whether each detail is true (**T**), false (**F**), or not discussed (**ND**).

___T___ 1. Unfamiliar words can scare Fantasia.

___T___ 2. Fantasia says she made a big mistake dropping out of school.

___T___ 3. Fantasia sees a difference between being smart and being educated.

___ND___ 4. Fantasia was a success in her Broadway debut.

___F___ 5. Fantasia is happy with how her parents disciplined her.

___F___ 6. Fantasia had no difficulty filling out job applications.

___T___ 7. Fantasia regrets spending time watching TV instead of studying.

___ND___ 8. Fantasia encourages her daughter to read instead of watching TV.

___F___ 9. Fantasia enjoys reading to her daughter.

___F___ 10. None of Fantasia's friends learned anything in school.

Major Details

Directions: Fill in the word or words that correctly complete each statement.

1. Fantasia really regrets _____dropping_____ out of school.

2. Fantasia won a _____free_____ car.

3. Fantasia made it to the _____ninth_____ grade.

4. Fantasia has a _____four_____-year-old daughter.

5. Fantasia refers to herself as a functioning _____illiterate_____.

6. Fantasia won the *American* _____Idol_____ competition.

Vocabulary in Context

Dictionary Definitions

Directions: Write the letter of the choice that best gives the meaning for each of the words or phrases as they are used in the selection. Numbers in parentheses indicate in which paragraph the words may be found.

_____d_____ 1. pay for it (1)
        a. give money in exchange for something
        b. retaliate against
        c. make a call or visit
        d. suffer or be punished

_____b_____ 2. to sound the letters out (1)
        a. to blow a horn
        b. to make certain noises with the voice
        c. to measure the depth of water
        d. to play a piano

_____a_____ 3. to figure out (1)
        a. to find the answer
        b. to draw pictures
        c. to solve a math problem
        d. to gain weight

_____d_____ 4. from my heart (1)
        a. with warm emotion
        b. with complete sincerity
        c. with true feeling
        d. all of the above

_____d_____ 5. grades (2)
        a. the amount of slope in a road
        b. classes of people
        c. standards of food based on quality
        d. marks or scores on tests or in school courses

_____d_____ 6. business (3)
        a. what a person does for a living
        b. store, office, or factory
        c. buying and selling goods or services
        d. something personal or private

_____c_____ 7. cool (3)
        a. feeling a little bit cold
        b. not being friendly
        c. being smart and superior
        d. being mean

_____c_____   8. papers (3)
  a. material used to decorate
  b. official documents
  c. written pieces of schoolwork such as compositions or reports
  d. newspapers or journals

_____b_____   9. chain reaction (4)
  a. an expensive necklace
  b. one thing causing another thing, which causes something else
  c. a range of mountains
  d. an explosion

_____a_____ 10. self-esteem (5)
  a. feelings of self-worth
  b. singing ability
  c. financial situation
  d. fame

_____a_____ 11. contract (5)
  a. a legal agreement
  b. an arrangement for a hired assassin
  c. a new song
  d. a role in a play

_____b_____ 12. fool the world (6)
  a. make people laugh
  b. keep something hidden
  c. make people angry
  d. make others look bad

In Your Own Words

1. In this excerpt from her autobiography, Fantasia describes some problems caused by her illiteracy. Specifically, she discusses being unable to fill out job applications, obtain a driver's license, and read scripts. Can you think of any other situations where an inability to read well could be limiting? What about reading menus in a restaurant or following a recipe in a cookbook? Can an inability to read threaten your health? What about reading directions on prescription labels?

2. Do you know anyone who is illiterate? If so, how has it affected his or her self-esteem? Is the person dependent on others for continual help?

3. Do you think that teachers should accept some responsibility for widespread illiteracy?

4. Look carefully at the cartoon on the following page. What main idea from the selection does the cartoon illustrate?

Copyright © 1993 Gary Brookins, Richmond Times-Dispatch.

Written Assignment

What advice would you give Fantasia? What are some concrete steps that she can take to solve her reading problems? Write a letter to her giving her advice.

Internet Activity

1. Visit the Fantasia Barrino website at

    http://www.fantasiabarrinoofficial.com/

    What do you find interesting about the site?

2. Visit the Literacy Volunteers of America website at

    http://www.literacyvolunteers.org/conference

    Write a paragraph describing what you learned about the organization.

READING

*"So no matter how much it bugs you when kids do it,
fidgeting can be a healthy thing to do."*

GETTING FOCUSED

As adults we "mature" and leave childish things behind. But looking at the world through a child's eyes and behaving like children may be just what we all need. In the following article, Joe Kita demonstrates that children may just be smarter than we think.

READING *continued*

BIO-SKETCH

Joe Kita, who lives in Schnecksville, Pennsylvania, with his wife and children, has been a writer and editor for *Men's Health,* a magazine with editions in 20 countries. He has the ability, as you will see in the following article, to combine humor with serious health issues. Two of his latest books are *GuyQ: 1035 Totally Essential Secrets You Either Know or You Don't* and *Another Shot: How I Relived My Life in a Year.*

TACKLING VOCABULARY

ingest to take into the body

munch to chew in a noisy, steady way

bliss utter joy or contentment

rejuvenate to make fresh, young, or new again

fidgeting moving restlessly

wretched very unhappy or troubled; miserable

innately inborn; existing from birth

bliss supreme happiness

Wiffle ball a plastic ball with small holes or cutouts often used in place of a baseball or golfball

DOING WHAT COMES NATURALLY

Joe Kita

Here are ten ways children are more knowledgeable about healthful living than you are. Learn from them.

2 **1. They prefer to eat five or more small meals a day.** This is called grazing, and nutritionists now recognize it as the most efficient way to eat. If you take the typical amount of food you ingest in three daily meals and spread it across five or six, you'll find you won't be as hungry, you'll be less inclined to overeat, and your energy level will remain fairly constant. Cleaning your plate when you're already full not only taxes your digestive system and promotes fat storage, it also redirects blood from your brain to your stomach, making you feel tired and dull. So as long as the snacks are nutritious, munching between meals is ideal.

3 **2. They never sit still.** Fidgeting is a form of unintentional exercise that can help people stay thin. In a recent study at the Mayo Clinic, in Rochester, Minnesota,

researchers fed 16 volunteers an extra 1,000 calories a day for eight weeks. Those who fidgeted the most burned nearly 700 extra calories a day and gained the least amount of weight. So no matter how much it bugs you when kids do it, fidgeting can be a healthy thing to do.

4   **3. They take naps.** Kids eventually do stop napping because they observe that it's not something big boys or girls do. But that's an American attitude. Many other cultures know that it's natural to have a longer period of sleep at night and a short snooze in the afternoon. In fact, says sleep expert Rubin Naiman, Ph.D., a clinical psychologist in Tucson, a 20- to 30-minute nap is key for keeping energy and creativity in high gear.

5   **4. They don't like tobacco, alcohol, or coffee.** Remember your first sip of beer, your first swig of coffee, or your first nervous puff on a cigarette? Chances are, you wrinkled your nose, made a face, spit the wretched substance out, and wondered how adults could ever enjoy that stuff. The reason? Taste is, for the most part, learned. When it comes to such vices, kids seem to be innately programmed to dislike what can harm them most.

6   **5. They have best friends.** Ask any child to name his best buddies and he'll quickly list a bunch. Ask any adult, especially a man, and chances are he won't be able to come up with even one best friend (other than, perhaps, his spouse), though he may be able to name a few social pals. This lack of intimate social support and the loneliness that results can adversely affect health. In a study conducted in Sweden last year, researchers x-rayed 131 women ages 30–65 who had been hospitalized for heart disease. They found that those with close personal relationships and broad social ties had fewer fatty deposits lining their arteries.

"Animals are such agreeable friends—they ask no questions, they pass no criticism."

—George Eliot

7   **6. They collect pets.** Puppies, kittens, birds, bugs—kids seek them out, name them, and love them. Parents often complain about the zoo their house becomes, but many studies have shown that adopting these creatures may actually lower the whole family's stress level. In addition, most doctors now agree that pets can help people live longer by relieving feelings of isolation.

8   **7. They make exercise a part of life.** For kids, exercise isn't something that's squeezed into 40-minute sessions three times a week; it's the way life is lived. Most children ride their bikes to visit friends, walk to the corner store, and literally run errands. Natural movement like this is the ideal, never-get-bored way to stay fit.

9   **8. They cry.** A sobbing 6-year-old is usually told to grow up and stop acting like a baby. But what parents don't realize is that an honest release of emotion, whether it's tears, anger, or yes, even the occasional bloodcurdling scream, is truly beneficial to the soul. It's when we keep everything bottled up inside that stress builds and our physical and mental health slide.

10   **9. They live in the present.** When a child is doing something, she is totally focused. There is no past or future, only the moment. This is called mindfulness, and it's a form of meditation that has been shown to reduce stress. It's the state of bliss that Buddhist monks strive to reach. But instead of celebrating mindfulness,

we urge our kids to hurry up. We need to remember that losing ourselves in anything, no matter how trifling the hobby or chore, is the most enjoyable and restorative experience possible.

11   **10. They play.** Try it sometime. Organize a game of Wiffle ball in your backyard. Sneak off to the local toy store and buy something for yourself. Stop thinking of your noontime work break as lunch hour and start viewing it as recess. Play rejuvenates. It calms you down. It spurs creativity. It's like sleep, only a lot more fun. In fact, a St. Louis-based company called Play Works organizes play breaks for employees in stressful occupations, with the result being greater job satisfaction and productivity.

12   So the next time you're about to correct kids for doing something you've told them a hundred times before not to do, pause for a moment to consider whether the behavior might actually be beneficial in some subtle way. Then try a bit of fidgeting yourself to see what you might be able to create from what's left of your broccoli and mashed potatoes.

> "Doing What Comes Naturally" by Joe Kita from *Parents* magazine, December 1999. Reprinted by permission of the author.

COMPREHENSION CHECKUP

True or False

Directions: Write **T** for each true statement and **F** for each false statement.

_____F_____ 1. According to nutritionists, grazing is the least efficient way to eat.

_____T_____ 2. Eating nutritious snacks between meals is a healthy habit.

_____T_____ 3. Exercise is a part of most children's lives.

_____T_____ 4. Most children eventually give up taking naps.

_____F_____ 5. Adopting pets probably will raise a family's stress level.

Agree or Disagree

Indicate whether the author is likely to agree or disagree with each of the following statements by writing **A** for agree or **D** for disagree in the blank provided.

_____A_____ 1. The Mediterranean custom of closing down businesses in the early afternoons for a short rest period makes sense.

_____D_____ 2. The state of mindfulness is a complete waste of time.

____A____ 3. A patient in a nursing home may benefit from having a pet.

____D____ 4. Wriggling about is a bad habit that should be eliminated.

____D____ 5. Always clean your plate.

____A____ 6. Riding your bike to work every day is better than taking one long bike ride on Saturdays.

____A____ 7. Having close friends is beneficial to your health.

____D____ 8. It's better to hold in your emotions than let them out.

____A____ 9. It would be a good idea for corporations to set up play rooms for their employees.

Vocabulary in Context

Directions: Look through the paragraphs indicated in parentheses to find the word that matches each of the definitions below.

1. people who are trained in the science of nourishment (2) ____nutritionists____

2. a short sleep or nap (4) ____snooze____

3. amount of liquid taken in one swallow (5) ____swig____

4. very close or familiar (6) ____intimate____

5. of little value or importance (10) ____trifling____

6. capable of renewing health or strength (10) ____restorative____

In Your Own Words

In Your Own Words

1. Do you have children of your own or children you spend time with on a regular basis? If so, give some examples of how these children demonstrate the trafor mentions in the selection.

2. Large numbers of American children are overweight. What can parents do to help children keep their weight under control? What can school districts do?

Written Assignment

Make a list of suggestions that you think could help people get more out of life. Give a specific reason for the inclusion of each item on your list.

Internet Activity

Consult one of the following websites and write a few paragraphs summarizing the information presented.

www.eating-disorder.com (eating disorders)

www.mcspotlight.org (anti-McDonald's)

www.mayoclinic.org/news (Mayo Clinic)

STUDY SKILLS
SQ3R, Scanning, and Skimming

Suppose your instructor handed out a quiz like this on your first day of class and told you   to "survey" the quiz before answering the questions. How would you respond?

_____

1. Write your name, last name first. _____

2. Write today's date according to the following model: 4 May 2007.

   _____

3. On the back of this paper, add the numbers 5,422 and 9,348.

   _____

4. What year did the Civil War officially end? _____

5. How many days are there in a leap year? _____

6. Multiply your answer to question 4 by your answer to question 5.

   Write your answer on the line. _____

7. Count the letters in your first and last name and write the number.

   _____

8. Answer only question 1. This question supersedes all others.

_____

Unless you read all the questions to the quiz first, you probably wasted quite a bit of time. The word *survey* means "to view or examine something in detail." This is an example of why surveying what you are going to read is important.

In previous warm-ups, we introduced techniques to help you "learn to read" more effectively. We discussed phonics, word structure, and the features of dictionaries. This warm-up is about learning techniques that will help you to more effectively "read to learn." One of those techniques is surveying.

Most of the reading you do in college will be for the purpose of learning. You will be reading material so that you can absorb information for use in tests, papers, or presentations. Three strategies that will help you to "read to learn" more efficiently are SQ3R, scanning, and skimming. As you will see below when we discuss the SQ3R process in more detail, the first step of SQ3R is surveying.

SQ3R: OVERVIEW

SQ3R is a five-step system for reading and studying textbook material that was developed by Dr. Francis P. Robinson. The acronym SQ3R stands for the following steps: survey, question, read, recite, and review. Research shows that the SQ3R method can help you improve both your reading comprehension and your grades.

A. **Survey**
   1. Become familiar with the way the material is organized.
   2. Read introductory and summary paragraphs.
   3. Read headings and subheadings.
   4. Look at illustrations and tables.
   5. Compare the material in front of you to previous material you may have read and to your own knowledge and experience.

B. **Question**
   1. Compose at least one question that you'd like to have answered by the reading.
   2. Turn headings and subheadings into questions that you can answer as you read.

C. **Read**
   1. Look for answers to your questions.
   2. Underline or highlight key words or phrases.
   3. Make notes in the margins.
   4. Explain the key points in your own words.

D. **Recite**
   1. Stop after each main heading and recite the key information.
   2. If you can't remember it, go back over the material.

E. **Review**
   1. Practice answering your original questions.
   2. Test yourself on the material more than once.
   3. Review the material frequently.

SQ3R: PRACTICE

You are going to be practicing the SQ3R techniques with a selection titled *Using Time Effectively,* on page 100 which is taken from a popular health textbook.

Step 1: Survey

A. Write the title of the selection and the author's name on the line below.

   Using Time Effectively by Wayne A. Payne
   _____

B. Think about what you know about using time effectively from personal experience. Write one sentence below.

   Answers will vary.
   _____

C. Read the first paragraph. Answer the following true/false questions.

   ___T___ 1. Many students feel that good time-management skills can lead to academic success.

   ___T___ 2. Managing your time effectively will help you control stress.

D. Now glance over the headings and subheadings and write the third subheading below.

   Use a Planner
   _____

E. Read the first and last sentence of each paragraph and answer the following true/false questions.

___T___ The first step on the road to time management is to figure out how you are spending your time.

___T___ Step two is keeping a daily planner.

___T___ It is only important to set goals for each day; forget about trying to plan for a whole week.

F. Read the last paragraph of the selection and answer the following true/false question.

___T___ The key to effective time management is breaking the large tasks down into manageable chunks and then doing them in order of importance.

Step 2: Question

A. After surveying the selection, you should have at least one question about the material. Write your question below.

Answers will vary.

_____

B. Now try turning the subheadings into questions. For instance, for subheading 2 you might ask, "Why should I assess my habits?" or "How should I assess my habits?" Write a question for subheading 4 below.

Answers will vary.

_____

Step 3: Read

A. Now read the entire selection. Try to answer the questions you posed previously. Underline what you consider the main points in the selection. You might also want to make some notes in the margins. Try to answer the following questions. If you have difficulty, read the material again.

1. When should your study time be scheduled? Schedule study time during the most productive part of your waking hours.

2. What is one method of task management? the ABC method of task management

Step 4: Recite

A. See if you can recite the answers to the following questions out loud.

1. What are the steps involved in keeping a daily planner?

2. How long does it take to establish good time-management habits? Why should you bother trying?

Step 5: Review

Continual review leads to success. Test yourself on the material over and over again. Can you still give the answers to your original questions? Do your notes still make sense? How about the material that you underlined? See if you can put the material aside and sum up the author's key points. Or exchange your notes with a classmate and have them quiz you on the material.

Can you fill in the missing details below?

The A tasks are those that _____ must be done today _____.

The B tasks can wait _____ 24 _____ hours.

The C tasks can wait _____ a few days to a week _____.

READING

"Managing your time effectively can help you cope with stress by enabling you to feel more in control of your life."

USING TIME EFFECTIVELY

Wayne A. Payne

An overwhelming number of students identify time management as the reason for their academic success or failure. Setting priorities and goals, balancing academic life with your social life, and finding time for sleeping, eating, exercising, and working along with studying is an essential aspect of managing stress effectively.

"What may be done anytime will be done at no time."

—Scottish proverb

Time Management

2 Managing your time effectively can help you cope with stress by enabling you to feel more in control in your life. Establishing good time management habits can take two to three weeks. By using specific systems, even the most disorganized persons can make their lives less chaotic and stressful.

Assess Your Habits

3 The first step is to analyze how you are spending your time. What are your most productive and least productive times of day and night? Do you tend to

underestimate how long something will take you to complete? Do you waste time or allow interruptions to take you off task? Carrying a notebook with you for a week and writing down how you spend your time might provide you with some insight into the answers to these questions and how you spend your time. You might find that you've been devoting most of your time to less important tasks. Perhaps it is tempting to do your laundry rather than to start writing that term paper, but this is probably not the best use of your time.

Use a Planner

4 Keeping a daily planner to schedule your time is the next step in managing your time more effectively. First block off all of the activities that are consistent, regular, weekly activities, such as attending classes, eating meals, sleeping, going to meetings, exercising, and working. Then look at the open, available time remaining. Schedule regular study time, relaxation time, and free time. Remember to schedule your study time during the more productive part of your waking hours. When you have a one-hour block of time, what can you realistically get done in that time? This could be a good time to review your notes from class, pay bills, or get some reading done.

Set Goals and Prioritize

5 Set goals for the week as well as for each day. If something unexpected interferes with your time schedule, modify your plans but don't throw out the entire schedule.

6   Making a to-do list can be helpful, but it is only the first step. Breaking the large tasks into smaller, more manageable pieces and then prioritizing them is the key to effective time management. When you prioritize your tasks, try the ABC method of task management. The A tasks are those items that are most urgent and must be done today. Then the B tasks are those things that are important but, if need be, could wait 24 hours. The C tasks are activities that can easily wait a few days to a week. Don't fall into the C trap, which is when you do the less important tasks because they are quick and can be checked off your list with ease. This can lead to putting off the more important A activities, leaving them until you feel stressed and overwhelmed.

> Excerpts from *Understanding Your Health,* 9th ed., by Wayne A. Payne et al. Copyright © 2007 The McGraw-Hill Publishing Companies, Inc. Reprinted by permission of The McGraw-Hill Companies, Inc.

This Is the Week That Was

Your next assignment is one that is going to take you a week to do. It involves keeping track of how you spend your time each day for a week. Each evening fill in the following calendar as best you can showing how you spent your time that day. Also keep track of how much sleep you get each night. *Be honest, and work on your calendar each day—don't wait until several days have passed.* At the end of the week, determine the total number of hours you spent on each of the following activities. Fill in your totals in the Hours Per Week Chart on page 103 and answer the questions that follow. You may find the results surprising. We hope you will also find them useful.

THIS IS THE WEEK THAT WAS

Name _____   Date _____

	MONDAY	TUESDAY	WEDNESDAY	THURSDAY	FRIDAY	SATURDAY	SUNDAY
6:00–7:00							
7:00–8:00							
8:00–9:00							
9:00–10:00							
10:00–11:00							
11:00–12:00							
12:00–1:00							
1:00–2:00							
2:00–3:00							
3:00–4:00							
4:00–5:00							
5:00–6:00							
6:00–7:00							
7:00–8:00							
8:00–9:00							
9:00–10:00							
10:00–11:00							
11:00–12:00							

Hours Per Week Chart

Sleep	_____	(You should sleep about 6–8 hours per night, or about 50 hours.)
Classes	_____	(This number will equal actual hours in class.)
Homework	_____	(We recommend that you spend two hours outside of class for every hour in class.)
Social Activities	_____	
Family Activities	_____	
Work	_____	
School Activities	_____	(Field trips, digs for archeology, painting for art class, softball practice, games.)
Grooming	_____	(Include time spent on personal care.)
Transportation	_____	(Include time spent driving or waiting for buses.)
Eating	_____	
Exercise	_____	(Don't overlook the need for this.)
Other	_____	(This may include church or other activities.)
TOTAL	_____	(This number should be 168 because there are 168 hours in a week.)

Now answer the following questions: Answers will vary.

1. What categories did you spend too much time on? _____

_____

_____

2. What categories did you spend too little time on? _____

_____

_____

3. How much time did you spend on classes, homework, and school activi-

   ties? How does this number compare with the time you spent

   on other activities, such as social activities and work? _____

   _____

   _____

4. What result surprises you the most? _____

   _____

   _____

Now reread the selection *Using Time Effectively* and answer the following questions:

1. What were the most useful time management strategies you learned from

   the reading? _____

   _____

   _____

2. What is the most productive time of the day for you to study? _____

   _____

   _____

3. If you have a one-hour block of time, what would be the best way for you

   to use it?_____

   _____

   _____

4. On a separate sheet of paper, make a to-do list for one day next week.
   Break the large tasks into manageable pieces and prioritize them using
   the ABC method of task management.

Vocabulary in Context

Directions: Using the vocabulary words below, fill in the crossword puzzle.

chaotic	insight	overwhelm	task
cope	manageable	priority	urgent
enable	modify	productive	

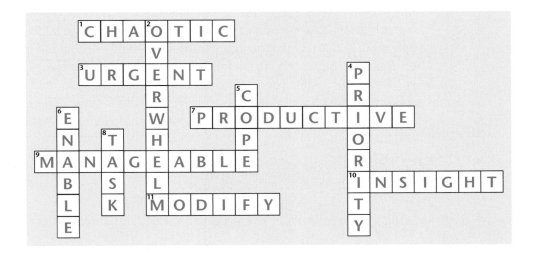

ACROSS CLUES
1. confused or disordered
3. requiring immediate action; pressing
7. fruitful
9. capable of being controlled
10. intuitive understanding
11. amend; change somewhat

DOWN CLUES
2. burden excessively
4. something given special attention
5. to face and deal with problems
6. make possible or easy
8. chore

USING YOUR COMPUTER AND THE INTERNET

To do well in college today, you need to have a basic proficiency with computers and the Internet. The Internet is a powerful tool for communicating with others, doing research for papers, and completing other classroom projects. As one expert has said, "Don't let that little glowing screen become an adversary. If you plan correctly, the computer can become your most useful tool at college—next to your brain." And of course your computer and Internet skills also will serve you well when you leave college and enter the workforce. More and more jobs require at least minimal computer skills, and many jobs are going to require higher levels of computer skills. Your mastery of basic computer skills is important for achieving college—and ultimately occupational—success.

READING

"Because minimal computer skill is the only expertise a person needs to set up a Web page, there may be as much misinformation on the Web as there is information."

GETTING FOCUSED

Practice your SQ3R techniques with this reading selection. Read the first paragraph, the first sentence of subsequent paragraphs, the subheadings, the information in bold type, the graphic material, and of course the cartoons. Then read the questions at the end. What do you already know about this topic? Before you start reading, come up with some questions of your own. As you are reading the selection, highlight (or underline) the definitions for each of the key terms. Use the margins for any notes you wish to make.

BIO-SKETCH

Robert S. Feldman is a professor of psychology at the University of Massachusetts, Amherst. In addition to the study skills book from which the following article is taken, he has written several psychology textbooks.

TACKLING VOCABULARY

virtual   of, existing on, or by means of computers
savvy   practical understanding; shrewdness or intelligence; common sense

MOVING BEYOND YOUR COMPUTER: THE INTERNET AND THE WEB

Robert S. Feldman

The Internet and Web have already revolutionized communication. And we haven't seen anything yet: Visionaries say it won't be too long before it will allow our refrigerators to order milk when supplies are running low or permit our physicians to constantly monitor our vital organs.

2   The **Internet** is the electronic network connecting millions of computers together. Hooking up to this network permits a user to share information with virtually anyone else who has a computer. Internet resources available to users are vast; from your home desktop you can access information from institutions at the farthest-flung corners of the earth. In fact, that's an understatement: Live images from as far away as the planet Mars have been transmitted to users via the Internet. The Internet is already the central storehouse for information in the 21st century.

3   The Internet provides the backbone of virtual communication. Among its specific features are the following:

● **E-mail.** The most widely used aspect of the Internet is **e-mail,** short for "electronic mail." E-mail offers a way for people to send and receive messages with incredible speed. On some college campuses, e-mail is the most common form of communication among students and faculty.

- **Instant messaging**. If you want to communicate in real time with friends and instructors, use instant messaging. With **instant messaging** (IM for short), you create a list of other users with whom you wish to communicate. If others on your list are online at the same time you are, you'll know instantly, and you'll be able to send messages back and forth. Instructors sometimes hold virtual office hours using instant messaging, and businesses increasingly use instant messaging in order to facilitate employee communication.

- **The World Wide Web**. Want to order flowers for your girlfriend in Dubuque? Find a long-lost friend? Hear the opening theme of Schubert's Unfinished Symphony? Read the latest health bulletin from the Centers for Disease Control? You can do all of these—and much, much more—on the **World Wide Web** (or, increasingly commonly, just **Web** for short) which provides a graphical means of locating and browsing through information on the Internet. Accessing the Web is rapidly becoming the standard way to find and use such information. The Web provides a way to transmit typewritten text, visual material, and auditory information—graphics, photos, music, sound-bites, video clips, and much more.

- **Newsgroups**. The Internet contains thousands of electronic **newsgroups,** where people can read and post messages relevant to a particular topic. For example, there are newsgroups devoted to the stock market, snowmobiles, the *Real World*, the New York Yankees, Jennifer Lopez, and Shakespeare's sonnets.

- **Listservs.** A **listserv** is a subscription service that automatically e-mails messages on general topics of shared interest to people who have added their names to its mailing list. Members can respond to messages by replying to the listserv, and their responses will be distributed automatically to everyone on the mailing list. (In most cases, it's also possible to respond directly to an individual who posts a message of interest, without sending that response to all members of the listserv.) Among the thousands of listservs online are those relating to jazz, tourism, privacy issues, and libertarianism.

The World Wide Web

4 As its name implies, the Web is vast—sometimes frustratingly so. In fact, no one knows how much material exists on the Web. Not only is more information added to the Web every day, but the information also resides on thousands of individual computers. Anyone with minimal Web savvy and access to a *server* (a computer with a permanent Internet connection) can set up a personal web site.

5   The fact that anyone can put information on the Web is both the biggest asset and the greatest disadvantage of using the Web as an information source. Because minimal computer skill is the only expertise a person needs to set up a Web page, there may be as much misinformation on the Web as there is information. Consequently, keep the usual consumer rule in mind: Buyer beware. Unless the Web site has been established and is maintained by a reliable organization, the information it contains may not be accurate.

6   There are a number of key factors involved in each Web search. They include a browser, Web pages, links, and search engines.

- **Browsers**. To use the Web, your computer has to have a browser. A **browser**, as its name implies, is a program that provides a way of looking at the information on the Web. A mong the major browsers are Microsoft's Internet Explorer, Netscape's Navigator, and Firefox's Mozilla.

  Using a browser is a bit like taking a taxi: once you get in, you get to where you want to go by providing an address. The address, also known as a URL (Uniform Resource Locator), identifies a unique location on the Web, a *Web site* or a *Web page* (one of the parts of a site.)

  Web addresses are combinations of letters and symbols. They typically start off with "**www.[domain_name].xxx**"—the address of the hosting Web site (e.g., **www.iastate. edu**, the home page for Iowa State University). The last three letters (.edu, .com, .gov, etc.) indicate the type of site (educational, commercial, governmental, etc.). Web addresses will become increasingly longer and more detailed in order to refer to more specific Web pages within a Web site. Because most addresses begin with "http://," this part of the address is often dropped in references to a site.

- **Web pages.** Web pages are the heart of the Web. A **Web page** is a document that presents you with information. The information may appear as text on the screen, to be read like a book (or more accurately, like an ancient scroll). It might include a video clip, an audio clip, a photo, a portrait, a graph, or a figure. It might offer a news service photo of the president of the United States or a backyard snapshot of someone's family reunion.

- **Links.** Web sites typically provide you with **links**—embedded addresses of other sites or documents that, at a click, cause your browser automatically to "jump" there. Just as an encyclopedia article on forests might say at the end, "See also Trees," Web pages often refer to other sites on the Web—only it's easier than with a book. You just have to click on the link with your mouse and—*poof!*—you're there.

- **Search engines.** A **search engine** is simply a computerized index to information on the Web. When you know what information you want to find but don't have an address for it, a search engine

"*Go ask your search engine.*"

"*First, they do an on-line search.*"

Traditional Library   **World Wide Web**

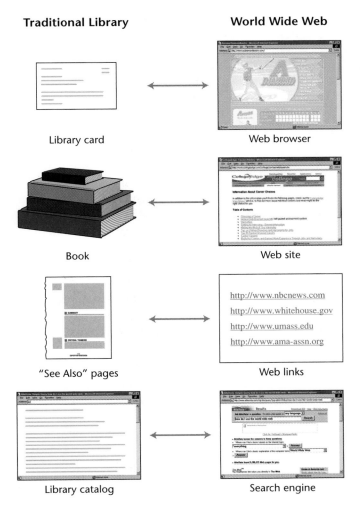

Library card   Web browser

Book   Web site

"See Also" pages   Web links

Library catalog   Search engine

can often steer you toward relevant sites. There is no central catalog of contents of the Web; instead, there are a number of different search engines. Furthermore, depending on the search engine you use and the type of search you do, you'll identify different information. Search engines themselves are located on the Web, so you have to know their addresses. Each search engine operates a little differently so you need to try some out and see which works best for you. Some of the more popular search engines are Google, MSN, Yahoo, Alta Vista, Ask Jeeves, and Dogpile.

7   The various parts of the Web are similar to the components of traditional libraries, as illustrated here. A Web browser is equivalent to a library card; it gives you access to vast quantities of material. Web sites are like the books of a library; Web pages are the book pages, where the content resides. Links are analogous to "see also" portions of books that suggest related information. And search engines are like a library's card catalog, directing you to specific locations.

WORK THE WEB: INFORMATION, PLEASE!

Try to find the answer to the first question below on Yahoo! (**www.yahoo.com**), Google (**www.google.com**), and Dogpile (**www.dogpile.com**). Then use the search engine you prefer to find answers to the remaining questions.

1. What was the French Revolution and when did it occur?

    an event to overthrow the monarchy and establish a republic in 1789

2. Who is Keyser Soze? a fictional character in the 1995 movie *The Usual Suspects.*

3. What are the first words of Dr. Martin Luther King Jr.'s "I Have a Dream" speech?

    "I am happy to join with you today . . ."

4. Is the birthrate in the United States higher or lower than that in Brazil?

    lower

How easy was it for you to find the answers to the questions? What search engine(s) did

you prefer, and why? <u>Answers will vary.</u>

_____

Excerpts from *Power Learning*, 3rd ed., by Robert S. Feldman. Copyright © 2007 The McGraw-Hill Companies, Inc. Reprinted by permission of The McGraw-Hill Companies, Inc.

COMPREHENSION CHECKUP

Understanding the Material

1. What is the selection about? <u>using computers and the Internet</u>

2. List four of the five popular features of the Internet below.

   a. <u>e-mail</u>

   b. <u>instant messaging</u>

   c. <u>World Wide Web</u>

   d. <u>newsgroups, also listservs</u>

3. List the essential components of the World Wide Web below and briefly explain the purpose of each.

   a. <u>browser</u>   <u>program that provides a way of looking at information</u>

   <u>on the Web</u>

   b. <u>Web page</u>   <u>a document that presents information</u>

   _____

   c. <u>link</u>   <u>embedded address to another site</u>

   _____

   d. <u>search engine</u> <u>a computerized index to information on the Web</u>

   _____

True or False

Directions: Indicate whether each statement is true or false by writing **T** or **F** in the space provided.

_____F_____ 1. There are exactly 3.3 billion unique pages on the World Wide Web.

_____F_____ 2. The author considers e-mail to be a slow method of communicating information.

_____T_____ 3. It is necessary to have a browser to be able to access the World Wide Web.

_____F_____ 4. According to the author, there is only one good search engine.

_____F_____ 5. The World Wide Web version of a library card catalog is a Web browser.

Vocabulary Matching

Directions: Match the vocabulary words in column A with the definitions in column B. Place the correct letter on the line provided.

Column A

1. ___d___ Internet

2. ___i___ e-mail

3. ___h___ link

4. ___b___ browser

5. ___f___ Web page

6. ___j___ search engine

Column B

a. an electronic Internet area in which users may post and read messages relevant to a particular topic

b. a program that provides a way of navigating around the information on the World Wide Web

c. a subscription service through which members can post and receive messages via e-mail on topics of shared interest

d. an electronic network connecting millions of computers

e. a means of communicating in real time

f. a document that presents you with information

7. __g__ World Wide Web   g. a graphical interface that permits users
to locate and browse through informa-
tion on the Internet

8. __a__ newsgroup   h. a means of "jumping" automatically
from one Web page to another

9. __e__ instant messaging   i. electronic mail

10. __c__ listserv   j. a computerized index to information on
the World Wide Web

Vocabulary in Context

Directions: Choose one of the following words to complete each of the sentences below. Use each word only once. Be sure to pay attention to the context
clues provided.

asset	embedded	facilitate	resides	unique
components	expertise	minimal	understatement	vast

1. Both Alaska and Texas have _____vast_____ expanses of unspoiled
wilderness.

2. Karen currently _____resides_____ in an apartment, but she is hoping
to buy a home shortly.

3. Ryan's new TV came with so many separate _____components_____ that it
took him almost three hours to assemble it.

4. He had a great deal of _____expertise_____ in computer information
systems but none in business management.

5. It is an _____understatement_____ to say that Sarah did okay in school when
she was the class valedictorian.

6. It takes more than a _____minimal_____ amount of knowledge about
photography to use a digital camera.

7. Having a college degree will be a definite _____asset_____ when
entering the job market.

8. Television journalists are now sometimes _____embedded_____ into military units in Afghanistan and Iraq.

9. Restaurants are now required to have restrooms that will
_____facilitate_____ people in wheelchairs using them.

10. The New York Giants football team came up with a _____unique_____
play to win the game in the last ten seconds.

In Your Own Words

1. Do you use the computer primarily for fun or for other purposes?
Explain your answer.

2. Do you have primarily negative or positive feelings about computers?
Explain why you feel this way.

3. What are some of the benefits and drawbacks you see for people in the
"information age"?

Written Assignment

Bill Gates has proposed funding a school in which all learning would take
place by means of computers. Drawing upon your school experience and
maybe the school experiences of your children, do you think his idea is a
good one? What do you believe would be the positive outcomes of using computers for all school learning? What would be the negative results of such a
program?

Internet Activity

Many colleges have a website. Go to a search engine and type in the name of
your college. If your college has a website, see if you can find the academic
calendar for your present term. Are the dates for final exams listed? If so,
what are those dates? What dates are listed as academic holidays? When does
registration for the next term open and end? Can you find anything else of
interest or help to you in your college's website?

SCANNING

Scanning is the process of quickly searching reading material in order to
locate specific bits of information. When you scan, you don't start at the beginning and read until you get to the end. Instead, you run your eyes rapidly
over the material to find the information that is important to you. Most of us
use scanning techniques when we search the telephone book for a number,
or the TV guide for the time and channel of a favorite show.

Techniques for Scanning

1. Think about what you are looking for. How is it likely to be expressed?
Are there specific words, phrases, or numbers you can search for?

2. Quickly look over the material in its entirety to get a sense of how it is
organized. Did you see the language you were looking for? Where in the
material is the item you are looking for most likely to be found?

3. You might find the item you are looking for right away. If you miss what you are looking for on your initial passes over the material, you may need to slow down a bit or focus on different areas.

4. When you find your item, read to confirm that the information is what you need.

Exercise 1: Car Advertisement

Directions: Scan the car advertisement on the next page and answer the questions that follow.

1. How many new Fords are priced at $14,995? 5

2. How many new models are there for $19,995? 6

3. Where is Mel Clayton Ford located? N. 16th Street and Camelback Rd.

4. What is the telephone number? 1-800 NEW FORD

5. What is the lowest price for a pre-owned vehicle? $4,995

Exercise 2: Yellow Pages

Directions: Read the page from the phone book on page 116 and answer the questions that follow.

1. What is the phone number for Outdoor Furniture & Acccessories?

   480-464-1767

2. How many locations are listed for Paddock Pools, Patios & Spas?

   12

3. Does Inside/Out sell to retail customers? No

4. All American Pool & Patio has two stores located on ____Bell____ Road.

5. What three other types of businesses are found on this page?

   Pattern Makers, Pavement & Floor Marking, and Pavers: Stone, Brick,

   Interlocking, Etc.

(Dex Official Directory, Qwest, Metro Phoenix, M–Z, 2007, p. 1437)

Mel Clayton Ford
Call 1-800-NEW FORD
North 16th Street and Camelback Road
Shop online 24/7 at www.melclaytonford.com

Copyright © 2009 by The McGraw-Hill Companies, Inc.

SKIMMING

Skimming is not a substitute for careful reading. Its purpose is to gain a quick overview of the author's key points. When you are skimming, you do not read every word. Instead, you move quickly through the material, skipping the parts that seem unrelated to a general understanding of the author's meaning. You might want to examine the introduction, the headings and subheadings, and the summary or conclusion. Skimming is very similar to the survey part of SQ3R (see page 97).

Exercise 3: Practice with Skimming and Scanning

Directions: Skim the selection on bats by science writer Anastasia Toufexis by quickly reading the first and last sentences of each paragraph. You should also read the first and last paragraphs in their entirety. Then answer the questions that follow.

READING

"The bat, say scientists, is actually one of nature's most dazzling and precious creations."

BATS' NEW IMAGE

Anastasia Toufexis

If ever a creature seemed conjured by the forces of darkness, it is the bat. With webbed wings and a feral face, the furry little beast appears to be the offspring of some monstrous union of bird and rodent. Over the years legend has had it that bats are filthy and nasty (they feed on human blood) and that they possess spooky supernatural powers (they shift shape from bat to man). No wonder they have been a staple of countless horror tales and films.

2   The image, however, is the product of imaginative folklore, stubborn myth and terrible public relations. The bat, say scientists, is actually one of nature's most dazzling and precious creations. Today researchers are striving to correct common misapprehensions about them—and racing to save them from extinction.

THE WEIRD AND WONDERFUL WORLD OF BATS

3 While most species of bats live in vast colonies in caves or trees, some nest in spider webs; others fashion "tents" out of leaves. In southern India, for example, the male short-nosed fruit bat spends as long as two months painstakingly chewing the veins of leaves and palm fronds until they collapse into a shelter that will house him and a harem of as many as 20 females.

4   Bat pups can weigh as much as a quarter of their mother's heft—the equivalent of a 100-pound woman giving birth to a 25-pound baby.

5   Most mammals wean their young when they reach 40% of adult size, but bats continue nursing their offspring until they are almost fully grown. The reason: pups need the extra time to attain the large wingspan and extra wing surface required to fly.

6   Bats' built-in echolocation system is so finely tuned that it can detect insects' footsteps, changes in air currents caused by vibrating insect wings, even the ripple in a pond as a minnow's fin breaks the surface.

7   According to the fossil record, bats were soaring in the sky at least 55 million years ago. These ancient flyers, says evolutionary biologist Nancy Simmons of New York City's American Museum of Natural History, were "virtually indistinguishable from today's echolocating bats." Though laymen think they most resemble rodents, bats' closest cousins are primates. Modern bats are amazingly diverse; about 1,000 species account for nearly a fourth of all mammal species. The only known group of flying mammals, they range in size from Thailand's tiny bumblebee bat, weighing less than a penny, to Indonesia's giant flying fox, with wingspans of nearly six feet. Many bats feed on insects, while others prefer fruit, nectar, or pollen. A few feast on fish, frogs, rodents, and yes, blood. Contrary to legend, however, vampire bats, which dwell in Latin America, suck the blood of grazing cattle and horses, not sleeping humans.

8   Essentially docile, bats play a vital role in maintaining ecological balance. For one thing, they protect crops from marauding insects. The 20 million Mexican tree-tailed bats that roost in Bracken Cave near San Antonio, Texas, from spring to fall consume 250 tons of insects every night as they swarm to altitudes of 10,000 feet. Farmers are not the only ones who benefit. A single little brown bat can speedily clear a suburban backyard of pesky mosquitoes, lapping up 600 bugs an hour.

9   Flower-browsing bats are prodigious pollinators and spreaders of seeds. When bats were kept away from an area in Curacao, researchers found that one type of cactus produced 90% less fruit and another produced no fruit at all. "The whole island fauna—birds and animals—relies on the cactus fruit to get through the dry season," observes zoologist Merlin Tuttle, founder of Bat Conservation International, based in Austin, Texas. In North America, long-nosed bats pollinate more than 60 species of agave, including those used by Mexico's tequila industry.

10   While folklore has enshrined the notion that bats are blind, all of them can see, and some species, such as Asia's fruit bats, boast extraordinary night vision, which they use to find food. But most bats rely on echolocation, emitting pulses of ultra-high-frequency sound some 10 times a second, then decoding the sound waves that bounce back from objects. "The time delay and the angle together give the bat the position of the target," explains neurobiologist Uli Schnitzler of the University of Tubingen in Germany. "The scans are so discriminating that "bats can discern the scales on a moth or the difference between a rock and a beetle," notes Boston University biologist Thomas Kunz. And so fast—the brain analyzes the data in microseconds—that a bat can snatch two insects within a single second.

11   Despite such stunning skills, bats are struggling for survival. Pollution and human encroachment are destroying their habitats. New Mexico's Carlsbad Caverns, once home to 8.7 million bats, now harbor fewer than a million. More than 40% of the U.S.'s 44 species are threatened or endangered. Fear has also

taken a heavy toll. In Latin America, people routinely dynamite and burn caves and roosts. "They think every bat is a vampire bat, and they kill all they can find," laments Kunz.

12   Scientists are lobbying hard to save the bat. Captive-breeding programs have been established in the Philippines as well as on several islands in the Indian Ocean. In India, legislation is being pushed to remove bats from the vermin category. The Convention on International Trade in Endangered Species bans traffic in fruit bats in the Pacific, where some people eat them.

13   In the U.S., Bat Conservation International has spearheaded education efforts, offering workshops for government officials and distributing books and videos to the public. More than 100 iron gates have been installed at cave mouths and over mine shafts to let bats in while keeping vandals and spelunkers out. On a smaller scale, Americans are busily erecting bat houses in their backyards along with the birdhouses.

14   Nowhere has the change of heart been more visible than in Austin. In 1980, when repairs under the Congress Avenue bridge inadvertently created attractive roosts for more than a million Mexican free-tailed bats, frightened citizens demanded their ouster. Familiarity, however, bred content. The bridge has now become a tourist attraction, and others like it are being built.

Anastasia Toufexis, *Time* Magazine, Volume 146, August 21, 1995, p. 58–59

Skimming Exercise

True or False

Directions: Answer the following questions using **T** for true and **F** for false.

_____F_____   1. Bats are evil, filthy creatures.

_____T_____   2. Most species of bats live in caves or trees.

_____F_____   3. Technically, bats are small flying rodents.

_____T_____   4. Bats play a role in ecological balance by protecting crops from insects.

_____T_____   5. Some types of bats pollinate and spread seeds.

_____F_____   6. The expression "blind as a bat" is a true one.

_____T_____   7. Most bats rely on echolocation to spot their prey.

_____T_____   8. Pollution and destruction of habitat has taken a toll on the bat.

_____F_____   9. Scientists have abandoned the effort to save the bat.

Scanning Exercise

A. **Directions:** Scan the selection to find the following information:

1. How long do fossil records indicate bats have been in existence?

   55 million years
   _____

2. How many Mexican free-tailed bats live in Bracken Cave?

   20 million
   _____

3. How many bats currently live in New Mexico's Carlsbad Caverns? fewer

   than a million
   _____

4. What percentage of bat species in the United States are threatened or en-

   dangered? more than 40%
   _____

5. What is the name of a U.S. conservation group that has promoted educa-

   tion about bats? Bat Conservation International
   _____

B. **Directions:** For each of the descriptions below, scan the paragraph indicated to find the word that fits the description given.

1. Find a word in paragraph 1 meaning "savage." feral
   _____

2. Find a word in paragraph 7 meaning "persons not belonging to or skilled

   in a given profession." laymen
   _____

3. Find the word in paragraph 8 meaning "raiding or plundering."

   marauding
   _____

4. Find the word in paragraph 9 meaning "extraordinary in quantity or de-

   gree" or "amazing." prodigious
   _____

5. Find the word in paragraph 10 meaning "cherished" or "held as sacred."

   enshrined
   _____

6. Find the word in paragraph 11 meaning "mourns" or "regrets

deeply." laments _____

7. Find the word in paragraph 12 meaning "pest." vermin _____

8. Find the word in paragraph 13 meaning "persons who explore caves as a

hobby." spelunkers _____

9. Find the word in paragraph 14 meaning "removal." ouster _____

Discovering Meaning Through Structure

"*Winning can be defined as the science of being totally prepared.*"

—*George Allen*

CHAPTERS IN PART 2

1 Identifying Topics, Main Ideas, and Supporting Details

© ZITS Partnership, King Features Syndicate.

The most important point the author makes is the **main idea.** The main idea can be directly stated, meaning that you can locate it somewhere in the passage or selection, or it can be implied, meaning that you, the reader, must infer it by uniting the key supporting details. **Supporting details** are specific bits of information that answer the question words: who, what, where, when, why, and how. Supporting details provide reasons and examples that support and explain the main idea.

As an illustration of the difference between main ideas and supporting details, study the Zits cartoon above. In it, the main idea is that Jeremy wants to attend a concert with his friends. The supporting details answer the question words.

TOPIC

In order to determine the main idea, it is helpful to first identify the topic the author is discussing. The **topic** is what the passage is about. It is the subject of the passage. The topic is not a complete sentence you can find in the passage. It can usually be summed up in a word or brief phrase similar to a title. It is sometimes the noun that is mentioned most frequently in the passage or selection. You can identify the topic by asking the question: What is this about? The answer is the topic.

Once you have identified the topic, ask the question: What is the most important point the author wants me to know about the topic? The answer is the main idea.

Main ideas are general statements, and supporting details are specific pieces of information. Supporting details back up and support the main idea. If you think of the main ideas as being similar to the roof of a house, then the supporting details are the pillars or support beams holding up the house.

In the exercises that follow, you are going to be determining the difference between general and specific, identifying topics, and working with main ideas and supporting details. The main ideas that you encounter in this chapter can all be directly stated. In the following chapter, you will be working with implied main ideas.

Distinguishing Between General and Specific

In order to be able to recognize a topic, a main idea, and supporting details, you must be able to determine the difference between something that is general and something that is specific.

Exercise 1: Underlining the Most General Term

Directions: In the following exercise, underline the most general term in each group of words.

1. dresser, sofa, dining table, recliner, <u>furniture</u>

2. grape juice, <u>beverages</u>, coffee, tea, milk

3. parakeet, goldfish, <u>pets</u>, dog, cat

4. Hearts, Canasta, Crazy Eights, <u>card games</u>, Old Maid

5. Spanish, Russian, Chinese, <u>languages</u>, English

Exercise 2: Identifying the Topic

Directions: Identify the topic, or general term, that best sums up each group of items below. Be sure to ask the question: What is this about?

Example
General: fruit
Specific: strawberries
             bananas
             grapes

In the example above, fruit is the general term, because there are many different kinds of fruit. Strawberries, bananas, and grapes are all specific types of fruit. Answers will vary.

1. super heroes; comics
   Superman
   Batman
   X-Men

2. U.S. presidents
   Ulysses S. Grant
   Theodore Roosevelt
   Jimmy Carter

3. countries (South America)
   Brazil
   Argentina
   Ecuador

4. teeth
   incisors
   canines
   molars

5. astrological signs
   Capricorn
   Pisces
   Aries

6. milk products
   butter
   yogurt
   ice cream

7. track and field events
   pole vault
   long jump
   shot put

8. rivers
   Nile
   Amazon
   Mississippi

9. insects (that sting)
   wasp
   hornet
   bee

10. punctuation marks
    period
    colon
    apostrophe

11. bones in the body
    radius
    ulna
    femur

12. planets
    Jupiter
    Saturn
    Mars

13. college degrees
    associate
    bachelor's
    master's

14. Monopoly properties
    Boardwalk
    Park Place
    Baltic Avenue

15. <u>Disney heroines</u>

Cinderella

Snow White

Belle

16. <u>state capitals</u>

Austin

Sacramento

Des Moines

Exercise 3: General and Specific

Directions: Number the following lists from the most general (1) to the most specific (4).

Example

_1_ artist

_4_ Picasso

_2_ painter

_3_ twentieth-century painter

A. _2_ nail polish

 _1_ cosmetics

 _4_ Revlon pink nail polish

 _3_ pink nail polish

B. _2_ children's movies

 _1_ movies

 _3_ children's Disney movies

 _4_ *Beauty and the Beast*

C. _4_ Toyota Highlander

 _2_ vehicles

 _3_ SUVs

 _1_ transportation

D. _1_ baseball players

 _3_ Cy Young award winners

 _4_ Roger Clemens

 _2_ pitchers

E. _4_ Sandy the golden retriever

 _3_ golden retriever

 _2_ dogs

 _1_ animals

F. _3_ Spanish classes

 _1_ community college

 _2_ foreign language department

 _4_ Spanish 101

G. _3_ rap

 _1_ media

 _2_ music

 _4_ Eminem

H. _1_ entertainment

 _4_ *Desperate Housewives*

 _2_ television shows

 _3_ dramedies

I. _2_ produce

 _1_ food

 _4_ pears

 _3_ fruit

J. _3_ star

 _2_ constellation

 _4_ North Star

 _1_ galaxy

Exercise 4: Choosing the Best Topic

Directions: Find the best topic for each list of words.

Example

horses	a. large animals
cows	b. small animals
pigs	c. animals
sheep	d. farm animals
hens	

Hens are not large animals. Horses and cows are not small animals. *Animals* is too broad a word because it includes many other kinds of animals, such as kangaroos and giraffes. Answer d is correct. All of the animals are farm animals.

c   1.

surfboarding	a. water
swimming	b. winter sports
sailing	c. water sports
scuba diving	d. sports
snorkeling	

a   2.

Guillermo	a. male names
John	b. female names
Carlos	c. names
Edward	d. Spanish names
Matthew	

c   3.

football	a. games
baseball	b. male sports
basketball	c. ball games
soccer	d. kicking games
tennis	

d   4.

San Francisco	a. U.S. state capitals
Chicago	b. Eastern cities
Baton Rouge	c. small cities
Atlanta	d. cities
Little Rock	

a   5.

chicken	a. meat
pork	b. food

turkey	c. poultry
beef	d. fowl
ham	

_d_ 6.

nose	a. body parts
ear	b. sensory organs
eyes	c. head and torso
cheeks	d. face parts
mouth	

_a_ 7.

canvas	a. art supplies
easel	b. supplies
brush	c. art
paint	d. office supplies
charcoal	

_d_ 8.

mittens	a. clothing
parka	b. indoor clothing
ski hat	c. knit clothing
muffler	d. outdoor clothing
galoshes	

_b_ 9.

checkers	a. games
chess	b. board games
Clue	c. children's games
Monopoly	d. sports
Sorry	

_d_ 10.

May	a. summer months
July	b. winter months
December	c. calendar
October	d. months with 31 days
August	

Exercise 5: Identifying Topics in Paragraphs

Directions: Read each paragraph and look for the topic. Remember to ask the question: What is this about? The topic is going to be a word or brief phrase, similar to a title.

"It is in games that many discover their paradise."

—Robert Lynd

1.   Bed racing is anything but a yawn, and races are springing up across the country. At the sixth annual Pineapple Grove Bed Race & Festival, in Delray Beach, Florida, more than 40 teams competed in 2003. The stakes are high: a total of $25,000 in cash prizes. Each team has five members. Four of them push "the queen," who rides on the bed as it speeds down Pineapple Grove Way. The fastest four-wheeled bed across the finish line wins. In this race, if you snooze, you definitely lose!

Topic: bed racing

2.   The first Virginia City (Nevada) International Camel Races began as a joke. A newspaper editor published a made-up account of a camel race to be held in September of 1959. But because so many people asked about entering, the race went off the next year. Camel racing is similar to horse racing, but more difficult in many ways. A jockey straddles the camel as it runs around a 175- to 200-yard track. Unlike horses, camels can be uncooperative and moody. They have been known to complete half the race, turn around, and return to the starting gate.

Topic: camel racing

3.   Volleyballers get down and dirty at the University of Connecticut's Oozeball Tournament, which is held each April. Four wooden-framed courts are filled with 250 tons of dirt that have been wet down by a fire hose. After oozing around in the eight-inch-deep slop, players are completely filthy. Teams play one match. The first team to earn 12 points advances. Each match is six-on-six, but each team must have three female players on the court at all times. The winning team gets about $150 and, one hopes, a shower.

Topic: Oozeball Tournament

4.   They shoot. They score! And they do it underwater. In underwater hockey, two teams of six players each shoot a plastic-coated lead puck into goals at opposite ends on the bottom of a pool. Substitutions are made frequently because players usually can't hold their breath for more than 30 seconds. Games are divided into 15-minute halves, and equipment consists of fins, a diving mask, a snorkel, a foot-long wooden stick, and a protective glove. Underwater hockey was invented by the British Navy in the 1950s to increase the physical fitness of its sailors. Today, the sport is played in 25 countries, and teams from Australia and New Zealand rule the pool.

Topic: underwater hockey

5.   Extreme ironing is a "sport" for those who crave adventure, excitement—and freshly pressed clothing. The activity was founded by Phil "Steam" Shaw, in England in 1997. Shaw decided to combine the chore of ironing with his rock-climbing hobby. The idea caught on in England and expanded around the globe. Competitors carry irons (battery powered or electric with long extension cords) and ironing boards to remote locations and press several pieces of clothing. The locations may be mountains and rocks (preferably after a difficult climb), ski slopes, or river

rapids. World championships were held in Germany, in 2002. Eighty competitors from 10 countries were judged on the difficulty of their athletic feat and the crispness of the creases in their laundry. Aren't there easier ways to let off steam?

Topic: extreme ironing

6.   You've heard of arm wrestling. But *toe* wrestling? Of course! The sport was invented in 1976, in Wetton, England, and has gained a foothold in organized sports. Today, world championships for men and women are held every year. Before a match, competitors ceremoniously remove their shoes and socks. Then they sit across from each other on a "toedium." Matches begin when two wrestlers lock big toes and the referee shouts "Toes away!" The first wrestler to turn his competitor's foot over and touch it to the "toe rack" is the winner. Feet fly but rear ends must be touching the toedium at all times. A player may yell "toe much" if he or she is in pain. Each match is the best toe . . . er, two . . . out of three.

Topic: toe wrestling

Information from Carter, Andre, and Nicholls, Shawn, *You Call* That *a Sport?*, New York: *Time* Inc., 2003

Exercise 6: Book Topics

Directions: Read each of the tables of contents below to determine the topic of the book it came from. Then choose the title from the list of book titles at the end of the exercise that best matches the topic and write it on the line provided.

1. *Don't Know Much About American History*

   Contents
   Chapter 1 Brave New World   8
   Chapter 2 A Little Rebellion   28
   Chapter 3 Growth of a Nation   50
   Chapter 4 The Way West   67
   Chapter 5 The War of Brothers   88
   Chapter 6 How the West Was Won and Lost   108
   Chapter 7 America Builds an Empire   130

2. *The Worst-Case Scenario Survival Handbook: College*

   Contents
   1. Getting Settled   15
        How to Avoid Going to the Wrong College   16
        How to Take on a New Identity   21
        How to Avoid a Disaster Mattress   28
        How to Decorate Your Room When You're Broke   31
   2. Room and Board   39
        How to Survive in a Small Room   40
        How to Deal with a Nightmare Roommate   43

How to Deal with a Promiscuous Roommate   45
How to Eat When You're Broke   53
How to Ask Your Parents for Money   57

3. *Ants at Work*

Contents

Introduction   vii
1. The rhythms of the landscape   1
2. The growth of an ant society   13
3. Food and the foreign relations of ant society   41
4. A forest of ant colonies   75
5. In the society of ants   95

4. *Call of the Mall*

Contents

Prologue   1
Introduction   3
1. America Shops   7
2. You Are Here   13
3. A Mouse Hole   17
4. Dude, Where's My Car?   23
5. Why Malls Fear Freedom   29
6. I Brake for Meanderthals   37

5. *On Death and Dying*

Contents

Preface   xi
  I. On the Fear of Death   1
 II. Attitudes Toward Death and Dying   10
III. First Stage: Denial and Isolation   34
IV. Second Stage: Anger   44
 V. Third Stage: Bargaining   72

6. *Chocolate*

Contents

The God's Breakfast   3
Chocolate for Turkeys   67
The Chocolate Coast   105
Belgium: Hobbit Chocolate   187
Chocolate Soldiers   263
Camp Cacao   287
Acknowledgments   291

7. *The Working Poor*

Contents

Preface   IX
Introduction: At the Edge of Poverty   3
Chapter One: Money and Its Opposite   13

8. *Teaching Your Children Good Manners*

Table of Contents

9. *All Your Worth*

Contents

10. *Coach*

Contents

Book Titles

All Your Worth by Elizabeth Warren & Amelia Warren Tyagi
Ants at Work by Deborah Gordon
Call of the Mall by Paco Underhill
Don't Know Much About American History by Kenneth C. Davis
On Death and Dying by Elisabeth Kübler-Ross
Chocolate by Mort Rosenblum

Teaching Your Children Good Manners by Lauri Berkenkamp
Coach by Andrew Blauner
The Working Poor by David K. Shipler
The Worst-Case Scenario Survival Handbook: College by Joshua Piven et al.

Exercise 7: Identifying Topics in Textbook Paragraphs

Directions: Write the topic of each of the following paragraphs on the lines provided.

1.   Do you believe—or know people who believe—in psychic phenomena, such as mental telepathy (transmitting thoughts between individuals) and precognition (foretelling the future)? Surveys around the world reveal widespread public belief in psychic phenomena. But, when tested under controlled conditions in well-designed experiments and replications, claim after claim of psychic ability has evaporated. At present there is no generally accepted scientific evidence to support the existence of psychic phenomena.

Topic: psychic phenomena

"What's done to children, they will do to society."

—Karl Menninger

2.   As a child, were you spanked for misbehaving? And, as someone who may one day become a parent or may already be one, do you believe that there are times when parents should spank their children? If you grew up in the United States, odds are high that your answers to both questions are yes. In one national survey of American parents, 94 percent reported that by the time their children reached the age of 4, they had spanked them. Yet your answers would likely be different if you grew up in Sweden, which banned spanking of children in 1979. Other countries, including Austria, Denmark, and Norway, have since passed similar bans.

Topic: spanking children

3.   Given that children are language sponges, it seems obvious that a second language would be learned best and spoken most fluently when acquired early in life. If you start to learn a second language in childhood, then by the time you reach age 25 or 30, let's say, you will have had many more years of exposure to that language than if you had first started to learn it in your late teens. In general, it is more difficult to learn a second language in adulthood than in childhood.

Topic: learning a second language

4.   From the moment of birth, infants differ from one another in temperament. Some infants are calm and happy; others are irritable and fussy; others are shy and inactive. Most infants can be classified into three groups. "Easy infants" ate and slept on schedule, were playful, and accepted new situations with little fuss. "Difficult infants" were irritable,

were fussy eaters and sleepers, and reacted negatively to new situations. "Slow-to-warm-up infants" were the least active, had mildly negative responses to new situations, but slowly adapted over time.

Topic: <u>types of infants</u>

5.   Suicide is the willful taking of one's own life. The World Health Organization estimates that worldwide, nearly 500,000 people commit suicide each year—almost 1 per minute. Ten times that number engage in nonfatal suicide attempts. In the United States, suicide is the second most frequent cause of death (after accidents) among high school and college students. Women attempt suicide about 3 times more often than men, but men are 3 times more likely to actually kill themselves. The suicide rate for both men and women is higher among those who have been divorced or widowed. Women's suicides are more likely to be triggered by failures in love relationships, whereas career failures more often prompt men's suicides.

Topic: <u>suicide</u>

6.   The three pounds of protein, fat, and fluid that you carry around inside your skull is the real you. It is also the most complex structure in the known universe and the only one that can wonder about itself. Although your brain accounts for only about 2 percent of your total body weight, it consumes about 25 percent of your body's oxygen and 70 percent of its glucose. Moreover, your brain is the most active energy consumer of all your body organs. It never rests. In fact, when you dream, the brain's metabolic rate actually increases slightly. Even more amazing, this rather nondescript blob of grayish tissue can discover the principle of relativity, build the Hubble Space Telescope, and produce great works of art, music, and literature.

Topic: <u>your brain</u>

7.   Sleep deprivation is a way of life for many college students and other adults. What do you think happens to students who pull all-nighters or cut back their sleep claiming they will still perform as well as ever? Researchers found that college students deprived of one night's sleep performed more poorly on a critical-thinking task than students allowed to sleep—yet they incorrectly thought that they had performed better. The researchers concluded that students underestimate the negative effects of sleep loss on performance. In general, it takes several nights to recover from extended sleep deprivation, and we do not make up all the sleep time that we have lost.

Topic: <u>sleep deprivation</u>

8.   Close relationships go through good times and bad, persisting or dissolving over time. Consider marriage. This union is often fragile, and many marriages end in divorce. Happily married couples experience conflict and anger but keep the negativity from getting out of control. Instead,

they make frequent "repair attempts" to resolve their differences in a spirit of mutual respect and support. Happily married couples maintain a much higher ratio of positive to negative interactions than couples headed for divorce, and this history provides a positive "emotional bank account" that helps them repair and recover from their immediate anger and conflict. They also strive to get to know each other deeply and they continually update their knowledge. Such behavior contributes to an essential aspect of happy marriages: an intimate friendship between the partners.

Topic: happy marriages

Passer, Michael W., and Smith, Ronald E., *Psychology,* 3rd edition, New York: McGraw-Hill, 2007

MAIN IDEAS AND DETAILS

The **main idea** of a paragraph is the most important point the author wants to make about the topic. **Supporting details** are specific pieces of information such as examples, facts, statistics, descriptions, and reasons that back up and support the main idea. Asking who, what, where, when, and why questions will help you identify the supporting details in a paragraph.

"Oh, no! Who, what, where, when?"

Each sentence in the paragraph is going to talk about the topic. To find the main idea, which is a general statement, ask yourself, "What is the most important thing the author wants me to know about the topic?" The *main idea sentence,* also known as the *topic sentence,* is a broad statement that includes all the other more specific sentences. The more specific sentences are the supporting details, and they provide the reasons the author uses to explain and support the main idea.

Exercise 8: Identifying the General or Main Idea Sentence

Directions: Put a check mark beside the most general statement in each group of statements.

A. _____ 1. It seems that there is never enough time to attend class, study, and work enough hours to pay the bills.

___✓___ 2. College students are stressed.

_____ 3. Some students are trying to cope with the demands of adapting to a new living environment, new peers, and academic pressure. (p. 1)

B. ___✓___ 1. Many stressors can combine to create a stressful home environment for the college student.

_____ 2. Many students live at home and share rooms with younger siblings and don't have a place where they can read and study undisturbed.

_____ 3. Other students report having to share the family computer that is often located in the family room where it is difficult to concentrate and work effectively. (p. 63)

C. _____ 1. For example, sleep loss as a result of noise can cause high blood pressure and an irregular heart beat.

___✓___ 2. Noise is associated with a variety of negative health outcomes.

_____ 3. Sleep loss as a result of noise can cause increased fatigue, depressed mood, and decreased performance. (p. 69)

D. _____ 1. For instance, the body needs several weeks to adjust fully to a switch from a day shift to a night shift.

_____ 2. Police officers, airline crews, and firefighters change shifts much more often than that.

___✓___ 3. Some jobs impose excessive time demands on workers. (p. 76)

E. _____ 1. Getting stuck in a dead-end job can be a major source of stress.

___✓___ 2. Career concerns can cause a great deal of stress.

_____ 3. Forced transfers can be very stressful to businessmen, businesswomen, and their families. (p. 79)

Information from Blonna, Richard, *Coping with Stress in a Changing World*, 4th edition, New York: McGraw-Hill, 2007

Exercise 9: Working with Main Ideas and Details in Ads

Directions: For each of the following ads, write the main idea and supporting details on the appropriate line. Look at the example and see how asking who, what, where, when, and why questions helps you to identify the supporting details.

Example
Chihuahuas For Sale, short　　　　　　　　*Jason (623) 745-1909*
coats, Male and Female,　　　　　　　　　*9 AM to 3 PM ONLY*
8 wks old. $400 Cash Only—　　　　　　　*1511 Westlake Drive,*
Special Price if you take　　　　　　　　　*Collinsville, IL*
both. First Shots, Adorable.　　　　　　　*MOVING—MUST SELL*
Health Guaranteed!

Main Idea:　　　　　　　　　　　Chihuahuas are for sale.

Who is selling something?　　　　Jason

What is being sold?   <u>short-haired, 8-week-old male and</u>

                                       <u>female Chihuahuas</u>

Where are they being sold?   <u>1511 Westlake Drive, Collinsville, IL</u>

When are they being sold?   <u>9 AM to 3 PM</u>

Why are they being sold?   <u>Moving (needs cash)</u>

Ad 1

Apartments For Rent   3 Sparkling Pools plus Spa
Brand NEW!   W/D provided, Covered
Carlyle Management Team   Parking, Pets Welcome!
First month FREE   Free Utilities and Cable
1 bdrm as low as $620 $199 Moves You In
2 bdrm as low as $725   Available Immediately in
Superior Fitness Cntr   Glendale and Arrowhead.

Main Idea: <u>Apartments are for rent.</u>

Who is renting something?   <u>Carlyle Management Team</u>

What is being rented?   <u>1- and 2-bedroom apartments</u>

Where is it being rented?   <u>Glendale and Arrowhead</u>

When is it being rented?   <u>immediately</u>

Why is it being rented?   <u>brand new—vacant</u>

Ad 2

A BIG Sale   Sofa and 2 Chairs,
Moving to Texas next month   Plasma TV, Bar
New job   Original Cost $5,000
3 Rms of Furniture   Will Sell $1,500
All Nearly New   Call (480) 623-3750
Pillowtop Mattress,   Tom or Ashley
Bedroom Set, Dining   1940 W. Marshall
Table and Hutch,

Main Idea: <u>There is a moving sale.</u>

Who is moving?   <u>Tom and Ashley</u>

What are they selling?   <u>furniture</u>

Where are they moving?	Texas
When are they moving?	next month
Why are they moving?	new job

Ad 3

For Sale—Toyota 02 Camry Fully Loaded, One Owner, Warranty Available, Power Windows/Locks, CD, Extra Clean, White Exterior, Blue interior.

$13,495 or best offer. Must Sell— Lots Overflowing! Call Jeff 580-915-6211 Mesa Toyota 9 AM–10 PM

Main Idea:	A used Toyota is for sale.
Who is selling something?	Jeff
What is he selling?	Toyota 02 Camry
Where is he selling it?	Mesa Toyota
When is he selling it?	9 AM–10 PM
Why is he selling it?	lots overflowing with cars

Ad 4

Resort/Hotel Opening in Oct. Housekeeping Positions Available Scenic location in Taos, New Mexico Both AM and PM needed. Benefits Package, $8.00/hr. Free Meals

Call TODAY for an appointment (602) GOPLAZA Drug-Free Workplace Pleasant Environment Join a Winning Team! Good investment opportunities. Contact J. R. Tuttle Development

Main Idea:	A housekeeping position is available at a new hotel.
Who is in charge?	J. R. Tuttle Development
What is available?	housekeeping positions for AM and PM
Where is the hotel located?	Taos, New Mexico

When is the hotel opening?   October

Why would people want to   pleasant environment, benefits, free meals

work there?

**Exercise 10: Main Idea and Detail Practice
in a Newspaper Article**

Directions: Use the newspaper article to answer the following detail questions about the Wal-Mart shooting and to identify the main idea of the piece.

2 SHOT DEAD AT WAL-MART

Pat Flannery, David Madrid
and Christine Romero

The Arizona Republic

A northwest valley man seething with anger turned a Wal-Mart Supercenter parking lot into a shooting gallery Tuesday, police said, leaving two store employees dead and investigators stumped for a motive.

2   "He just went crazy," said Chuck O'Leary, 26, of Peoria, whose wife, Kara, 28, witnessed part of the mayhem as she walked into the store shortly after 1 P.M. "She said the guy just went ballistic and starting firing off shots."

3   The suspect, identified by police as Ed Lui, 53, was tracked to a nearby retirement community and arrested a few hours later.

4   Dead at the scene of the fusillade were Anthony Spangler, 18, and Patrick Graham, 18 or 19. Both Glendale men were collecting grocery carts in the parking lot near 83rd Avenue and Union Hills Drive when, according to police, Lui drove into the parking lot and angrily pumped them full of bullets without any known motive. Witnesses said one of the men appeared to have tried to crawl under a car for protection before being shot.

5   "For some unknown reason, he decided to tragically end these guys' lives," Officer Mike Peña, a Glendale police spokesman, said at a late-evening news conference.

6   "There's no motive at all," he said. "It's a random act."

7   David Kost, 25, said he was in his vehicle in the parking lot when he heard about seven shots fired. He ducked to the floorboards and came out when the firing stopped.

1. Who was shot and killed?

   Anthony Spangler, 18, and Patrick Graham, 18 or 19

2. Where did the shootings occur?

   Wal-Mart Supercenter parking lot

3. What were the victims doing when the suspect drove into the parking lot?

collecting grocery carts in the parking lot

4. When did the shooting take place?

shortly after 1 P.M.

5. Why did the suspect shoot the victims?

no motive, random act, just went crazy

6. What is the suspect's name and age?

Ed Lui, 53

7. According to an eyewitness, how did the suspect behave at the scene of the crime?

just went ballistic and started firing off shots

8. Write the main idea of the newspaper article below.

For unknown reasons, two Wal-Mart employees were killed in the Supercenter

parking lot by Ed Lui.

Exercise 11: Locating Topics and Main Ideas in Textbook Material

Directions: Determine the topic of each paragraph and find the main idea sentence. Remember, the main idea sentence is the most general sentence in the paragraph, the one that all the other sentences relate to and support. Write your answers on the designated lines.

"Habit is stronger than reason."
—George Santayana

1.   The foods people eat, along with the customs they observe in preparing and consuming their meals, say a great deal about their culture. In some cultures such as that of Papua, New Guinea, roast pork is a delicacy reserved for feasts; in other cultures it is forbidden food. In U.S. culture, genetically modified food is accepted without much question, but in Europe it is banned. Because Swedish people put great value on natural, organic foods, 99 percent of mothers in Sweden breast-feed their infants—a rate much higher than in the United States.

Topic: culture and food

Main Idea: first sentence—The foods people eat . . .

2.   He works. She works. Both are physicians—a high-status occupation with considerable financial rewards. He makes $140,000. She makes $88,000. Take air traffic controllers. He makes $67,000; she earns $56,000. Or housekeepers: he makes $19,000; she earns $15,000. What about teacher's assistants? He makes $20,000; she earns $15,000. Across the board, in occupation after occupation, there is a substantial gender gap in the median earnings of male and female full-time workers.

Topic: gender gap in income

Main Idea: last sentence—Across the board . . .

3.   Voters today of all ages and races appear to be less enthusiastic than ever about elections, even presidential contests. For example, in the presidential election of 1896, almost 80 percent of eligible voters in the United States went to the polls. Yet by the 2000 election, turnout had fallen to less than 51 percent of all eligible voters. Voter turnout is particularly low among members of racial and ethnic minorities. In post-election surveys, fewer African Americans and Hispanics than whites report that they actually voted. Particularly troubling is the low turnout among young people. Turnout among this group was 55 percent in 1972, but only 42 percent in 2000.

Topic: voter turnout

Main Idea: first sentence—Voters today of all ages . . .

4.   Cheating has become a hot issue on college campuses. Professors who take advantage of computerized services that can identify plagiarism, such as the search engine Google, have been shocked to learn that many of the papers that students hand in are plagiarized in whole or part. Most students today use personal computers to do their research online. Apparently, the temptation to cut and paste passages from Web site postings and pass them off as one's own is irresistible to many. Surveys done by the Center for Academic Integrity show that from 1999 to 2001, the percentage of students who approved of this type of plagiarism rose from 10 percent to 41 percent. At the same time, the percentage who considered cutting and pasting from the Internet to be a serious form of cheating fell from 68 percent to 27 percent.

Topic: cheating

Main Idea: first sentence—Cheating has become . . .

5.   The Sherpas—a Tibetan-speaking Buddhist people in Nepal—live in a culture that idealizes old age. Almost all members of the Sherpa culture own their own homes, and most are in relatively good physical condition. Typically, older Sherpas value their independence and prefer not to live with their children. Among the Fulani of Africa, however, older men and women move to the edge of the family homestead. Since this is where people are buried, the elderly sleep over their own graves, for they are viewed socially as already dead. The treatment of the elderly varies from

culture to culture with one society treating older people with great reverence, while another sees them as unproductive and difficult.

Topic: treatment of elderly

Main Idea: last sentence—The treatment of the elderly varies . . .

6.   What can make a boring job tolerable or even enjoyable? In his often cited "banana time" study, sociologist Donald Roy examined the worker satisfaction of a small group of machine operators. He discovered that the group used "themes" to break up the long days of simple repetitive work. For example, the workers divided their food breaks into coffee time, peach time, banana time, fish time, Coke time, and lunch time. Each break involved conversation, horseplay, jokes and insults. In conclusion, positive relationships with co-workers help make repetitive jobs enjoyable.

Topic: coping with boring jobs

Main Idea: last sentence—In conclusion . . .

7.   The e-mail carried the subject line "Travelers Beware!" Its message was to warn those planning to go to the Mardi Gras in New Orleans in 1997 that a highly organized crime ring there was drugging tourists, in order to remove organs from their bodies and sell them on the black market. The rumor circulated throughout the country via e-mail and fax, causing an avalanche of calls to the New Orleans Police Department. Of course, an investigation turned up absolutely no evidence of an organ-snatching ring. The department finally set up a Web site to squelch the rumors. Rumors serve many functions, but one is to reinforce people's suspicions.

Topic: rumors

Main Idea: last sentence—Rumors serve many functions . . .

8.   In times of danger, the affluent and powerful have a better chance of surviving than people of ordinary means. For example, when the supposedly unsinkable British ocean-liner *Titanic* hit an iceberg in 1912, it was not carrying enough lifeboats to accommodate all passengers. Plans had been made to evacuate only first- and second-class passengers. About 62 percent of the first-class passengers survived the disaster. Despite a rule that women and children would go first, about a third of those passengers were male. In contrast, only 25 percent of the passengers in third class survived. In a more recent example, when Hurricane Katrina hit the Gulf Coast of the United States in 2005, affluent and poor people alike became its victims. However, poor families who did not own automobiles were less able than others to evacuate in advance of the storm.

Topic: survival

Main Idea: first sentence—In times of danger . . .

Information from Schaefer, Richard T., *Sociology*, 10th edition, New York: McGraw-Hill, 2007.

Exercise 12: Locating Details in Textbook Material

Directions: Read each of the following paragraphs. Then fill in the answers to each of the question words to identify the supporting details. If there is no answer to a question word, put an X on the line beside it. You don't have to use complete sentences.

"Primum non nocere—*first do no harm.*"

—Plaque on the wall of the University of Chicago Hospital

1.   The great majority of early Americans had little contact with physicians, or even midwives, and sought instead to deal with illness on their own, confident that their own abilities were equal to those of educated physicians—which, given the state of medical knowledge, was often true. Seventeenth and eighteenth century physicians had little or no understanding of infection and sterilization. As a result, many people died from infections contracted during childbirth or surgery from dirty instruments or dirty hands. In addition, because communities were unaware of bacteria, many were plagued with infectious diseases transmitted by garbage or unclean water.

Who or What? 17th and 18th century physicians

Did What? may have infected people

When? 17th and 18th centuries

Where? America

Why? little knowledge of bacteria

How? not using sterilization

2.   Doctors practiced medicine on the basis of the prevailing assumptions of their time, most of them derived from the theory of "humoralism" popularized by the great second-century Roman physician Galen. Galen argued that the human body was governed by four "humors" that were lodged in four bodily fluids: yellow bile (or "choler"), black bile ("melancholy"), blood, and phlegm. In a healthy body, the four humors existed in balance. Illness represented an imbalance and suggested the need for removing from the body the excesses of whatever fluid was causing the imbalance. That was the rationale that lay behind the principal medical techniques of the seventeenth and eighteenth centuries: purging, expulsion, and bleeding. Bleeding was the most destructive of the treatments. George Washington's death in 1799 was probably less a result of the minor throat infection that afflicted him than of his physicians' efforts to cure him by bleeding and purging.

Who or What? Galen's theory of humoralism

Did What? said body governed by four humors

When? 17th and 18th centuries

Where? America

Why? Illness indicated an imbalance in body.

How? removing excess fluid by bleeding, expulsion, purging

3.   Among the many fads and theories about human health in the 1830s and 1840s, one of the most popular was the idea that bathing in warm, sulphurous water was restorative. Wealthy men and women visited health spas for the celebrated "water cure" (known to modern scientists as hydrotherapy), which was supposed to improve health through immersing people in hot or cold baths or wrapping them in wet sheets. Visitors to "warm springs" all over the United States and Europe "took the baths," drank the foul-smelling water, and sometimes stayed for weeks as part of a combination vacation and "cure." Although the water cure in fact delivered few of the benefits its promoters promised, it did have some therapeutic value and some forms of hydrotherapy are still in use today.

"Most things get better by themselves. Most things are better by morning."

—Lewis Thomas

Who or What? hydrotherapy

Did What? immersed people in hot or cold baths

When? 1830s, 1840s

Where? U.S., Europe

Why? to improve health

How? by visiting "warm springs"

4.   Other Americans adopted new dietary theories. Sylvester Graham, a Connecticut-born Presbyterian minister and committed reformer, won many followers for his prescriptions for eating fruits, vegetables, and bread made from coarsely ground flour instead of meat. Graham's prescription for good health is very similar to some dietary theories today. (The "Graham cracker" is made from a kind of flour named for him.) Graham accompanied his dietary prescriptions with moral warnings about the evils of excess and luxury.

Who or What? Sylvester Graham

Did What? won followers

When? 1830s, 1840s

Where? U.S. (Connecticut)

Why? to promote good health

How? prescriptions for eating fruit, vegetables, bread

5.   Perhaps strangest of all to modern sensibilities was the widespread belief in the new "science" of phrenology, which appeared first in Germany. Phrenology became popular in the United States beginning in the 1830s through the efforts of Orson and Lorenzo Fowler, publishers of the Phrenology Almanac. Drawing from the concepts of the German writer Johann Gaspar Spurzheim, American phrenologists argued that the shape of an individual's skull was an important indicator of his or her character and intelligence. Phrenologists made elaborate measurements of bumps and indentations to calculate the size (and, they claimed, the strength) of different parts of the brain, each of which they argued, controlled a specific kind of intelligence or behavior. For a time, phrenology seemed to many Americans an important vehicle for improving society. It provided a way of measuring an individual's fitness for various positions in life. The theory is now universally believed to have no scientific value at all.

Who or What? phrenology

Did What? looked at shape of skull

When? 1830s

Where? Germany and United States

Why? to judge fitness for various positions

How? made elaborate measurements

Brinkley, Alan, *American History*, 11th edition, New York: McGraw-Hill, 2003, pp. 69, 329

Paragraph Diagrams

"The most technologically efficient machine that man ever invented is the book."

—Northrop Frye

A directly stated main idea is most often located at either the beginning or end of a paragraph. However, the main idea may also appear in the middle, or at both the beginning and the end. Wherever the main idea is located, it is supported by details such as examples, reasons, facts, or statistics.

The topic of each of the following paragraphs is the Harry Potter books. For each paragraph, a diagram shows the locations of the main idea and supporting details. The main idea in each paragraph is underlined.

1.   The Harry Potter books have changed the world of publishing. Sales of children's literature have picked up markedly since Potter's debut in 1998. The publishing industry loves the books because they bring people, including adults, into bookstores, where other titles might catch their eye. *The New York Times* was forced to establish a new best-sellers list, exclusively for children's literature, because the Potter books were taking up too much of the adult list.

In paragraph 1, the main idea is stated in the first sentence. The examples that follow all back up the main idea. A diagram of this type of main idea is a triangle with the point aiming downward. The main idea is represented by the horizontal line at the top.

2.	By the time the fifth book in the series, *Harry Potter and the Order of the Phoenix*, hit the bookstores in the summer of 2003, more than 200 million copies of the first four books had been sold worldwide, 80 million of those in the United States, and the first two had been made into blockbuster movies. The books had been translated into 55 languages (including Greek, Latin, and "Americanized English") and were available in 200 countries. The books' influence was truly global.

In paragraph 2, the main idea is given in the last sentence as a conclusion. The examples are given in the beginning. A diagram of this type of paragraph places the main idea at the bottom of the triangle.

3.	The most important contribution of the Harry Potter books is that they have gotten children to read. Even boys ages 9 to 12, the segment of the population least likely to read anything, dive into the Potter book as if they were the latest video game. They like the characters J. K. Rowling has created, and they like to talk about them in the schoolyard the next day. Harry Potter, the little wizard, has not only defeated the evil Lord Voldemort, but has managed to launch a million readers, and that is a singular achievement.

(George Rodman, *Mass Media in a Changing World,* 2006, p. 38)

In paragraph 3, the author begins with the main idea, gives several examples to illustrate it, and then restates the main idea in the final sentence. A diagram of this type of paragraph would have an hourglass shape.

4.	What has been Harry Potter's impact on reading? A 1999 survey of U.S. reading habits found that only 45% of readers read anything (books, newspapers, magazines, cereal boxes) for more than 30 minutes a day. The National Endowment for the Arts issued its report, *Reading at Risk*, in July 2004. It noted that fewer than half of all Americans over 18 years old read novels, short stories, plays, or poetry. The number of consumers buying books of all kinds was in decline. Harry Potter, with his huge impact on reading, has managed to change all that. Soon after the release of *The Prisoner of Azkaban* in 1999, the Gallup polling organization found that 84% of all Americans said they had read a book all the way through in the previous year. *Newsweek*'s Anna Quindlen said that he [Harry Potter] had helped "create a new generation of inveterate readers." Author Stephen King agreed, writing, "If these millions of readers are awakened to the wonders and rewards of fantasy at 11 or 12 . . . well, when they get to age 16 or so, there's this guy named King."

Stanley J. Baran, *Introduction to Mass Communication*, 4th edition, 2006, p. 74

In paragraph 4, the author begins with facts and statistics illustrating the decline in reading, states the main idea that the Potter books have managed to reverse that trend, and then concludes with facts and statistics supporting that reversal. Because the main idea is in the middle, the diagram resembles a diamond.

Exercise 13: Topics, Main Ideas, and Diagrams

Directions: Read each paragraph below. Write the topic for each paragraph. Then, underline the main idea sentence in each one and draw a diagram that illustrates the location of the main idea and details.

1.   Potatoes develop an exciting flavor when cooked on a barbecue grill. Corn, peppers, and onions can be cooked over an open flame. And how about unusual vegetables like eggplant, artichoke, asparagus, and fennel? Many vegetables can be made delicious by grilling. Tomatoes, mushrooms, and squash develop a delicious sweet taste when cooked on the barbecue grill, but they take a little more effort than firmer vegetables. Care must be taken that they don't fall through the spaces of the open grill. You might want to use a grilling basket to keep them out of the fire.

Topic: grilling vegetables   Diagram: ◇

2.   Yesterday was one of those days when everything went wrong. I left my freezer door open by mistake before I went to work. Of course, when I came home, everything had thawed. And I was late getting home because I had a flat tire on the way. And then when I got out of the car at home, I noticed a long scratch and a dent on the right side. Someone must have hit my car while I was inside at work. Of course, no note was left. At least the warmed-up food in my freezer didn't go to waste. My dog discovered the open door, and he had been helping himself all day!

Topic: bad day   Diagram: ▽

3.   In the time of the Romans, toothaches, lost teeth, and gum disease were very common and many remedies were suggested. Celsus, a Roman doctor, suggested chewing unripe pears or apples or the use of a weak vinegar solution as a cure for gum disease. For a sore tooth, he recommended a hot sponge compress. One Roman citizen, Pliny the Elder, suggested touching a sore tooth with a lizard's bone when the moon was full. He also suggested that the teeth be cleaned with a piece of wool dipped in a mixture of honey and anise, the flavoring in licorice.

Topic: Roman teeth   Diagram: ▽

4.   Om Prakash Singh of India stood still for 20 hours, 10 minutes and 6 seconds. In 1992, Paul Lynch performed 124 one-finger push-ups in London. America's Tim Johnston, 12, balanced 15 spoons on his face for 30 seconds in 2005. A young man named Michael Gallen set the record by eating 63 bananas in 10 minutes. Sarah Walker worked a yo-yo more than 4,053 times in one hour and broke the world record. In 1990, Gary Stewart did 177,737 pogo stick jumps in California. The USA's Robert Foster held his breath for 13 minutes 42.5 seconds in 1959. In 2001, Ashrita Furman balanced 75 pint beer glasses on her chin for 10.6 seconds in

New York. People are always trying to break the Guinness World Record for one thing or another.

Topic: breaking Guinness world records   Diagram: △

5.   Most of us are born with five main senses that enable us to learn about ourselves and the world we live in. Your sense of hearing may alert you to danger when you hear a horn honk while you are crossing the street. Your sense of smell may tell you that a pie is baking in the oven. Put on an itchy sweater, and your sense of touch will probably cause you to change sweaters. Your sense of sight lets you see where you are going. Your sense of taste will tell you if you've accidentally used shaving cream on a hot fudge sundae instead of whipped cream.

Topic: our five senses   Diagram: ▽

6.   A young boy or girl who enjoys keeping fish in an aquarium may someday become a marine biologist. A young rock collector might become a geologist. A child who likes to build with blocks or LEGOS may be a future architect. Doctors, nurses, and veterinarians often tell of loving and caring for sick or helpless creatures when they were children. Teachers often talk about teaching their younger brothers and sisters or their toy animals when they were young. At 8, Steven Spielberg began playing with his father's 8mm camera. He started writing scripts, complete with special effects, and everyone in his family was assigned a part. Neighborhood friends also participated. As you can see, hobbies often turn into full-time careers for many young people.

Topic: hobbies and careers   Diagram: △

Exercise 14: Topics, Main Ideas, Diagrams, and Details

Superstition I

Directions: Read the following paragraphs on superstitions. For each one, write the topic and the number of the main idea sentence. Then draw the appropriate main idea diagram on the lines provided.

THE FAMILY CIRCUS.   By Bil Keane

9-29
©1995 Bil Keane, Inc.
Dist. by Cowles Synd., Inc.

"How can that rabbit's foot bring you luck? It didn't work for him and he had FOUR of 'em!"

A.   (1) There are a number of superstitions involving animals. (2) For instance, many people believe that if a black cat crosses your path evil will soon befall you. (3) The evil will be canceled if you spit right away. (4) Rabbit's feet are considered good luck because they are associated with spring and the return of plants and flowers. (5) But the shriek of an owl is an omen of death or bad luck for whoever hears it.

Topic: animal superstitions

Main Idea Sentence #: 1   Diagram: ▽

B.   (1) A long time ago gypsies found the mule with the longest ears and asked it whether someone loved them. (2) If the mule shook its head, the answer was yes; if the mule moved one ear, the answer was maybe; and if the mule did not move at all, the answer was no. (3) A more modern version involves the daisy. (4) As you pull the petal off a daisy, say "He (or she) loves me." (5) Then pull another petal and say, "He (or she) loves me not." (6) What you say when you pull out the last petal gives you the true answer. (7) For a sure-fire method, pull a hair from a loved one's head. (8) The person may get mad, but according to the superstition, they'll love you back. (9) As you can see, there are many superstitions dealing with love.

Topic: _love superstitions_____

Main Idea Sentence #: _9_____   Diagram: _△_____

C.   (1) Ordinary household items are the subject of many superstitions. (2) Be sure to knock on wood to ward off evil spirits if you've boasted about something. (3) If a button falls off a shirt and you sew it on again without taking the shirt off, you'll have bad luck for the rest of the day. (4) If you break a mirror it's even worse. (5) You'll have seven years of continuous bad luck. (6) And whatever you do don't get out of bed on the wrong side, which is the left side, or you'll be in for a very bad day. (7) However, the most unlucky of accidents is spilling salt, unless you quickly pick some of it up and toss it over your left shoulder.

Topic: _household superstitions_____

Main Idea Sentence #: _1_____   Diagram: _▽_____

Supporting Details

Directions: A supporting detail has been omitted from each paragraph above. Look at the supporting details below and match each one to its correct paragraph. Put the letter of the correct paragraph on the line.

___B___ 1. To dream of what your future husband will look like, sleep with a mirror under your pillow.

___C___ 2. Don't ever purchase a broom in the month of May. "Brooms bought in May sweep the family away."

___A___ 3. To bring good luck, the horseshoe must be hung over a door with the open end up so that the good fortune doesn't spill out.

Superstition II

Directions: Read the following paragraphs on wedding superstitions. For each one, write the number of the main idea sentence on the line provided. Then draw the appropriate main idea diagram.

A.   (1) In the United States, there is a tradition of the bride ensuring good luck in her marriage by wearing something old, something new, something borrowed, and something blue. (2) Something old belonging to the bride's family is worn to represent a link to the past. (3) Something new is worn to represent good fortune and success in the bride's future life. (4) Something borrowed is worn to remind the bride that friends and family will be there for her when help is needed. (5) Something blue is worn to symbolize her faithfulness and loyalty to her future spouse.

Main Idea Sentence #: 1_____   Diagram: ▽_____

B.   (1) As a symbol of both happiness and luck, a bride usually carries a beautiful bouquet of flowers. (2) The lucky single woman who catches the bouquet is believed to be the next to marry. (3) Many brides wear a garter on their right leg just above the knee. (4) The groom traditionally removes the garter from the bride's leg and throws it to the unmarried men. (5) The lucky man who catches it is thought to be the next to marry. (6) The circular wedding ring, symbolizing everlasting unity, is placed on the fourth finger of the left hand. (7) For many centuries, it was believed that a special vein ran from this finger directly to the heart. (8) Therefore, it was considered to be the most suitable finger to bear a symbol of love. (9) Finally, most couples make the first cut of their wedding cake together to symbolize their shared future. (10) As you can see, a wedding ceremony has many symbolic meanings.

Main Idea Sentence #: 10_____   Diagram: △_____

C.   (1) The veil was first worn by Roman brides. (2) It was thought that it would disguise the bride and thereby outwit evil spirits. (3) Bridesmaids were dressed to resemble the bride for the same reason. (4) The bridesmaids were thought to act as decoys to confuse evil spirits and thus protect the bride. (5) Traditionally, brides have been thought to be particularly vulnerable to evil spirits, and so many of the customs associated with weddings are meant to provide protection. (6) This is also why the married couple is often showered with flowers, petals, rice, or grains. (7) The custom of throwing rice, which is a symbol of health and fertility, originated when people thought rice could appease the evil spirits. (8) In addition, cars carrying the bridal couple were decorated with tin cans and other noisemakers to chase away evil spirits.

Main Idea Sentence #: 5_____   Diagram: ◇_____

D.   (1) Many wedding traditions have faded into the past. (2) Once a wedding date was set, it was considered bad luck to change it. (3) It was also bad luck for a groom to see the bride in her wedding gown before the ceremony. (4) It used to be traditional for the groom to carry the bride over the threshold when they entered their home for the first time. (5) This was because it was believed bad luck would follow if the bride tripped. (6) A bride was also supposed to put a penny in her shoe to ensure prosperity in her marriage. (7) Most of these traditions are no longer observed.

Main Idea Sentence #: 1, 7_____   Diagram: ⊠_____

Superstition III

Directions: Read the following paragraphs on New Year's superstitions. For each one, write the specific topic, the number of the main idea sentence, and the appropriate main idea diagram on the lines provided.

New Year's Superstitions

A.   (1) Many people believe that they can influence the luck they will have during the coming year by what they eat on the first day of the new year. (2) A traditional New Year's custom observed by many southerners in the U.S. is the eating of black-eyed peas on New Year's Day. (3) They often eat the peas with turnip greens, kale, or spinach. (4) The peas represent good luck and the greens represent money and prosperity. (5) The Dutch eat do-nuts because they believe that anything in the shape of a ring is good luck. (6) To ensure good health and good luck in the coming year, the Chinese eat candied melon, the Vietnamese eat watermelon, and the Germans eat pork.

Topic: food and New Year's superstitions

Main Idea Sentence #: 1   Diagram: ▽

B.   (1) Ozark families always open their windows at midnight for a few min-utes regardless of the temperature outside or the weather condition. (2) This is thought to release the accumulated bad luck of the old year while inviting in the good luck of the new. (3) Well before New Year's Day, Chinese families thoroughly clean their homes. (4) They do this to drive away bad spirits from the old year, and make room for good ones for the new year. (5) But on New Year's Day, they do not sweep or dust so that good fortune will not be removed. (6) After New Year's Day, the floors may finally be swept. (7) As you can see, many people believe that how they treat their homes can affect good fortune in the coming new year.

Topic: homes and New Year's superstitions

Main Idea Sentence #: 7   Diagram: △

C.   (1) It is said that the first person to set foot inside a Scottish home on New Year's Day will decide the family's luck for the rest of the year. (2) The person most welcome on New Year's morning is a tall, dark-haired man. (3) As the "first-footer," he must not arrive empty-handed. (4) It is preferable if he arrives carrying a bottle of wine or other spirits and toasts the new year with each adult member of the family.

Topic: Scottish New Year's superstition

Main Idea Sentence #: 1   Diagram: ▽

D.   (1) Chinese Americans continue to practice traditional superstitions related to grooming. (2) People should not get a haircut on New Year's Day because good luck for the coming year could be cut off. (3) It is smart to wear the color red on New Year's Day, because that color brings good luck. (4) New shoes should be purchased well ahead of time. (5) This is because in Chinese, the word for shoes sounds a lot like the word for rough. (6) Any attempt to buy shoes on New Year's Day is likely to lead to a rough year ahead.

Topic: Chinese New Year's superstitions

Main Idea Sentence #: 1   Diagram: ▽

Supporting Details

Directions: One supporting detail has been omitted from each paragraph above. Look at the supporting details below, match each one to its correct paragraph, and then put the letter of the correct paragraph on the line.

  B   1. The Scots prepare for the new year by cleaning their houses.

  D   2. The Chinese believe a long bath should be taken on New Year's Eve, but never on New Year's Day lest good fortune be washed away.

  A   3. A Spanish custom is to eat 12 grapes (one for each month of the coming year) at midnight on New Year's Eve for good luck.

  C   4. Disaster is likely to follow if the first person across the threshold on New Year's Day is a woman, especially if she arrives without liquid refreshment.

READING

"According to Randi, cold-readers often interview people while they are waiting to get on the show."

GETTING FOCUSED

Have you ever received an e-mail from a friend that contains an uplifting message, but at the end it says something like, "If you pass this message on to five people, within three days you will be the recipient of tremendous good luck"? That kind of promise often makes people feel unsettled, so many pass the e-mail on without thinking that they are behaving superstitiously. Will they really have good luck if they pass it on? Will they have bad luck if they don't? The following selection describes another kind of superstitious behavior. Many fall victim to the claims made by psychics. Ever wonder how a psychic can know so much about people? Read the selection to find out how it's done.

BIO-SKETCH

John Santrock is a professor of psychology and human development at the University of Texas at Dallas. In addition to writing the general psychology

(*continued*)

textbook from which this reading is taken, he has also written textbooks on life-span development and educational psychology.

TACKLING VOCABULARY

fish story   an improbable, boastful tale. The expression refers to the tendency of fishermen to exaggerate the size of their catch

supernatural   above and beyond what is explainable by natural law

SHOULD WE BELIEVE THE CLAIMS OF PSYCHICS?

John Santrock

A woman reports that she has power over the goldfish in a 50-gallon tank. She claims that she can will them to either end of the tank.

2   Under the careful scrutiny of James Randi, this woman's account turned out to be just another fish story. The woman had written Randi, a professional magician who has a standing offer of $1,000,000 to anyone whose psychic claims withstand his analysis. In the case of the woman and the goldfish, Randi received a letter from her priest validating her extraordinary power. Randi talked with the priest, who told him that the woman would put her hands in front of her body and then run to one end of the tank. The fish soon swam to that end of the tank. Since the fish could see out of the tank just as we could see into it, Randi suggested that the woman put opaque brown wrapping paper over one end of the tank and then try her powers. The woman did and called Randi to tell him that she had discovered something new about her powers: Her mind could not penetrate brown paper. The woman, believing she had magical powers, completely misunderstood why Randi had asked her to place the brown paper over the fish tank.

3   To date, no one has met Randi's $1,000,000 challenge, but he has investigated hundreds of reports of supernatural and occult powers. Recently he has evaluated *cold-reading*, a popular technique among psychics (people who claim to have extrasensory perception). When cold-reading, the psychic tells the person nothing but makes guesses, puts out suggestions, and asks questions. For example, if the "reader" says, "I am visualizing an older woman," the person usually gives some reaction. It may be just a nod, somebody's name, or even identification of a sister, aunt, mother, or grandmother. The important thing is that this information is supplied by the person, not the reader. Of course, almost everyone will show some reaction to such a general statement, giving the reader new information to incorporate into subsequent comments or questions. Alternatively, the reader may say, "Mary? Do you recognize this person?" If there is a Mary, the person will give more helpful information to the reader. If no Mary is immediately recognized, the reader moves on. If "Mary" is remembered later, she is incorporated into the reader's comments. The reader can try many names, confident that the person will likely remember only suggested names that are meaningful to him or her. In this way, the person may well end up volunteering what he or she wants to hear.

4   According to Randi, cold-readers often interview people while they are waiting to get into the show. Then, when the show begins, they can choose to work with people they have already talked to. Suppose a person approaches the reader before the show and says he has a question about his deceased wife. That person can later be selected during the show and be asked, "Is your question about your dead wife?" To other people who are not aware of the previous conversation, the reader's question can seem miraculous.

5   Randi also says that when cold-readers are not allowed to speak to anyone in advance, or to be asked or told anything in advance, and people are allowed to answer only "yes" or "no" when asked direct questions, they fail miserably. In general, according to Randi, cold-readers have a way of leading people to believe that they knew something they didn't.

6   Randi makes a distinction between the tricks of magicians, such as himself, and the work of psychics and others who claim extraordinary ESP powers. He says that magic is done for entertainment; the other for swindling.

Excerpts from *Psychology,* 7th ed., by John Santrock. Copyright © 2003 The McGraw-Hill Companies, Inc. Reprinted by permission of The McGraw-Hill Companies, Inc.

✔ COMPREHENSION CHECKUP

Multiple Choice

Write the letter of the correct answer on the blank provided.

_____c_____ 1. The topic of the reading is
      a. cold-readers.
      b. controlling fish.
      c. investigating psychic claims.
      d. magicians vs. psychics.

_____b_____ 2. The main idea of the reading is
      a. Some people will believe anything.
      b. James Randi has debunked many claims made by individuals who believe they have supernatural powers.
      c. People often volunteer information to psychics.
      d. Many people have paranormal abilities.

_____b_____ 3. James Randi is a(n)
      a. psychic.
      b. magician.
      c. author of this reading.
      d. swindler.

_____d_____ 4. The word *cold* in the term *cold-reading* means
      a. low temperature.
      b. lacking in enthusiasm.
      c. lifeless or extinct.
      d. without preparation.

___d___   5. Which of the following techniques are psychics likely to use?

    a. They may interview people prior to a show.

    b. They may make general statements to people and wait for a response.

    c. They may suggest various names in hope of getting a response.

    d. All of the above.

True or False

Indicate whether each statement is true or false by writing **T** or **F** in the blank provided.

___T___   1. James Randi has offered $1,000,000 to any person who can prove to his satisfaction the presence of a supernatural power.

___T___   2. Psychics often ask preliminary questions to find out the background of a person before giving a reading.

___F___   3. James Randi believes that certain people really do have psychic powers.

___T___   4. The priest believed that the woman could will the fish to either end of the fish tank.

___T___   5. James Randi thinks that people who claim to have ESP powers are often swindlers.

___T___   6. If someone is *deceased*, they are dead.

___F___   7. Something *opaque* is transparent.

___T___   8. If you *scrutinize* something, you are probably giving it a careful examination.

___F___   9. A *subsequent* comment is one that comes before.

___F___   10. Cold-readers are most successful when those interviewed respond with yes or no answers only.

Vocabulary Word-Parts Review

Directions: Match the word-part definitions in column B with the underlined word parts in column A. Write the letters of the word-part definitions in the appropriate blank. You may refer back to the lists of word parts on pages 41–44 to refresh your memory on the meaning of word parts.

	Column A	Column B
e	1. mi<u>s</u>understood	a. full of
b	2. <u>inter</u>view	b. between; among
f	3. <u>super</u>natural	c. before
i	4. <u>re</u>action	d. apart; away
j	5. <u>in</u>vestigated	e. badly
d	6. <u>dis</u>tinction	f. above; over
h	7. informa<u>tion</u>	g. see
g	8. <u>vis</u>ualizing	h. condition or result
c	9. <u>pre</u>vious	i. again; back
a	10. help<u>ful</u>	j. in; into

In Your Own Words

1. Do you think James Randi's $1,000,000 prize will ever be claimed? Why or why not?

2. Why do you think people continue to believe in psychic phenomena when confronted with contradictory evidence produced by Randi and others?

Written Assignment

1. You have probably driven down a street and seen a sign in front of a store window or small house advertising palm readings or fortune telling. Do you believe that palm readers and fortune tellers have psychic powers?

2. What kind of research would be necessary to establish that a particular psychic phenomenon is genuine?

Internet Activity

Read more about the Amazing Randi's skeptical approach to supernatural phenomena at his website:

www.randi.org

Watch one of his videos at

www.randi.org/images/081304-ForkBend.mpg

Can you tell whether you are watching a psychic phenomenon or magic? Write a paragraph describing your reaction.

2 Implied Main Ideas and Paraphrasing

"Phone for you, Al."

Copyright © The New Yorker Collection 1963 James Stevenson from cartoon bank.com. All Rights Reserved.

Implied Main Idea

Not all main ideas are directly stated, as you can see in the cartoon above. Instead, some main ideas are **implied,** which means that the reader must figure out the most important point the author is making from the details provided. You may recall from the previous chapter that the first step in identifying a directly stated main idea is to identify the topic. You do this by asking, "What is this about?" or "Who is this about?" The first step in determining an implied main idea is exactly the same. In the cartoon, the topic is "a skywriting mistake." Two key details in the cartoon help the reader to determine the main idea. The most important detail is the misspelled word *Pespi.* The other key detail that is important is the "Sky-Writers" sign written on the side of the plane that Al is walking away from. Together these details suggest an implied main idea sentence something like this: Al has incorrectly written the word *Pepsi* in the sky, and someone is calling to tell him about it.

In order to write your own **implied** main ideas, you need to understand the difference between something that is implied, meaning it is hinted at or suggested in the text, and something that is directly stated. Look at the following two statements made by Mark's mother. Which statement is implying something and which one is directly stating it?

Statement 1: Mark, your room is a mess. You said you were going to clean it up and you didn't. You also didn't feed the dog or take out the trash, and I had to do both.

Statement 2: Mark, you are not doing your part to help out around the house.

The first statement is implying what the second sentence is directly stating.

Exercise 1: Implied Versus Directly Stated

Directions: Write **D** on the blank provided if the statement is directly stated and **I** if it is implied.

___D___ 1. Carl, I want you to fill my car with gas.

___I___ 2. I did all of these errands for you today, and now my car is out of gas.

___D___ 3. I need a new computer.

___I___ 4. Computers are really cheap right now, and mine is pretty much worn out.

___I___ 5. I've heard good things about the Will Smith movie. Maria and Carlos just went to see it, and they said it was terrific.

___D___ 6. I want to go see the new Will Smith movie.

PARAPHRASING

To write a good implied main idea sentence, you need to be able to paraphrase the author's words. When you **paraphrase** something, you express the author's meaning using *your own words*. Key words such as names are left the same.

Exercise 2: Paraphrasing Quotations by Benjamin Franklin

Directions: Paraphrase the following quotations. When you are finished, check to make sure the meaning of both statements is the same.
Answers will vary.

Example: Hunger never saw bad bread.

Paraphrase: When we are hungry, we will eat just about anything.

1. He that lies down with dogs shall rise up with fleas.

   Bad friends can have a harmful influence on you.

2. Love your neighbor; yet don't pull down your hedge.

   Be friendly to your neighbor but don't get too close.

3. Well done is better than well said.

   Actually doing something is better than just talking about it.

4. A friend in need is a friend indeed.

   If someone needs help, they'll be your friend.

5. Love your enemies, for they tell you your faults.

   Listen to even unfriendly criticism.

6. He that goes a borrowing goes a sorrowing.

   Don't borrow so much that you get into trouble.

7. Little strokes fell big oaks.

   To accomplish something big, take a lot of little steps.

8. Be slow in choosing a friend, slower in changing.

   Choose friends with care and then keep them.

9. Lost time is never found again.

   Don't waste time because you can't get it back.

10. Fish and visitors smell in three days.

   Limit the amount of time you spend in people's homes. Don't overstay your

   welcome.

STRATEGIES FOR IDENTIFYING THE IMPLIED MAIN IDEA

The following strategies are methods for using the given information in a paragraph to write a main idea sentence.

Asking Questions

Read the paragraph below on the topic of the Salem witchcraft trials.

> Belief in witchcraft was a common feature of New England society. To the Puritans, witchcraft seemed not only believable, but scientifically rational. Their world was filled with invisible forces and supernatural beings that could interrupt the order of nature. This widely shared belief allowed for the unfolding of the notorious witchcraft trials in Salem Village. There, in the early months of 1692, a group of adolescent girls used the white of a raw egg suspended in a glass of water as a kind of crude crystal ball to divine what sorts of men their future husbands might be. Somehow, the séance went sour and the frightened adolescents began behaving in ways that other villagers took to be signs of bewitchment. Crying out in pain and terror, the afflicted women claimed to see specters of witches, whom they recognized as fellow villagers. In the hysteria that followed, hundreds of accusations of witchcraft led to the trial and execution of 20 innocent men and women.

By asking who, what, where, when, and why questions about the topic of this passage, we get the following information:

Who was involved? — adolescent girls and innocent men and women

What happened? — the girls accused innocent villagers of witchcraft and 20 of them were executed

Where did the event happen? — in Salem Village

When did it happen? — in the late 1600s

Why did the event happen? — teenage girls claimed to see specters of witches who they identified as fellow villagers

By combining these key details, the main idea looks something like this:

> **Implied Main Idea:** In Salem Village in the late 1600s, innocent people were executed because teenage girls accused them of practicing witchcraft.

Combining Sentences

Sometimes implied main ideas can be constructed by combining two or more sentences in a passage. Read the following paragraph on the topic of the Salem witchcraft trials.

> Research into the background of accused witches by historians reveals that most were middle-aged women, often widowed, with few or no children. Many accused witches were involved in domestic conflicts, and were considered annoying by their neighbors. Others were women who, through inheritance or hard work, had come to own a great deal of land and property on their own and so challenged the gender norms of the community. These women were vulnerable to accusations because they seemed threatening to people who were accustomed to women as subordinate members of the community. Puritan society had little tolerance for "independent" women.

The main ideas here are contained in the first and last sentences. The rest of the sentences have details that support the notion that the Puritans viewed independent women as threatening. Combining the key points in the first and last sentences results in a main idea that looks like this:

> **Implied Main Idea:** Historians have tried to discover the causes behind the Salem episode and have concluded that many of the women accused of witchcraft were considered too independent.

Summing Up Important Ideas into One Sentence

This method involves summing up the important information from the paragraph into one main idea sentence. Read the paragraph below on the topic of the Salem witchcraft trials.

> The first accused witches were questioned by informal magistrates instead of in a formal court setting recognized under English law. When the magistrates began collecting evidence, they did something highly unusual. Instead of conducting their examinations in private, the magistrates questioned the accused witches in front of throngs of villagers and the afflicted girls themselves. As a result of these examinations, the crisis spread and many suspected of witchcraft were put in jail. In May, the Official Court made up of seven judges chose not to re-hear the earlier evidence. It rushed through the trials and executed several of the convicted townspeople while overlooking many procedures. By October, the court had hanged

14 women and 5 men and pressed another man to death with stones for refusing to plead either guilty or innocent. Five years later, twelve of the jurors acknowledged there had been "insufficient" basis for their convictions. And in 1711, the colony reversed all the guilty verdicts and made restitution to those falsely accused and to the descendants of those executed.

Information from Alan Brinkley, *American History*, 12th edition , 2007, pp. 88–89; James West Davidson, *Nation of Nations*, 5th edition, 2005

Implied Main Idea: The witch trials were run without regard for traditional courtroom rules, and as a result many of the accused had little chance for a fair trial.

For all three methods of creating an implied main idea, you will often have to use some of your own words, as well as the important words of the author. The key thing to remember is that you are expressing the author's most important point. Do not worry if your words are not exactly the same as someone else's. Keep in mind that there are many different ways to express the same point.

Making Sure You Have Correctly Identified the Implied Main Idea

It is important to be sure you have correctly identified the implied main idea of a paragraph. Some key points to remember:

1. **Make sure that you have correctly identified the topic.** What is the main thing the author is talking about in the paragraph?

2. **Look at the details in the paragraph.** What one idea do they all relate to?

3. **Make sure the implied main idea you write covers all of the supporting details in the paragraph, but does not go beyond them.**

Note: Remember that the implied main idea, like the directly stated main idea, is always written as only one complete sentence.

Implied Main Idea Practice

Exercise 3: Identifying the Topic and Choosing the Implied Main Idea

Directions: Read each paragraph below and identify the topic. Write the topic on the given line. Then determine the implied main idea from the choices below and put the correct letter on the line provided.

a. Avoid issuing ultimatums in fights.

b. While low-income families are often unable to save money, middle and upper-income families are able to.

c. How people greet each other can vary greatly from culture to culture.

d. Alcohol exacts a great toll on American families.

e. As education increases, income also increases.

f. Involved fathers are good for their children.

g. When fighting, resist giving the silent treatment.

h. There is a difference in the average income of males and females with men making more than women.

1. According to a 2002 U.S. Census Bureau report, the average American male working full-time earned $38,275. The average American woman working full-time earned only $29,215, a difference of about $9,000. The discrepancy between the incomes of males and females in Black, Hispanic, and Asian families is slightly smaller than that in White families.

   Topic: _____income differences_____   Implied Main Idea: _____h_____

2. Individuals completing 9 years of schooling or less averaged $17,932 in yearly income. Those with 9 to 12 years averaged $20,823. High school graduates averaged $28,106. College graduates averaged $45,856. Those people with professional degrees beyond college make salaries almost double those of a college graduate. When you look at the total income individuals achieve in a lifetime of working full-time, those with a high school education earn about $1.2 million in a lifetime, whereas those with a college degree earn almost twice that amount.

   Topic: _____value of education_____   Implied Main Idea: _____e_____

3. Most poverty-level and lower-income families are incapable of saving much money. They spend a high percentage of their income to meet basic needs such as food, clothing, shelter, and utilities. However, middle- and upper-income families are in a good position to save something each month.

   Topic: _____saving money_____   Implied Main Idea: _____b_____

4. An ultimatum is a nonnegotiable demand—"You do this or else"—and is a hallmark of dirty fighting. Ultimatums generally lead to counter-ultimatums, leaving little room for genuine negotiation. An ultimatum puts the receiver in the child position and the sender in the parent position. Neither person gets a chance to negotiate from the adult position.

   Topic: _____ultimatums_____   Implied Main Idea: _____a_____

5. Refusing to talk—the silent treatment—is an attempt to get even with or to manipulate a partner. Shutting out another person emotionally in

the hope that she or he will give in is a form of psychological torture and an approach that rarely resolves conflict. Disagreements don't go away by themselves; they may lie dormant for awhile but they eventually resurface, often in a less manageable form than before. The shut-out partner's anger and frustration might also increase, even though that might not have been the intent of the "silent" partner.

Topic: _____silent treatment_____   Implied Main Idea: _____g_____

6.   In most Latin countries, from Venezuela to Italy, the *abrazo* (hug) is as common as a handshake. Men hug men; women hug women; men hug women. In Slavic countries, this greeting is better described as a bear hug. In France, the double cheek-to-cheek greeting is common among both men and women. A traditional bow from the waist is the standard greeting for the Japanese, who are averse to casual touching. Many Americans, however, feel uncomfortable with bowing, but to the Japanese it means, "I respect your experience and wisdom."

Topic: _____greetings_____   Implied Main Idea: _____c_____

7.   The more fathers are involved in the routine activities of their children, the more likely the children will have fewer behavior problems, be more sociable, and do better in school. Across different ethnic groups, fathers tend to assume the important role of economic provider and protector. When fathers provide economically for their children, they also stay more involved with their children, even if they live apart. In addition, fathers who pay child support tend to have children who behave better and do better in school.

Topic: _____role of fathers_____   Implied Main Idea: _____f_____

8.   An estimated 100,000 Americans die each year from alcohol abuse. Alcohol abuse also directly affects the marital relationship. A national sample of more than 2,000 couples found in general that the more often a spouse was drunk, the greater likelihood there was of physical violence in the marital relationship. At the very least, tension and verbal conflict are likely to be frequent. In dealing with an alcohol-abusing member, families commonly go through predictable stages. First, the family attempts to deny the problem and then later to eliminate it. If there is no resolution, the sober spouse attempts to escape the problem through separation or divorce.

Topic: _____effects of alcohol_____   Implied Main Idea: _____d_____

Olson, David and DeFrain, John, *Marriage and Families,* 5th edition, New York: McGraw-Hill, 2006

Exercise 4: Asking Questions to Find Implied Main Ideas

Letters to Aunt Janet

Directions: Try asking questions (who? what? where? when? why?) to determine the implied main idea of each of the following letters to Aunt Janet.

Letter 1

Dear Aunt Janet,

I'm having a lot of problems with my boss. I'm a single mother of two children and sometimes the babysitter is late getting to my house and so I'm a little late to work. I always make up for it by working a little bit later, but my boss is always yelling at me about this. I would quit my job and get another one, but it's really close to my house so I can walk. This saves me a lot of time and money. What can I do to get my boss to treat me more respectfully?

Topic: work problems

Implied Main Idea: A woman is late to work and her boss is angry.

Your Advice:

Letter 2

Dear Aunt Janet,

My 24-year-old son has recently moved back home. He's a college graduate, has a job, and owns a car, but he couldn't seem to make it on what he earned. In some ways he's good company, but his room is never picked up, he leaves dirty dishes everywhere, and he comes in at all hours. He was paying me about $100 a month to help with grocery expenses, but he's stopped that. The situation is starting to drive me crazy. What do you think I should do?

Topic: problem with son

Implied Main Idea: The person is having trouble adjusting to her adult son

living at home.

Your Advice:

Letter 3

Dear Aunt Janet,

I'm an adopted child. I was told about my adoption around age 3 when I noticed that everyone in my family had blue eyes except for me. My parents have been wonderful to me and treated me just like I was their biological child. However, I sometimes feel like I don't really belong because I'm so different from everybody else in my family. Do you think I should try to contact my birth parents? They never married but provided Mom and Dad with their phone numbers and addresses. I just turned 18. Should I wait until I'm 21? Also, how can I bring up the subject without hurting Mom and Dad? I'm so confused. Please advise me what to do.

Topic: adopted child _____

Implied Main Idea: The person is having a problem dealing with adoption. _____

Your Advice: _____

_____

Letter 4

Dear Aunt Janet,

My problem is my daughter. She is slightly overweight for her age and height. I tell her she is just big-boned and takes after her father, but she is starting to feel bad about herself. I think I make the situation worse because I seem to be able to eat whatever I want and my weight never changes. How can I help her to feel better about herself and not hate me because I'm thin?

Topic: overweight daughter _____

Implied Main Idea: She wants to know how to deal with her overweight _____

daughter. _____

Your Advice: _____

_____

Letter 5

Dear Aunt Janet,

My mother-in-law is driving me nuts! She comes over all the time without calling ahead, and she is always offering unasked-for advice. When she comes over, she expects everybody to drop whatever they're doing and pay attention to her. She gets very insulted if we have other plans and have to leave. How can I get her to call ahead before she visits? We make a habit of never just dropping in on her. Also, how can I get her to keep her well-meaning advice to herself?

Topic: <u>mother-in-law</u>

Implied Main Idea: <u>She is having problems coping with her mother-in-law's</u>

<u>rude behavior.</u>

Your Advice: _____

_____

Letter 6

Dear Aunt Janet,

I knew all about my husband's drinking problem before I married him. My parents warned me about him, but I believed him when he told me he would stop drinking after we got married. He claimed that he was just lonely and bored and that's why he drank. He said that when we started living together he would be so happy that he'd forget all about going out to bars. Now he wants to have children, and he says he'll stop drinking when they arrive. What should I do? I don't think I trust him to stop anymore.

Topic: <u>husband who drinks</u>

Implied Main Idea: <u>She wants to know what to do about her husband, who</u>

<u>has a drinking problem.</u>

Your Advice: _____

_____

Letter 7

Dear Aunt Janet,

I was recently diagnosed with cancer. Actually, it's a recurrence of cancer I had three years ago. My husband and daughter are just going on with their lives as if nothing is different. Neither one will even take time off from work to take me to my appointments. They just say "been there, done that." Only my son is supportive. I can't help feeling hurt by their behavior, and I worry that my negative feelings will interfere with a cure. Can you give me some advice about what to do?

Topic: <u>cancer</u>

Implied Main Idea: <u>She feels bad about the way her husband and daughter are</u>

<u>treating her cancer recurrence.</u>

Your Advice: _____

_____

Exercise 5: Combining Sentences to Find Implied Main Ideas

Directions: Two specific-detail sentences are given in each of the exercises below. Working in a group, try to write a main idea sentence that will cover both of the details.

1. Restaurant meals are not as healthy as home-cooked ones.

   A. Meals eaten out are usually 20% to 30% lower in fiber, calcium, and iron.

   B. Fat supplies about one-fifth more calories in restaurant or take-out meals than in meals that have been prepared at home.

2. A nap can have cognitive benefits.

   A. Research demonstrates that people become more alert after as little as a 15-minute nap.

   B. A study by the National Aeronautics and Space Administration showed that pilots who slept for 30 minutes during a long flight, while their co-pilots took over the controls, were better at landing the plane.

3. Movies and songs depict substance abuse.

   A. Ninety-eight percent of the top 200 movie rentals of 2004 and 2005 depicted substance abuse.

   B. Twenty-seven percent of the 1,000 most popular songs of 2006 contained a reference to either drugs or alcohol.

4. Men are more likely to be stressed by shopping than women.

   A. Stress levels skyrocket for males who find themselves in noisy, crowded stores.

   B. A survey found that nearly all men experience increases in blood pressure and heart rates when doing holiday shopping, but only 25% of the women registered any change at all.

5. Cameras are watching you more often than you think.

   A. If you run a red light in many major cities, your illegal act will be recorded by a camera.

   B. Go to the bank, the airport, a neighborhood convenience store, or into the dressing room of a department store, and it's increasingly likely that a camera is filming you.

6. Gambling is popular with teenagers and young children.

   A. An estimated 80% of teenagers gamble in some form.

   B. The lottery and private bets on sporting events are favored forms of gambling by the very young.

7. Even though handwashing curbs the spread of disease, not enough people do it.

   A. More than 95% of people surveyed say they always wash their hands after using restroom facilities, but researchers discovered only 67% actually do.

   B. Handwashing is the simplest, most effective thing people can do to reduce the spread of infectious diseases.

8. People are developing poor manners.

   A. The phrases "thank you" and "excuse me" are disappearing.

   B. Many people have developed the habit of chewing with their mouths open.

Exercise 6: Summing Up Important Ideas in One Sentence

Directions: Reduce the key information in each paragraph to one sentence.

The Scotty Who Knew Too Much

(1) Several summers ago there was a Scotty who went to the country for a visit. He decided that all the farm dogs were cowards, because they were afraid of a certain animal that had a white stripe down its back.

A Scotty who visited the country looked down on the farm dogs because they

were scared of a skunk.

(2) "You are a chicken and I can whip you," the Scotty said to the farm dog who lived in the house where the Scotty was visiting. "I can whip the little animal with the white stripe, too. Show him to me." "Don't you want to ask any questions about him?" said the farm dog. "Naw," said the Scotty. "*You* ask the questions."

The Scotty decided to beat up the skunk without knowing anything about him.

---

(3) So the farm dog took the Scotty into the woods and showed him the white-striped animal and the Scotty closed in on him, growling and slashing. It was all over in a moment and the Scotty lay on his back. When he

came to, the farm dog said, "What happened?" "He threw poison," said the Scotty, "but he never laid a glove on me."

The Scotty lost to the skunk because of the spray.

_____

(4) A few days later the farm dog told the Scotty there was another animal all the farm dogs were afraid of. "Lead me to him," said the Scotty. "I can lick anything that doesn't wear horseshoes." "Don't you want to ask any questions about him?" said the farm dog. "Naw," said the Scotty. "Just show me where he hangs out."

The Scotty agreed to fight another animal the farm dogs were afraid of.

_____

(5) So the farm dog led him to a place in the woods and pointed out the little animal when he came along. "A clown," said the Scotty, "a pushover," and he closed in, leading with his left and exhibiting some mighty fancy footwork. In less than a second the Scotty was flat on his back, and when he woke up the farm dog was pulling quills out of him. "What happened?" said the farm dog. "He pulled a knife on me," said the Scotty, "but at least I have learned how you fight out here in the country, and now I am going to beat _you_ up."

The Scotty was defeated by a porcupine and now is going to fight a farm dog.

_____

(6) So he closed in on the farm dog, holding his nose with one front paw to ward off the poison and covering his eyes with the other front paw to keep out the knives. The Scotty couldn't see his opponent and he couldn't smell his opponent, and he was so badly beaten that he had to be taken back to the city and put in a nursing home.

Unable to defend himself well, the Scotty ended up in a nursing home.

_____

(7) MORAL: _It is better to ask some of the questions than to know all the answers._

It's a good idea to not act like you know everything.

_____

Thurber, James, _Fables For Our Time_

Exercise 7: Summing Up Important Ideas in One Sentence

Directions: Reduce the key information in each paragraph to one sentence.

The Princess and the Tin Box

(1) Once upon a time, in a far country, there lived a king whose daughter was the prettiest princess in the world. Her eyes were like the cornflower, her hair was sweeter than the hyacinth, and her throat made the swan look dusty. From the time she was a year old, the princess had been showered with presents. Her nursery looked like Cartier's window. Her toys were all made of gold or platinum or diamonds or emeralds. She was not permitted to have wooden blocks or china dolls or rubber dogs or linen books, because such materials were considered cheap for the daughter of a king. She walked in silver slippers to a sapphire-and-topaz bathroom and slept in an ivory bed inlaid with rubies.

A king had a beautiful daughter who was showered with luxurious items from the

time she was small.

(2) On the day the princess was eighteen, the king sent a royal ambassador to the courts of five neighboring kingdoms to announce that he would give his daughter's hand in marriage to the prince who brought her the gift she liked the most.

The king pledged to marry his daughter to the prince who gave her the gift she

liked best.

(3) The first prince to arrive at the palace rode a swift white stallion and laid at the feet of the princess an enormous apple made of solid gold which he had taken from a dragon who had guarded it for a thousand years. It was placed on a long ebony table set up to hold the gifts of the princess's suitors. The second prince, who came on a gray charger, brought her a nightingale made of a thousand diamonds, and it was placed beside the golden apple. The third prince, riding on a black horse, carried a great jewel box made of platinum and sapphires, and it was placed next to the diamond nightingale. The fourth prince, astride a fiery yellow horse, gave the princess a gigantic heart made of rubies and pierced by an emerald arrow. It was placed next to the platinum-and-sapphire jewel box.

The first four princes all gave the princess expensive gifts.

_____

(4) Now the fifth prince was the strongest and handsomest of all the five suitors, but he was the son of a poor king whose realm had been overrun by

mice and locusts and wizards and mining engineers so that there was nothing much of value left in it. He came plodding up to the palace of the princess on a plow horse and he brought her a small tin box filled with mica and feldspar and hornblende which he had picked up on the way.

The fifth prince, who was poor, gave her a tin box with rocks in it.

_____

(5) The other princes roared with disdainful laughter when they saw the tawdry gift the fifth prince had brought to the princess. But she examined it with great interest and squealed with delight, for all her life she had been glutted with precious stones and priceless metals, but she had never seen tin before or mica or feldspar or hornblende. The tin box was placed next to the ruby heart pierced with an emerald arrow.

The princess liked the gift of the fifth prince because she'd never seen anything like it

before.

(6) "Now," the king said to his daughter, "you must select the gift you like best and marry the prince that brought it." The princess smiled and walked up to the table and picked up the present she liked the most. It was the platinum-and-sapphire jewel box, the gift of the third prince.

The princess liked the gift of the third prince the most.

_____

(7) "The way I figure it," she said, "is this. It is a very large and expensive box, and when I am married, I will meet many admirers who will give me precious gems with which to fill it to the top. Therefore, it is the most valuable of all the gifts my suitors have brought me and I like it the best." And so the princess married the third prince that very day in the midst of great merriment and high revelry.

She thought his gift was the most valuable so she married him the same day.

_____

(8) MORAL: *All those who thought the princess was going to select the tin box filled with worthless stones instead of one of the other gifts will kindly stay after class and write one hundred times on the blackboard "I would rather have a hunk of aluminum silicate than a diamond necklace."*

If you thought she was going to pick something worthless instead of something

valuable, go write on the blackboard.

Thurber, James, *The Beast in Me and Other Animals*, New York: Harcourt Brace & Company, 1974, pp. 34–36

READING

"In many parts of the world, including the U.S., fishermen release their first catch of the day for good luck."

GETTING FOCUSED

Superstitions have long been a part of sports. And the sport of fishing is no exception. Did you know that wishing a fisherman good luck brings bad luck? Or that according to ancient lore, fish may not bite if a red-headed woman crosses the path of a fisherman? Read the following selection to learn more about fishing and superstition.

TACKLING VOCABULARY

angler   a person who fishes with a hook and line

breaking taboo   doing something forbidden or prohibited

lee   the side or part that is sheltered or turned away from the wind

FISHIN' SUPERSTITION: IT'S MORE THAN JUST LUCK

Don't *even* think about bringing bananas on board; you'll jinx the trip!

Associated Press

New Orleans—It was dawn, and fishing guide Nash Roberts III was going over his gear, like a pilot in his preflight routine:

2   Rods. Check.

3   Reels. Check.

4   Lures. Check.

5   Sunscreen, water, rain gear, food: Check, check, check and check.

6   Now he had one final blank to fill in before shoving off.

7   "Anyone bring any eggs on board?" Roberts asked his anglers, his tone courtroom-serious. Anything at all egg-related?

8   "Hard-boiled eggs? Egg-salad sandwiches? Anything with an egg in it?"

9   There was a puzzled silence from the clients, before they began shaking their heads:

10   "No."

11   "OK," the guide said. "We can go fishing."

12   The story didn't surprise Roberts' friend and fellow guide, Joe Courcelle.

13   "Nash is very superstitious about eggs and fishing," Courcelle said. "He won't go fishing with an egg on board. And if he finds an egg on board while he's fishing, he'll throw it out, or throw you out.

14   "And you know what? I'm with him on this. It's the one superstition I believe in, because I've seen terrible things happen when you have an egg on board."

15 Like boats burning to the ground. Motors quitting. Terrible weather. Gear breaking. And, most important of all, not catching fish.

16 As it turns out, people are as superstitious about fishing as they are about baseball, motor sports, golf, gambling or any other activity in which chance has a role. Some of its participants believe their fate can be altered by specific habits.

17 They religiously follow routines that preceded happy outcomes and passionately avoid anything associated with a bad day. The superstition tradition is deep-rooted in fishing, dating to the days when the oceans were a great and terrifying mystery to all men, and fishing was a very risky occupation. Breaking taboo, such as saying a superstitious word, could lead not only to a poor catch but death.

18 In 19th-century England, for example, there was a deep superstition against wishing a fisherman "good luck." An unknowing visitor to an English seaport who good-naturedly uttered that wish might end up with a bloodied nose.

19 Bringing a pig aboard a ship was forbidden throughout Western Europe. In some cities, a crewman who even spoke the word "pig" might be set adrift. Similarly, having a woman aboard was considered an invitation to disaster, as was the practice of carrying another person across the gangplank.

20 It didn't stop there. Bad things would happen if someone started a voyage on a Friday, or continued a voyage after a hawk, owl, or crow had landed on the rigging. Empty nets or personal tragedy would follow if a looking glass was broken, a hatch was dropped, or nails were driven on a Sunday.

21 Naturally, that tradition spilled over into recreational angling. In Ireland, many anglers believe letting a red-haired girl cross your path on your way to fishing will bring bad luck. And if someone steps over your fishing rod, you might as well stay home—or go home.

22 In Iceland, anglers believe if someone drops a knife while cleaning fish, and the knife points to land, the next fishing trip will be a bummer. Conversely, if the knife points to the sea, you'll catch a limit the next time out.

23 In the Bahamas, anglers never bring a banana on a fishing trip. It's a prevalent superstition in the United States as well.

24 In many parts of the world, including the U.S., fishermen release their first catch of the day for good luck. They also spit on baited hooks; never carry a fishing pole into the house; never let their shadow fall on the water; never tell anyone how many fish they've caught while they're still fishing; never put the anchor out while fish are biting; won't fish after hearing an owl hoot; won't curse during a lightning storm; make their first cast to a spot certain not to hold fish, because catching a fish with your first cast means the rest of the day will come up empty.

25 On the other hand, anglers feel lucky if they see cows grazing in the morning, chickens oiling their feathers, or aquarium fish active and feeding as they leave for the outing.

26 Many superstitions are based on natural events that actually affect fish behavior. For instance:

- "A cloudy day is good for fishing," is tied to the fact that fish are more active when barometric pressure is falling.

- "Fish bite best during a full moon," corresponds to large tidal waves, which tend to promote fish activity.

- "Casting into the wind brings luck" because an angler will be tossing his bait on the lee shoreline, where protected waters are clearer and fish can see the bait.

27 Of course, most superstitions have no science behind them, only emotions. After taking the lead in the 1999 BASS Masters Classic in New Orleans, Davy Hite never changed his lucky "charm"—a pair of boxer shorts with heart prints. Hite had a streak going, he explained, and didn't want to risk a change. He won the three-day tournament with an all-time record stringer!

"Fishin' Superstition: Its more than just luck" is reprinted by permission of ESPN Internet Ventures.

COMPREHENSION CHECKUP

Multiple Choice

Directions: Write the letter of the correct answer on the blank provided.

_____c_____   1. What is the main idea of this selection?
- a. Nash Roberts III is very superstitious about eggs and fishing.
- b. Many fishing superstitions are based on scientific fact.
- c. Anglers are prone to superstitious and ritualistic behavior.
- d. Fishing has always been a very risky undertaking.

_____d_____   2. According to the selection, why is it a good idea to fish on a cloudy day or during a full moon?
- a. Fish are more likely to be active when barometric pressure falls.
- b. Lightning storms agitate fish, making them easier to catch.
- c. Large tidal waves are correlated with increased fish activity.
- d. Both a and c.

_____b_____   3. If something is *prevalent* it is likely to be
- a. rare.
- b. common.
- c. unusual.
- d. both a and c.

_____d_____   4. Based on the information in the selection, choose the answer that best completes this sentence: Anglers believe that
- a. women on board a fishing vessel bring good luck.
- b. having good luck is not something to be taken lightly.
- c. on a fishing trip, words as well as actions can lead to disaster.
- d. both b and c.

_____d_____   5. The supporting ideas in the last paragraph tell you
- a. the 1999 BASS Masters Classic was held in New Orleans.
- b. Davy Hite won the 1999 BASS Masters Classic.
- c. Davy Hite wore the same pair of boxers for three days straight.
- d. all of the above.

___a___   6. In the United States, the first catch of the day is likely to be

    a. released.

    b. used for bait.

    c. given to the poor.

    d. kept as a trophy.

Working with Details

Directions: Fill in the word that correctly completes each statement.

1. Both Nash Roberts III and Joe Courcelle won't go fishing with an
   _____egg_____ on board.

2. At one time, breaking _____taboos_____ by saying a forbidden word
   could lead to death.

3. In 19th-century England, it was considered unwise to wish a fisherman
   _____good_____ _____luck_____ .

4. Throughout Western Europe it was dangerous to say the word
   _____pig_____ or to bring one aboard a vessel.

5. The Irish have many fishing superstitions, such as staying home if someone steps over your _____fishing_____ _____rod_____ .

6. In the Bahamas and the United States, fishermen won't allow
   _____bananas_____ on board.

7. Good luck apparently follows those who see chickens
   _____oiling_____ their feathers.

8. In the U.S., it might not be a good idea to fish after hearing an owl
   _____hoot_____ .

Vocabulary

Directions: Fill in the blank with the word that correctly completes each statement.

dawn   altered   preceded   fate   uttered   adrift   correspond

1. After her move to New York City from a town of only 400 people,
   Veronica felt lonely and _____adrift_____ .

2. With the storm raging, everyone in Newport worried about the
   _____fate_____ of the ship still at sea.

3. Marla unexpectedly _____preceded_____ her older sister Elizabeth to
   the altar.

4. He _____uttered_____ an obscenity on TV, which was immediately bleeped from the telecast.

5. Some people get up at the crack of _____dawn_____ and others like to sleep until noon.

6. I like to vote for public officials whose views on the key issues _____correspond_____ to mine.

7. After so much plastic surgery, her appearance was _____altered_____ beyond recognition.

In Your Own Words

What do you think of the following superstitions? Can you think of any sound reasons for respecting some of them?

Sailing Superstitions

For Sailors, It Was Lucky

- to smash a bottle against the boat just before sailing.
- for sailors to have tattoos.
- to throw an old pair of shoes overboard just after launch.
- to have a black cat on board.
- for sailors to wear gold hoop earrings.
- to step aboard using the right foot first.

For Sailors, It Was Unlucky

- to have the bottle not break when used in the launch ceremony.
- to change the name of a boat.
- to sail on a green boat.
- to sail on a Friday.
- to see rats leaving a ship.
- to have someone die on the ship.
- to cross an area where another ship once sank.

Other Sailing Superstitions

- Women and clergymen as passengers bring bad luck.
- The word *drown* can never be spoken at sea, or it may summon up the actual event.
- Horseshoes on a ship's mast help turn away storms.
- Whistling, cutting nails, and trimming beards at sea will cause storms.

Written Assignment

How would you feel about going fishing or sailing with someone who was superstitious? Would you get off the boat? Would you become a believer in superstitions? Describe what you think your reactions would be sailing with one of the superstitious people mentioned in the reading selection.

Internet Activity

Do research on the Internet to find superstitions associated with other sports. For instance, what superstitions are associated with football, golf, or horse racing?

READING

"The beauty of the Hope diamond will continue to awe visitors, and the legacy of the curse will always surround it with mystique."

GETTING FOCUSED

It has long been thought that precious stones have great powers. Many people collect crystals of various shapes and colors because they are reputed to have curative powers. Still others proudly wear their birthstones because they are supposed to confer magical properties. The jewel described below was once thought to bring terrible luck to those who possessed it.

BIO-SKETCH

The well-known journalist Russell Smith currently lives in Toronto where he writes the weekly "Virtual Culture" column for the *Globe and Mail*. He is the author of the novels *How Insensitive, Noise, Young Men,* and *The Princess and the Whiskheads*.

TACKLING VOCABULARY

desecration   an act of disrespect toward something regarded as sacred

mystique   an aura of mystery or mystical power

THE HOPE DIAMOND

Russell Smith

It's a gem of incredible beauty, the largest, deep blue diamond in the world, now permanently resting at the Smithsonian Institution's Janet Annenberg Hooker Hall of Geology, Gems, and Minerals (try saying that fast three times).

Millions of years old, the Hope diamond only has a definite historical track to humans since 1830. It was in that year a fabulous blue diamond was sold in London to Henry Philip Hope, who gave the stone its famous name.

2 Gem experts who saw the 45-carat Hope diamond in 1830 were almost certain it had been re-cut from a much larger diamond owned by French kings in the 17th and 18th centuries. And that diamond had itself been cut from an original rough-cut diamond that weighed a staggering 112 carats.

3 Historians believe that the original gem was mined in India and somehow was obtained by a French trader named Jean Baptiste Tavernier in 1666. Unsubstantiated reports have either Baptiste or a hired thief stealing the diamond from the eye socket of a Hindu god statue near Mandalay, India. Later in its ownership trail, this desecration began to loom large as the birth of the legendary curse of the Hope diamond.

4 The curse of the stolen diamond began to work its magic as Baptiste brought the diamond back to France in 1668 and sold it to King Louis XIV. Various tales of the legend have Baptiste going bankrupt, nearly drowning, and finally returning to India where a pack of wild dogs killed him. Almost all of the historical accounts of the diamond report that this is how Baptiste died. But there is one notable exception.

5 The Smithsonian curator of the museum in which the Hope diamond now resides disagrees. Jeffrey Post, who has written a book called *The National Gem Collection,* asserts Baptiste died of natural causes.

"Riches serve a wise man but command a fool."

—Old saying

6 The new owner of the diamond, twenty-five-year-old King Louis XIV, had the diamond cut down into a heart shaped 67-carat stone. Louis XIV would reign longer than any other European monarch (1643–1715), and thus isn't exactly the typical owner of the fabled diamond. He named the stone the Blue Diamond of the Crown. The diamond passed to the Sun King's great-grandson Louis XV, and finally to King Louis XVI and his Austrian wife Marie Antoinette. By now the beautiful crown jewel had acquired another popular nickname, the French Blue. This time the curse did seem to work its charm with these owners (Marie had reputedly worn it in a necklace and Louis wore it in a crown) as they fell victim to the violence of French Revolution and were tried for treason and beheaded in January of 1793.

7 Before their death, their jewels, including the French Blue, had been stolen in a robbery. Some of the crown jewels were recovered, but not the French Blue.

8 For 38 years, the gem was missing and never did reappear in the form of the French Blue. It is conjectured that a Dutch diamond cutter named Wilhelm Fals cut the French Blue down to its present weight. In keeping with the growing legend of the diamond's curse, Wilhelm supposedly died of grief after his son stole the diamond. Then his thieving son committed suicide.

9 One interesting side-note to the lost years of the big blue diamond is that a portrait painted by Goya in 1800 of Queen Maria Louisa of Spain shows her with a diamond that looks much like the Hope diamond. At any rate, a 45-carat, deep blue diamond appeared in London in 1830 and was bought by Henry Hope.

10 At this stage the Hope diamond began another mad whirlwind tour of new owners and the historical accuracy dims once again. Reputedly a Russian prince gave it to his girlfriend, Mademoiselle Ladrue, and then shot and killed her.

11 The story then goes that a Greek owner and his family were all killed when their car went off a cliff. The next reputed owner was Turkish sultan Abdul Hamid II, and he repeated the performance of the Russian prince by killing his girlfriend, Zobeida. Abdul was toppled from power by a rebellion in 1909.

12 Finally, the much-traveled gemstone arrived in America and was acquired by the famous jeweler Pierre Cartier. Now the tale becomes more reliable.

13 Cartier quickly resold the Hope diamond in 1911 to an American, Mrs. Evalyn Walsh McLean, who lived in Washington, D.C. Contrary to popular belief, her husband did not perish on the *Titanic*. However, he did die in a mental hospital. And we do know her daughter died from an overdose of sleeping pills in 1946, and her son died in a car accident.

14 Another intriguing story about Mrs. McLean and the Hope diamond is that she hocked it in a Virginia pawnshop in 1932 to obtain ransom money, which she used in an unsuccessful attempt to recover the kidnapped Lindbergh baby. A confidence man named Gaston Means, who was unconnected with the actual kidnapping, conned her out of the money. She later recovered her diamond and Means went to prison.

15 About a year after her daughter's death, Mrs. McLean passed away at the age of 60. Soon afterward, the famed New York jeweler Harry Winston made a sealed bid offer to the bank controlling her estate. He bought it and kept it until 1958 when he donated it to the Smithsonian, where it has remained ever since. One final note about the diamond's cursing effect is that the mailman who delivered the diamond from Winston later lost his wife, his house, and a leg. There the curse appears to have ended.

16 And the value of the Hope diamond? It was appraised at $100,000 when Mrs. McLean hocked it in 1932. But today it is the most famous museum piece in the world (over 5 million people view it each year, surpassing even the number of visitors to the Louvre in Paris). The official Smithsonian line is that it has "inestimable value." Even Bill Gates couldn't buy this world treasure.

17 The beauty of the Hope diamond will continue to awe visitors, and the legacy of the curse will always surround it with mystique.

"Hope Diamond" by Russell Smith is reprinted by permission of Russell Smith.

✔ COMPREHENSION CHECKUP

Main Idea

___a___ 1. The main idea of the selection is

    a. the Hope diamond has had a long and colorful history.

    b. philanthropists like Harry Winston make it possible for millions of people to enjoy looking at something beautiful and rare.

    c. the Hope diamond should be restored to its rightful owners.

    d. the Hope diamond has been responsible for bringing misfortune to its owners.

Supporting Details

True or False

Directions: Indicate whether each statement is true or false by writing **T** or **F** on the blank.

____F____   1. The Hope diamond was cut thousands of years ago.

____F____   2. The Hope diamond currently resides in the Louvre in Paris.

____T____   3. An *unsubstantiated* report is one that has not been confirmed.

____F____   4. Jeffrey Post, the curator of the Smithsonian, believes that Baptiste was killed by wild dogs.

____F____   5. Louis XVI had a diamond cut into a heart-shaped stone weighing 67 carats.

____T____   6. Henry Hope purchased a diamond weighing 45 carats.

____T____   7. Pierre Cartier was the first in America to have possession of the blue Hope diamond.

____T____   8. Historians do not know for sure whether the French blue diamond appeared in a painting by Goya.

____F____   9. Despite possession of the Hope diamond, Evalyn Walsh McLean lived well into her eighties.

____T____   10. Something of *inestimable* value is priceless.

____T____   11. The words *reputedly* and *supposedly* are synonyms.

Sequence

Directions: Number the following sentences in correct time order sequence from first (1) to last (8).

____7____   In 1932, the Hope diamond, then valued at $100,000, is hocked to pay ransom money.

____8____   In 1958, Harry Winston donates the Hope diamond to the Smithsonian.

____2____   Louis XIV names the diamond the Blue Diamond of the Crown.

____5____   In 1909, Abdul Hamid II is removed from power by a rebellion.

_____4_____   Henry Philip Hope purchases the blue diamond.

_____3_____   The French Blue is stolen from King Louis XVI and his wife Marie Antoinette.

_____6_____   Pierre Cartier sells the blue diamond to Evalyn Walsh McLean.

_____1_____   Jean Baptiste Tavernier sells a diamond to King Louis XIV.

Vocabulary in Context

Directions: Decide whether or not the word in italics is used correctly in the following sentences. Write **C** if it is used correctly and write **I** if it is used incorrectly.

_____C_____   1. He *staggered* under the weight of the heavy piece of lumber.

_____C_____   2. With final exams *looming*, Serena knew she would have to buckle down and study hard.

_____C_____   3. After two years without a job, Mark was forced to declare *bankruptcy*.

_____I_____   4. She is such a *notable* author that almost no one has heard of her.

_____C_____   5. People say that Helen of Troy had a *fabled* beauty. It is said that her face launched a thousand ships.

_____I_____   6. Something *intriguing* is not worth bothering with.

_____C_____   7. The young child first built a large tower of bricks and then *toppled* it.

_____C_____   8. If you *hock* something, you no longer have it in your possession.

_____I_____   9. If a character on a TV sitcom *perishes*, you are likely to see that character again.

_____C_____ 10. The elderly have to be careful not to be *conned* out of their life savings.

In Your Own Words

1. Some people speculate that the curse was entirely invented by Pierre Cartier to drive up the value of the diamond. What do you think?

2. Why do you think the Hope diamond is such a tourist attraction at the Smithsonian?

3. How do you feel about owning valuable jewelry? Does it make you uncomfortable? Or do you just put it on and wear it? Does it make you feel attractive or successful?

Written Assignment

1. Did you know that the Heart of the Ocean in the movie *Titanic* was based on the Hope diamond? If you had a diamond in your possession that was alleged to be cursed, what would you do with it? Would you return it to the ocean, give it away, donate it to a museum, or keep it and take your chances?

2. Here are some sentences from the reading. Paraphrase them by rewriting each one in your own words in the space provided.

   A. Gem experts who saw the 45-carat Hope diamond in 1830 were almost certain it had been re-cut from a much larger diamond owned by French kings in the 17th and 18th centuries. And that diamond had itself been cut from an original rough-cut diamond that weighed a staggering 112 carats. Answers will vary,

   _____

   _____

   _____

   _____

   B. For 38 years, the gem was missing and never did reappear in the form of the French Blue. It is conjectured that a Dutch diamond cutter named Wilhelm Fals cut the French Blue down to its present weight. In keeping with the growing legend of the diamond's curse, Wilhelm supposedly died of grief after his son stole the diamond. Then his thieving son committed suicide. Answers will vary.

   _____

   _____

   _____

   _____

   C. About a year after her daughter's death, Mrs. McLean passed away at the age of 60. Soon afterward, the famed New York jeweler Harry Winston made a sealed bid offer to the bank controlling her estate. He bought it and kept it until 1958 when he donated it to the Smithsonian, where it has remained ever since. One final note about the diamond's cursing effect is that the mailman who delivered the diamond from

Winston later lost his wife, his house, and a leg. There the curse appears to have ended. Answers will vary.

_____

_____

_____

_____

Internet Activity

1. Do research to discover the symbolic meaning of other gemstones. What does the opal signify? Or the ruby or emerald or garnet?

2. Find out more about James Todd, the mailman who delivered the Hope to the Smithsonian. Did you know that despite having his wife die of a heart attack, his house burning down, and his dog dying (all in quick succession), he never became a believer in the curse?

READING

"Though it was freezing, Jordan remained crouched down by the boy until his father could take a picture."

GETTING FOCUSED

In 1984, Michael Jordan, a graduate of University of North Carolina, was the National Basketball Association's rookie of the year. As the leader of the Chicago Bulls, number 23 helped the Bulls win six NBA championships. The murder of his father in 1993 caused Jordan to retire from the game he loved. He returned to the NBA in 1995 after a brief stint as a minor league baseball player, and amazingly won another championship his first full year back. Many consider "Air" Jordan to be the greatest player of all time. But there is another side to Jordan, which this selection describes. His caring attitude toward others who are not as fortunate has not been as well documented as his athletic skill.

BIO-SKETCH

Bob Greene, a syndicated columnist, has written several best-selling books including *Hang Time, 50-Year Dash, Chevrolet Summers, Dairy Queen Nights*.

TACKLING VOCABULARY

shagging balls   retrieving the balls

dribbling   controlling the ball while moving by means of short bounces of the basketball

STADIUM NIGHTS

By Bob Greene

In my time as a reporter, I have witnessed some impressive, moving, and emotional things. But I had never seen anything like what I experienced during time spent with Michael Jordan in 1990 and 1991. Though his purely athletic feats were well-documented, I often saw things that made all the athletic heroics fade away.

2   One night after a game, Jordan approached his car, which the security guards had readied. There were so many people and so much noise, and about twenty feet away was a little boy in a wheelchair. Jordan was clearly in a hurry; he had his own son with him. So he opened his car door, and somehow saw the boy. He walked over, got down on the ground beside him and spoke. Jordan comforted the child, talking slowly. This was not something that had been set up by the team; the boy's father had just brought him there to get a close glimpse of Jordan. Though it was freezing, Jordan remained crouched down by the boy until his father could take a picture. Only then did he return to his car. You can't set out to learn how to do this. No one can tell you how or advise you on it; it comes from something deep inside. If nothing else good ever happens for that little boy, he will always know that, on that night, Michael Jordan included him in his world.

3   At another game, I met Carmen Villafane. Her disabilities were so severe, her physical limitations so pronounced, that strangers tended to avert their eyes. I wondered how she was able to have her wheelchair positioned on the floor behind the Bulls bench at every game. *She must come from a family with a lot of pull*, I thought.

4   Well, not exactly, I learned.

5   In talking to her, I discovered that about a year earlier she had made a valentine for Jordan. She had managed to get tickets to a game and give it to him. He opened it right there in front of her, read it, and thanked her.

6   Months later, she saw him at an auto show, and he asked her why she hadn't been at any more games. When Jordan learned Carmen had only had that single ticket, he instructed her to call his office. Without much hope, she did, and the office staff knew all about her. They mailed tickets for the remainder of the season. The following season, Jordan sent her more tickets and a handwritten note. The letter said: "I hope you enjoy the season ahead. I'm looking forward to seeing you at every game—Michael."

7   Carmen was not the only one touched by Jordan. One time I got to the stadium early and found him on the playing surface of the stadium with hours to go before game time. He grabbed a basketball and motioned to two of the teenage ball boys to guard him. They glanced at each other; this was new. They were accustomed to shagging balls for him, but tonight he was inviting them to play. I watched as the two ball boys dribbled and passed. Jordan chased them into a corner of the court, laughing with them, reaching for the ball, slapping it out of their hands. The unspoken, priceless message he was sending them was that they were good enough for this—they were good enough to play around with him.

8   Another time, I had written a column about a random act of kindness I had seen Jordan do for a child outside the arena. It was when all this was new to me, before I knew that he did this kind of thing all the time.

9   A reader called in response and told me he and his wife had been to a Bulls game and their car had broken down. "We were four blocks from the stadium, in a bad area, and at the corner under a streetlight was Jordan's car," he said. "He was standing outside the car, talking with some neighborhood boys. It was late at night and they were just talking."

10   Later I asked Jordan about these boys. He said the year before, he'd seen them waiting outside the stadium in terrible weather, wanting a glimpse of the Bulls. He brought them in with him to the game. "Now they wait for me on that corner every night. . . . They're just kids who seem like they really need someone to talk to," he told me. Jordan's wife later told me he asks the boys to show him their grades to make sure they are keeping up with their schoolwork.

11   Jordan remembers that once he was a kid learning how to lift a basketball into the air. He was once a boy who was told that he wasn't good enough. He remembers every detail of being cut from the basketball team when he was a high school sophomore. Jordan told me: "We stood there and looked for our names. Mine wasn't on the list. I looked and looked. It was almost as if I didn't stop looking, it would be there."

12   When reality set in that morning he was cut, Jordan went through the rest of the day numb. "Then I hurried into my house and I closed the door of my room and I cried so hard. It was all I wanted, to play on that team."

"We must accept finite disappointment but never lose infinite hope."

—Martin Luther King.

13   At the end of that high school season, Jordan worked up the nerve to ask the coach if he could ride along on the bus with the team to a district tournament. "The coach told me no. But I asked again, and he said I could come. When we got there, he told me the only way I could go in was to carry the players' uniforms. So that's what I did."

14   Jordan told me he was glad the episode happened because it taught him what disappointment felt like, and he never wanted to feel that way again.

15   In those years that I spent with Jordan, the world I wrote about had become no less grim, no less dismaying than it had been the first time I'd walked into the stadium. Nothing was going to change that; if anything, this world of ours keeps spinning itself into crueler and more sorrowful shape.

16   But there is more than one way to look upon that world. Of all the things I'd taken away fom all those stadium nights, maybe that was the most important: the knowledge that, if you look closely enough, amid the merciless and the bitter, there is always the chance that you may find comfort and the promise of something good.

"Stadium Nights" by Bob Greene. Copyright © 1992 by Bob Greene. Reprinted by permission of the author.

COMPREHENSION CHECKUP

1. The topic of the selection is Michael Jordan

2. The implied main idea of paragraph 2 is Michael Jordan selflessly talked to

    a boy in a wheelchair after the game

3. The overall implied main idea of the selection is Michael Jordan is a loving

    and caring individual

Multiple Choice

Directions: Write the letter of the correct answer on the blank provided.

___c___   1. The suffix *less* in the words *priceless* and *merciless* means

     a. more

     b. study of

     c. without

     d. full of

___d___   2. Which of the following is discussed in the selection?

     a. Jordan's success as a basketball coach.

     b. Jordan's success as a baseball player.

     c. Jordan's success as a manager.

     d. Jordan's disappointment in not making the basketball team his sophomore year in high school.

___b___   3. According to the context of paragraph 3, *avert* means

     a. to turn towards

     b. to turn away

     c. to close

     d. to stare at

___c___   4. In paragraphs 11 and 12, *cut* according to the context of the selection means

     a. to slice with a sharp instrument

     b. to split into two parts with a sharp instrument

     c. to be eliminated from

     d. to shorten by omitting parts

___d___   5. According to the selection, Michael Jordan gave season tickets to

     a. the four boys he met on the street corner.

     b. the ball boys he played with at the gym.

     c. the boy in the wheelchair.

     d. Carmen Villafane.

___a___   6. The prefix *un* in the word *unspoken* means

     a. not

     b. with

     c. together

     d. again

___d___ 7. A *random act of kindness*

        a. is usually spontaneous.

        b. is a selfish act.

        c. is a selfless act.

        d. both a and c.

True or False

Directions: Indicate whether the statement is true or false by writing **T** or **F** on the blank provided.

___T___ 1. If something is *well-documented* it is well supported by evidence.

___F___ 2. Michael Jordan was always successful as a basketball player.

___T___ 3. Bob Greene, the author of this selection, feels that acting kindly to strangers is innate to Michael Jordan's character.

___T___ 4. Jordan encouraged the academic success of some local boys he befriended.

___T___ 5. A synonym for the word *dismaying* in paragraph 15 is *discouraging*.

___T___ 6. Greene does not think the world is a hospitable place.

___F___ 7. If you have a *lot of pull*, you have very little influence.

___T___ 8. A *feat* is a remarkable deed.

___T___ 9. Michael Jordan often played basketball with the ball boys.

___T___ 10. Michael Jordan met Carmen for the second time at a car show.

Vocabulary in Context

Directions: Using the vocabulary words below, fill in the crossword puzzle.

amid	crouched	glimpse	impressive	pronounced
bitter	episode	grim	numb	random

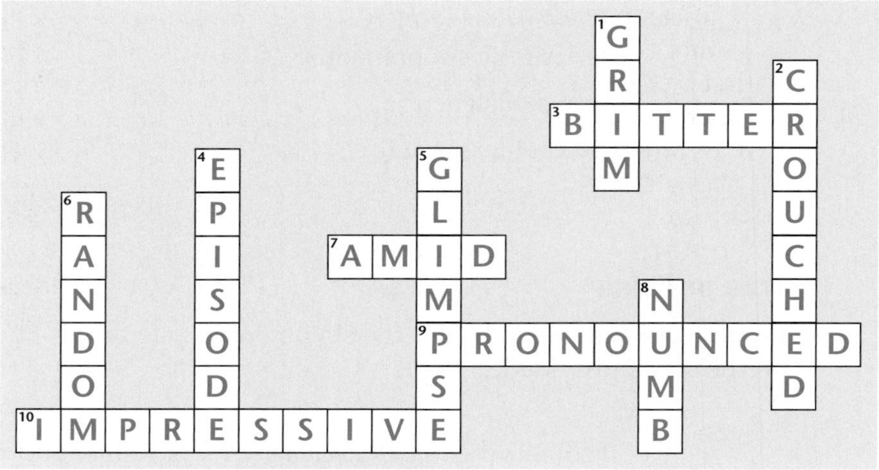

(crossword puzzle grid)

Across answers shown in grid: BITTER, AMID, PRONOUNCED, IMPRESSIVE
Down answers shown in grid: GRIM, CROUCHED, EPISODE, GLIMPSE, RANDOM, NUMB

ACROSS CLUES

3. full of sorrow, pain,

7. among

9. clearly marked; definite

10. arousing admiration or respect

DOWN CLUES

1. cruel; harsh

2. stooped with the legs bent close to the ground

4. any incident that forms part of a life, history

5. to get a quick look at

6. made or done without planning or purpose

8. not able to feel

In Your Own Words

1. Jordan was known as an extremely hard worker. He was constantly practicing his shots. Do you think the frustration of being cut from the team his sophomore year in high school pushed him to develop a strong work ethic?

2. What are the reasons Greene gives for admiring Michael Jordan?

Written Assignment

To many people, Michael Jordan is the measuring stick for great accomplishments in basketball. To be "Jordanesque" or "Like Mike" is very high praise. After reading this selection, you know that Jordan wasn't always great and that he even encountered adversity along the way. How does Jordan's story demonstrate a positive way to handle disappointments? What lessons can we learn from the way he dealt with the difficulties in his life, including the death of his father?

Internet Activity

Pull up a website devoted to Michael Jordan and list the highlights of his long career. How long did he have to play before he finally won a championship? What has he been doing since he officially retired in 2003?

REVIEW TEST 1: IDENTIFYING THE DIRECTLY STATED MAIN IDEA

Directions: Identify the topic of each paragraph and the letter of the main idea sentence and write them on the designated lines. Then draw a diagram of the paragraph.

1.   (a) How do you choose your friends? (b) Do you think "birds of a feather flock together"? (c) Or do "opposites attract"? (d) Research reports that college students who get A's are usually more comfortable around other A students. (e) The political liberal or conservative likes to hang out with others who have similar political beliefs. (f) The engineering major relates better to friends who are interested in engineering than to those who are majoring in something else. (g) At work, the workaholics are more likely to be attracted to each other. (h) Your friends are also likely to be the same age, race, religion, and socioeconomic status. (i) Despite the increasing diversity in the United States, similarity plays a key role in choosing friends.

Topic: choosing friends

Main Idea Sentence: i   Diagram: △

2.   (a) Music has been essential to man since the very earliest times. (b) Our early ancestors probably tried to imitate the sounds of the ocean, wind, rain, and thunder, and also bird songs and animal cries. (c) The first music was probably made by prehistoric man producing sounds by banging bones together or hitting them on a rock. (d) Some 5,000 years ago, Egyptians played harps, flutes, zithers, and castanets to accompany their dancing on special occasions. (e) In ancient Greece, lyres, trumpets, horns, and oboes were used for religious ceremonies and funerals. (f) The Romans added cymbals, gongs, and trumpets for banquets and plays.

Topic: music

Main Idea Sentence: a   Diagram: ▽

3.   (a) California has Death Valley, the lowest point in the United States, and Mt. Whitney, the highest point in the contiguous United States. (b) While the Mojave Desert occupies one-fifth of the state, the fertile soil of Imperial Valley produces a larger volume of agricultural products than any other state. (c) California is truly a land of contrasts. (d) The California coastline includes some of the most beautiful shoreline imaginable, but is also highly unstable, with many faults or fractures, the most prominent of which is the San Andreas Fault. (e) The diversity of vegetation includes Coast Redwoods, the world's tallest trees, and the giant Sequoia. (f) Finally, the state's wine-grape vineyards produce a large percentage of the wines made in the U.S.

Topic: California

Main Idea Sentence: c   Diagram: ◇

4.   (a) Have you ever been the victim of identity theft? (b) Someone who steals your account numbers can buy big-ticket items, such as computers

and cars, and have you charged for them. (c) They can take out loans or establish phone or wireless service in your name. (d) They can even drain your current bank account and open up a new one in your name. (e) If you think you're a victim of identity theft, you need to close your bank or credit card accounts immediately. (f) You should also file a report with your local police department and a complaint with the Federal Trade Commission. (g) Identity theft is a big problem that can hurt people financially, but there are ways to combat it.

Topic: identity theft

Main Idea Sentence: g_____   Diagram: △_____

5.   (a) Hand washing is the most important thing you can do to prevent disease. (b) Throughout the day, people pick up germs from other people, from contaminated surfaces, and from animals. (c) If you don't take the time to wash your hands, you transfer those germs to yourself when you touch your eyes, nose, or face. (d) Colds and flu are easily spread in this manner. (e) Serious diseases, such as hepatitis A and meningitis, are also spread in this same way. (f) Despite repeated warnings from the Center for Disease Control, one out of every three people still don't wash their hands after using the restroom. (g) If you want to prevent the spread of disease, do everyone a favor by remembering to wash your hands.

Topic: hand washing

Main Idea Sentence: a, g_____   Diagram: ⋈_____

6.   (a) Tattooing and body piercing should only be done after careful consideration of the facts. (b) Both can cause infection and diseases such as hepatitis B or C. (c) If you decide to have your tattoo removed later, the process is painful, expensive, and not always successful. (d) In body piercing, the removal of the object frequently results in scarring. (e) Most importantly, before getting a tattoo or doing body piercing, be sure to visit the place where the procedure will be done to determine if it is safe, clean, and professional-looking.

Topic: tattooing and body piercing

Main Idea Sentence: a_____   Diagram: ▽_____

REVIEW TEST 2: IDENTIFYING THE IMPLIED MAIN IDEA

Directions: Write the implied main idea for each of the following paragraphs.

1.   What would you do if a friend or a relative asked you to cosign a loan? Did you know that you may be required to pay up to the full amount of the debt if the borrower doesn't pay? Or that you may have to pay late

fees and collection costs, which increase this amount? Be sure you can afford to pay if you have to. Also, be very sure that you want to accept this responsibility. Keep in mind that the creditor can sue you or garnish your wages. And if the debt is ever in default, that fact may become a part of *your* credit record.

Implied Main Idea: Be very careful before agreeing to cosign a loan, because

it could cause you problems.

2.   To establish relationships they hope will extend well beyond the college years, credit card marketers are offering students everything from free T-shirts to chances to win free airline tickets as enticements to sign up. As a result, some 14 percent of students have balances of $3,000 to $7,000 according to Nellie Mae, a nonprofit student loan provider in Braintree, Massachusetts. "Students who have no history with credit are being handed it on a silver platter," says Gerri Detweiler, education adviser for Debt Counselors of America, a consumer advocacy group in Rockville, Maryland. Now 21 and a senior at Georgetown University in Washington, Jason Britton wracked up $21,000 in debt on 16 cards over four years. "When I first started at 18, my attitude was: 'I'll get a job after college to pay off all my debt,'" he says. He realized he dug himself into a hole when he couldn't meet the minimum monthly payments. Now he works three part-time jobs, and his parents are helping him pay his tuition and loans.

Implied Main Idea: Credit card marketers target students, who can get

themselves into real financial difficulty.

3.   Can you imagine saving 25 cents a week and having it grow to over $30,000? As hard as that may be to believe, that's exactly what Ken Lopez was able to do. Putting aside a quarter a week starting in second grade, he built up a small savings account. These funds were then invested in various stocks and mutual funds. While in college, Ken was able to pay for his education while continuing to save between $50 and $100 a month. He closely monitored spending. Ken realized that the few dollars here and there for snacks and other minor purchases quickly add up. Today, at age 27, Ken works as a customer service manager for an online sales division of a retailing company.

Implied Main Idea: By saving a small amount of money every week, Ken Lopez

amassed over $30,000.

4.   Would you pay $8 to cash a $100 check? Or pay $20 to borrow $100 dollars for two weeks? Many people without ready access to financial

services (especially low-income consumers) commonly use the services of check-cashing outlets. Desperate borrowers also go to payday loan stores. Offers of "quick cash" and "low payments" attract consumers without a bank account or credit cards. Many consumers pay annual interest rates of as much as 780 percent and more to obtain needed cash from payday loan companies. The most common users of payday loans are workers who have become trapped by debts run up by free spending or have been driven into debt by misfortune.

Implied Main Idea: Many people are forced to use check-cashing outlets or payday loan stores because they are desperate.

Jack Kapoor, *Personal Finance,* 8th edition, New York: McGraw-Hill, 2007

REVIEW TEST 3: IDENTIFYING THE MAIN IDEA

Directions: Write the directly stated or implied main idea for each paragraph.

1.   Most children want their parents to watch them perform in sports. Many children whose parents do not come to watch them play in sporting events feel that their parents do not adequately support them. However, some children become extremely nervous when their parents watch them perform, or they get embarrassed when their parents cheer too loudly or make a fuss. If children request that their parents not watch them perform, parents should respect their children's wishes.

Main Idea: Although most children want parents to watch them perform in sports, some become nervous or embarrassed.

2.   Parents should compliment their children for their sports performance, even if the child has limited abilities. In the course of a game, there are dozens of circumstances when the child has done something positive. Parents can tell their children how much the children hustled in the game and how enthusiastically they played. Even if the child strikes out in a baseball game, a parent can say, "That was a nice swing."

Main Idea: first sentence

3.   Parents need to carefully monitor their children as they participate in sports for signs of developing stress. Parents should ask themselves the following questions: Is the sport in which the child is participating the best one for the child? Can the child handle the competitive pressures of this particular sport? If the problems appear to be beyond the intuitive skills of a volunteer coach or parent, a consultation with a counselor or clinician may be needed.

Main Idea: first sentence

4. Above all, parents and coaches of children in sports should make sports fun so that children will want to play. It is never appropriate for a parent or coach to yell or scream at a child or to ridicule a child for poor play. The goal for an adult is to be a positive role model. Children don't learn new things immediately, so remember that it's okay for them to make mistakes; it means they are trying.

    Main Idea: Parents and coaches should be good role models for children so

    that they want to play.

5. Outstanding athletes reach their peak physical performance before the age of 30, often between the ages of 19 and 26. Even though athletes keep getting better than their predecessors—running faster, jumping higher, and lifting more weight—the age at which they reach their peak performance has remained virtually the same. Most gymnasts and swimmers reach their peak in their late teens. Many athletes, including track performers in sprint races, peak in their early to mid-twenties. Golfers and marathon runners peak in their late twenties or even early thirties.

    Main Idea: first sentence

6. No matter how well individuals take care of themselves, aging eventually produces declines in biological functions. However, aging individuals who are active and healthy perform motor skills at a higher level than their less active, less healthy counterparts. For example, one recent study found that walking regularly appears to protect older adults against a loss in mobility.

    Main Idea: Even though everyone eventually ages, active individuals perform

    motor skills at a higher level than those who are less active.

    John Santrock, *Human Adjustment*, New York: McGraw-Hill, 2006

Recognizing Transition Words and Patterns of Organization

When you are driving down the street, you encounter road signs along the way that signal what is coming up ahead. **Transition words** are like road signs in that they help the reader understand the direction of the author's thoughts and they signal the author's intent.

Authors don't just randomly put down their thoughts and ideas on paper. Instead, they organize their thoughts in ways designed to help them achieve their purpose and convey their main ideas to their readers. A **pattern of organization** is a method for organizing information in a specific format. For example, an author might decide to describe the steps in the process of a lab experiment (steps in a process pattern) or explore the events that caused a tragic disaster to occur (cause and effect pattern).

Authors use transition words to connect one idea to another. They also serve as a link between one paragraph and another. These transition words provide signals to an author's pattern of organization. Understanding an author's organizational structure makes it easier for you to understand the author's main ideas.

TRANSITION WORDS

Following is a list of transition words and the patterns of organization they introduce.

Transition Words

WORDS TO SHOW CLASSIFICATION AND DIVISION (CATEGORIES)

break down	classify	divide	split
categorize	combine	lump	group

WORDS TO SHOW CAUSE AND EFFECT

as a result	because	bring about	consequently
for this reason	since	so	resulting
then	therefore	outcome	hence

WORDS TO SHOW COMPARISON

all	and	as	both
just as	like	similarly	in comparison

WORDS TO SHOW CONTRAST

although	but	however	instead
nevertheless	unlike	in contrast	yet
on the other hand			

WORDS TO SHOW STEPS IN A PROCESS AND CHRONOLOGY

after	first, second	next	finally
at this stage	now	then	at last

WORDS TO SHOW EXAMPLE

for example	for instance	such as	to illustrate
specifically	in other words	in particular	to demonstrate

WORDS TO SHOW DEFINITION

is defined by	means	is called	refers to
derives from			

Exercise 1: Introduction to Transition Words

Directions: In the following paragraphs, provide transition words or phrases that relate to the pattern of organization indicated in parentheses. Use the transition words chart on page 197. The first item has been completed for you.

1. Each of us will spend some 25 years of life asleep. (cause) _Because_ sleep is familiar, many people think they know all about it. Contrary to common belief, you are not totally unresponsive during sleep. (example) _For example_, you are more likely to awaken if you hear your own name spoken instead of another. Likewise, a sleeping mother may ignore a siren outside (contrast) _but_ wake at the slightest whimper of her child. It's even possible to do simple tasks while asleep. In one experiment, people learned to avoid an electric shock by touching a switch each time a tone sounded. Eventually, they could do it without waking. This is much like the basic survival skill of turning off your alarm clock without waking.

2. A microsleep is (definition) _defined by_ a brief shift in brain activity to the pattern normally recorded during sleep. When you drive, remember that microsleeps can lead to macro-accidents. By the way, if you are struggling to stay awake while driving, you should stop, quit fighting it, and take a short nap. Coffee helps too, but briefly giving in to sleep helps more. There is a near epidemic of sleep problems in our society. Worry, stress, and excitement are responsible for temporary insomnia. Insomnia (definition) _means_ difficulty in falling asleep, frequent nighttime awakenings, or waking too early. To promote sleep, try eating a snack that is nearly all starch. Good sleep-inducing snacks are cookies, bread, oatmeal, pretzels, bagels, and dry cereal. If you really want to drop the bomb on insomnia, try eating a baked potato (which may be the world's largest sleeping pill!).

3. Is there any way to stop a recurring nightmare? A bad nightmare can be worse than any horror movie. Most nightmares can be banished by following three simple steps. (steps in a process) _First_, write down your nightmare describing it in detail. (steps in a process) _Then_, change the dream any way you wish, being sure to spell out the details of the new dream. (steps in a process) _Finally_, mentally rehearse the changed dream before you fall asleep again.

4. We can (classification/division) _divide_ dream experts into two groups: those who believe that dreams have deeply hidden meanings, and those who regard dreams as no more meaningful than ordinary thinking. In general, dreams show few signs of directly expressing hidden wishes. Most dreams probably don't have hidden meanings. They are probably just carryovers from ordinary waking events. (contrast) _But_, dreams do tend to reflect a person's current concerns. And there seems to be little doubt that they can make a difference in our lives. (example) _For example_, sleep researcher William Dement once dreamed that he had lung cancer. At the time, Dement was smoking two packs of cigarettes a day. Dement quit smoking the next day.

Information from Coon, Dennis, *Psychology*, 10th edition, Belmont, CA: Wadsworth, 2006, pp. 219, 226, 228, 229, 230

COMMON PATTERNS OF ORGANIZATION

In the sections that follow, we will discuss these common patterns of organization.

1. Classification and division
2. Cause and effect
3. Comparison and contrast
4. Steps in a process and chronology
5. Example
6. Definition

Classification and Division Pattern

Classification and division is the process of organizing information into categories. A category is created by noticing and defining the common characteristics of a group of items. Larger categories may be divided into smaller categories (or subdivisions) by finding additional common characteristics.

Most of us are already familiar with classification and division. Whenever we do the laundry, most of us classify and divide. We sort articles of clothing into piles before putting them in the washing machine. For example, we may have separate piles of whites and colors. And then we might divide the whites into separate piles for underwear and bedding. We might divide the colors into separate piles for casual clothes and work clothes.

Grocery shopping is made much easier because stores organize products by categories. Stores group dairy products in one aisle, fresh fruits and vegetables in another, and breads and bakery items in another. Most grocery stores have a broad category of like items and then further subdivide the category as much as needed. For instance, once you locate the cereal aisle, you will find hot cereals, cold cereals, and breakfast bars.

Our daily lives are made much easier because of classification and division. The following words are clues to the classification and division pattern: *classify, group, combine, divide,* and *split.*

The exercise below organizes traits into six clusters or families.

Exercise 2: Taking Stock—An Exercise in Classification

The following exercise from the textbook *The Career Fitness Program* illustrates how classification works.

Directions: Answer each question quickly, "off the top of your head." The longer you think about your answer, the less reflective the answer is of your true feelings. Answers will vary.

1. I am _____.

2. I need _____.

3. I want _____.

4. If all goes well in the next five years, I will be doing the following things:

   _____.

5. If things go poorly in the next five years, I will be doing

   _____.

6. Reviewing past jobs or volunteer experiences I have had, what did I like best/least about each one? Is there a pattern?

   _____

   _____

7. What subjects in school do I like?

   _____

   _____

8. What books or magazines do I read? What kind of music, art, movies do I like? What are my favorite websites?

   _____

   _____

9. What do I like to do for fun? How do I spend my free time?

   _____

   _____

The following skills are divided into six related clusters or families: **realistic, investigative, artistic, social, enterprising,** and **conventional.** Circle those adjectives in each cluster that best describe you. Place an **X** in front of those adjectives that least describe you.

Realistic	**Investigative**	**Artistic**
practical	careful	emotional
athletic	achieving	expressive
rugged	curious	imaginative
stable	precise	unordered
frank	independent	creative
persistent	introverted	impulsive
conforming	confident	flexible
down-to-earth	analytical	idealistic
self-reliant	intellectual	original

Social	Enterprising	Conventional
helpful	energetic	conscientious
insightful	driving	persistent
kind	ambitious	organized
friendly	assertive	obedient
tactful	enthusiastic	dependable
understanding	adventurous	moderate
popular	powerful	orderly
cooperative	persuasive	efficient
responsible	competitive	detailed
flirtatious		thorough

Next, review the adjectives you circled. Which groups of adjectives best describe you?

From which three of the six groups do most of your adjectives come? Rank the group from which most of them come as 1, the second most as 2, and the third most as 3.

1. _____ 2. _____ 3. _____

Each of the following groups of adjectives describe a certain kind of person. What kinds of people do you like to be around? Rank the top three types of people you like to be around.

1. _____ 2. _____ 3. _____

Doers

(Realistic-R) These types like jobs such as automobile mechanic, air traffic controller, surveyor, farmer, electrician. They like to work outdoors and to work with tools. They prefer to deal with things rather than with people.

Thinkers

(Investigative-I) These types like jobs such as biologist, chemist, physicist, anthropologist, geologist, medical technologist. They are task-oriented and prefer to work alone. They enjoy solving abstract problems and understanding the physical world.

Creators

(Artistic-A) These types like jobs such as composer, musician, stage director, writer, interior designer, actor/actress. They like to work in artistic settings that offer opportunities for self-expression.

Helpers

(Social-S) These types like jobs such as teacher, clergy, counselor, nurse, personnel director, speech therapist. They are sociable, responsible, and concerned with the welfare of others. They have little interest in machinery or physical skills.

Persuaders

(Enterprising-E) These types like jobs such as salesperson, manager, business executive, television producer, sports promoter, buyer. They enjoy leading, speaking, and selling. They are impatient with precise work.

Organizers

(Conventional-C) These types like jobs such as bookkeeper, word processing technician, banker, cost estimator, tax expert. They prefer highly ordered activities, both verbal and numerical, that characterize office work.

The following is a list of some majors that correlate with the six clusters mentioned above. According to the exercise, which major would best suit you?

_____

Realistic

drafting, engineering, forestry, criminal justice, dietician, medical technology

Investigative

biology, chemistry, computer science, economics, electronics, geography, geology, law, paralegal, physics, psychology

Artistic

art, computer animation, design, music, theater

Social

anthropology, child care, communications, dental hygiene, elementary and secondary education, English, foreign languages, history, nursing, sociology, speech

Enterprising

business, finance, law enforcement, marketing, public administration, real estate

Conventional

accounting, computer information systems, court reporting, legal/medical office management, library science, word processing

Information from Sukiennik, Diane, et al., *The Career Fitness Program*, 7th edition, New Jersey: Pearson/Prentice Hall, 2004, pp. 15, 18, 75–77

Cause and Effect Pattern

In a **cause-and-effect** relationship, one event or condition causes another. The second event is the effect or result of the first. Watch for the transition word *because*. It often signals that a cause-and-effect relationship is being explained.

Read the following anecdote and underline the cause-and-effect relationships. Do you think the incident described really happened?

A Green Snake

A couple in Sweetwater, Texas, had a lot of outdoor potted plants. During a recent cold spell, the wife decided to bring them indoors to protect them from a possible freeze. It turned out that a green garden snake was hidden in one of the plants. When it had warmed up, it slithered out, and the wife saw it go under the sofa. Consequently, the wife screamed very loudly.

The husband ran into the living room to see what the problem was. Because his wife told him there was a snake under the sofa, he got down on the floor on his hands and knees to look for it. The family dog came and nosed him on the rear. As a result, he thought the snake had bitten him, and he fainted.

Since his wife thought he'd had a heart attack, she called 911. An ambulance arrived, and the attendants loaded him on a stretcher.

About that time, the snake came out from under the sofa, and one of the emergency medical technicians saw it and in reaction dropped his end of the stretcher. That's when the husband broke his leg and why he went to the hospital.

The wife still had the problem of the snake in the house, so she called a neighbor. He volunteered to capture the snake. Armed with a rolled-up newspaper, he began poking under the sofa. Unable to locate the snake, he concluded the snake had fled. Reassured, the wife sat down on the sofa. But as her hand dangled in between the cushions, she felt the snake wriggling around. As a result, she screamed and fainted, and the snake rushed back under the sofa.

The neighbor seeing her lying there tried to use CPR to revive her. The neighbor's wife, who had just returned from grocery shopping, saw her husband's mouth on the woman's mouth, and this led to her hitting him on the back of the head with a bag of groceries. An ambulance was called to determine whether he needed stitches.

The ambulance arrived and took away the neighbor and his sobbing wife. Just then the green snake crawled out from under the couch, and, as a result, one of the policemen drew his gun and fired at it. He missed the snake and hit the leg of the end table next to the sofa. The table fell over and the lamp on it shattered. The bulb broke and started a fire in the drapes.

The fire quickly spread from the drapes to the walls until the whole house was ablaze. For this reason, neighbors called the fire department. The speeding fire engine started raising the ladder when it was halfway down the street. The ladder tore out the overhead wires and disconnected telephone lines in a ten-square city block.

Time passed.

Power was restored, both men were discharged from the hospital, the house was re-built, and all was right with the world!

P. S. This incident helps explain why nobody in Sweetwater brings outside plants indoors.

Do you think this incident really occurred as described?

probably not

Exercise 3: Cause and Effect

Directions: Rewrite the following sentences using the transition word *because*. Then write in the cause and effect of each event on the lines provided.

Example: Marcus couldn't change the tire on his car because he had broken his arm.

Cause: Marcus had broken his arm.

Effect: He couldn't change the tire.

1. Ford Motor Company is going to close 14 factories. Many people will lose their jobs.

   Many people will lose their jobs because Ford Motor Company is going to close

   14 factories.

   Cause: closing factories

   Effect: loss of jobs

2. You did not do your household chores. I am very angry.

   I am very angry because you did not do your household chores.

   Cause: didn't do chores

   Effect: I'm angry.

3. Luis studied with a tutor every day for three months. He passed his GED.

   Because Luis studied with a tutor every day for three months, he passed his

   GED.

   Cause: studied with a tutor

   Effect: passed GED

4. The hurricane's storm surge was very powerful. Many people lost their homes.

   Because the hurricane's storm surge was very powerful, many people lost their

   homes.

   Cause: powerful storm surge

   Effect: homes lost

5. He failed to separate his red sweatshirt from his white T-shirts. All of his clothes turned pink in the wash.

Because he failed to separate his red sweatshirt from his white T-shirts, all of his clothes turned pink.

Cause: didn't separate clothes

Effect: clothes turned pink

6. Caroline lost 20 pounds when she stopped eating junk food and started exercising.

Caroline lost 20 pounds because she stopped eating junk food and started exercising.

Cause: stopping eating junk food, started exercising

Effect: lost 20 pounds

7. He stayed out past his curfew and his parents grounded him.

Because he stayed out past his curfew, his parents grounded him.

Cause: stayed out past his curfew

Effect: got grounded

8. Kevin called the tow truck when his car wouldn't start.

Kevin called the tow truck because his car wouldn't start.

Cause: car wouldn't start

Effect: called tow truck

Exercise 4: Cause and Effect

How does the cartoon on the next page illustrate a cause-and-effect relationship?

Because Jon stuffed a breadstick up his nose, his date was a disaster.

GARFIELD © Paws, Inc. Reprinted with permission of Universal Press Syndicate. All rights reserved.

Comparison and Contrast Pattern

When you **compare** two things, you show the similarities between them. When you **contrast** two things, you highlight the differences between them. Sometimes a writer both compares (tells the similarities) and contrasts (tells the differences) at the same time. In the paragraphs that follow from *The Meaning of Sports*, the author compares and contrasts war to the sport of football. Can you find the similarities and differences? Look for the following comparison and contrast transition words: *and, both, just as, like, but, yet.*

"Pro football is like nuclear warfare. There are no winners, only survivors."

—Frank Gifford

War involves the organized, deliberate use of force to attain a goal, often the control of territory. And so does football. At the heart of every football game are violent physical encounters between and among players on the opposing teams. The offensive team blocks the defensive side, trying to clear the way for the teammate carrying the ball or to allow time for their quarterback to throw a forward pass. In football, the goal of the defense is to knock to the ground the offensive player in possession of the ball.

Like opposing armies, football teams seek to conquer and defend territory. Each half of the field is said to be the "property" of the team defending the goal at its end. A touchdown is the method of scoring with the highest value, and thus roughly corresponds to the capture of an important city in war.

Just as war is composed of a series of battles, so a football game consists of a series of individual plays. Like most battles, football plays have a beginning and an end, after which the outcome can be assessed.

Football and war have yet another common feature: Both are dangerous. Injuries to football players are normal byproducts of the game. And of course, injuries in war are commonplace.

Of course, football games are less lethal versions of battles. And while warfare is among the oldest of human institutions, football is recent. Furthermore, war is a full-time year-round undertaking but football is played only during the fall and winter.

Michael Mandelbaum, *The Meaning of Sports*, New York: Public Affairs, 2004, p. 128

Exercise 5: Similarities and Differences

Directions: List five ways in which the author of the above passage indicates that football and war are alike (similar) and five ways in which he suggests they are different. Answers will vary.

Similarities	Differences
1. Both are organized.	Football uses a ball.
2. Both have deliberate use of force.	Football has touchdowns.
3. Both have assessment at the end.	War is year-round.
4. Both have a series of plays/battles.	Football is recent.
5. Both are dangerous.	Football is less lethal.

Exercise 6: Comparing

Directions: For each pair of items below, complete the sentence by telling how the items are alike.

1. A fox and a dog are both animals, have four legs, have fur.

2. A peach and an apricot are both fruits.

3. A car and a pair of skates have four wheels.

4. A guitar and a bird both make music and song.

5. An auditorium and a gymnasium both hold people.

Exercise 7: Comparing and Contrasting

Directions: Each sentence below compares two items, or shows how they are alike. On the line provided, write a sentence that contrasts the two items, or shows how they are different.

1. A cranberry is similar to a cherry in color. However, <u>a cranberry is</u>

   <u>smaller.</u>

2. Coffee and milk are both liquids. However, <u>they have different colors</u>

   <u>and different tastes.</u>

3. A committee and a mob are both composed of people. However,

   <u>a committee is organized and a mob is unruly.</u>

4. A pencil and a computer both enable someone to write. However,

   <u>a computer can store information.</u>

5. A whisper and a yell are both ways to communicate. However,

   <u>a whisper is soft and a yell is loud.</u>

6. A rhinestone and a diamond can both be made into earrings.

   However, <u>a diamond is harder than a rhinestone.</u>

7. A flower and a tree are both plants. However, <u>a tree has a trunk and a</u>

   <u>flower has a stem.</u>

8. An A and a D are both letter grades. However, <u>an A is a higher grade</u>

   <u>than a D.</u>

9. A triangle and a square are both geometric forms. However, <u>a triangle has</u>

   <u>three sides and a square has four.</u>

10. An eagle and a robin are both birds. However, <u>an eagle is larger than a</u>

    <u>robin.</u>

READING

"The care and feeding of heroes is solely in the hands of the public. Not all winners are heroes."

GETTING FOCUSED

In this selection, Erma Bombeck uses comparison and contrast to illustrate her opinion on what makes a hero and who should be called one. In the first paragraph of *Heroes*, Bombeck refers to the 1981 Wimbledon Tournament in which John McEnroe, frequently referred to as McNasty, beat Bjorn Borg.

Copyright © 2009 by The McGraw-Hill Companies, Inc.

READING *continued*

BIO-SKETCH

Erma Bombeck died in 1996 at age 69 after a kidney transplant. For over 30 years, she wrote a widely syndicated humor column. In addition, she is the author of numerous books, including *Eat Less Cottage Cheese and More Ice Cream* and *If Life Is a Bowl of Cherries, What Am I Doing in the Pits?* For years she was referred to as America's Funniest Mother.

TACKLING VOCABULARY

rhetoric   exaggerated language

Mount Rainier   Washington's highest mountain

come to grips with   confront squarely; deal decisively with

HEROES

Erma Bombeck

On the first Saturday of last month, a 22-year-old U.S. tennis player hoisted a silver bowl over his head at Centre Court in Wimbledon.

2   The day before, five blind mountain climbers, a man with an artificial leg, an epileptic, and two deaf adventurers stood atop the snowcapped summit of Mount Rainier.

3   It was a noisy victory for the tennis player, who shared it with thousands of fans, some of whom had slept on the sidewalks outside the club for six nights waiting for tickets.

4   It was a quiet victory for the climbers, who led their own cheering, punctuated by a shout from one of them that echoed on the winds: "There's one for the epileptics!"

5   There was a lot of rhetoric exchanged at Wimbledon regarding "bad calls."

6   At Mount Rainier they learned to live with life's bad calls a long time ago. The first man to reach the mountaintop tore up his artificial leg to get there.

7   Somehow, I see a parallel here that all Americans are going to have to come to grips with. In our search for heroes and heroines, we often lose our perspective.

8   We applaud beauty pageant winners; we ignore the woman without arms who paints pictures with a brush in her teeth. We extol the courage of a man who will sail over 10 cars on a motorcycle; we give no thought (or parking place) to the man who threads his way through life in a world of darkness or silence.

9   The care and feeding of heroes is solely in the hands of the public. Not all winners are heroes. Not all people with disabilities are heroes. "Hero" is a term that should be awarded to those who, given a set of circumstances, will react with courage, dignity, decency, and compassion—people who make us feel better for having seen or touched them.

"Being a hero is about the shortest-lived profession on earth."
—Will Rogers

10 I think the crowds went to the wrong summit and cheered the wrong champion.

"Heroes" by Erma Bombeck is reprinted with permission from the Aaron M. Priest Literary Agency.

▼ COMPREHENSION CHECKUP

1. What is Erma Bombeck's primary purpose in writing this selection?

   to persuade people to reserve the word "hero" for unique individuals

2. If Erma Bombeck was reading this selection orally, her tone of voice

   would probably be serious, critical, angry   .

3. Erma Bombeck compares the quiet victory of the climbers who labored

   without public support to John McEnroe's victory celebrated by thou-

   sands. Who does she think is the real hero? The group of climbers or John

   McEnroe? Why? the climbers because they overcame real hardships to succeed

   _____

4. What are the "bad calls" that John McEnroe complained about? What are

   the "bad calls" that the climbers might have complained about but didn't?

   McEnroe complained about bad calls from the referee. The climbers could have

   complained about their disabilities but didn't.

5. According to Bombeck, we celebrate the feats of a daredevil but give lit-

   tle thought to the accomplishments of a blind person. Do you agree with

   Bombeck that people react this way? Explain your answer. Answers will vary.

   _____

6. According to Bombeck, who decides who the heroes are? _____

   the public does

7. Does Bombeck believe that all popular heroes are real heroes?

   No, she says that not all winners are heroes.

8. According to Bombeck, what traits does a real hero have? <u>courage,</u>

   <u>dignity, decency, compassion</u>

9. List the ways in which the two events discussed in the reading are different.

   Tennis Match: Climbing Mount Ranier:

   <u>the match was noisy</u>   <u>the summit was quiet</u>

   <u>others cheered at the match</u>   <u>the group led their own cheer</u>

   <u>a lot of complaints</u>   <u>few complaints</u>

Vocabulary in Context

Directions: In the blanks below, write the word from the list that best completes the sentence. Use each word only once.

artificial	extol	perspective	solely
compassion	hoisted	punctuated	summit
echoed	parallel	rhetoric	threads

1. If you're tired of sweeping up pine needles, then an <u>artificial</u> Christmas tree may be just what you need.

2. Her scream of fright <u>echoed</u> in the empty house.

3. Positive political ads <u>extol</u> the virtues of particular candidates.

4. He <u>hoisted</u> the young child on his shoulders and galloped around with her.

5. It took the expedition days to reach the <u>summit</u> of the mountain.

6. He was <u>solely</u> to blame for the accident.

7. Around election time, you can expect a lot of empty <u>rhetoric</u> from political commentators.

8. Growing up poor might give you a different <u>perspective</u> from someone who grew up rich.

9. The silence was <u>punctuated</u> by the sound of gunfire.

10. The professor drew a <u>parallel</u> between Winston Churchill and Abraham Lincoln.

11. The president, shaking hands with the people closest to him,
    _____threads_____ his way through the crowd.

12. She felt deep _____compassion_____ for the children who had lost their
    loved ones in the war.

Written Assignment

In the following chapter, you will read a selection about Lance Armstrong. Think about Lance Armstrong and his victories in the Tour de France and his battle against cancer. Do you think Armstrong meets Bombeck's definition of a real hero? Why or why not? Write a paragraph giving your opinion.

Internet Activity

Erma Bombeck, a cancer survivor, raised millions of dollars for cancer research. In addition, she donated the proceeds from one of her books to aid children suffering from cancer. Her donation to the Phoenix Children's Hospital enabled the establishment of a pediatric kidney center. Do some research on Erma Bombeck. Write a paragraph discussing her accomplishments. Do you think she qualifies as a hero?

Steps-in-a-Process and Chronology Pattern

One of the easiest patterns to recognize is time order, also called chronological order, sequence, or steps in a process. In this pattern, ideas are presented in the order in which they occur in time. The **steps-in-a-process** pattern is used to explain the specific steps involved in completing a procedure and the order in which they should be performed. The task could be as simple as making the perfect grilled cheese sandwich or as complex as how to build your own home from scratch. Transition words such as *first, second, third, then, next*, or *finally*, which indicate time order, are often used to introduce the different steps in a process, as it is usually important that they occur in a certain sequence.

    Chronological order is used in reporting news stories or historical events. It is often found in textbooks and reference books such as encyclopedias.

    In the excerpt that follows, Dennis Coon uses the step-by-step pattern to explain his method for "catching a dream."

HOW TO CATCH A DREAM

1. First, before going to sleep, plan to remember your dreams. Keep a pen and paper or a tape recorder beside your bed.

2. If possible, arrange to awaken gradually without an alarm. Natural awakening almost always follows soon after a REM period.

3. If you rarely remember your dreams, you may want to set an alarm clock to go off an hour before you usually awaken. Although less desirable than awakening naturally, this may let you catch a dream.

4. Upon awakening, lie still and review the dream images with your eyes closed. Try to recall as many details as possible.

5. If you can, make your first dream record (whether by writing or by tape) with your eyes closed. Opening your eyes will disrupt dream recall.

6. Review the dream again and record as many additional details as you can remember. Dream memories disappear quickly. Be sure to describe feelings as well as the plot, characters, and actions of the dream.

7. Finally, put your dreams into a permanent dream diary. Keep dreams in chronological order and review them periodically. This procedure will reveal recurrent themes, conflicts, and emotions. It almost always produces valuable insights.

Coon, Dennis, *Introduction to Psychology*, 8th edition, Belmont, CA: Thomson Wadsworth, 2006, pp. 253–254

Exercise 8: Steps in a Process—Changing a Tire

Directions: The following is meant to be an account of someone's experience changing a flat tire, but the steps are out of order. Use the transition words in the sentences and other clues to put it together in the correct sequence, numbering the steps in order from first (1) to last (12).

_____11_____ Then she lowered the rear of the car to the ground.

_____1_____ Clunk! Clunk! Clunk!

_____8_____ Off came the lug nuts and the flat tire.

_____12_____ Finally, after putting the tools and the bad tire into the trunk, Rosalba headed for a garage to have the tire repaired.

_____3_____ She stopped the car in a safe place well off the road and began the task of changing the tire.

_____2_____ Rosalba knew from that sound that she had a flat tire.

_____10_____ Then she replaced and hand-tightened the lug nuts and replaced the hub cap.

_____6_____ Next, she went to work on the right rear tire, which was completely deflated.

_____5_____ Second, for safety, she placed the block in front of the front wheels.

_____9_____ She lifted and pushed the spare tire into place.

_____7_____ She removed the hub cap, loosened the lug nuts with the lug wrench, and carefully jacked the rear wheels of the car off the ground.

_____4_____ First, she opened her trunk and removed a jack, a lug wrench, a spare tire, and a block.

Exercise 9: Chronological Order

Directions: Number the events listed below in the correct time order, numbering the steps in order from first (1) to last (10).

___5___ In 1919, the Indian Packing Company provided $500 for uniforms and equipment and allowed the team to use the company field for practices. This is considered to be the beginning of the Green Bay Packers. That first year the Packers were 10-1.

___3___ The Arizona Cardinals began as the Morgan Athletic Club. The team stayed in Chicago for 62 years before moving to St. Louis, and then under the ownership of William Bidwill, to Phoenix, Arizona. Because the team was started in 1899, it is considered to be the oldest continuing professional football team.

___1___ In 1892, Pittsburgh, Pennsylvania, was the scene of an intense rivalry between two local athletic clubs, the Pittsburgh Athletic Club (P.A.C.) and the Allegheny Athletic Association (A.A.A). There was only one paid player on the field, William Heffelfinger, who received $500 from the A.A.A., which won by a score of 4-0.

___6___ In 1920, the American Professional Football Association was formed with eleven teams pledging $100 as a membership fee. (No team ever paid the fee.)

___8___ On January 12, 1969, an AFL team won the Super Bowl for the first time when "Broadway Joe" Namath's New York Jets beat the Baltimore Colts 16-7.

___4___ In 1906, Dan (Bullet) Riley made football history by becoming the first man to ever catch a forward pass in a professional football game.

___2___ The first football game featuring all professionals was played in Latrobe, Pennsylvania, in 1897.

___9___ Dallas won their third Super Bowl title when they defeated the Pittsburgh Steelers in Super Bowl XXX at Sun Devil Stadium in Tempe, Arizona, on January 28, 1996.

___10___ In 2001, following the September 11 terrorist attacks, President Bush designated Super Bowl XXXVI as a "National Security Event." All security for the game was supervised by the Secret Service.

___7___ The Bears and the Giants played the first championship game in Chicago in 1933. The Bears were victorious with a score of 23-21.

Definition and Example Pattern

A paragraph of **definition** will clarify or explain a key term or concept. Definitions can be developed by providing dictionary meanings or personal meanings. They can also be developed by means of **examples** or by comparing or contrasting the term being defined to other words. Definitions are often introduced by the following transition words: *means, is called, refers to,* or *derives from.* The definition and example pattern is frequently found in textbooks where authors are trying to introduce the reader to the key terminology in a specific subject area.

In the following textbook excerpt, the writer defines the term *hypertension.*

> **Hypertension** occurs when blood moves through the arteries at a higher presfsure than normal. Also called high blood pressure, hypertension is sometimes called a silent killer because it may not be detected until it has caused a heart attack, stroke, or even kidney failure. Hypertension is present when the systolic blood pressure is 140 or greater or the diastolic blood pressure is 90 or greater.

Mader, Sylvia S., *Human Biology,* 9th edition, New York: McGraw-Hill, 2006, p. 88

Exercise 10: Definition and Examples

Directions: For each word, choose the correct definition from the list on the right and place the letter on the top line. Then choose the specific examples that illustrate the definition from the list and write that letter on the bottom line. The first one is done for you.

1. **sport**

    ___i___   a. 1, 2, 3

    ___l___   b. one of the positive or negative numbers

2. **abode**   c. Hawaii, Maui, Oahu, Kauai

    ___h___   d. dwelling, home, residence

    ___d___   e. perch, carp, salmon

    f. an article of dress that completes or enhances an outfit

3. **accessory**   g. a tract of land completely surrounded by water

    ___f___   h. a place in which a person resides

    ___j___   i. any athletic activity requiring skill or physical prowess

4. **fish**   j. gloves, earrings, hat

    ___k___   k. a cold-blooded aquatic vertebrate having fins and gills

    ___e___   l. archery, tennis, baseball

5. **integer**

    _____ b _____

    _____ a _____

6. **island**

    _____ g _____

    _____ c _____

Exercise 11: More Definition Practice

Directions: The paragraph below defines the word *malapropism*. Read the paragraph and then study the cartoon that follows. How many malapropisms can you identify? Try for at least ten. Hint: "The Creped Crusader" should read "The Caped Crusader."

   Malapropism is derived from the French phrase *mal a propos*, meaning "out of place." A malapropism is an incorrect usage of a word by substituting a similar sounding word with a different meaning. The effect is often humorous. In his 1775 comedy, *The Rivals*, playwright Richard Sheridan introduced a humorous character by the name of Mrs. Malaprop. The self-educated Mrs. Malaprop was always using words incorrectly.

Frank and Ernest

© 1999 Thaves. Reprinted with permission. Newspaper dist. by NEA, Inc.

1. hi-trek _____

2. flaptop commuter _____

3. inflammation age _____

4. windex 98 _____

5. knee mail _____

6. smell checker _____

7. food processor _____

8. smurf the internet _____

9. cider space _____

10. carpool tunnel syndrome, loser friendly _____

Examples (illustrations) are often provided to help a reader better understand statements, general ideas, and unfamiliar words. A paragraph of examples usually gives the main idea and then provides specific concrete examples to support the main idea. *For example* and *for instance* are common transition words used to introduce this pattern. Here is a definition of the term *yogiisms*, followed by examples that illustrate exactly what they are.

Yogiisms are statements made by Yogi Berra, who, besides being a baseball player, was also famous for fracturing the English language. The following are some of the best-known examples of Yogi's unique speaking style.

"It ain't over till it's over."

This quotation is the best-known Yogiism. Yogi was referring to the 1973 National League pennant race.

"I want to thank you for making this day necessary."

This was said at Yogi Berra Day in St. Louis in 1947. It is supposed to be the first Yogiism. Yogi apparently asked a teammate to write a short speech for him, and when he delivered the speech he misspoke, replacing the word *possible* with *necessary*.

"When you get to a fork in the road, take it."

Berra insists that this is part of some driving directions to his house. In his hometown of Montclair, New Jersey, there is a fork in the road, but either way you take will direct you to his house. Many people believe the quotation means that when you find a challenge, overcome it.

"I never said half the things I said."

Yogi can't even escape creating a Yogiism in his disclaimer for not creating all of the Yogiisms. He was pointing out that he didn't say everything that people think he said.

"Tomorrow night is another day."

Yogi said this when his team lost a night game. He knew they would play better the following day.

Some additional examples of Yogi quotes:

"You can observe a lot by watching."
"If you don't know where you're going, you'll wind up somewhere else."

Yogi has also become famous in the world of advertisements. Television commercials have taken advantage of Yogi's fame in speaking and have scripted some Yogiisms for him to say.

For instance, in an Entenmann's commercial, Yogi says, "You can taste how good these cookies are just by eating them" and "This box is always open until it's closed."

And in an AFLAC commercial, Yogi says, "If you get hurt and miss work, it won't hurt to miss work. And they give you cash, which is just as good as money."

Exercise 12: Identifying Patterns of Organization and Transition Words

Directions: This is an excerpt from *A Fashionable History of Makeup and Body Decoration*. Read each section looking for transitional words and the patterns of organization they are associated with and then answer the questions that follow.

A FASHIONABLE HISTORY OF MAKEUP AND BODY DECORATION

A. The Eyes Have It

Eye paint dates back to antiquity and originally may have been believed to have magical properties that protected the eyes. By ancient Egyptian times, however, vanity had taken over and eye makeup was used by both men and women as a beauty aid. Egyptians used powdered minerals in their eye makeup. Eyes were either outlined in kohl, made from black galena (a lead ore), or with green malachite (a copper ore).

2   Ideas about beauty changed over the centuries, with some strange practices coming and going. Queen Elizabeth I (1533–1603) used drops of the nightshade plant, which is a deadly poison, to make her pupils larger and her eyes appear brighter. Fashionable women continued this practice for centuries afterward.

3   In the 18th century, stylish women shaved off their eyebrows and applied artificial ones made from mouse skin! By the 19th century, makeup was frowned upon, and it was only worn in an obvious way by the kind of women considered disreputable, such as actresses and prostitutes.

1. In paragraph 1, what transition word is used to indicate a contrast?

however

_____ b _____ 2. In paragraph 3, the use of the words *18th century* and *19th century* indicate
     a. definition.
     b. chronological order.
     c. cause and effect.

_____ a _____ 3. In paragraph 3, the phrase *such as* indicates
     a. example.
     b. comparison.
     c. contrast.

B. Lovely Lips

Lip paint is another beauty aid that dates back to ancient times. Neatly packaged lipsticks weren't available in those days, of course, and cosmetics were made by the wearer or a servant. The ancient Egyptians ground up a mineral called red ochre, while the Greeks mashed up seaweed and mulberries.

2   Bold use of lip paint has gone in and out of vogue over the years. Roman women loved bright lips, for example, but in the Middle Ages a more natural look was preferred.

3   In 17th- and 18th-century Europe, the nobility of both sexes applied lip paint as a mark of their social rank. Lip paints were often made from colored plaster of Paris. After the French Revolution, however, Europe was swept by a new passion for simplicity in clothing and general appearance. Men stopped wearing lip paint, and there was a sharp decline in its use by women that continued throughout much of the Victorian era.

4   Although during much of the 19th century makeup was frowned upon, from the 1890s onward, suffragettes campaigning for votes for women sometimes adopted red lip paint. It was a symbol of their defiance of traditional ideas about acceptable female behavior.

5   In the early 20th century, discreet lip paint was again being used by society ladies. Lip crayons had been around since the 16th century, but most lip paints came in pots, were greasy, and needed a skillful hand to apply them. In 1915, the first lipstick in a sliding metal tube was patented. This easy-to-apply product was an immediate success and was soon being manufactured in a wide range of red tints. By the 1920s, the wearing of lipstick was commonplace among stylish women, and has remained so until the present day.

4. What transition words are used in paragraph 2?

for example, but _____

5. In paragraph 3, what transition word is used to indicate contrast?

however _____

6. In paragraph 4, what transition word is used to indicate contrast?

although _____

7. In paragraph 5, what transition word is used to indicate contrast?

but

8. The overall pattern of organization for paragraphs 3 to 5 is chronological

order. List four transition words or terms that indicate chronological

order. after, 19th, 1890s, early 20th, 16th, 1915, 1920s, present

C. The Painted Face

In the Western world up until the early 20th century, pale skin was a sign of wealth and status. Suntans were abhorred because they were associated with outdoor work and lower status. The wealthy painted and powdered their faces the palest shades of white.

2   Recipes for whitening the skin and hiding blemishes have been around since Roman times. Although some ingredients were harmless, others such as powdered white lead were definitely dangerous. Elizabeth I, for instance, whitened her face with a thick layer of toxic, lead-based paint. Mild lead poisoning caused headaches, nausea, and stomach cramps. The worst cases ended in insanity, paralysis, or death.

3   When makeup fell from favor in the 19th century, the use of harmful products such as white lead declined. When makeup came back in vogue in the early 20th century, a more natural look was in and women began wearing flesh-toned cosmetics.

4   Throughout history, face paints have long been used in war—either as a very visible message of identity or to camouflage soldiers, helping them blend into the background. The Celtic peoples of ancient Britain made a blue paint from the leaves of the woad plant, a kind of mustard. They used it to make themselves look even more terrifying in battle, as seen on Mel Gibson in the movie *Braveheart* (1995).

9. In paragraph 1, what transition word is used to indicate cause and effect?

because

10. In paragraph 2, what transition phrases are used to indicate example?

such as, for instance

11. In paragraph 3, what transition phrase is used to indicate example?

such as

12. What reasons are given for the use of face paint in war?

a. as a message of identity _____

b. to camouflage soldiers _____

c. to look more terrifying _____

D. Body Art

In India and North Africa, henna, a plant dye, has been used for centuries to create elaborate body art for weddings and other ceremonies. Henna is now often used for temporary tattoos.

2   Scarring and piercing have also been practiced for centuries. Scarring techniques differed, but they often involved scratching patterns into the skin with a sharp object such as a stone or a shell. Wood ash was then rubbed into the cuts, leaving behind raised bumps and ridges after the skin healed.

3   Body piercing is far more widespread than scarring, and it has been done on virtually every part of the body. Through the pierced holes, ornaments made from metal, bone, shell, or glass are inserted. Lip plugs were worn by the Maya of ancient Mexico and the Inuit of Alaska. Nose rings have long been traditional in India, Pakistan, and many other countries. Piercing the septum, or center of the nose, was most common among warrior cultures. Nose plugs can be almost an inch thick.

4   In the 1980s, when people took up multiple ear-piercing, they revived a practice that has been around for 4,000 years. Today, in addition to ears, it is not uncommon to see piercing done on the nose, eyebrow, lip, tongue, and navel.

5   Tattooing, a cross between painting and scarring, is another permanent form of body art. Patterns are made by pricking tiny holes, through which colored pigments seep into the skin. In the past, tattoos were done by hand, using a sharp stick, bone, or needle. In the early 1890s, the practice was revolutionized by the invention of the electric tattoo machine. Modern tattoo machines can make as many as 3,000 tiny holes per minute.

6   Like other forms of body art, tattoos have been used in different ways by different cultures. Sometimes tattooing is done purely to decorate the body, and other times to communicate social status. One of the oldest known examples of tattooed skin was found on the body of Utzi the Iceman, who died more than 5,200 years ago in the mountains between Italy and Austria. Tattoos have also been discovered on 4,000-year-old Egyptian mummies.

7   In the West, interest in tattoos was revived by the voyages of Captain James Cook (1728–1779) into the Pacific during the 1760s and 1770s. Because they became fascinated by the customs of the Pacific Islanders, some of Cook's crew had themselves tattooed. This started a trend among sailors.

8   In Japan, tattooing began to flourish as an art form in the 18th century. Inspiration for the elaborate images came from woodcuts and watercolors. Modern tattooists usually plan complex designs on paper first. Then using a stencil, the design is transferred to the skin to guide the tattoo needle.

9   Although common among Western sailors by the early 19th century, tattoos were seen as highly exotic by most landlubbers. Tattooed women and men were

a popular exhibit at fairgrounds and circuses, and people paid money to gasp and stare.

13. In paragraph 2, what transition phrase is used to introduce the sharp

    objects used to scratch patterns into the skin? such as _____

14. What cause-and-effect relationship in paragraph 7 is indicated by the transition *because*? Write the cause and effect below.

    Cause: They became fascinated. _____

    Effect: They got tattooed. _____

15. In paragraph 8, what transition words are used to indicate steps in a

    process? first, then _____

E. The Body Beautiful

In each culture and era, people have had different ideas about beauty. In the West in the late 19th century, for instance, women used corsets and bottom-enlarging bustles to create voluptuous S-shaped curves.

2 In some cultures, the pursuit of the perfect body shape led to more drastic actions. Until the custom was banned in 1911, young girls in well-to-do Chinese families had their feet bound to restrict their growth. In some African and North American communities, the practice of head shaping dates back hundreds of years. For example, the Chinook people of northwestern North America practiced head shaping by strapping their children's heads between wooden planks.

16. In paragraphs 1 and 2, what transition phrases are used to introduce

    examples? for instance, for example _____

F. Tooth and Nail

Many a beauty's smile was marred by rotten or missing teeth before the 19th century, when modern dental science began to develop and people began to understand the causes of tooth decay. In the past, the cheapest solution was to have rotten teeth extracted—an excruciatingly painful business before anesthetics were invented in the 1840s.

2 The first known sets of false teeth were made in Italy around 2,700 years ago, by the Etruscans. The use of dentures had died out by the Middle Ages, however, and when they were reintroduced in the 17th century, only the wealthy could afford them. More ornamental than practical, early dentures often fell out and had to be removed for eating. Early false teeth were carved from animal bone, ivory, or mother-of-pearl, or cast in silver or gold. Human teeth were also used, either pulled from the dead or sold by poor people from their own mouths.

3   Throughout history, clean hands and buffed, filed fingernails have been considered a sign of the leisured upper classes. On the other hand, at times it was also fashionable for the aristocracy to show that they didn't need to work by growing extremely long nails, clearly unsuitable for manual labor. In China, in particular, it was once the custom for noblewomen to grow their nails more than 9 inches long. Sometimes the nails were sheathed in gold or silver to protect them.

17. In paragraph 2, what transition word is used to indicate contrast?

     however

18. In paragraph 3, what transition words are used to indicate contrast?

     on the other hand

G. Hairy Faces

Men's moustaches and beards have come in and out of fashion over the centuries. Ancient Egyptian men were usually clean-shaven. Nevertheless, as part of their royal regalia, pharaohs wore a false beard tied around the chin with a strap.

2   In ancient Greece, in contrast, beards were common until the 5th century B.C.E., after which they were mainly worn only by old men and philosophers to symbolize their freedom from worldly concerns. Roman men were obsessed with having a clean shave. Viking men, on the other hand, wouldn't have been caught dead without a beard.

3   When beards and moustaches were in fashion, men often experimented by altering their shape. For the noblemen of medieval Europe, for instance, a neatly trimmed and waxed forked beard was stylish for many decades.

4   Upturned moustache tips and a goatee beard were all the rage in the first half of the 17th century. As the nineteenth century progressed, luxuriant facial hair came to symbolize the Victorian ideals of seriousness and sobriety. In many religions, full facial hair has long been a sign of piety.

5   Men have often suffered for the sake of a smooth chin. For centuries, the only practical razor was a straight razor or cutthroat (a long blade with a handle), and shaving accidents were a daily hazard. The breakthrough in shaving technology came in 1901, when the American King C. Gillette (1855–1932) patented the first safety razor with a disposable blade. The final step toward facial freedom came in the 1920s with the invention of the electric razor.

A Fashionable History of Makeup and Body Decoration, Raintree, a division of Reed Elsevier, Inc., Chicago, Illinois, 2003

19. In the first two paragraphs, what transition words are used to indicate

     contrast? nevertheless, in contrast, on the other hand

20. In paragraph 3, what example of a beard is given?

     forked beard

21. What pattern of organization is paragraph 5?

   steps in a process

22. What year was the safety razor patented? 1901

23. When was the electric razor invented? 1920s

READING

> *"All Ralston had in mind was a weekend break from*
> *his job at an Aspen mountaineering store."*

GETTING FOCUSED

Many of us have faced problems that offered no easy solutions. In this excerpt from *Between a Rock and a Hard Place*, mountaineer Aron Ralston, facing near-certain death, saves his own life by amputating his right hand and wrist.

BIO-SKETCH

Thomas Fields-Meyer is a writer and associate editor for *People* magazine. In addition to writing for *People* magazine, Vicki Bane is the author *of Dr. Laura: The Unauthorized Biography*. Jason Bane has written for the *St. Louis Post-Dispatch* and *Inside Education* magazine.

TACKLING VOCABULARY

ingenuity   the quality of being clever or resourceful

AWOL   an acronym meaning "absent without official leave." An acronym is a word formed from the first letters of two or more words. The military applies the acronym AWOL to soldiers who leave their military duties without permission

trailhead   the beginning point of a hiking trail

cronies   close friends or associates

Aspen   a ski resort in Colorado

adrenaline   a hormone the body often secretes when a person is under extreme stress. Adrenaline often causes increased heart rate, blood pressure, and cardiac output

gumption   courage

dude   a slang term meaning "person"

THE SURVIVOR

Thomas Fields-Meyer

Climber Aron Ralston lost his arm but saved his life, thanks to luck, guts—and levelheaded ingenuity.

2   Peering down from a helicopter at the Utah desert, Mitch Vetere assumed the worst. Hours earlier, the Emery County Sheriff's department sergeant had been summoned to help search for a hiker missing near Canyonlands National Park. Aron Ralston had been AWOL for five days; that morning a park worker had spotted his truck at a remote trailhead. Says Vetere: "I'm thinking, when you have somebody there that many days, this is going to be a recovery, not a rescue."

3   Vetere didn't know Ralston. The team spent about 90 frustrating minutes in the air scouring the craggy landscape when they suddenly spotted two hikers frantically trying to wave down the chopper—and with them, a man with his right arm in a makeshift sling. As the pilot touched down, Vetere and a sheriff's deputy scrambled toward the man. "He told us, 'I'm the one you're looking for,'" says Vetere, 43.

4   Now people across the globe recognize Ralston, 27, who made headlines for saving his life by severing his right lower arm, crushed by a massive boulder, and escaping to safety. Long before that, though, climbing cronies knew Ralston for the savvy and the stamina that propelled him up Alaska's Mount McKinley and 54 of Colorado's 14,000-ft. peaks, often alone in winter. "I don't think any of us could comprehend what he went through," says Daniel Hadlich, 33, a close friend. "He endured a terrible ordeal and found the strength inside himself to live."

5   All Ralston had in mind was a weekend break from his job at an Aspen mountaineering store. After parking his truck and pedaling his mountain bike 15 miles through Horseshoe Canyon, he briefly joined up with two women he encountered on the trail before heading alone to climb through barren Bluejohn Canyon.

6   Within half an hour, Ralston was descending, without ropes, through a steep "slot" between rock faces in a challenging maneuver that required him to snake over and under boulders that blocked his path. Deep in the slot, where sunlight penetrated for no more than a couple of hours a day, Ralston began to navigate a 10-ft. drop between ledges when a large stone shifted. Ralston had time to pull his left hand away, but his right hand became pinned between the boulder and the side of the slot. "The adrenaline was pumping very, very hard through my body," he would later say at a press conference at the Grand Junction, Colorado, hospital where he was taken for treatment. "It took some good, calm thinking to get myself to calm down and stop throwing myself against the boulder."

7   That was 2:45 on Saturday afternoon, April 26. Ralston knew the situation was dire. A desert rainstorm, common at this time of year, would surely have flash-flooded the canyon, drowning him on the spot. And yet with only a liter of drinking water, Ralston feared dehydration. It wasn't until Tuesday morning, April 28, that friends began to worry in earnest after he didn't show up for work. They began calling law-enforcement offices across Colorado and Utah. Meanwhile, Ralston tried vainly to budge the rock, finally concluding that his only hope was to sever the limb.

8   "I began laying plans for what I would do . . . taking stock of what I had with me. The next five days . . . I spent going through each option I had. . . . On Tuesday morning . . . I took my pocket knife, after preparing myself, went through the motions of applying a tourniquet. I had my biking shorts so I had those to use as absorbent padding. I started sawing back and forth and didn't even break the skin. I couldn't even cut the hair off my arm, the knife was so dull at that point. . . . I drank the last of my water. I settled back in, spent another day. It occurred to me that I might be able to break my bones up at the wrist where they were pinched between the rock and the canyon wall. And upon maneuvering myself for about five minutes, really wrestling with it and applying torque . . . I was able to first snap the radius. And then, within minutes snap the ulna at the wrist. I had the knife out [to cut through the remaining soft tissue] and applied the tourniquet. I felt pain and I coped with it."

9   Once Ralston was found, he boarded the rescue chopper with minimal aid, but blood was dripping out of both ends of the sling he had fashioned from a Camelback water-carrying backpack. During the 12-minute flight to a Moab, Utah, hospital, he requested only water, though all he had eaten in days was part of an Oreo given to him by the hikers he had encountered on the trail. And though he had coolly gathered the gumption to sever his own hand, when Ralston arrived at the ER he was alarmed to see a nurse preparing an injection of morphine. "I heard him say, 'I really don't like needles,'" recalls Vetere. "And I said 'Aron that's the least of your worries right now.'"

10   While Ralston recovered, Terry Mercer, the Utah Highway Patrol chopper pilot, and a crew headed back to find his severed hand. "There was a lot of blood splashed across the rock," said Mercer, who noticed Ralston had rigged ropes and pulleys to try to move the rock. "He had done virtually everything in his power to get out." They also found the three words Ralston carved in the rock with a knife apparently just before he wrenched his own bones apart: "Good Luck now." Three days later a crew of 13 took an hour to hoist the boulder enough to recover the hand, which was taken to a mortuary.

11   Though some criticized Ralston's decision to tackle such dangerous territory alone, search-and-rescue volunteer Bego Gebhart, a veteran climber, feels he understands the young man, now recovering at his parents' Centennial, Colorado, home. "Cutting off his hand will stop him for a month, and that's about it," says Gebhart. "It's the mountain-high thing. If it gets you, you can't stop. What a dude."

"The Survivor" by Thomas Fields-Meyer et al. from *People* magazine, May 26, 2003.

✔ COMPREHENSION CHECKUP

Multiple Choice

Directions: Write the letter of the correct answer on the blank provided.

_____c_____   1. The best title for this selection would be

      a. "The Life of Aaron Ralston."

      b. "Lost in the Wilderness."

      c. "Losing a Hand, Saving a Life."

      d. "Problems with Rock Climbing."

_____d_____   2. Which of the following can you conclude from paragraph 4?
        a. After the incident described, Ralston became well-known.
        b. Ralston's friends thought he had a lot of physical and mental endurance.
        c. Ralston was not afraid to climb solo in the winter months.
        d. All of the above.

_____b_____   3. Mitch Vetere is an employee of
        a. the Canyonlands National Park.
        b. the Emery County Sheriff's department.
        c. a helicopter company.
        d. the Utah Highway Patrol.

_____a_____   4. Which of the following people probably knew Ralston the best?
        a. Daniel Hadlich
        b. Terry Mercer
        c. Bego Gebhart
        d. Mitch Vetere

_____d_____   5. Ralston's situation was dire because
        a. a flash-flood could have drowned him.
        b. he was low on drinking water.
        c. the rock that trapped him would not budge.
        d. all of the above.

True or False

Directions: Indicate whether the statement is true or false by writing **T** or **F** on the blank provided.

_____T_____   1. A person who is *savvy* is shrewd and canny.

_____F_____   2. Ralston had plenty of food and water.

_____F_____   3. Ralston was an inexperienced rock climber.

_____T_____   4. Colorado has more than 50 peaks higher than 14,000 feet.

_____T_____   5. A *makeshift* structure is likely to be temporary.

_____F_____   6. Ralston's story takes place in the middle of winter.

_____T_____   7. Vetere did not expect to see Ralston alive.

_____F_____   8. Ralston used his knife to cut through his bone.

_____T_____   9. A person who is *levelheaded* is sensible.

_____T_____   10. The human body can quickly *dehydrate* in hot, dry weather.

Sequencing

Directions: Number the events in correct time order sequence.

____5____   Terry Mercer finds Ralston's severed hand.

____1____   Ralston encounters two women.

____2____   Ralston navigates a 10-ft. drop.

____4____   A helicopter picks up Ralston and transports him to a hospital.

____3____   Ralston tries to move the boulder.

Vocabulary in Context

Directions: Choose one of the words in the following list to complete each of the sentences below. Use each word only once.

assumed	dire	massive	peering	stamina
barren	frustrating	minimal	pinned	steep

1. No trees or plants could be seen across the _____barren_____ landscape.

2. I gasped for breath as I climbed the _____steep_____ path.

3. King Kong is a _____massive_____ gorilla.

4. If you only do the _____minimal_____ requirements for the class, you are likely to get a poor grade.

5. The wrestler _____pinned_____ his opponent to the mat.

6. My financial situation is _____dire_____: I have no money to pay my rent, and I am about to be evicted from my apartment.

7. It's _____frustrating_____ to be in a dead-end job with no opportunity for advancement.

8. When you told me to meet you at the movie at noon, I _____assumed_____ you would be there.

9. _____Peering_____ down the drain with a flashlight, Tina thought she could see the glint of her wedding ring.

10. Raquel is trying to develop the _____stamina_____ to run in the Rock and Roll Marathon.

Dictionary Usage

Each word below can have different meanings depending on how it is used in a sentence. Referring to a dictionary, write out the correct definition for each of the following words as they are used in this selection. The number in parentheses indicates the paragraph in which the word appears.

1. Scouring (3) searching

2. scrambled (3) climbed or moved quickly using one's hands and feet

3. globe (4) the planet earth; the world

4. navigate (6) to find one's way

5. sling (9) a loop of cloth hanging down from around the neck, for holding an injured arm

6. chopper (9) a helicopter

7. wrenched (10) twisted suddenly or sharply

In Your Own Words

1. How does Aron Ralston illustrate the Jerry Garcia song lyric, "You've got to love the life you live, and live the life you love"?

2. Do you think it's a good idea to publicize risk-taking exploits like Aron Ralston's? Does it encourage dangerous behavior?

3. Did Aron have any responsibility to those who worked to rescue him?

Written Assignment

Since his accident, Aron Ralston has resumed climbing with a specially made prosthetic device that he helped to design. His goal is to solo climb all 59 of the Colorado 14,000-foot peaks in winter. Asked to express his philosophy of life he said, "Our purpose as spiritual beings is to follow our bliss, seek our passions, and live our lives as inspirations to each other." In a few paragraphs, discuss your reactions to Aron's philosophy. What is your personal philosophy?

Internet Activity

For more information and pictures of Bluejohn Canyon, go to the Google search engine, type in "Bluejohn Canyon," and then click on "Images." What did you learn about the canyon from looking at the photos? What additional information, if any, did you find out about Bluejohn Canyon and Aron Ralston's adventure?

READING

"But if we can recognize and reduce our weaknesses, we will feel more in control, and our relationships will improve."

GETTING FOCUSED

Is it easy for someone to get you to do something that you don't really want to do? In the selection that follows, Baldwin divides people into categories: those who can be easily manipulated by others and those who can resist manipulative techniques. He then lists each of the most common types of vulnerabilities.

BIO-SKETCH

Bruce A. Baldwin received his doctorate in psychology from Arizona State University. After a teaching career at the University of North Carolina School of Medicine, Baldwin became head of Direction Dynamics. His stated goal is to teach people effective ways of managing their lives so that they can become successful both personally and professionally. He is also the author of *The Hurry Sickness*.

TACKLING VOCABULARY

reinforced   strengthened; supported

scott-free   no punishment at all

monosyllabic   having only one syllable

STAND UP FOR YOURSELF

Bruce A. Baldwin

"Men trip not on mountains, they stumble on stone."

—Old saying

At a store, five-year-old Sam spots a toy truck. His mother knows the ritual:
2   "Can I have this truck?"
3   "Not now."

4   Sam bursts into tears. "You *never* let me have anything!" he cries. Mrs. Brown bought Tommy a truck."

5   "Oh, all right," his mother says. "Just this once." Sam is used to getting things this way. He has learned to use emotional pressure to manipulate his mother. Because Sam's maneuvers work so well, his manipulative behavior is reinforced—and will be used again.

6   If a child of five can manipulate others by discovering their vulnerabilities, think what a savvy adult can do! This is the way it works:

7   Locating an emotional vulnerability, often by trial and error, the manipulator exploits that knowledge to arouse our emotions and create internal pressure. We lose objectivity and make decisions to appease the one who has created the pressure—rather than do what is right. Then we feel used.

8   But if we can recognize and reduce our weaknesses, we will feel more in control, and our relationships will improve.

9   To help you close up the chinks in *your* emotional armor, consider the following list of vulnerabilities.

10   1. *You feel guilty.* Inducing guilt is the most common form of manipulation. Martyrs are masters of this kind of emotional blackmail.

11   2. *You fear conflict or anger.* Many nonassertive men and women agree to almost anything to avoid a fight. Sometimes a person's early family life was so filled with parental conflict that he or she learned to abhor differences of any kind. Other parents so carefully hide conflict that their children grow up with an unrealistic idea of a "good relationship."

12   3. *You consistently fall for a "hard luck" story.* Some people become expert at the game of "woe is me." They "hook" others into taking care of them. When confronted by this kind of manipulator, ask yourself: "Is this person playing on my emotions? How should I respond to help him help himself?

13   Tears are also a favorite ploy. Children can turn tears off and on like a faucet and use them selectively on the parent who is most vulnerable. (Don't forget that some adults can cry on demand too.)

14   4. *You fall for flattery.* When little Johnny is about to be punished, he professes undying love for his parents with bear hugs and sloppy kisses. His parents melt, and Johnny gets off scott-free. Similar cons are used in adult relationships. Flattery distorts your perception and makes you want to please.

15   5. *You fear disapproval.* It's surprising how many otherwise bright and insightful people can't stand the thought of not being liked by someone. So they give in. These unrealistic adults have never learned that the price for their need for approval is self-respect—and the respect of others.

16   6. *You feel insecure in your role.* In a defined role (as parent, manager or supervisor) you have been given responsibilities, prerogatives and boundaries. Another person, usually one who makes an unfair or unwarranted demand, makes accusations ("You don't like me!") or threats ('I'm going to report you to your supervisor!"). The recipient of the threats becomes insecure in the assigned, defined role and gives in.

17   7. *You can't stand silence.* Here a manipulator's responses are formal, monosyllabic. As time passes, feelings of rejection grow within you. To deal with this power play, avoid participating: pressure the pouter to end the game by going about your business as usual.

18   8. *You're afraid to be different.* At work there is a feeling that if you're different, you're somehow wrong. Two facts should be considered, however. First,

what everyone else is doing isn't necessarily right. Second, when your major frame of reference is other people, you lose the capability to define and live by your own values.

19 How do you reduce your vulnerabilities? Begin by thinking about occasions when you gave in to others or felt used. What feelings were dominant? What did others say or do to arouse those emotions? Who in particular arouses such feelings?

20 Once you pinpoint situations, people and feelings that influence your decisions, you can use two strategies to avoid being manipulated. The best is to resolve the underlying issue that makes you vulnerable. For example, you can define your role in a given situation so that no one can make you insecure. Or you can decide what you owe yourself so that others can't make you feel "selfish."

21 Even if you can't completely stifle your vulnerability, you can still resist manipulation. Define the feelings that lead to your exploitation, and then use them as cues to be cautious. For instance, if you are susceptible to guilt, *any* feelings of guilt should make you wary. Do what is right to avoid being manipulated in spite of your feelings.

22 By outmaneuvering your manipulators, you regain control, and your decisions reflect what's right for you. This feels good, and others learn to respect you. It's interesting that those who are easily manipulated are well-liked but not respected. By working through your emotional weak spots, you create a basis for respect *and* approval.

"Stand up for Yourself" by Bruce Baldwin as published in *PACE* magazine, Piedmont Airlines, February 1987. Reprinted by permission of the author.

COMPREHENSION CHECKUP

1. What is the author's main idea?

   We need to be able to understand our vulnerabilities so that we can resist

   being manipulated.

2. In the example of Sam and his mother, what is the cause-and-effect relationship?

   Cause: Sam bursts into tears.

   Effect: His mother buys Sam a toy truck.

3. Baldwin writes, "If a child of five can manipulate others by discovering their vulnerabilities, think what a savvy adult can do!" Rewrite this sentence using your own words.

   If a 5-year-old can get other people to do what he or she wants by finding

   out what their weak areas are, imagine what a clever adult is capable of.

4. In paragraph 7, Baldwin describes the process that manipulators use to get us to give them what they want. Explain the process in your own words.

   The manipulator finds our weak spots and exploits them. We no longer do

   what we think is right and instead do anything to get the other person to

   stop making us feel uncomfortable.

5. In paragraph 8, what does the transition word *but* signal?

   In contrast, on the other hand—it doesn't have to be this way.

6. Give an example of four of the eight types of vulnerabilities listed.
   Examples will vary.

   a. _____

   _____

   b. _____

   _____

   c. _____

   _____

   d. _____

   _____

Vocabulary in Context

Directions: Choose the best definition for the italicized word, and write the appropriate answer letter on the blank.

___c___ 1. His mother knows the *ritual* (paragraph 1)

   a. ceremony

   b. religious law or custom

   c. repeated act; routine

___b___ 2. his *manipulative* behavior is reinforced (paragraph 5)

   a. operating with the hands

   b. controlling by unfair means

   c. operating by mechanical means

___a___   3. make decisions to *appease* (paragraph 7)
   a. to calm or pacify
   b. to sacrifice principles
   c. to have an outward aspect

___c___   4. *chinks* in your emotional armor (paragraph 9)
   a. a sharp metallic sound
   b. a narrow beam of light
   c. small cracks or fissures

___a___   5. list of *vulnerabilities* (paragraph 9)
   a. areas open to criticism
   b. relating to the common people
   c. lacking in taste

___b___   6. *abhor* differences of any kind (paragraph 11)
   a. to give up
   b. to hate
   c. to make briefer

___a___   7. *unwarranted* demand (paragraph 16)
   a. inexcusable
   b. not tired
   c. not alert

___b___   8. *stifle* your vulnerability (paragraph 21)
   a. to deprive of oxygen
   b. to stop or curb
   c. to encourage

___a___   9. *susceptible* to guilt (paragraph 21)
   a. lack of ability to resist
   b. to regard with awe
   c. temporarily remove

___c___   10. should make you *wary* (paragraph 21)
   a. declare with certainty
   b. clean
   c. cautious

In Your Own Words

1. Do you think that children can act as if they are helpless to manipulate others? Can adults do the same? Can you give some examples?

2. Do you think that people who appear to be helpless can actually be very controlling?

3. Do you think people who have high self-esteem are less vulnerable to manipulation? Why or why not?

4. What advice would you give to someone who feels manipulated? How can you stop someone from "pulling your strings"?

Written Assignment

1. Study the first example about Sam and the toy truck. Describe his mother's vulnerabilities and how Sam used them to manipulate her. Be specific!

2. Study the list of vulnerabilities provided by Baldwin. Which ones are you especially susceptible to? Write a paragraph describing the "chinks in your emotional armor." Give examples.

Internet Activity

Do some research on self-esteem. Why is self-esteem important? What traits contribute to positive self-esteem?

4 Identifying the Author's Tone and Purpose

It is not so much what you say as the manner in which you say it;

It is not so much the language you use as the tone in which you

   convey it.

"Come here," I sharply said, and the child cowered and wept.

"Come here," I sweetly said, and to my lap he crept.

Words may be mild and fair but the tone may pierce like a dart;

Words may be soft as the summer air but the tone may break my

   heart;

For words come from the mind, grow by study and art—

But tone leaps from the inner self, revealing the state of the heart.

Whether you know it or not, whether you mean it or care,

Gentleness, kindness, love and hate, envy and anger are there.

—Anonymous

The poem above describes the importance of **tone.** The word *tone* refers to the emotional quality of a piece of written material. Just as a speaker's voice can convey a wide range of feelings, so can a writer's voice. Authors vary tone to express their attitude toward a topic. In this way, authors can express an opinion without directly stating it.

Authors have a **purpose** in mind when they compose a piece of writing. They want their written work to have a certain effect on the people who are going to read it, their **audience.** In general, authors write for the purpose of informing, entertaining, or persuading.

An author's purpose will affect his or her choice of tone. An author writing to entertain might choose a humorous or ironic tone.

An author writing to inform might choose a matter-of-fact tone. An author writing to persuade might choose an alarmed or angry tone.

You can't fully understand the meaning of a piece of writing without taking into account the author's tone and purpose.

Do you think the author's purpose for the poem is to inform, entertain, or persuade?

IDENTIFYING TONE

To appreciate the differences in tone that writers can employ, read the following versions of a murder confession. Notice how the words and details chosen by the authors lead to contrasting tones.

"I just shot my husband five times in the chest with this .357 Magnum." (*Tone:* matter-of-fact, objective)

"How could I ever have killed him? I can't believe I did that!" (*Tone:* surprised)

"Oh, my God. I've murdered my husband. How can I ever be forgiven for this dreadful deed?" (*Tone:* regretful)

"That dirty rat. He's had it coming for years. I'm glad I finally had the nerve to do it." (*Tone:* revengeful)

Langan, John, *Improving Reading Comprehension Skills*, Townsend Press, 1992, p. 308

Here is a list of words that are sometimes used to describe tone. A brief definition is provided for each.

Tone Words

admiring   (*respecting*)
alarmed   (*suddenly afraid*)
amused   (*entertained*)
angry   (*showing strong displeasure*)
arrogant   (*feeling superior*)
bitter   (*extremely resentful*)
caring   (*showing worry or concern*)
charming   (*very pleasing*)
cheerful   (*happy*)
confused   (*bewildered*)
courteous   (*polite; thoughtful of others*)
critical   (*disapproving*)

cruel   (*causing great pain*)
cynical   (*doubting that people are ever sincere, honest, or good*)
depressed   (*gloomy*)
excited   (*stirred up*)
friendly   (*liking and trusting people*)
humorous   (*funny or amusing*)
ironic   (*meaning the opposite of what is expected or said*)
loving   (*warmly affectionate*)
objective   (*neutral, matter-of-fact*)
optimistic   (*looking on the bright side*)
peevish   (*cross or irritable*)
pessimistic   (*expecting the worst*)
regretful   (*full of sorrow over something that happened, that one did*)
revengeful   (*feeling or showing a desire to get even*)
sarcastic   (*mocking*)
self-pitying   (*feeling sorry for oneself*)
sentimental   (*having tender, gentle feelings*)
serious   (*not joking or fooling around*)
solemn   (*very serious*)
surprised   (*struck by a sudden feeling of wonder by something unexpected*)
tragic   (*involving death, grief, or destruction*)
vindictive   (*wanting to get even*)
whiny   (*complaining or begging*)
witty   (*clever in an amusing way*)

Exercise 1: Tone

A. Working with Tone Words

Directions: Match each of the words in the following list with the sentence that best illustrates them.

Example: *pessimistic*   I have always assumed I would die young.

angry	cruel	friendly	sentimental
confused	depressed	humorous	tragic
courteous	excited	pessimistic	vindictive

confused   1. Luz couldn't make up her mind what dress to wear to the party.

depressed   2. After attending the funeral service for her best friend, Cindy came home and cried.

angry   3. Bill gave a nasty look to the driver of the car that cut in front of him.

excited   4. Yumiko's heart started pounding when she heard she had won the lottery.

vindictive   5. When Sara discovered that Karen had ruined her favorite dress, she deliberately broke Karen's favorite vase.

pessimistic   6. Miguel always thinks the worst is going to happen.

tragic   7. After working hard all of his life, Tony was killed by a hit-and-run driver two days before he was to retire.

cruel   8. Cinderella's wicked stepmother did mean and vicious things to her.

sentimental   9. Sue can't get rid of any of the things her children made for her.

humorous   10. While reading the Sunday comics, Zach couldn't stop giggling.

friendly   11. Thanh likes to be with people.

courteous   12. Maria is always polite to both friends and strangers.

B. Synonyms

Directions: Write a synonym for each of the words in Part A of this exercise on the lines below. Answers will vary.

1. bewildered

2. gloomy

3. mad

4. elated

5. vengeful

6. negative

7. disastrous

8. harsh

9. touching

10. funny

11. sociable

12. polite

C. Choosing the Appropriate Tone

Directions: Based on the title, what is the likely tone of the following passage?

serious

Now read the passage and answer the question that follows.

AN EASY EXERCISE TO HELP BUILD MUSCLE STRENGTH IN THE ARMS AND SHOULDERS

For best results do three days a week.

Begin by standing on a comfortable surface where you have plenty of room on each side.

With a five-pound potato sack in each hand, extend your arms straight out from your sides and hold them there as long as you can. Try to reach a full minute, then relax. Each day, you'll find that you can hold this position for just a bit longer.

After a couple of weeks, move up to ten-pound potato sacks. Then fifty-pound potato sacks. And then eventually try to get to where you can lift a one hundred-pound potato sack in each hand and hold your arms straight for more than a full minute.

Once you feel confident at that level, put a potato in each of the sacks.

What is the tone of the passage? humorous

Exercise 2: Tone

Directions: A football team won the NFL championship game for the first time in 30 years. Below are the reactions of some people to this news. Find the word in the list of tone words at the beginning of the chapter that best describes the tone of each of the comments below. Answers will vary. Sample answers provided.

Tone   **Comment**

excited   1. Wow! I can't believe it! What a great day for our city! This is awesome!

admiring   2. The team's owner, manager, and coach have had a lot of influence throughout this season. They all deserve a lot of credit for this victory.

bitter   3. The game was completely unfair. The crowd was hostile and nasty, and they had the advantage of the loudest stadium in the NFL.

surprised 4. What! They won? Are you kidding me? They've played so poorly for so long. I never guessed that this would happen.

sentimental 5. This brings back wonderful memories of when I was a boy. I was just a kid the last time they won. I remember it like it was yesterday.

critical 6. It couldn't have been skill because they don't have that. Their quarterback is a joke. And their running game is nonexistent. The whole thing is puzzling. The other team must have forgotten to show up. It's the only possible explanation for why they won.

objective 7. I think they could be good for a long time. They've got young players and a good organization.

Working with Irony

Irony is the use of words to say something different or even the opposite of what the actual words mean. For example, a person who sees rain pouring down outside might say, "Looks like we're getting a drop or two of rain today." The statement is ironic because both he and the person he's talking to know that it's raining a lot more than one or two drops.

Writers often use irony in a humorous way. But they need to be careful when they do this because irony can easily be misunderstood when the intonation of regular speech is missing. As a result, the reader could misunderstand the writer's real meaning.

What is ironic about the following statement by Mark Twain?

"When I was a boy of fourteen, my father was so ignorant I could hardly stand to have the old man around. But when I got to be twenty-one, I was astonished at how much the old man had learned in seven years."

Exercise 3: Recognizing Irony

Directions: Read each comment below. If the comment involves irony, write **I** (irony) on the line. If it does not involve irony, write **NI** (no irony) on the line.

_I_ 1. The builder was so clever he didn't omit a single mistake in our new home.

_NI_ 2. Even though we had the heaviest rain of the year, our roof didn't leak.

_NI_ 3. Over the Memorial Day weekend, the park is usually crowded with people on picnics.

___I___   4. Demonstrating his usual cheerful, sunny personality, Mike snarled at everyone he met.

___NI___   5. When the policeman heard the sound of the siren, he began stopping traffic to let the emergency vehicle pass.

___I___   6. After trying hard all season, switch hitter Don Adams finally broke the record for most strike-outs in one year.

___NI___   7. Sara is a good nurse who has many grateful patients.

___NI___   8. The November day was so perfect that we decided to go for a walk.

___I___   9. Martha is so well-coordinated that she looks like an elephant crossing a rocky stream.

___I___   10. Our team seems determined to keep its string of glorious defeats unbroken.

___NI___   11. She is such a polite, well-mannered person.

___I___   12. The best substitute for experience is being 16.

___NI___   13. I had a wonderful dinner at my favorite restaurant last night.

___I___   14. My brother's light dinner consisted of a 16-ounce steak, two baked potatoes, a half-gallon of milk, an apple pie, and a quart of ice cream.

___I___   15. "Thanks a lot," said Maria to her son when he offered to help with the dishes just as she was putting away the last one.

Exercise 4: Humor and Irony

Directions: In what way are these signs ironic? Write your answers on the lines provided.

1. Notice in health food shop window: CLOSED DUE TO ILLNESS.

   We expect people in the health food business to be healthy.

   _____

2. Message on a flyer: IF YOU CANNOT READ, THIS FLYER WILL TELL YOU HOW TO GET LESSONS.

   You need to be able to read in order to read the flyer.

   _____

3. On a repair shop window: WE CAN REPAIR ANYTHING.
(PLEASE KNOCK HARD ON THE DOOR. THE BELL DOESN'T
WORK.)

The repair shop should be able to repair its own bell.

What is it about these newspaper headlines that make them humorous?

1. Something Went Wrong in Jet Crash, Expert Says.

Obviously something went wrong or the jet would not have crashed.

2. Police Begin Campaign to Run Down Jaywalkers.

It sounds like the police are going to hit the jaywalkers with their cars.

3. Red Tape Holds Up New Bridge.

It sounds like tape is keeping the bridge from falling. They mean they are "officially"

stalled.

4. Explain the irony in the following cartoon.

The animal rights group is going to be trampled by the animals it is trying

to save.

Satire

Satire is a kind of writing that makes use of ridicule, sarcasm, or irony to create awareness of human weaknesses or foolishness. The author's goal is to bring about change. Almost anything can be satirized, including people, places, and institutions. Because satire often exaggerates and distorts to expose human foolishness, it often has a humorous effect.

Note the following examples on the topic of golf:

"Golf—a good walk spoiled."—Mark Twain

"Long ago when men cursed and beat the ground with sticks, it was called witchcraft! Today it's called golf." —Will Rogers

As you can see, neither author has a favorable opinion of golf.

READING

"Today of course, thanks to the educational efforts of the bottled-water industry, we consumers are terrified of our tap water."

GETTING FOCUSED

The following satire by noted humorist Dave Barry takes on the bottled-water industry. Are consumers getting good value for their money? Or are they getting ripped off?

BIO-SKETCH

Dave Barry, a 1998 winner of the Pulitzer Prize for commentary, is well known for his humorous writing. Although he no longer writes a syndicated column for the *Miami Herald*, he still continues to write novels. Two of his latest books are *Dave Barry's History of the Millenium* and *Secret of Rundoon*.

TACKLING VOCABULARY

hyperactive   unusually or abnormally active

ingest   to take into the body, as food or liquid

dehydrate   to lose body fluids or water

secretions   substances, such as perspiration, that are released from the body

intangible   not able to be touched or grasped; vague

Hindenburg **dirigible disaster**   A *dirigible* is a floating airship that can be steered. The term *dirigible* is most often used as a synonym for a blimp. Today dirigibles or blimps contain helium, a lighter-than-air nonexplosive chemical, but dirigibles used to be filled with hydrogen, which is highly explosive when combined with oxygen. The *Hindenburg* dirigible exploded in 1937 killing 35 people

pristine   having its original purity

impurities   not pure or clean; contaminated

WATER EVERYWHERE BUT NOT A DROP TO DRINK FOR FREE

Dave Barry

Gatorade is now making water. I know this because I saw a Gatorade commercial that asks the intriguing question: "What if Gatorade made water?" (Intriguing answer: Gatorade will charge you a dollar for a small bottle of it.)

2   The commercial features the usual cast of hyperactive Gatorade people, who have to constantly ingest massive quantities of fluids, or they shrivel up like dead toads on hot asphalt. Gatorade people dehydrate rapidly because they are fanatically dedicated to exercise, and as a result, perspiration-wise, they are human fire hydrants. Even when they stand still, sweat gushes from their every pore, so that within seconds they're surrounded by an expanding puddle of their own bodily secretions. People are constantly slipping and falling around them, but the Gatorade people don't notice. That's how dedicated they are.

3   The Gatorade people are similar to the Nike-commercial people, another group of fierce, focused, grunting competitors who give a minimum of 175 percent and would not hesitate to elbow their own grandmother in the teeth if she stood between them and their objective (usually, a ball). The message of these commercials is that Nike people are winners, because they have heart, willpower, and the one "intangible" asset that all true champions possess: severely overpriced sneakers.

4   Here's an intriguing question: What if a Gatorade man married a Nike woman? THAT would be a competitive wedding. The happy couple would race each other down the aisle, the bride gaining a momentary advantage by jamming her bridal bouquet into the groom's eye, then the groom countering by stomping on her bridal train, snapping her head back like a Pez dispenser, while the guests cheered and jumped up and down in their sweat puddles. At the reception, everybody would eat a wedding cake made entirely out of Power Bars, and take turns bench-pressing members of the band. Blood would be shed during the limbo competition.

5   But getting back to my point: Gatorade is now making water. It joins the rapidly growing list of companies, including Coke, Pepsi and (any day now) Yoo-Hoo, getting into the highly profitable, multi-billion-dollar business of making water.

6   Of course, when I say that these companies "make" water, what I mean is that they "do not make" water. There's no need to actually MAKE water, because there's already water all over the planet—water in lakes, water in rivers, water falling from the sky, water in your home plumbing system, water escaping from your home plumbing system causing your ceiling to collapse when you're away on vacation, water just EVERYWHERE.

7   What the bottled-water companies do is get some of this water, put it in bottles, give it a brand name, sell it to consumers, then smack themselves in their corporate foreheads and say, "We can't BELIEVE we're getting away with this! Do you think they'd buy air? How about dirt?"

8   Incredible as it may seem, there was a time, years ago, when people right here in America actually drank the water that came out of their taps. Back then, if you had tried to "brand" water and sell it, people would have laughed and squirted you with garden hoses.

9   Today, of course, thanks to the educational efforts of the bottled-water industry, we consumers are terrified of our tap water, because we know that it contains some of the most deadly substances known to man: chemicals. To cite one example: Bottled-water-industry researchers recently issued an alarming report stating that virtually every sample of tap water they tasted contained large quantities of hydrogen, which is a type of atom believed to have caused the *Hindenburg* dirigible disaster.

10   "We're not saying that people who drink tap water will explode in massive fireballs," assured the researchers. "We're just saying they should avoid open flames."

11   This is why millions of consumers now prefer bottled water, which—we know this, because we have seen it with our own eyes, in commercials— bubbles up from pristine underground mountain springs, and thus does not contain any impurities, unless of course you count worm droppings.

12   I mean, let's face it, underground is where worms live, and very few worm species wear diapers. Also, your mountains are frequented by your mountain goats, which drink from the springs, and if you know anything about goats, you know they drool. "He drools like a goat" is a common mountain expression.

13   But big deal, bottled-water consumers! Ingesting goat saliva and worm poop (which is very low in fat) is a small price to pay for the security of knowing you are drinking water that is backed by the highest scientific quality of marketing campaign, right? So let's raise our glasses of brand-name water in a toast to health and fitness!

14   OK, you Gatorade people, please put your arms back down.

"Water Water Everywhere and Not a Drop for Free" by Dave Barry. Copyright © 2000 Dave Barry. Reprinted by permission of the author, and not to be duplicated without the author's permission.

COMPREHENSION CHECKUP

Multiple Choice

Directions: Write the letter for the correct answer to each question on the lines provided.

___b___   1. Dave Barry's reason in writing this selection was to
   a. argue that beverage companies should be regulated by the federal government.
   b. poke fun at the beverage and bottled-water industry.
   c. persuade readers to avoid drinking bottled water.
   d. persuade Gatorade to discontinue making bottled water.

___c___   2. The topic of this selection is
   a. Gatorade.
   b. the beverage industry.
   c. the selling of bottled water.
   d. our watery planet.

_d_   3. The tone of the selection is
            a. sentimental and sad.
            b. alarmed and fearful.
            c. bitter and resentful.
            d. humorous and witty.

_d_   4. The author mentions all of the following *except*
            a. Gatorade is now making water.
            b. some people are terrified of tap water.
            c. worms live underground.
            d. people drink too much water.

_c_   5. The author would probably agree that
            a. Gatorade sells good bottled water.
            b. tap water might explode because it contains hydrogen.
            c. buying bottled water may be a waste of money.
            d. none of the above.

_c_   6. What did the *Hindenburg* contain to make it rise in
            the air?
            a. water
            b. helium
            c. hydrogen
            d. Gatorade

_d_   7. If Gatorade people "shrivel up like dead toads on hot asphalt,"
            they
            a. become weak.
            b. wither.
            c. are energized.
            d. both a and b.

_c_   8. Saying that Gatorade people "are human fire hydrants" means
            that they
            a. are prepared for emergencies.
            b. are strong and sturdy.
            c. produce a lot of perspiration.
            d. are flushed and clammy.

_a_   9. According to Barry, someone who "drools like a goat"
            a. drools a lot.
            b. drools very little.
            c. needs to drink more fluids.
            d. none of the above.

_a_ 10. In paragraph 3, Barry compares Gatorade people to Nike people by implying that both
   a. are fierce competitors who want to win.
   b. wear overpriced sweat suits.
   c. don't like to be around their grandmothers.
   d. don't like to get dirty.

_d_ 11. When Barry says, "So let's raise our glasses of brand-name water in a toast to health and fitness," he is being
   a. satirical.
   b. sarcastic.
   c. humorous.
   d. all of the above.

True or False

Directions: Indicate whether each statement is true or false by writing **T** or **F** in the space provided.

_F_ 1. The author believes that Nike's sneakers are appropriately priced.

_T_ 2. People in the United States used to drink plain tap water.

_F_ 3. According to the author, Gatorade people are reluctant to exercise.

_T_ 4. "Competitors who give a minimum of 175 percent" is an example of exaggeration.

_T_ 5. Selling bottled water can be highly profitable.

Vocabulary in Context

Directions: In the paragraphs indicated in parentheses, find the words that correctly match each of the definitions below and write them in the spaces provided.

1. arousing curiosity or interest (1)   intriguing

2. large in amount (2)   massive

3. wholly committed; devoted (2)   dedicated

4. a useful and desirable thing (3)   asset

5. purpose; goal (3)   objective

6. unbelievable (8)   incredible

7. If the italicized word is used correctly, write **C** on the line. If it is used incorrectly, write **I** on the line.

____C____ a. Were you so *hyperactive* as a child that you were unable to sit still in class?

____C____ b. It is easy to become *dehydrated* when exercising in the hot summer months.

In Your Own Words

Do you think that it is worth it to buy bottled water? Why or why not?

Written Assignment

What does the author really mean when he refers to the "educational efforts of the bottled-water industry" in paragraph 9?

Internet Activity

The government has not placed many regulations on the bottled-water industry. Some bottled water is not as chemically pure as tap water. Do you think that the government should more closely regulate the selling of bottled water? Now go to the following website and decide whether your opinions about bottled water have changed.

http://www.nrdc.org/water/drinking/nbw.asp

DETERMINING THE AUTHOR'S PURPOSE

Most of the writing you will encounter will fall into one of three categories: to **inform,** to **entertain,** or to **persuade.** To determine the author's purpose, ask yourself the following question: "Why did the author write this?" Look for clues in the title, headings and subheadings, introductory and concluding statements, and source information to answer this question.

Writing to Inform

Writing meant to **inform** is likely to have an objective or matter-of-fact tone. The purpose of informative writing is to explain, instruct, or share knowledge. In presenting information, the author does not care if you agree or disagree. Textbooks are usually written to inform, as are encyclopedias, research articles, and articles in newspapers. The following is an example of a paragraph whose purpose is to inform.

A **quiz** is a brief assessment, usually covering a relatively small amount of material. Although a single quiz usually doesn't count very much, instructors often add quiz scores together, and collectively they can become a significant part of the final course grade. A **test** is a more extensive, more heavily weighted assessment than a quiz, covering more material. An **exam** is the most substantial kind of assessment. Exams are usually weighted quite heavily because they are meant to assess knowledge of the course material covered up to that point.

Feldman, Robert S., *Power Learning*, 3rd edition, p. 125

What clues are given by the author to indicate that the tone is meant to inform?

explains three terms objectively

Writing to Entertain

If the author's purpose is to **entertain,** the tone is often humorous, or ironic, or both. The author may rely on **hyperbole** (exaggeration). Or the author may use **understatement** (saying less about a subject than the reader might expect). The following is an example of a paragraph whose purpose is to entertain.

Dawn reported for her final examination, which consisted entirely of True/False answers. She took her seat in the classroom, stared at the test, and then in a bit of inspiration, took a quarter out of her purse. She started tossing the coin and marking the answer sheet "True" for heads and "False" for tails. Within twenty minutes she was done. During the last few minutes of the exam period, she again frantically started flipping the coin. The instructor, concerned about what she was doing, stopped by her desk and asked if everything was all right. "Oh yes, I'm fine," Dawn said. "I finished the exam a while ago, but I'm going back through and checking my answers."

What clues are given by the author to indicate the tone is meant to entertain?

tone is humorous, reads like a joke

Writing to Persuade

If the author's purpose is to **persuade,** the author is trying to get the reader to view a subject in the same way that he or she does. In this case, we might say the author has "an ax to grind." The author's tone might be one of anger or outrage. Newspaper editorials are written with a persuasive purpose in mind. The following is an example of a paragraph whose purpose is to persuade.

Tests may be the most unpopular part of academic life. Students hate them because they produce fear, anxiety, and a focus on grades instead of learning for learning's sake. However, there's another reason you might dislike tests: You may assume that tests have the power to define your worth as a person. If you do badly on a test, you may be tempted to believe that you've received some fundamental information about yourself from the professor and the college, information that says you're a failure in some significant way. This is a dangerous—and wrong-headed—assumption. If you do badly on a test, it doesn't mean you're a bad person. Or stupid. Or that you'll never do better again, and that your life is ruined. If you don't do well on a test, you're the same person you were before you took the test—no better, no worse. You just did badly on a test. Period.

Feldman, Robert S., *Power Learning*, 3rd edition, p. 123

What clues are given by the author to indicate the tone is meant to persuade?

highly opinionated language _____

Exercise 5: Identifying Purpose

Directions: Label each paragraph according to its general purpose: to inform (**I**), to entertain (**E**), or to persuade (**P**).

1. **Skin Cancer** ___I___

   Three forms of skin cancer exist: basal cell cancer, squamous cell cancer, and melanoma. More than 1 million cases of basal cell and squamous cell cancers occur each year in the United States. Most of these are curable. Melanoma is a less common but more serious form of skin cancer. The most effective way to prevent melanoma is to avoid sun exposure, especially during childhood and adolescence. Recommended ways of achieving this goal, in order of importance, are staying out of the sun during midday (10:00 a.m. to 4:00 p.m.), wearing protective clothing (including a hat to shade the face and neck, long sleeves, and long pants), using sunscreen with a sun protective factor (SPF) of 15 or higher, and wearing sunglasses that offer UV protection.

   Teague, Michael, et al., *Your Health Today*, New York: McGraw-Hill, 2007, p. 613

2. **Proper Skin Care** ___E___

   Your skin's number one enemy is Mister Sun, whom we used to think of as a friend. Remember? Of course we now realize, thanks to advances in scientific knowledge, that Mr. Sun is bombarding us with tiny vicious invisible rays called "ultraviolets" that are slowly heating up the Earth to the point where they may ultimately destroy all life on the planet. And what is worse, they cause *dry skin*.

Even as you read these words, scientists from many nations are working feverishly to develop some practical solution to this problem, such as launching a giant orbiting plastic squeeze tube that would squirt humongous gobs of Clinique number 74 sunblock all over the planet. But for now it's up to you to deal with the problem yourself.

Step One is never go out in the daylight. Your role model here is the vampire community, whose members keep their skin attractively smooth and waxy for thousands of years. Step Two is don't even look at the sun *on television*, or stand in a room with bright wallpaper, or hum "Here comes the Sun," unless you're wearing a layer of UV-blocking cream thick enough to conceal a set of car keys in.

Dave Barry Turns 40, New York: Ballantine, 1990, pp. 38–39

3. Tanning Salons ___P___

Stay away from tanning salons! Despite advertising claims to the contrary, the lights used in tanning parlors are damaging to your skin. Tanning beds and lamps emit mostly UVA radiation, increasing your risk of skin aging and skin cancer. If you *must* have a tan, use sunless self-tanning lotions to achieve that bronze look.

Insel, Paul M., *Core Concepts in Health,* 10th edition, New York: McGraw-Hill, 2006, p. 402

4. Walking ___I___

Walking is generally considered as a lifestyle physical activity and is very effective in promoting metabolic fitness and health benefits. If cardiovascular fitness is desired, walking must be done intensely enough to elevate the heart rate to target zone levels. As people grow older, walking often provides the intensity necessary for building and maintaining cardiovascular fitness. For younger people, walking would have to be quite brisk to promote cardiovascular fitness.

Corbin, Charles B., *Concepts of Fitness and Wellness*, 4th edition, New York: McGraw-Hill, 2002, p. 135

5. Walking Like a Dork ___E___

Walking like a dork has become very popular among older people who used to jog for their health but could no longer afford the orthopedic surgery. The object of dork-walking is to make a simple, everyday act performed by millions of people every day, namely walking, look as complex and strenuous as Olympic pole-vaulting. To do this, you need to wear a special outfit, which includes high-tech color-coordinated shorts and sweat-clothes, headbands, wristbands, a visor, little useless weights for your hands, and special dork-walking shoes that cost as much per pair as round-trip airfare to London.

But the most important thing is your walking technique. You have to move your arms and legs as stiffly as possible and swing them violently forward and back. You'll know you're doing it right when passing motorists laugh so hard that they drive into trees.

Dave Barry Turns 40, New York: Ballantine, 1990, p. 140

6. Stationary Exercise Machine ___E___

Making a pledge of pulmonary well-being means not only getting on one of these things but actually *staying* on it, ideally for a duration long enough to figure out how it works. Begin by entering your age, weight, mother's maiden name, gravitational expansion ratio of molecular digitalization, etc. Then begin pedaling, stair climbing, or getting your shoelace caught in the rotary mechanism and being sucked under the conveyor belt until you are crushed and killed (advanced workout only). When evaluating which device is right for you, I recommend looking only for one that is located in front of a TV.

Zevin, Dan, *The Day I Turned Uncool*, New York: Villard Books, 2002, p. 24

7. Pedestrians ___P___

Take care when you lace up those shoes, because "Yea, you may be walking through the valley of the shadow of death." The fact is, as you cruise around on your Harley humming "Born to Be Wild," you're much safer than you are on a leisurely stroll. When it comes to methods of locomotion, a simple walk is one of the most likely to end in sudden death. When you add it up, pedestrian accidents end the lives of more people than plane, train, and ship accidents combined. So, please remember the lesson from kindergarten: Look both ways when crossing the street. The bottom line: "Yea, though you walk through the valley of the shadow of death, fear not." Just remember to pay attention and don't listen to a radio, tape, or CD on headphones while walking!

Lee, Laura, *100 Most Dangerous Things in Everyday Life and What You Can Do About Them*, New York: Eye Quarto, Inc., 2004, p. 230

8. Pedestrians ___I___

About one in seven motor vehicle deaths involves pedestrians, and more than 80,000 pedestrians are injured each year. The highest rates of death and injury occur among the very young and the elderly. Nearly 45% of pedestrian deaths occur when people cross or enter the roadway between intersections. Alcohol intoxication plays a significant role in up to half of all adult pedestrian fatalities.

Insel, Paul M., *Core Concepts in Health*, 10th edition, New York: McGraw-Hill, 2006, p. 668

Exercise 6: Purpose and Book Covers

Directions: Can you determine an author's purpose by examining the cover of a book? Look at all the available clues on each of the book covers below and on page 255, and then write your answers below each one.

1. *The Wall Street Journal Guide to Understanding Money & Investing*

2. *All Your Worth: The Ultimate Lifetime Money Plan*

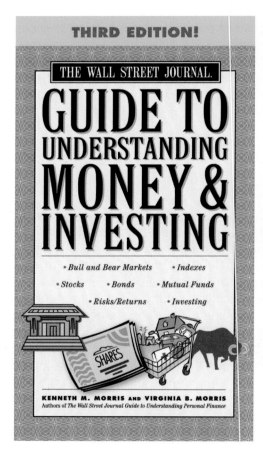

Purpose: inform

Purpose: inform/persuade

3. *Dave Barry's Money Secrets Like: Why Is There a Giant Eyeball on the Dollar?*

4. *Strapped: Why America's 20- and 30-Somethings Can't Get Ahead*

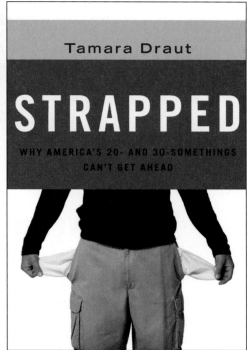

Purpose: entertain _____   Purpose: inform _____

READING

> *"When those men digest my words, they will feel better for it.*
> *Somehow the city will benefit from their happiness."*

GETTING FOCUSED

In this selection, Art Buchwald uses his friend as an example to demonstrate what is wrong with New York City and, of course, the larger society as a whole. Do you think it would make a difference in the world if people were to "practice random acts of kindness" as a popular bumper sticker encourages?

BIO-SKETCH

Art Buchwald, a recipient of the Pulitzer for humorous commentary, was widely known for his long-running column in the *Washington Post*. The author of over 30 books, Buchwald was born in Mt. Vernon, New York, in 1925 and died in Washington, DC, in 2007. His final book is entitled *Too Soon to Say Goodbye*.

TACKLING VOCABULARY

nut   The word *nut* was first used as a slang term for "head" around 1820. Gradually it acquired the meaning of "something wrong in the head."

(*continued*)

The Man from LaMancha   a literary reference to *Don Quixote*, a novel written in the seventeenth century by Miguel Cervantes. The character Don Quixote reads too many romance novels and begins to believe that he is a knight whose destiny lies in reviving the age of chivalry. Quixote is often referred to as "the man from LaMancha."

LOVE AND THE CABBIE

Art Buchwald

"The most exquisite pleasure is giving pleasure to others."

Jean de La Bruyère

I was in New York the other day and rode with a friend in a taxi. When we got out, my friend said to the driver, "Thank you for the ride. You did a superb job of driving."

2   The taxi driver was stunned for a second. Then he said, "Are you a wise guy or something?"

3   "No, my dear man, and I'm not putting you on. I admire the way you keep cool in heavy traffic."

4   "Yeah," the driver said and drove off.

5   "What was that all about?" I asked.

6   "I am trying to bring love back to New York," he said. "I believe it's the only thing that can save the city."

7   "How can one man save New York?"

8   "It's not one man. I believe I have made that taxi driver's day. Suppose he has 20 fares. He's going to be nice to those 20 fares because someone was nice to him. Those fares in turn will be kinder to their employees or shopkeepers or waiters or even their own families. Eventually the goodwill could spread to at least 1,000 people. Now that isn't bad, is it?"

9   "But you're depending on that taxi driver to pass your goodwill to others."

10   "I'm not depending on it," my friend said. "I'm aware that the system isn't foolproof so I might deal with ten different people today. If out of ten I can make three happy, then eventually I can indirectly influence the attitudes of 3,000 more."

11   "It sounds good on paper," I admitted, "but I'm not sure it works in practice."

12   "Nothing is lost if it doesn't. It didn't take any of my time to tell that man he was doing a good job. He neither received a larger tip nor a smaller tip. If it fell on deaf ears, so what? Tomorrow there will be another taxi driver I can try to make happy."

13   "You're some kind of a nut," I said.

14   "That shows how cynical you have become. I have made a study of this. The thing that seems to be lacking, besides money of course, for our postal employees, is that no one tells people who work for the post office what a good job they're doing."

15   "But they're not doing a good job."

16 "They're not doing a good job because they feel no one cares if they do or not. Why shouldn't someone say a kind word to them?"

17 We were walking past a structure in the process of being built and passed five workmen eating their lunch. My friend stopped. "That's a magnificent job you men have done. It must be difficult and dangerous work."

18 The workmen eyed my friend suspiciously.

19 "When will it be finished?"

20 "June," a man grunted.

21 "Ah. That really is impressive. You must all be very proud."

22 We walked away. I said to him, "I haven't seen anyone like you since *The Man from LaMancha*."

23 "When those men digest my words, they will feel better for it. Somehow the city will benefit from their happiness."

24 "But you can't do this all alone!" I protested. "You're just one man."

25 "The most important thing is not to get discouraged. Making people in the city become kind again is not an easy job, but if I can enlist other people in my campaign . . ."

26 "You just winked at a very plain-looking woman," I said.

27 "Yes, I know," he replied. "And if she's a school-teacher, her class will be in for a fantastic day."

"Love and the Cabbie" by Art Buchwald. Reprinted by permission of the Estate of Art Buchwald.

COMPREHENSION CHECKUP

Understanding the Material

Directions: Write the letter for the correct answer to each question on the lines provided.

___c___ 1. Which of the following best expresses Art Buchwald's main idea?
   a. Postal workers are often mistreated by others.
   b. Meanness is a serious problem in the United States today.
   c. Love will be brought back to New York City when people who live there start treating one another with kindness.
   d. The reasons why people are cruel to others are complicated.

___c___ 2. What was the author's purpose in writing this article?
   a. to inform people about life in New York City
   b. to entertain people with amusing stories about New Yorkers
   c. to persuade people to try to be kind to one another
   d. to explain New York to people unfamiliar with it

___d___ 3. The author's tone in this article could be described as
   a. formal.
   b. witty.
   c. humorous.
   d. both b and c.

Vocabulary in Context

Directions: Write the letter for the correct answer to each question on the lines provided.

_b_ 1. The word *superb* as used in paragraph 1 most likely means
   a. proud.
   b. wonderful.
   c. rich.
   d. noble.

_c_ 2. The word *stunned* as used in paragraph 2 most likely means
   a. rendered unconscious.
   b. made dizzy.
   c. shocked or astonished.
   d. bewildered by noise.

_d_ 3. The expression *putting you on* as used in paragraph 3 most likely means
   a. teasing.
   b. misleading.
   c. hinting.
   d. both a and b.

_a_ 4. The word *goodwill* as used in paragraphs 8 and 9 most likely means
   a. a friendly or kindly attitude.
   b. willingness.
   c. common sense.
   d. rewards.

_a_ 5. The phrase *sounds good on paper* as used in paragraph 11 most likely means that something
   a. seems like a good idea.
   b. is written well.
   c. is practical.
   d. none of the above.

_c_ 6. The word *cynical* as used in paragraph 14 most likely means
   a. sarcastic.
   b. sneering.
   c. negative.
   d. optimistic.

___b___ 7. The word *digest* as used in paragraph 23 most likely means

    a. to summarize.

    b. to think over and absorb.

    c. to change food into a form that can be absorbed by the body.

    d. to abridge or shorten.

In Your Own Words

1. What does Buchwald see as the source of the troubles experienced by postal employees? What do you think the expression "going postal" means?

2. What does Buchwald mean by his reference to *The Man from LaMancha*?

Written Assignment

1. Paraphrase this paragraph:

> "I'm not depending on it," my friend said. "I'm aware that the system isn't foolproof so I might deal with ten different people today. If out of ten, I can make three happy, then eventually I can indirectly influence the attitudes of 3,000 more."

2. List five of the author's main ideas.

Internet Activity

Check out some of Art Buchwald's quotations. Type "Art Buchwald quote page" into Google, select several quotes, and then explain what they mean to you.

READING

"But I'm not remarkable; I'm like anybody else, and if you catch me at the wrong time I'm not good for much."

GETTING FOCUSED

In the following excerpt, Lance Armstrong, a cancer survivor, discusses his feelings about being a role model for others fighting the disease. He shares a personal experience in which he thinks he may have been less than inspirational and discusses what he sees as his purpose in life.

BIO-SKETCH

On July 24, 2005, Lance Armstrong ended his professional bicycling career with his seventh consecutive Tour de France victory. Diagnosed with testicular cancer in 1996, Armstrong won his first tour in 1999. Later that year, he wrote the best-selling book *It's Not About the Bike*, which describes his personal struggles with the disease. Because of his full recovery and spectacular achievements, he serves as an inspiration to cancer survivors everywhere. His new goal, as a member of the President's Cancer Panel, is to raise enough

(continued)

funds to help beat the disease. He feels that "it is the responsibility of the cured to help those not so lucky." To date millions of dollars have been raised by the Lance Armstrong Foundation, which aids cancer survivors through the sale of yellow Livestrong bracelets.

TACKLING VOCABULARY

protocol custom, etiquette

epiphany insight into essential meaning of something

IT'S NOT ABOUT THE BIKE

Lance Armstrong

"Growth begins when we start to accept our own weaknesses."

—Jean Vanier

An athlete has to somehow figure out how to enrich the people around him, and not just himself. Otherwise he's purposeless.

2   I'm still sorting out what I can and can't do for other people. I can be a good-luck charm, a hopeful example, a companion in suffering, an advisor, and a good listener. I can try to win the Tour de France over and over again, and in doing so, pound cancer into the ground. I can tell people the one thing I know for sure about the disease, which is that they aren't alone: the illness is so big, so widespread, and so common, that it affects nearly everybody—friends, family, people in the workplace or at your school. Mainly, I can just try to be helpful.

3   But sometimes, I'm not so helpful. There are occasions when I simply don't know what to say to someone experiencing the ravages of the disease. In September of 2002, I went to the White House to promote cancer research and make a plea for more resources and funding. Before the presentation, someone in the White House press office arranged for me to meet privately with a Hodgkin's Disease patient named Paul de la Garza, a journalist from the *St. Petersburg Times* who was undergoing chemo. After he was diagnosed, a friend had given him a copy of *It's Not About the Bike,* and he followed the Tour. When he heard that I would be visiting the White House to promote cancer research, he arranged for a meeting through a contact. He wrote later of our meeting: "Who better, I thought, to give me a moral boost or a morale boost than the world's most remarkable cancer survivor?"

4   But I'm not remarkable; I'm like anybody else, and if you catch me at the wrong time I'm not good for much. As I was introduced to de la Garza, we were ushered into a small anteroom near the Blue Room to talk, but the White House was on a very strict schedule and the protocol was very clear: There wasn't a lot of time, and I was nervous over the prospect of meeting with the president. I tried to listen as I was given some things to sign, posters and magazines.

5   De la Garza began to ask me some very specific questions about his cancer, what to do, what not to do. I fumbled for replies. I didn't have the $64,000 answer for every cancer question, but I gave him my standard one, which I believe to my core: find the best doctors you can, and trust the hell out of them.

6   "How do I survive this?" he asked.

7   I answered honestly, "Listen to your doctors. Get the very best treatment."

8   But that advice, as he put it later in an article he wrote about the experience, was "not exactly an epiphany."

9   His left arm was hurting, his veins were burning, and other parts of his body were rebelling against the treatment. But the main part of him that was rebelling was his mind. He had seven chemo treatments left, and he was getting weaker with each one. I knew exactly what he was experiencing—the nausea, and the taste of tin in the roof of his mouth. I could still smell the stuff myself. He was demoralized, and he had come to meet me hoping for something else.

10   "How do I survive when I can't stand the thought of another IV in my arm?" he asked.

11   "The misery is part of getting better," I said. "You have to welcome it."

12   What I meant was this: the misery is the cure. You must embrace it, because it's what may save you. You can alter any experience with your mind—it's up to you to determine what the quality of each moment is. Concentration and belief can make even chemo, no matter how sickening it is, a positive experience. It takes practice, but it's possible. I used to tell myself, when I threw up or when it burned so badly to urinate, that the sensations represented the cancer leaving my body. I was pissing it out, puking it out, coughing it out. I wasn't going to dwell on whether I was going to die. There were those in medicine and those outside it who thought I *would* die—but I chose to be around doctors and nurses who believed I could make it.

13   I had help from LaTrice Haney, my oncology nurse. Once, deep in misery of chemo, I asked LaTrice if I would ever get out of the hospital. LaTrice said, "Lance, each time you walk in here, you will walk out again. And there will be a time when you don't come here anymore at all—because you'll be cured."

14   I should have told all of these things to Paul de la Garza. Or maybe I'd have been better off just sympathizing with his plight and telling him the simple, stark truth: yeah, cancer was the best thing that ever happened to me—but I don't want to do it again.

15   Instead, all I said was, "Whenever the treatment is over, you bounce back quick. At least, I did."

16   Then a White House staffer interrupted us and I was ushered into the Blue Room for my brief address with the president. De la Garza was left in the anteroom, clearly disappointed in our meeting.

17   "That was it," he wrote:

> Our meeting lasted maybe five minutes. While I appreciated his time—
> I later learned it was his 31st birthday—and relished the trappings of the
> White House, he really didn't say anything that knocked my socks off,
> the sort of nugget I was fishing for to get me through the tunnel. Still,
> the meeting helped, because it made me realize something else. On the
> drive home from work the night before, I actually had tears in my eyes
> in anticipation of our meeting. I was counting on him for some revela-
> tion to make everything better. Because of his story I was treating him
> as if he held the secret for my cancer cure. But what I discovered almost
> immediately, before I walked out the gates of the White House even,
> is that I don't have to turn to the rich and famous, to the heroes of the

"The greater part of our happiness or misery depends on our own dispositions and not our circumstances."

—Martha Washington

sports world, to get me through the anxiety, the depression, and the fear of the what-ifs. My heroes are right in front of me, ordinary folks who every day make my life better. At the top of the list I include my wife, kids . . . my family, my friends, my co-workers, my nurses, my doctors.

18 He was right; heroism is impossible to fulfill—the bar is too high. If some people want a revelatory experience, I can't answer the request. More often than not, a hero is a person who acts without thinking, anyway. If ten people, or a million people, want to say that you're a hero, the only thing you can do is say thank you, just keep going about your day, and understand that *trying* to be a hero is not the most useful purpose you can serve.

19 The most useful purpose I can serve is to tell people who are suffering that it's an absolutely important human experience to be ill, that it can change how you live, and that it can change other lives, too.

> Excerpt from *Every Second Counts* by Lance Armstrong and Sally Jenkins. Copyright © 2003 by Lance Armstrong. Used by permission of Broadway Books, a division of Random House, Inc.

▼ COMPREHENSION CHECKUP

Multiple Choice

Directions: Write the letter for the correct answer to each question on the lines provided.

_c_   1. Armstrong says that he can be helpful to people by serving as all of the following *except*

   a. a hopeful example.

   b. an advisor.

   c. a miracle worker.

   d. a good-luck charm.

_b_   2. Armstrong thinks that he was not very helpful to de la Garza for all of the following reasons *except*

   a. he was nervous about meeting the president.

   b. he didn't like de la Garza.

   c. there wasn't a lot of time.

   d. he didn't have answers for de la Garza's specific questions.

_d_   3. When speaking with de la Garza, Armstrong was

   a. in a small anteroom.

   b. given things to sign.

   c. feeling hurried.

   d. all of the above.

c 4. Armstrong would agree with all of the following *except*

   a. if you are suffering from cancer, you need to find the very best doctors you can.

   b. the misery of chemotherapy is the cure, and it must be embraced.

   c. cancer was the worst thing that ever happened to him.

   d. you can make a painful experience into something positive with your mind.

d 5. Lance Armstrong believes that cancer

   a. affects nearly everybody.

   b. can change how you live.

   c. only happens to people with unhealthy life styles.

   d. both a and b.

a 6. Lance Armstrong believes

   a. that his best response to people who treat him like a hero is to just keep going about his day.

   b. that he is a hero because he possesses secrets that can cure cancer.

   c. that he needs to act like a hero because that's what people expect from him.

   d. becoming a hero is a worthwhile goal.

b 7. Paul de la Garza

   a. was a personal friend of Armstrong's.

   b. was able to arrange a meeting with Armstrong at the White House.

   c. worked in the White House.

   d. went to the White House with Armstrong to meet the president.

d 8. At the time he met Armstrong, de la Garza

   a. was counting on Armstrong for an epiphany.

   b. had seven cancer treatments left.

   c. was searching for a morale boost.

   d. all of the above

Vocabulary in Context

Directions: Choose the definition that best fits the meaning of the italicized words as they are used in the selection.

___b___ 1. In paragraph 1, Armstrong says that he wants to "enrich the people around him." Choose the best definition of the word *enrich* according to the way that Armstrong is using it.
  a. to supply with riches or wealth
  b. to add greater value or meaning to
  c. to adorn or decorate
  d. to provide with vitamins and minerals

___c___ 2. An antonym for *widespread* as used in paragraph 2 is
  a. common.
  b. far-reaching.
  c. rare.
  d. sweeping.

___d___ 3. When de la Garza was *demoralized*, he felt (paragraph 9)
  a. discouraged.
  b. enthusiastic.
  c. disheartened.
  d. both a and c.

___d___ 4. When you *dwell* on something, you (paragraph 12)
  a. focus on it.
  b. become preoccupied with it.
  c. go on and on about it.
  d. all of the above.

___b___ 5. An antonym for the word *stark* in paragraph 14 is
  a. harsh.
  b. pleasant.
  c. grim.
  d. severe.

True or False

___T___ 1. To *knock the socks off* means to amaze or overwhelm.

___F___ 2. To *bounce back* means to recover slowly.

___F___ 3. You are sure of the correct answer if you are *fumbling* for a reply.

___F___ 4. A *plight* is a pleasant situation.

___T___ 5. When something is *relished*, it is greatly appreciated.

___T___ 6. When the *bar* is set too high, the goal is impossible to accomplish.

___T___ 7. An *oncologist* specializes in the diagnosis and treatment of cancer.

___T___ 8. A *standard* answer is one that is usual or customary.

In Your Own Words

1. How is Armstrong coping with his fame? Do you think other famous athletes should follow his example?

2. What characteristics or attitudes do you think helped Armstrong withstand the rigors of chemotherapy? How might his training as an athlete have been beneficial to him in his fight against cancer?

3. In the first paragraph of the selection, Armstrong describes his purpose in life. What do you think of that purpose? Does that purpose pertain only to athletes?

Written Assignment

How do you define a hero? Do you agree with Armstrong that "more often than not, a hero is a person who acts without thinking"? Do you agree with de la Garza that heroes are "ordinary folks who every day make my life better"? Write a paragraph giving your opinion.

Internet Activity

To learn more about the Lance Armstrong Foundation, visit

www.livestrong.org

Write a paragraph describing the mission of the foundation.

READING

"Some people believe Sanders saved the lives of more than 200 kids that day."

Coach Sanders

GETTING FOCUSED

On April 20, 1999, at Columbine High School in Littleton, Colorado, two teenage students, Eric Harris and Dylan Klebold, killed 12 fellow students and a teacher. In addition, they wounded 24 others before committing suicide.

Although there have been similar incidents in which young students have opened fire on their fellow students, the Columbine massacre has become symbolic of this particular type of catastrophe. The selection below describes the brave teacher who became a victim as he sought to protect the students under his care.

(continued)

READING *continued*

BIO-SKETCH

For over 20 years, Rick Reilly has been a writer for the magazine *Sports Illustrated*. During that time, he has been named National Sportswriter of the Year nine times.

TACKLING VOCABULARY

shrapnel   fragments scattered by a bursting shell, mine, or bomb

sitting ducks   easy targets. Ducks that are sitting still in one spot present an easy target for a hunter. This is in direct contrast to the difficulty a hunter faces in trying to shoot a duck that is already in flight.

chopper   an informal term for a helicopter

paramedic   a person who is trained to give first aid or other health care in the absence of a physician

SWAT team   a group of police officers who are trained and equipped to deal with especially dangerous or violent situations. SWAT is an acronym for Special Weapons And Tactics

THE BIG HERO OF LITTLETON

Rick Reilly

May 3, 1999—As usual, coach Dave Sanders spent Tuesday of last week at Columbine High hanging around the kids.

2   One kept constant pressure on the gaping gunshot wounds in Sanders's shoulders, using T-shirts off other kids' backs. Another made a pillow from kids' sweatshirts for his head. Others covered his shivering body with more shirts.

3   Outside the science room bullets and shrapnel were still flying, but inside, where Sanders lay, the kids were quietly keeping him talking, conscious, alive.

4   "Who's this?" they whispered, going through his wallet, showing him his own pictures.

5   "My . . . wife . . . Linda," he said with what little breath he had. They asked him about the pictures of his daughters Angela and Connie. They asked him about coaching the Columbine girls' basketball team. They asked him about coaching the girls' softball team. They asked him about all of the boys' and girls' teams he used to coach. A man coaches just about every team at a school over 25 years, there's a lot to cover.

6   Every high school has a Coach Sanders, the giving one, the joking one, the one who sets up the camps, sacrifices his nights to keep the gym open, makes sure the girls have the weight room to themselves twice a week. RUN,

"We cannot live only for ourselves. A thousand fibers connect us with our fellow men."

—Herman Melville

GUN, AND HAVE FUN is what the girls' basketball T-shirts said last season and it worked. The Rebels had their best record in a decade. So when he ran into the cafeteria on Tuesday morning at 11:30, his face bright red, and yelled, "Get out! Get out! They're shooting!" the hundreds of kids in there took him seriously.

7   Some people believe Sanders saved the lives of more than 200 kids that day. Witnesses say he led many to the kitchen, to the auditorium, to safety. "He saved my life," says Brittany Davies, one of his jayvee basketball players, "and then he kept running, cutting across the lunchroom, telling people to get down. He left himself in the open where he could get shot."

8   Columbine English teacher Cheryl Lucas told the *Rocky Mountain News*, "He was the most responsible for saving a bunch of lives. . . . They would've been sitting ducks if not for Mr. Sanders." But that wasn't enough for Sanders. There must have been a dozen ways out of the cafeteria to safety. Instead, he ran up-stairs to warn more kids.

9   "I was standing in the science room, looking out the window [in the door leading to the hall]," says Greg Barnes, a varsity basketball player. "Then I saw Coach Sanders turn around, take two shots, right in front of me. Blood went fly-ing off him and he fell."

10   Sanders got up and staggered into the science room. Teeth were knocked out when he fell. Blood was pouring from his shoulders and his chest. A roomful of kids leaped back. Eagle Scout Aaron Hancey, a junior who videotapes boys' basketball games, began applying pressure to the wounds.

11   An hour went by. The gunmen had tried to enter the room next to the sci-ence room but couldn't. Hancey talked to police on the science room phone, telling them where he and the others were, that Coach Sanders was badly wounded. The police said a SWAT team was coming.

12   A second hour went by. Someone crept to a science room window facing the parking lot and held up a sign that read 1 BLEEDING TO DEATH. Still, no SWAT team. No fire ladder to the window. No chopper.

13   Three hours and nothing. The kids in the science room weren't hearing ex-plosions anymore, but they dared not run for it. They figured the killers could be anywhere. How could they know that the killers had been dead for more than an hour?

14   Somehow, Sanders stayed alive, despite losing body heat, blood and breath. "He was a brave man," said Hancey. "He hung in there. He was a tough guy."

15   Finally, after three and a half hours, a SWAT team burst in. One member said he'd wait with Sanders until a stretcher came. "Even if they'd gotten him out then," says Hancey, "I think he would've made it."

16   Outside, in the hollow-eyed afternoon, there came a rumor that Sanders was in surgery at a Denver hospital. For hours Linda and the girls frantically called area hospitals. Nothing. Finally at about 9 P.M., Angela went live on a Den-ver TV station and pleaded, "Does anybody know where my father is?"

17   Her father was still in that science room. He died by the time paramedics reached him. He died a couple hundred yards from 300 cops and dozens of am-bulances. Only the kids in that terrifying room heard his last words: "Tell my girls I love them."

18   Everybody said Dave Sanders lived for kids.

19   Should've known he'd die for them, too.

"The Big Hero of Littleton" by Rick Reilly from *The Life of Reilly: The Best of Sports Illustrated's Rick Reilly*. Copyright © 2000. Originally published in *Sports Illustrated*, May 3, 1999.

✓ COMPREHENSION CHECKUP

True or False

Directions: Indicate whether each statement is true (**T**) or false (**F**).

___T___ 1. The author believes that the death of Dave Sanders was senseless.

___T___ 2. Coach Sanders's children did not know of his injury until it was too late.

___T___ 3. Coach Sanders's death was painful to his students.

___T___ 4. Coach Sanders's final words expressed concern for his girls.

___F___ 5. Because of the presence of the gunmen in a nearby room, students were unable to communicate with the police from the science room phone.

Multiple Choice

Directions: Select the best answer for each item.

___b___ 1. The author suggests that all of the following may have been responsible for Coach Sanders's death *except*
    a. the paramedics' failure to respond in a timely manner.
    b. the first aid given by the students.
    c. the long delay of the SWAT team in coming to the rescue.
    d. the two gunmen.

___d___ 2. We can assume that the students tending to Coach Sanders were
    a. thoughtless and irresponsible.
    b. concerned and sympathetic.
    c. fearful and agitated.
    d. both b and c.

___d___ 3. The author's tone conveys
    a. anguish about what happened to Coach Sanders.
    b. respect for Coach Sanders.
    c. outrage over the police response.
    d. all of the above.

___c___ 4. All of the following are true of this selection *except*
    a. Coach Sanders was concerned for the welfare of the students.
    b. Coach Sanders fell to the ground with such force that he knocked out teeth.
    c. after one hour, Coach Sanders was rescued by the SWAT team.
    d. Coach Sanders had a long involvement with athletics at Columbine High.

    <u> a </u>   5. One can assume from reading the selection that
Coach Sanders was

      a. popular with the students.

      b. selfish and self-centered.

      c. a reclusive individual.

      d. foolish and vain.

Vocabulary in Context

Directions: Try to determine the meaning of the italicized words from context, and then write the definition on the line provided. The paragraph in which the words appear in the reading selection is indicated in parentheses.

1. *hanging around* (paragraph 1) being with _____

2. *gaping* gunshot wounds (paragraph 2) open _____

3. *constant* pressure (paragraph 2) unrelenting _____

4. *sacrifices* his nights (paragraph 6) gives up _____

5. *staggered into* (paragraph 10) fell into _____

In Your Own Words

1. Many people who watched the live coverage of the events of April 20, 1999, saw nearly 800 police officers gathered outside the high school grounds. Of those who watched the events unfold, many have been especially critical of the long wait to rescue students and faculty. Coach Sanders's daughter Angela is especially critical. "How many of those kids could have lived if they had moved more quickly?" she asks. "When 500 officers go to a battle-zone and not one comes away with a scratch, then something's wrong," said Dale Todd, whose son lay wounded inside the school. Sergeant Barry Williams, leader of the SWAT team, said that they tried to track Coach Sanders but were unable to locate the science room where a red rag was supposed to be tied to a doorknob as a signal. On the basis of the information provided in the selection, do you think the SWAT team acted appropriately? Or do you think that they should have done more?

2. What is the general purpose of this selection? Why do you suppose Reilly talks about the personal side of Coach Sanders's life? How does Reilly evoke a sense of sadness about the death of Coach Sanders?

3. The massacre provoked intense public debate on the issue of gun control and the availability of firearms in the United States. What is your opinion on the issue of gun control? Would gun control have helped in this particular instance?

4. A great deal of discussion was focused on the role of violent video games, television shows, movies, and music in American society. Do you think that violence in mass media has a share of responsibility for what happened at Columbine? Do you think greater effort should be taken to control teenage access to the media? Why or why not?

5. Apparently Klebold and Harris felt like outcasts at Columbine High and may have been bullied. Do you think a greater effort should be made to ban high school cliques and bullying?

6. Should the parents of Klebold and Harris be held accountable for the actions of their children?

Written Assignment

Have you experienced or observed a tragedy involving the misuse of firearms? Have you heard about such a situation in your community? If so, describe what happened.

Internet Activity

Today, largely in response to this school shooting and similar copycat crimes, many schools have a zero-tolerance philosophy toward possession of weapons and threats. Has the policy gone too far? Has it helped to deter crime or made it more likely? Do some research on this topic and write a few paragraphs summarizing your information.

Interpreting What We Read

"Find the grain of truth in criticism—chew it and swallow it."

—Don Sutton

CHAPTERS IN PART 3

The details in this photograph can help you answer some of the following questions. Answer the questions you can and write the clues that helped you answer them after your answers. Write "can't tell" after any question for which you do not think there are enough clues for you to answer it correctly.

1. How old are the children? <u>can't tell</u>

2. What are the children's names? <u>can't tell</u>

3. What grades are the children in? <u>can't tell</u>

4. Where are the children going? <u>probably trick-or-treating</u>

5. What state or country do the children live in? <u>can't tell</u>

6. What are the children dressed as? <u>boy a pirate; girl a princess or fairy</u>

7. Are the children happy or sad? <u>happy</u>

INFERENCE

When you answered these questions, you were making **inferences.** You made educated guesses and drew conclusions based on the indirect clues given in the questions. You had to "read between the lines" because nothing was directly stated. From this photograph, you could answer only questions 4, 6, and 7. The children are probably going trick-or-treating for Halloween because they are wearing costumes and carrying sacks. The boy in the picture is also carrying a flashlight to light the way as they make the rounds of houses or apartments. The boy is more than likely dressed as a pirate because of the striped pants and hat with the skull and crossbones. The girl is probably some kind of fairy or princess. You can also reasonably infer that they are happy since both are smiling. However, your inferences could still be wrong. Maybe the children are going to a costume party or playing dress-up. And maybe they are not really happy, but just dutifully smiling for the camera. Inferences, then, are only probable.

The ability to make accurate inferences is an essential part of reading critically. Drawing inferences from written material requires the same kind of thinking as drawing inferences from real-life situations. You must study the available clues and come to some sort of reasonable conclusion. To be accurate, your inference must accord with what you see.

In this chapter, you are going to have an opportunity to improve your skill at making inferences using a variety of materials.

Drawing Inferences from Droodles

Picture riddles are commonly called "droodles." The word *droodle* is a combination of doodle (a scribbled drawing) and riddle. In order to solve a droodle, you must infer from clues in the drawing what it is a picture of. Try to guess what the following droodle represents.

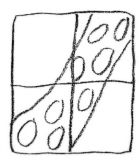

If you guessed that it is a drawing of a giraffe passing by a window, you are correct.

Picture riddles are thought to have originated in Italy in the seventeenth century. Here is an example of one of those early drawings. Can you make a logical guess about what the drawing is supposed to represent?

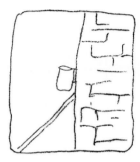

The drawing most likely depicts a blind beggar coming around the corner of a building. We can infer this because of the cane and the cup.

Let's see how good you are at solving the following droodles. Study each picture for no more than 1 minute and then write your inference on the line below. Compare your answers with a classmate's before trying to create your own droodle.

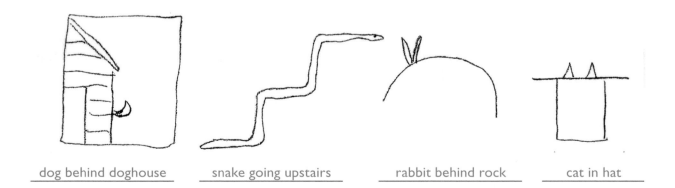

dog behind doghouse   snake going upstairs   rabbit behind rock   cat in hat

Exercise 1: Drawing Inferences

Directions: Write down what you might infer if you saw each of the following. Base your guess on the clues that are provided by the writer, your own experience, and logic.

1. Six people are seated at a restaurant booth. A small cake with one candle is in front of one of the people.

   Your inference: a birthday party

2. A policeman stops traffic as a line of cars with their lights on go through the intersection.

   Your inference: a funeral procession

3. One thousand people wearing running outfits and jogging shoes are gathered on a downtown city street.

   Your inference: beginning of a race or marathon

4. The neighbor across the street has set up tables in her carport. On each table are miscellaneous household items.

   Your inference: rummage sale or garage sale

5. Your neighbor, the elderly Mrs. Green, has not been seen for the past three days. Her newspapers and mail have not been collected.

   Your inference: She's sick or in the hospital or on a trip.

6. Firefighters are gathered around a large pine tree. A mewing sound is heard above.

   Your inference: A cat is stuck in a tree.

7. Cars are lined up outside every local gas station you pass.

   Your inference: gas shortage or cheap gas

8. Groups of children dressed in costumes go door-to-door while adults wait at the curb for them.

   Your inference: Halloween

9. Fifty people are gathered outside a department store 30 minutes before it is due to open.

   Your inference: big sale

10. A mini-van is packed with a stroller, porta-crib, high chair, diaper bag, and suitcases.

    Your inference: family going on a trip

Drawing Inferences from Cartoons

Exercise 2: Drawing Inferences from Cartoons

A. Directions: Study the cartoons below and answer the questions that follow.

George B. Abbott cartoon is reprinted by permission of the artist.

Art Bouthillier cartoon is reprinted by permission of the artist. Art Bouthillier is an Editorial Cartoonist for *The South Whidbey Record* and can be reached at art@whidbey.com

1. What do you infer about the cartoons that makes them funny?

   The parents are using signs to get their points across to their children.

   _____

   _____

2. Write the implied main idea of both cartoons.

   The parent of each young person is eager to have the child move out.

   _____

   _____

B. Directions: Study each of the following cartoons carefully and consider the statements below them. If a statement appears to be a good inference based on the details found in the cartoon, mark it **Y** for yes. If it appears to be an unlikely conclusion, mark it **N** for no.

"Dad, can you read?"

___Y___   1. The father has poor vision.

___Y___   2. The father watches a lot of TV.

___Y___   3. The son is reading a book.

___N___   4. The son wants the father to read to him.

___Y___   5. The father can read the *TV Guide*.

"*Mrs. Horton, could you stop by school today?*"

___N___   1. The person holding the drawing is the artist's mother.

___Y___   2. The artist watches a lot of TV.

___Y___   3. The teacher is concerned about the artist.

___Y___   4. Mrs. Horton is the mother of the artist.

___N___   5. The teacher is going to yell at Mrs. Horton.

Drawing Inferences from Epitaphs

Epitaphs are inscriptions carved on a tomb or grave marker in memory of the person buried there. They often provide clues to the person's personality and achievements, the cause of his or her death, and the relationships he or she had with others.

| Exercise 3: Drawing Inferences from Epitaphs |

Directions: Make use of inferential reasoning to answer the questions that follow each epitaph.

1. Stranger! Approach this spot with gravity!
   John Brown is filling his last cavity.

   What is the likely former profession of the deceased? <u>dentist</u>

2. Here lies a man named Zeke.
   Second fastest draw in Cripple Creek.

   How did Zeke die? <u>gun fight</u>

   Who killed him? <u>the fastest draw</u>

3. Here lies the body of our Anna
   Done to death by a banana.
   It wasn't the fruit that laid her low
   But the skin of the thing that made her go.

   What was the likely cause of Anna's death? <u>slipped on a banana peel</u>

4. John E. Goembel
   1867–1946
   "The defense rests."

   What is the likely former profession of the deceased? <u>attorney</u>

5. Here lies Bernard Lightfoot
   Who was accidentally killed
   in the 45th year of his age.
   This monument was erected
   by his grateful family.

   How did Mr. Lightfoot's family feel about him? <u>disliked him</u>

6. Here lies
   Ezekiel Aikle
   Age 102
   The Good
   Die Young.

   How do those close to Mr. Aikle feel about him? <u>He wasn't a good</u>

   <u>person.</u>

7. See. I told you
   "I was sick."

What inference can you make about the deceased person's death?

Nobody believed that he was sick until he died.

8. Here lies the body of Jonathan Blake.
   Stepped on the gas
   Instead of the brake.

What was the likely cause of Mr. Blake's death? car accident

9. Tom Smith is dead, and here he lies,
   Nobody laughs and nobody cries,
   Where his soul's gone, or how it fares,
   Nobody knows, and nobody cares.

Tom Smith was likely what sort of person? He was a loner.

10. Beneath this slab
    John Brown is stowed.
    He watched the ads
    And not the road.
    (Ogden Nash)

What likely caused Mr. Brown's death? He was distracted while driving

and had an accident.

Drawing Inferences from Textbook Material

Exercise 4: Drawing Inferences from Textbook Material

Directions: Read each of the following excerpts from textbooks and use inferential reasoning to answer the questions that follow.

A.   The beer people drink today is an alcoholic beverage made by fermenting grains and usually incorporating hops, but the process of making it was discovered nearly 8,000 years ago, around 6,000 B.C.E., in Sumeria. The Sumerians made beer out of half-baked crusty loaves of bread, which they crumbled into water, fermented, and then filtered through a basket. Surviving records indicate that as much as fifty percent of each grain harvest went into the production of beer.

Literally hundreds of surviving tablets contain recipes for beer, including for a black beer, a wheat beer, a white beer, and a red beer. One surviving tablet, which is similar to modern advertising slogans, reads "Drink Ebla—the beer with the heart of a lion."

Janetta Benton, *Arts and Culture*, p. 18

   b   1. We can infer that
   a. beer-making is a recent phenomenon.
   b. a key process involved in making beer is fermentation.
   c. beer-making consumed a small amount of the typical Sumerian grain harvest.
   d. none of the above.

   a   2. We can infer that
   a. even in the past, good cooks sought to preserve their recipes by writing them down.
   b. the beer made by the Sumerians had a bitter taste.
   c. in Sumeria, only one type of beer was available.
   d. the Sumerians liked wine more than beer.

B.   Want to "bulk up" your muscles and be stronger, with more endurance? Just swallow a pill. That is the message to bodybuilders and other athletes from the purveyors of substances like "andro"—androstenedione—and THG—tetrahydrogestrinone (a chemical cousin of two anabolic steroids). Andro made news in 1998 when Mark McGwire admitted he used it during his successful attempt to break major league baseball's home run record. THG burst into the headlines when an international track star admitted using it, as did some professional football and baseball players.

       Cecie Starr, *Human Biology*, p. 105

   c   3. We can infer that
   a. THG and andro must be injected into the body with a syringe.
   b. Mark McGwire failed to break the home run record despite taking andro.
   c. both amateur and professional athletes are willing to take performance-enhancing drugs.
   d. THG did not work as well as andro.

C.   Each day, about 3,000 teenagers—most younger than 15—join the ranks of habitual smokers in the United States. The first time someone lights up, they typically cough and choke on the irritants in smoke. They may feel dizzy and nauseated, and get a headache.

    So why do smoking "recruits" ignore the threat signals their body is sending and keep on lighting up? Research tells us that teens take up the habit in order to fit in socially. At the time, the threat that tobacco use poses to their health and survival seems remote. And of course, the nicotine in cigarette smoke is addictive.

       Cecie Starr, *Human Biology*, p. 193

   b   4. We can infer that
   a. teenagers who smoke are particularly worried about lung cancer.
   b. smoking is typically an unpleasant experience for a first-time user.
   c. teens don't worry about being perceived as different than their peers.
   d. 15-year-olds are unlikely to become addicted to nicotine.

D.   In the United States, roughly 10 million people, including a growing number of musicians, have lost some hearing from damage caused by loud noise. The National Institutes of Health has estimated that high noise levels in the home, on the job, or in recreational pursuits put another 20 million Americans at risk of hearing loss. One-third of adults in the United States will suffer significant damage to their hearing by the time they are 65. Researchers believe that most cases are due to the long-term effects of living in a noisy world.

Cecie Starr, *Human Biology,* p. 261

___d___ 5. We can infer that
          a. a professional musician playing in a rock band might be at increased risk to suffer hearing loss in later years.
          b. a person who operates a jackhammer or leaf blower without earplugs might be at increased risk to suffer hearing loss in later years.
          c. hearing loss affects only people who are 65 and older.
          d. both a and b.

E.   Coffee is one drink that people enjoy the world over. Coffee was first used by nomads in Ethiopia where, according to legend, it was discovered by a goatherd who noticed that goats exhibited unusual energy after eating the red berries. The goatherd, named Kaldi, tried the berries himself and experienced an energy surge. Sometime between 1000 and 1300, coffee was made into a beverage by a monk from a nearby monastery who boiled the berries to make a drink. By the late fifteenth century, coffee had spread to the Muslim cities of Medina and Mecca, and by the seventeenth century it had been introduced to the Netherlands and to North America. During the eighteenth century, coffee became daily fare of people throughout the world, soon leading to a great number of coffee houses and coffee bars throughout Europe, and ultimately to the phenomenon of Starbucks and other specialty coffee merchants today.

Janetta Benton, *Arts and Culture,* p. 576

___d___ 6. We can infer that
          a. coffee was discovered by accident.
          b. coffee is an extremely popular drink.
          c. coffee leads to an increase in energy.
          d. all of the above.

___b___ 7. We can infer that
          a. coffee is a Western invention.
          b. coffee beans can be eaten without causing death.
          c. goats become ill when they eat coffee beans.
          d. it took coffee a long time to become popular because of its bitter taste.

F.   On April 10, 1912, the ocean liner *Titanic* slipped away from the docks of Southampton, England, on its first voyage across the North Atlantic to New York. A proud symbol of the new industrial age, the towering ship carried 2,300 passengers, some enjoying more luxury than most travelers today could imagine. Poor people crowded the lower decks, journeying to what they hoped would be a better life in the United States.

Two days out, the crew received reports of icebergs in the area but paid little notice. Then, near midnight, as the ship steamed swiftly westward, a stunned lookout reported a massive shape rising out of the dark ocean directly ahead. Moments later, the *Titanic* collided with a huge iceberg, as tall as the ship itself, that split open its side as if the grand vessel were a giant tin can.

Seawater flooded into the ship's lower levels, pulling the ship down by the bow. Within twenty-five minutes of impact, people were rushing for the lifeboats. By 2:00 A.M., the bow was completely submerged, and the stern rose high above the water. Clinging to the deck, quietly observed by those in lifeboats, hundreds of helpless passengers and crew solemnly passed their final minutes before the ship disappeared into the frigid Atlantic.

The tragic loss of more than 1,600 lives made news around the world. However, some categories of passengers had much better odds of survival than others. Those on the upper decks, passengers traveling on first-class tickets, were more likely to be saved. Very few of the third-class passengers, on the lower decks, escaped drowning. And it was an advantage to be a woman or a child since they boarded the lifeboats first.

John C. Macionis, *Society,* p. 192

____a____ 8. We can infer that
  a. passengers on the *Titanic* were more likely to survive if they were wealthy.
  b. passengers on the *Titanic* were more likely to survive if they were poor.
  c. the captain and crew members of the *Titanic* were more likely to survive.
  d. small children on the *Titanic* were more likely to perish because they didn't know how to swim.

____a____ 9. We can infer that
  a. despite its massive size, the *Titanic* sank within a few hours.
  b. the *Titanic* sank within 25 minutes of hitting the iceberg.
  c. the crew bears no blame for the sinking of the *Titanic.*
  d. the *Titanic* split into two pieces as it sank in the freezing water.

G.   Ancient Americans played a variety of games using balls of various sizes. In one of them the Hachtli players tried to shoot a rubber ball through a stone ring. The Olmecs left ball courts made around 1500 B.C.E., and colossal Olmec stone heads are sometimes shown wearing helmets presumed to have been worn in their ancient ball games.

Much more than a mere sport, in which onlookers sometimes made bets, ancient Mesoamerican ball games were rituals of religious significance. They were also a matter of life and death. A Mayan epic describes a ball game in which the Hero Twins descend into the underworld to defeat the Lords of Death and thereby save humanity.

Unlike modern-day basketball, which tends to be a high-scoring affair, with many baskets made by both teams, ancient ball games were rough defensive contests in which scoring was difficult, since use of the hands was not allowed.

A more serious difference between contemporary basketball and the ancient version is that modern players, when they fail at a crucial shot at game's end, come back to play another day, whereas members of losing teams in ancient Mesoamerica often found themselves offered as a ritual sacrifice.

Janetta Benton, *Arts and Culture*, p. 220

____c____ 10. We can infer that
   a. helmets are a twentieth-century invention.
   b. the Hero Twins invented basketball when they shot rubber balls through stone hoops.
   c. Mesoamerican players often put their lives on the line in ball games.
   d. ball games were not as popular as ritual sacrifice.

____b____ 11. We can infer that
   a. football was not as popular in Mesoamerica as basketball.
   b. Mesoamerican ball games sometimes involved gambling.
   c. it was easy to score in ancient ball games.
   d. hands could be used only when a contest was close.

H.   The ancient Greeks had a prescription for good living that is still popular today: "A sound mind in a sound body." The Greeks celebrated the human body and physical accomplishments as no other culture had before, particularly in sporting contests. The most enduring of all sporting contests was the Olympiad, begun in 776 B.C.E. These Olympic Games were held every four years. From the outset, the foot race was the most important event. Held in honor of Zeus, the course was six hundred feet in length (the length of the stadium at Olympia), about equivalent to a modern two-hundred meter race.

The first thirteen Olympic Games consisted solely of this race, but soon two lengths around the stadium was added (or about one time around a modern track), as well as a long-distance race of about two and a half miles. Over the years the pentathlon, consisting of five events (discus, long jump, javelin, running, and wrestling) was added. By the mid-fifth century, the games had been expanded to also include a chariot race.

Today the Olympic Games have become more than just an athletic contest. They are big business. The United States Olympic Committee has an annual operating budget of $388 million for funding the training and preparation of U.S. athletes. They are also usually a major economic boon to the community that hosts the games. When Atlanta hosted the 1996 Summer Games, for instance, 73,000 hotel rooms were filled within a ninety-minute radius of the Olympic Center, pumping over $5.1 billion into the local economy. After more than a century of being held outside Greece, the Olympics returned to Athens in the Summer of 2004.

Janetta Benton, *Arts and Culture*, p. 81

____d____ 12. We can infer that
   a. because of the high cost of security, modern Olympic Games are unlikely to make the host country much money.
   b. the pentathlon includes seven to eight physical contests.
   c. Olympic athletes from the United States have had to pay for their own training.
   d. the tradition of holding the Olympic Games every four years is a legacy from the Greeks.

Drawing Inferences from Popular Literature

Exercise 5: Drawing Inferences from Popular Literature

Directions: Read each of the following excerpts from popular literature, and use inferential reasoning to complete the sentences that follow.

A.   Within weeks, we had a hard time remembering what life had been like without our new boarder. Quickly, we fell into a routine. I started each morning before the first cup of coffee, by taking him for a brisk walk down to the water and back. After breakfast and before my shower, I patrolled the backyard with a shovel, burying his land mines in the sand at the back of the lot. I seldom left the house before ten, first locking Marley out in the concrete bunker with a fresh bowl of water, a host of toys, and my cheery directive to "be a good boy." Jenny came home on her lunch break, when she would give Marley his midday meal and throw him a ball in the backyard until he was tuckered out.

   John Grogan, *Marley & Me*, p. 26

Inference: Marley is likely to be a <u>dog</u>   .

B.   The trip to Arizona had begun early on a cloudy and cool October morning. It had taken many miles to put the cars and smog of Los Angeles behind me, but by the time I'd reached the California state line, Los Angeles seemed a world away. The flat, sepia-colored desert was quiet and looked lifeless through the windshield. I pulled into the small community of Miami, where I stopped for gas. As I stood beside the pump filling the tank, a stranger approached me and smiled. There was nothing unusual about this, but what happened next reminded me that I was not just starting a new job but a new life.
   "Hey, Kareem!" the man said. "How's your team?"
   I had to laugh at his enthusiasm. It was October 29, and the basketball season was still several days away.
   "Are they tall?" he asked.
   "I don't know," I told him. "I haven't even seen the guys yet."
   "Good luck, Coach," he said, turning to leave.
   I watched him go and let the word sink in: "Coach." It had a fresh and promising ring. During my long career as a high school player at Power Memorial in New York City, a college center at UCLA, and twenty years as a pro in the NBA, I'd been called many things by many people, but "Coach" wasn't one of them. Change was definitely in the damp autumn air, and not just when it came to basketball. "Coach Kareem." I liked the way that sounded.

   Kareem Abdul-Jabbar, *A Season on the Reservation*, p. 11

Inference: Kareem is traveling to Arizona to <u>coach a basketball team</u>   .

C.   My brother, who was normally quite an intelligent human being, saw an ad in *Mechanics Illustrated* that invited him to enjoy color television at home for 65 cents plus postage. He placed an order, and four weeks later received in the mail a multicolored sheet of transparent plastic that he was instructed to tape over the television screen and watch the image through.

Having spent the money, my brother refused to accept that it was a touch disappointing. When a human face moved into the pinkish part of the screen or a section of lawn briefly coincided with the green portion, he would leap up in triumph. "Look! Look! *That's* what color television's gonna look like someday," he would say. "This is all just experimental, you see."

Bill Bryson, *The Life and Times of the Thunderbolt Kid*, p. 8

Inference: When the author's brother faced disappointment, he would <u>try to</u>

make the best of a bad situation   .

D.   In 1981, when Dad turned fifty-five, he was eligible to retire from his city job. Now that his kids were grown, he thought that his newspaper job, together with his pension, might bring in enough income to live on. Even so, he kept debating whether or not to leave the Sanitation Department. I knew that this wasn't just about money, but I encouraged him to "retire," although that's an odd word to use for somebody who would still be working full-time. To bolster my argument, I sat down with him to go over the numbers.

"And then I have to figure out what to do with those sick days," he said.

"What do you mean?" I asked

"My sick days. I never took 'em."

I was stunned. Although in all my years at home I had never seen him miss a day of work, I had never thought of it in terms of sick days.

"Dad, everybody takes sick days."

"Well I didn't, and now I've got two hundred of them."

"Two *hundred*? Why didn't you take them?"

"Because I wasn't sick."

"Dad, those days are yours. They're made available to you."

"They're made available if you're sick.

"But there must have been times when you *were* sick."

"Sure, but if I took off from the morning job, and then I felt better and went to the afternoon job, how would that look? When I was sick, I worked it off and rode it out."

I went with him to city hall to work out his retirement package, which included partial compensation for all the sick days he never took. I shouldn't have been surprised, but I was. I've worked in government and the media all my life, and I've come to know many fine and hardworking people. But I can only imagine how much this country could achieve if everyone had Dad's work ethic.

Not long ago, an old family friend called to tell me that she had been reading a novel by Gail Goodwin, where she came across a line that struck her as a wonderful description of big Russ: "He lived his life by the grace of daily obligations."

Tim Russert, *Big Russ and Me*, New York: Miramax, 2004, pp. 72–74

Inference: The author's attitude toward his father can be described as

respectful; admiring   .

E.   Under Our Skin!

There once was an oyster, whose story I tell;
Who found that some sand had got into his shell.
It was only a grain, but it gave him great pain;
For oysters have feelings, although they are plain.

Now, did he berate the harsh workings of fate,
That had brought him to such a sad, sorry state?
"No," he said to himself, "since I cannot remove it,
I'll lie in my shell, and think how to improve it."

The years rolled around, as the years always do,
And he came to his ultimate Destiny . . . stew!
Now that small grain of sand that had bothered him so,
Was a beautiful pearl all richly aglow.

This tale has a moral, for isn't it grand,
What an oyster can do with a morsel of sand?
Think . . . What could WE do, if we'd only begin,
With some of the things that get under OUR skin?

—Anonymous

Inference: Just as the oyster turned the grain of sand into a pearl, we should

turn the annoyances in our lives into something positive   .

F.   A Real Loss

I was sitting in back of a little girl flying as an unaccompanied minor, put on the plane by a mother who put a stuffed bear in her arms and told her to remind Daddy to call when she got to California. The girl adjusted her seat belt and sniffed back a tear, bravely setting her jaw.

As we prepared for takeoff, the man next to the girl asked her the name of her bear and nodded in approval, saying "Furry" was a good name for a bear. When the little girl told him she was six years old, the man replied that he had a daughter who was six years old. His daughter was missing the same teeth, in fact. He asked how much money the tooth fairy was giving out in New York these days.

By the time we were in the air, the man and the girl were playing tic-tac-toe, and she revealed to him the names of her favorite friends. Somewhere over Ohio, I fell asleep, awakened by my mother instinct when I heard a child announce that she had to go to the bathroom.

"It's in the back, right?" I heard the girl say to the man. She looked hesitant. The flight attendants were busy collecting lunch trays.

"Do you want me to take you there?" the man asked, standing.

At once my antennae were up and, leaning into the aisle, I craned my neck, practically knocking heads with the woman in the seat across from me. For one moment our eyes locked. She had been listening too, and both of us had the same idea. Would this man go into the bathroom with the child? I held my breath as he held open the bathroom door. Suddenly he became transformed in my eyes—the dark business suit looked sinister, the friendly smile really a lure to something evil.

Then the man showed the little girl how the lock worked and waited outside the door. The woman and I sighed in relief. She said, "Well you can't be too careful these days."

I've thought about that man on the plane since then, and the image of him and the little girl always leaves an empty sorrow. I know that increased awareness about child molestation is in itself a good thing. I know that sexual abuse of children is awful, and that we must guard against it. But it saddened me that I looked at someone who understood a child's fear and saw a child molester. There is a real loss here for all of us when we must always be wary of the kindness of strangers.

Fern Kupfer, *Newsday*, September 27, 1987

Many times you have enough evidence to draw the correct inference. At other times, your initial inference may be incorrect, and you may need to change it as you collect more information.

1. What was the author's initial inference about the character of the man on

    the plane? a good, kind man
    _____

2. What evidence was her initial inference based on? He befriended the

    nervous little girl.
    _____

3. Halfway through the story, why does the author revise her initial infer-

    ence? The man is taking the girl to the bathroom.
    _____

4. Why does the author revert back to her original assessment of the man?

    He shows the girl how to lock the door.
    _____

5. What is the "real loss" the author is speaking about? It is a loss of trust

    in helpful people.
    _____

Directions: Study this excerpt and answer the questions that follow using the indirect clues from the story to help you.

G. When Fish Are Three Days Old

Helen thinks all her decisions are always right, but really, she is only lucky. For over fifty years I have seen this happen, how her foolish thinking turns into good fortune. It was like that at lunch yesterday. "Winnie-ah," she said, "have some more chicken." I told Helen I did not want to eat any more funeral leftovers—five days was enough. So we went shopping at Happy Super, deciding what new things to eat for last night's dinner.

Helen picked out a flat fish, pom-pom fish, she called it, only a dollar sixty-nine a pound, bargain bin.

And I said, "This kind of bargain you don't want. Look at his eye, shrunken in and cloudy-looking. That fish is already three days old."

But Helen stared at that fish eye and said she saw nothing wrong. So I picked up that fish and felt its body slide between my fingers, a fish that had slipped away from life long time ago. Helen said it was a good sign—a juicy, tender fish!

So I smelled that fish for her. I told her how all the sweetness of its meat had risen to the skin and turned stinky-sour in the air. She put that fish to her nose and said, "That's a good pom-pom smell."

She bought that three-day-old fish, the dinner I ate at her house last night. And when she served it, her husband poked out a fish cheek, popped it in his mouth, and praised its taste; then their son Frank swallowed the other cheek right away. And Helen took a piece near the tail, the thinnest section, and after smacking her lips, she said she had steamed it just right, not too long. Then she saw my bowl, how it held nothing but rice. She dipped her chopsticks once again, this time near the stomach, took the fattest part of the fish, and laid this on top of my rice.

"Winnie-ah don't be polite," she scolded. So I had to be polite and eat her fish. I tell you that fish made me so mad. It was sweet. It was tender. Only one dollar sixty-nine a pound. I started to think. Maybe Helen went back to Happy Super and exchanged that fish. But then I thought, Helen is not that clever. And that's when I remembered something. Even though Helen is not smart, even though she was born poor, even though she has never been pretty, she has always had luck pour onto her plate, even spill from the mouth of a three-day-old fish.

From *The Kitchen God's Wife* by Amy Tan, pp. 67–68

"Give and take makes good friends."

—Scottish proverb

Questions	Answer	Clue
1. Has there been a funeral recently?	Yes	funeral leftovers
2. Is this a friendship of long duration?	Yes	for over 50 years
3. Do you think Winnie is jealous of Helen?	Yes	"lucky"
4. Is one of the friends an optimist?	Yes	Helen bought a three-day-old fish
5. Are Helen and Winnie Asian?	Yes	rice, chopsticks

Drawing Inferences from Fables

A fable is a short story that teaches a lesson, or warns against commonly made mistakes. The main characters are usually, but not always, animals.

Exercise 6: Drawing Inferences from a Fable

Directions: Read this fable and answer the questions that follow.

THE FOX AND THE STORK

Aesop

"To throw away an honest friend is, as it were, to throw your life away."

—Sophocles

At one time the Fox and the Stork were on visiting terms and seemed very good friends. So the Fox invited the Stork to dinner, and for a joke put nothing before her but some soup in a very shallow dish. This the Fox could easily lap up, but the Stork could only wet the end of her long bill in it, and left the meal as hungry as when she began. "I am sorry the soup is not to your liking," said the Fox.

"Pray do not apologize," said the Stork. "I hope you will return this visit, and come and dine with me soon."

1. What do you think is going to happen next? Write your inference below.

   The stork will invite the fox to dinner and serve something that he is not able

   to eat.

2. Now read the rest of the fable. How close did you come to predicting what the stork would do?

   So a day was appointed when the Fox should visit the Stork; but when they were seated at the table all that was for their dinner was contained in a very long-necked jar with a narrow mouth, in which the Fox could not insert his snout, so all he could manage to do was to lick the outside of the jar.

   "I will not apologize for the dinner," said the Stork:

   "ONE BAD TURN DESERVES ANOTHER."

3. Do you think the stork behaved correctly in retaliating? How do you think these events affected the relationship between the fox and the stork? Write your answers below.

   It probably adversely affected their friendship. The stork should have turned

   the other cheek. Two wrongs do not make a right.

In fables, animals take on the traits and characteristics of human beings. Below is another version of The Fox and the Stork fable called "Two Friends Who Met For Dinner" by Alexander McCall Smith. In this African version, the main characters are actually humans. Do you think this changes the essential message of the fable? Can you still make a prediction about what is going to happen in the story based on the title?

Exercise 6: Drawing Inferences from a Fable Continued

Directions: Read this fable and answer the questions that follow.

TWO FRIENDS WHO MET FOR DINNER

Alexander McCall Smith

A man once asked a friend to have a meal with him. The friend was happy to receive this invitation, as he was never asked by anybody else to go anywhere. He spent a great deal of time making sure that he was smartly dressed for the meal so that his friend would be proud of him.

The guest arrived at his friend's house and was asked inside. Together they sat at the table and smelled the delicious smell of the food that had been cooked.

"All the food is in this calabash," said the host. "To get it out, you have to put your hand in the neck and take out a piece. I shall show you."

The host inserted his hand into the thin neck of the calabash and took out a morsel of food. It looked good, and the guest began to feel his mouth watering. Reaching across, he put his hand into the calabash and picked out a piece of food. Unfortunately, when he tried to take out his hand he found that it was too big to pass through the neck of the calabash with food in it. In order to get his hand out, he had to leave the food inside.

The host appeared not to notice the difficulty in which his guest found himself. He had small hands, and so he was able to take food out and put it into his mouth. He did not offer to give any food to his guest, although he handed him the calabash again and told him to help himself.

After a few minutes, the host had eaten all the food. He looked at his guest and smiled.

"I am sorry that you did not get much food," he said. "But if you have big hands, then that is one of the things that happens to you."

The guest said nothing. He was very sad that the only invitation that he had received for many years should have turned out to be such an unhappy occasion.

Some days later, the guest invited his host to dinner in his own hut. Before his friend arrived, however, he burned all the grass around his hut, so that the ground was black and charred with stubble.

The friend entered the hut and took off his hat.

"This is a good place," he said. "I am surprised that you do not have more friends, living in a comfortable place like this."

The other man smiled.

"The food is ready," he said. "But first, if you don't mind, you must wash your feet. People do not like dirty feet in this place."

The guest understood, and immediately walked off to the river to wash his feet. Then, when they were quite clean, he returned to the hut and found that the host had already started the meal. The host looked at the guest's feet and shook his head.

"I'm afraid that your feet are still very dirty," he said. "You will have to return to the river and wash them again. This is very good food here and I do not want it spoiled by dirty feet."

The guest knew that this was right, but he could not understand why his feet were so dirty after he had washed them so carefully. This time, he ran to the river's edge and washed both feet thoroughly. Then, checking to see that they were both quite clean, he ran back to the hut. On his way, of course, he passed through the middle of the charred stubble that surrounded his friend's hut. This soon covered his feet and made them dirty again.

"Oh dear," said the friend. "I must ask you to wash your feet one more time. Look at how dirty they are."

The friend was now becoming angry, but he ran back to the river and washed the dirty feet again. Then he returned to the hut.

The friend looked at him.

"I'm sorry," he said. "I have just finished all the good food I prepared for the meal. Also, I'm very sorry to tell you, your feet are still dirty."

Smith, Alexander McCall, *The Girl Who Married a Lion and Other Tales from Africa*,
New York: Pantheon Books, 2004, pp. 177–180

1. How do you think the events described in the fable affected the friend-

   ship of the two men? They probably strained or ended the friendship.

2. After the first dinner party, what is the mood of the guest?

   not happy

3. After the second dinner party, what is the mood of the guest?

   angry

4. What kind of person is the first guest? insecure

5. What kind of person is the second guest? self-centered

6. In this fable, what is the author trying to say about friendship? In what

   ways is the fable critical of human nature? A friend doesn't just

   think about himself or herself. The men are displaying selfish, petty traits.

Directions: Find the words in the fable that best complete each of the following sentences.

1. The guest dressed nicely because he wanted his friend to be ___proud___ of him.

2. The food was in a thin-necked ___calabash___ .

3. The host had hands that were ___small___ so he was easily able to obtain the food.

4. When the guest reciprocated by having his friend to dinner, he first burned the ___grass___ around his hut.

5. The guest washed his feet ___three___ times in the river, but they remained dirty because of the charred stubble around the hut.

6. The host finished all of the ___food___ by himself.

"You're a lucky fellow. You landed in a wood near the beach. You're in Brighton."

GETTING FOCUSED

This short story is a good example of an individual using inferences, or educated guesses, to determine his location and the seriousness of his situation. You, the reader, will also need to read between the lines in order to understand "Beware of the Dog."

BIO-SKETCH

Roald Dahl was born September 13, 1916, in Llandaff, South Wales. Dahl is best known as the author of the children's books *Charlie and the Chocolate Factory* and *James and the Giant Peach*. He is also well known for short stories for adults and his autobiographical descriptions of flying in World War II. His adult fiction, based on real-life situations, is noted for unexpected plot twists.

In 1939, Dahl joined the Royal Air Force training squadron in Nairobi, Kenya. He soon proved his skill as a fighter pilot engaging the Germans in battle near the Mediterranean Sea. While strafing a convoy of trucks near Alexandria, Egypt, his plane was hit by machine-gun fire. The plane crashed, and Dahl crawled from the wreckage as the gas tanks exploded. The crash left his skull fractured, his nose crumpled, and his eyes temporarily stuck shut. After six months of recovery, he returned to his squadron in Greece and shot down four enemy planes; however, frequent blackouts eventually rendered him unable to fly.

Dahl received numerous awards for his writing, including the Edgar Award from Mystery Writers of America and the *New York Times* Outstanding Books

(continued)

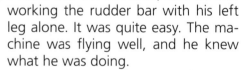

READING   *continued*

award. Many of his stories have been adapted for movies and television. The short story featured here was made into the movie *36 Hours* (1964) and also the movie *Breaking Point* (1989). Dahl died November 23, 1990, in Oxford, England.

TACKLING VOCABULARY

Channel   The English Channel is a body of water separating England from France. During much of World War II, France was occupied by Germany.

undulating   moving in waves

delirious   raving without making sense

RAF   Britain's Royal Air Force

Lancasters   Britain's bomber planes

Flying Fortresses   American bomber planes

Hurricane   British fighter plane

garde au chien   French for "beware of the dog"

Directions: Answer the questions following each section of the story by using the clues provided by the author.

BEWARE OF THE DOG

Roald Dahl

Down below there was only a vast white undulating sea of cloud. Above there was the sun, and the sun was white like the clouds, because it is never yellow when one looks at it from high in the air.

2   He was still flying the Spitfire. His right hand was on the stick, and he was

working the rudder bar with his left leg alone. It was quite easy. The machine was flying well, and he knew what he was doing.

3   Everything is fine, he thought. I'm doing all right. I'm doing nicely. I know my way home. I'll be there in half an hour. When I land I shall taxi in and switch off my engine and I shall say, help me to get out, will you. I shall make my voice sound ordinary and natural and none of them will take any notice. Then I shall say, someone help me to get out. I can't

do it alone because I've lost one of my legs. They'll all laugh and think that I'm joking, and I shall say, all right, come and have a look. Then Yorky will climb up onto the wing and look inside. He'll probably be sick because of all the blood and the mess. I shall laugh and say, for God's sake, help me out.

4   He glanced down again at his right leg. There was not much of it left. The cannon shell had taken him on the thigh, just above the knee, and now there was nothing but a great mess and a lot of blood. But there was no pain. When he looked down, he felt as though he were seeing something that did not belong to him. It had nothing to do with him. It was just a mess which happened to be there in the cockpit; something strange and unusual and rather interesting. It was like finding a dead cat on the sofa.

5   He really felt fine, and because he still felt fine, he felt excited and unafraid.

6   I won't even bother to call up on the radio for the blood wagon, he thought. It isn't necessary. And when I land I'll sit there quite normally and say, some of you fellows come and help me out, will you, because I've lost one of my legs. That will be funny. I'll laugh a little while I'm saying it; I'll say it calmly and slowly, and they'll think I'm joking. When Yorky comes up onto the wing and gets sick, I'll say, Yorky, have you fixed my car yet?

7   Then he saw the sun shining on the engine cowling of his machine. He saw the rivets in the metal, and he remembered where he was. He realized that he was no longer feeling good; that he was sick and giddy. His head kept falling forward onto his chest because his neck seemed no longer to have any strength. But he knew that he was flying the Spitfire, and he could feel the handle of the stick between the fingers of his right hand.

8   I'm going to pass out, he thought. Any moment now I'm going to pass out.

9   He looked at his altimeter. Twenty-one thousand. To test himself he tried to read the hundreds as well as the thousands. Twenty-one thousand and what? As he looked the dial became blurred, and he could not even see the needle. He knew then that he must bail out; that there was not a second to lose, otherwise he would become unconscious. Quickly, frantically, he tried to slide back the hood with his left hand, but he had not the strength. For a second he took his right hand off the stick, and with both hands he managed to push the hood back. The rush of cold air on his face seemed to help. He had a moment of great clearness, and his actions became orderly and precise. That is what happens with a good pilot. He took some quick deep breaths from his oxygen mask, and as he did so, he looked out over the side of the cockpit. Down below there was only a vast white sea of cloud, and he realized that he did not know where he was.

10   It'll be the Channel, he thought. I'm sure to fall in the drink.

11   He throttled back, pulled off his helmet, undid his straps, and pushed the stick hard over to the left. The Spitfire dipped its port wing, and turned smoothly over onto its back. The pilot fell out.

12   As he fell he opened his eyes, because he knew that he must not pass out before he had pulled the cord. On one side he saw the sun; on the other he saw the whiteness of the clouds, and as he fell, as he somersaulted in the air, the white clouds chased the sun and the sun chased the clouds. They chased each other in a small circle; they ran faster and faster, and there was the sun and the clouds and the clouds and the sun, and the clouds came nearer until suddenly there was no longer any sun, but only a great whiteness. The whole world was white, and there was nothing in it. It was so white that sometimes it looked black, and after a time it was either white or black, but mostly it was white. He

watched it as it turned from white to black, and then back to white again, and the white stayed for a long time, but the black lasted only for a few seconds. He got into the habit of going to sleep during the white periods, and of waking up just in time to see the world when it was black. But the black was very quick. Sometimes it was only a flash, like someone switching off the light, and switching it on again at once, and so whenever it was white, he dozed off.

1. What can we infer about the pilot's personality from his reaction to the loss of his leg? <u>He is trying to remain calm. He displays self-reliance and</u>

   <u>humor.</u>

2. Why does the pilot attempt to read the altimeter? <u>He is testing himself.</u>

   <u>He's trying to prove he's conscious and coherent.</u>

3. At the beginning of the story, the pilot is suffering from shock. What specific details from the story allow the reader to make this inference? What can we infer is happening to the pilot when his world keeps changing from black to white? <u>_____</u>

   <u>He is in and out of a state of consciousness.</u>

13 One day, when it was white, he put out a hand and he touched something. He took it between his fingers and crumpled it. For a time he lay there, idly letting the tips of his fingers play with the thing which they had touched. Then slowly he opened his eyes, looked down at his hand, and saw that he was holding something which was white. It was the edge of a sheet. He knew it was a sheet because he could see the texture of the material and the stitching on the hem. He screwed up his eyes, and opened them again quickly. This time he saw the room. He saw the bed in which he was lying; he saw the grey walls and the door and the green curtains over the window. There were some roses on the table by his bed.

14 Then he saw the basin on the table near the roses. It was a white enamel basin, and beside it there was a small medicine glass.

15 This is a hospital, he thought. I am in a hospital. But he could remember nothing. He lay back on his pillow, looking at the ceiling and wondering what had happened. He was gazing at the smooth grayness of the ceiling which was so clean and gray, and then suddenly he saw a fly walking upon it. The sight of this fly, the suddenness of seeing this small black speck on a sea of gray, brushed the surface of his brain, and quickly, in that second, he remembered everything. He remembered the Spitfire and he remembered the altimeter showing twenty-one thousand feet. He remembered the pushing back of the hood with both hands, and he remembered the bailing out. He remembered his leg.

16 It seemed all right now. He looked down at the end of the bed, but he could not tell. He put one hand underneath the bedclothes and felt for his knees.

He found one of them, but when he felt for the other, his hand touched something which was soft and covered in bandages.

17 Just then the door opened and a nurse came in.

18 "Hello," she said. "So you've waked up at last."

19 She was not good-looking, but she was large and clean. She was between thirty and forty and she had fair hair. More than that he did not notice.

20 "Where am I?"

21 "You're a lucky fellow. You landed in a wood near the beach. You're in Brighton. They brought you in two days ago, and now you're all fixed up. You look fine."

22 "I've lost a leg," he said.

23 "That's nothing. We'll get you another one. Now you must go to sleep. The doctor will be coming to see you in about an hour." She picked up the basin and the medicine glass and went out.

24 But he did not sleep. He wanted to keep his eyes open because he was frightened that if he shut them again everything would go away. He lay looking at the ceiling. The fly was still there. It was very energetic. It would run forward very fast for a few inches, then it would stop. Then it would run forward again, stop, run forward, stop, and every now and then it would take off and buzz around viciously in small circles. It always landed back in the same place on the ceiling and started running and stopping all over again. He watched it for so long that after a while it was no longer a fly, but only a black speck upon a sea of gray, and he was still watching it when the nurse opened the door, and stood aside while the doctor came in. He was an Army doctor, a major, and he had some last war ribbons on his chest. He was bald and small, but he had a cheerful face and kind eyes.

25 "Well, well," he said. "So you've decided to wake up at last. How are you feeling?"

26 "I feel all right."

27 "That's the stuff. You'll be up and about in no time."

28 The doctor took his wrist to feel his pulse.

29 "By the way," he said, "some of the lads from your squadron were ringing up and asking about you. They wanted to come along and see you, but I said that they'd better wait a day or two. Told them you were all right, and that they could come and see you a little later on. Just lie quiet and take it easy for a bit. Got something to read?" He glanced at the table with the roses. "No, well, nurse will look after you. She'll get you anything you want." With that he waved his hand and went out, followed by the large clean nurse.

4. How do you think the pilot feels about being in Brighton? <u>He feels like he</u>

<u>is in a safe place.</u>

5. What is the significance of the fly? <u>The fly reminds him of what happened.</u>

_____

30 When they had gone, he lay back and looked at the ceiling again. The fly was still there and as he lay watching it he heard the noise of an airplane in the distance. He lay listening to the sound of its engines. It was a long way

away. I wonder what it is, he thought. Let me see if I can place it. Suddenly he jerked his head sharply to one side. Anyone who has been bombed can tell the noise of a Junkers 88. They can tell most other German bombers for that matter, but especially a Junkers 88. The engines seem to sing a duet. There is a deep vibrating bass voice and with it there is a high-pitched tenor. It is the singing of the tenor which makes the sound of a JU-88 something which one cannot mistake.

31 He lay listening to the noise, and he felt quite certain about what it was. But where were the sirens, and where the guns? That German pilot certainly had a nerve coming near Brighton alone in daylight.

32 The aircraft was always far away, and soon the noise faded away into the distance. Later on there was another. This one, too, was far away, but there was the same deep undulating bass and the high singing tenor, and there was no mistaking it. He had heard that noise every day during the battle.

33 He was puzzled. There was a bell on the table by the bed. He reached out his hand and rang it. He heard the noise of footsteps down the corridor, and the nurse came in.

34 "Nurse, what were those airplanes?"

35 "I'm sure I don't know. I didn't hear them. Probably fighters or bombers. I expect they were returning from France. Why, what's the matter?"

36 "They were JU-88's. I'm sure they were JU-88's. I know the sound of the engines. There were two of them. What were they doing over here?"

37 The nurse came up to the side of his bed and began to straighten out the sheets and tuck them in under the mattress.

38 "Gracious me, what things you imagine. You mustn't worry about a thing like that. Would you like me to get you something to read?"

39 "No, thank you."

40 She patted his pillow and brushed back the hair from his forehead with her hand.

41 "They never come over in daylight any longer. You know that. They were probably Lancasters or Flying Fortresses."

42 "Nurse."

43 "Yes."

44 "Could I have a cigarette?"

45 "Why certainly you can."

46 She went out and came back almost at once with a packet of Players and some matches. She handed one to him and when he had put it in his mouth, she struck a match and lit it.

47 "If you want me again," she said, "just ring the bell," and she went out.

48 Once toward evening he heard the noise of another aircraft. It was far away, but even so he knew that it was a single-engined machine. But he could not place it. It was going fast; he could tell that. But it wasn't a Spit, and it wasn't a Hurricane. It did not sound like an American engine either. They make more noise. He did not know what it was, and it worried him greatly. Perhaps I am very ill, he thought. Perhaps I am imagining things. Perhaps I am a little delirious. I simply do not know what to think.

6. Why does the pilot become disturbed and agitated? What does he think

   is happening? He hears a German bomber. He thinks they are under attack.

7. Why does the pilot expect to hear sirens and guns? He expects his

countrymen to defend themselves.

8. What clues lead the reader to know that the story takes place during

World War II? names of the aircraft, participants in the conflict, fight over the

English Channel

49 That evening the nurse came in with a basin of hot water and began to wash him.

50 "Well," she said, "I hope you don't still think that we're being bombed."

51 She had taken off his pajama top and was soaping his right arm with a flannel. He did not answer.

52 She rinsed the flannel in the water, rubbed more soap on it, and began to wash his chest.

53 "You're looking fine this evening," she said. "They operated on you as soon as you came in. They did a marvelous job. You'll be all right. I've got a brother in the RAF," she added. "Flying bombers."

54 He said, "I went to school in Brighton."

55 She looked up quickly. "Well, that's fine," she said. "I expect you'll know some people in the town."

56 "Yes," he said, "I know quite a few."

57 She had finished washing his chest and arms, and now she turned back the bedclothes, so that his left leg was uncovered. She did it in such a way that his bandaged stump remained under the sheets. She undid the cord of his pajama trousers and took them off. There was no trouble because they had cut off the right trouser leg, so that it could not interfere with the bandages. She began to wash his left leg and the rest of his body. This was the first time he had had a bed bath, and he was embarrassed. She laid a towel under his leg, and she was washing his foot with the flannel. She said, "This wretched soap won't lather at all. It's the water. It's as hard as nails."

58 He said, "None of the soap is very good now and, of course, with hard water it's hopeless." As he said it he remembered something. He remembered the baths which he used to take at school in Brighton, in the long stone-floored bathroom which had four baths in a room. He remembered how the water was so soft that you had to take a shower afterwards to get all the soap off your body, and he remembered how the foam used to float on the surface of the water, so that you could not see your legs underneath. He remembered that sometimes they were given calcium tablets because the school doctor used to say that soft water was bad for the teeth.

59 "In Brighton," he said, "the water isn't. . ."

60 He did not finish the sentence. Something had occurred to him; something so fantastic and absurd that for a moment he felt like telling the nurse about it and having a good laugh.

61 She looked up. "The water isn't what?" she said.

62 "Nothing," he answered. "I was dreaming.

63 She rinsed the flannel in the basin, wiped the soap off his leg, and dried him with a towel.

64   "It's nice to be washed," he said. "I feel better." He was feeling his face with his hands. "I need a shave."

65   "We'll do that tomorrow," she said. "Perhaps you can do it yourself then."

9. What is the significance of the pilot's memory of Brighton? Why does he fail to complete his sentence to the nurse? His memory of

   Brighton doesn't fit with the information the nurse has given him.

10. What specific details make the pilot suspect he is not in Brighton, England? He remembers that Brighton had soft water not hard water.

_____

66   That night he could not sleep. He lay awake thinking of the Junkers 88's and of the hardness of the water. He could think of nothing else. They were JU-88's, he said to himself. I know they were. And yet it is not possible, because they would not be flying around so low over here in broad daylight. I know that it is true, and yet I know that it is impossible. Perhaps I am ill. Perhaps I am behaving like a fool and do not know what I am doing or saying. Perhaps I am delirious. For a long time he lay awake thinking these things, and once he sat up in bed and said aloud, "I will prove that I am not crazy. I will make a little speech about something complicated and intellectual. I will talk about what to do with Germany after the war." But before he had time to begin, he was asleep.

67   He woke just as the first light of day was showing through the slit in the curtains over the window. The room was still dark, but he could tell that it was already beginning to get light outside. He lay looking at the gray light which was showing through the slit in the curtain, and as he lay there he remembered the day before. He remembered the Junkers 88's and the hardness of the water; he remembered the large pleasant nurse and the kind doctor, and now the small grain of doubt took root in his mind and it began to grow.

68   He looked around the room. The nurse had taken the roses out the night before, and there was nothing except the table with a packet of cigarettes, a box of matches and an ashtray. Otherwise, it was bare. It was no longer warm or friendly. It was not even comfortable. It was cold and empty and very quiet.

69   Slowly the grain of doubt grew, and with it came fear, a light, dancing fear that warned but did not frighten; the kind of fear that one gets not because one is afraid, but because one feels that there is something wrong. Quickly the doubt and the fear grew so that he became restless and angry, and when he touched his forehead with his hand, he found that it was damp with sweat. He knew then that he must do something; that he must find some way of proving to himself that he was either right or wrong, and he looked up and saw again the window and the green curtains. From where he lay, that window was right in front of him, but it was fully ten yards away. Somehow he must reach it and look out. The idea became an obsession with him, and soon he could think of nothing except the window. But what about his leg? He put his hand underneath the bedclothes and felt the thick bandaged stump which was all that was left on the right-hand side. It seemed all right. It didn't hurt. But it would not be easy.

11. Why does the pilot decide to look out the window? <u>He has to prove to</u>

<u>himself whether he is right or wrong.</u>

70 He sat up. Then he pushed the bedclothes aside and put his left leg on the floor. Slowly, carefully, he swung his body over until he had both hands on the floor as well; and then he was out of bed, kneeling on the carpet. He looked at the stump. It was very short and thick, covered with bandages. It was beginning to hurt and he could feel it throbbing. He wanted to collapse, lie down on the carpet and do nothing, but he knew that he must go on.

71 With two arms and one leg, he crawled over towards the window. He would reach forward as far as he could with his arms, then he would give a little jump and slide his left leg along after them. Each time he did, it jarred his wound so that he gave a soft grunt of pain, but he continued to crawl across the floor on two hands and one knee. When he got to the window he reached up, and one at a time he placed both hands on the sill. Slowly he raised himself up until he was standing on his left leg. Then quickly he pushed aside the curtains and looked out.

72 He saw a small house with a gray tiled roof standing alone beside a narrow lane, and immediately behind it there was a plowed field. In front of the house there was an untidy garden, and there was a green hedge separating the garden from the lane. He was looking at the hedge when he saw the sign. It was just a piece of board nailed to the top of a short pole, and because the hedge had not been trimmed for a long time, the branches had grown out around the sign so that it seemed almost as though it had been placed in the middle of the hedge. There was something written on the board with white paint, and he pressed his head against the glass of the window, trying to read what it said. The first letter was a G, he could see that. The second was an A, and the third was an R. One after another he managed to see what the letters were. There were three words, and slowly he spelled the letters out aloud to himself as he managed to read them. G-A-R-D-E A-U C-H-I-E-N. Garde au chien. That is what it said.

73 He stood there balancing on one leg and holding tightly to the edges of the window sill with his hands, staring at the sign and at the whitewashed lettering of the words. For a moment he could think of nothing at all. He stood there looking at the sign, repeating the words over and over to himself, and then slowly he began to realize the full meaning of the thing. He looked up at the cottage and at the plowed field. He looked at the small orchard on the left of the cottage and he looked at the green countryside beyond. "So this is France," he said. "I am in France."

74 Now the throbbing in his right thigh was very great. It felt as though someone was pounding the end of his stump with a hammer, and suddenly the pain became so intense that it affected his head and for a moment he thought he was going to fall. Quickly he knelt down again, crawled back to the bed and hoisted himself in. He pulled the bedclothes over himself and lay back on the pillow, exhausted. He could still think of nothing at all except the small sign by the hedge, and the plowed field and the orchard. It was the words on the sign that he could not forget.

12. What is the significance of what the pilot finds? <u>He realizes he is in</u>

<u>France.</u>

13. Why does the pilot's leg suddenly begin to throb? He exerted himself

getting to the window. It also reflects his inner turmoil.

75 It was some time before the nurse came in. She came carrying a basin of hot water and she said, "Good morning, how are you today?"

76 He said, "Good morning, nurse."

77 The pain was still great under the bandages, but he did not wish to tell this woman anything. He looked at her as she busied herself with getting the washing things ready. He looked at her more carefully now. Her hair was very fair. She was tall and big-boned, and her face seemed pleasant. But there was something a little uneasy about her eyes. They were never still. They never looked at anything for more than a moment and they moved too quickly from one place to another in the room. There was something about her movements also. They were too sharp and nervous to go well with the casual manner in which she spoke.

14. Who does the pilot think the nurse is? He knows the nurse is an enemy.

78 She set down the basin, took off his pajama top and began to wash him.

79 "Did you sleep well?"

80 "Yes."

81 "Good," she said. She was washing his arms and his chest.

82 "I believe there's someone coming down to see you from the Air Ministry after breakfast," she went on. "They want a report or something. I expect you know all about it. How you got shot down and all that. I won't let him stay long, so don't worry."

83 He did not answer. She finished washing him, and gave him a toothbrush and some tooth powder. He brushed his teeth, rinsed his mouth and spat the water out into the basin.

84 Later she brought him his breakfast on a tray, but he did not want to eat. He was still feeling weak and sick, and he wished only to lie still and think about what had happened. And there was a sentence running through his head. It was a sentence which Johnny, the Intelligence Officer of his squadron, always repeated to the pilots every day before they went out. He could see Johnny now, leaning against the wall of the dispersal hut with his pipe in his hand, saying, "And if they get you, don't forget, just your name, rank and number. Nothing else. For God's sake, say nothing else."

85 "There you are," she said as she put the tray on his lap. "I've got you an egg. Can you manage all right?"

86 "Yes."

87 She stood beside the bed. "Are you feeling all right?"

88 "Yes."

89 "Good. If you want another egg I might be able to get you one."

90 "This is all right."

91 "Well, just ring the bell if you want any more." And she went out.

92 He had just finished eating, when the nurse came in again.

93 She said, "Wing Commander Roberts is here. I've told him that he can only stay for a few minutes."

94   She beckoned with her hand and the Wing Commander came in.

95   "Sorry to bother you like this," he said.

96   He was an ordinary RAF officer, dressed in a uniform which was a little shabby, and he wore wings and a DFC. He was fairly tall and thin with plenty of black hair. His teeth, which were irregular and widely spaced, stuck out a little even when he closed his mouth. As he spoke he took a printed form and a pencil from his pocket, and he pulled up a chair and sat down.

97   "How are you feeling?"

98   There was no answer.

99   "Tough luck about your leg. I know how you feel. I hear you put up a fine show before they got you."

100   The man in the bed was lying quite still, watching the man in the chair.

101   The man in the chair said, "Well, let's get this stuff over. I'm afraid you'll have to answer a few questions so that I can fill in this combat report. Let me see now, first of all, what was your squadron?"

102   The man in the bed did not move. He looked straight at the Wing Commander and he said, "My name is Peter Williamson. My rank is Squadron Leader and my number is nine seven two four five seven."

"Beware the Dog" from *Over To You: Ten Stories of Flyers and Flying* by Roald Dahl. Reprinted by permission of the Estate of Roald Dahl and the Watkins/Loomis Agency.

15. At the time of the story, what country occupies France? <u>Germany</u>

16. Who is the Wing Commander and what does he want from the pilot? Why did the nurse, doctor, and Wing Commander lie to the pilot?

   <u>The Wing Commander is an enemy. They wanted him to betray his</u>

   <u>country's military secrets.</u>

17. Why does the pilot decide to provide only basic information to the Wing

   Commander? <u>He remembers the intelligence officer telling him not</u>

   <u>to reveal any information if he is captured.</u>

18. At the end of the story, the reader can infer the pilot knows he is a prisoner of war. How does the reader come to this conclusion?

   <u>He gives only his name, rank, and serial number.</u>

19. Should the pilot be considered a hero? Why or why not? <u>Yes, he</u>

   <u>demonstrates bravery in battle and in the hospital. He protects his country.</u>

20. What do you think is going to happen to the pilot? <u>He is now a</u>

   <u>prisoner of war.</u>

Vocabulary in Context

Directions: Use the vocabulary words to complete the crossword puzzle.

absurd	giddy	jarred	slit	undulating
blurred	hoisted	obsession	speck	vast
crumpled	idly	precise	tenor	vibrating
delirious	interfere	shabby	throbbing	wretched

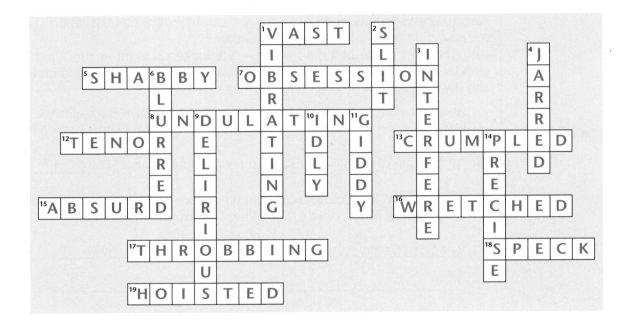

ACROSS CLUES
 1. very great or large
 5. old and worn out
 7. an idea that fills one's thoughts and can't be put out of mind
 8. rising and falling in waves
12. high pitch
13. crushed

15. unreasonable; ridiculous
16. worthless
17. pulsating
18. very small spot
19. raised

DOWN CLUES
 1. echoing; resounding
 2. narrow opening

 3. get in the way of
 4. jolted
 6. unclear; made less sharp
 9. hallucinating; raving incoherently
10. lazily; uselessly
11. dizzy
14. very careful; accurate

Written Assignment

How do you think you would behave if you were placed in a situation similar to the pilot's? Do you think you would divulge information about your squadron? Or do you think you would just give your name and serial number? Do you think being a prisoner of war would be harder on a male or a female? Write several paragraphs describing how you think you would conduct yourself.

Internet Activity

Senator John McCain is a well-known prisoner of war from the Vietnam conflict. Pull up information on Senator McCain's history as a P.O.W. Write a paragraph describing his ordeal.

Figurative Language

© ZITS Partnership. King Features Syndicate.

There are many expressions that can't be understood in a literal, word-by-word sense. These expressions are examples of **figurative language.** Authors use these expressions to make their writing more colorful or interesting and to create fresh effects.

In the cartoon above, the figurative expression "heads will roll" means that someone will be severely punished. There are many other figurative expressions that make reference to the word "head." What do you think the following expressions mean?

1. You'd better keep your head.

   keep control

2. Don't lose your head over that.

   lose control

3. You're head and shoulders above her.

   better than; superior to

4. Don't let it go to your head.

   feel dizzy or drunk; feel too proud

5. It's completely over your head.

   too hard to understand

6. You have your head in the clouds.

behaving absent-mindedly or impractically

7. Keep your head above water.

stay out of trouble

8. He's head over heels in love.

completely; thoroughly

FIGURATIVE LANGUAGE

Figurative language appeals to your senses, your imagination, and your emotions. As an illustration of the difference between figurative expressions and literal ones, look at the sentences below. In each example, the first expression is a figurative one and the second literal. Some figurative expressions, such as those in the examples below, are said so often they become trite or stale. When that happens, they become **clichés.**

Example 1

The test was a piece of cake.

I think I did pretty well on the test we took today.

Example 2

Over the weekend, she was as sick as a dog.

She was really sick over the weekend.

Exercise 1: Literal or Figurative Language

Directions: In the sentences below, if the language is meant literally, write an **L** on the blank. If the language is figurative, write an **F** on the blank. Then explain the meaning of the figurative expressions.

_____F_____ 1. I don't think you should say that to Pete. He's already mad, and

you'll just add fuel to the fire. make the situation worse

_____F_____ 2. Sarah is the apple of her mother's eye. is special to her mother

_____L_____ 3. If you're going to the store, can you get me some milk and eggs?

_____ L _____ 4. His insurance rates are going to go up because the accident was entirely his fault. _____

_____ F _____ 5. He's been goofing off all summer, but when school starts he's going to have to buckle down. work hard _____

_____ F _____ 6. She works around the clock at her job. I think she needs a long vacation. all the time _____

_____ L _____ 7. A healthful diet includes lots of fruits and vegetables.

_____

_____ L _____ 8. Their marriage probably isn't going to last. They're already considering a trial separation. _____

_____ F _____ 9. They haven't spoken for five years. I think it's time to bury the hatchet. forgive and forget – make peace _____

_____ L _____ 10. Registration for fall classes begins in August. _____

TYPES OF FIGURATIVE LANGUAGE

Many figurative expressions make comparisons by means of similes, metaphors, or personification.

DENNIS THE MENACE

Dennis the Menace © North American Syndicate.

"MY GRANDPA SAYS THAT LIFE IS LIKE MASHED POTATOES…ONCE IN A WHILE, THERE'S GONNA BE A LUMP."

Similes

A **simile** is a comparison between two unlike things that is introduced by the words *like, as,* or *as if.* For example, a writer might describe a stormy sky by saying, "The sky darkened and storm clouds towered like skyscrapers against the horizon." In this case, the writer is comparing tall buildings to clouds in order to convey the sense of how large and menacing the clouds appear. In the cartoon, Dennis makes use of a simile to explain "life" to his friend Joey.

What does Dennis mean when he uses the simile "Life is like mashed potatoes . . . Once in a while, there's gonna be a *lump*"?

There are going to be problems periodically. Life does not

always go smoothly.

Exercise 2: Similes

Directions: Fill in the blanks below to create similes. Answers will vary. Sample answers are given.
Example: He is as brave as <u>King Kong.</u>

1. Jennifer's eyes were as blue as <u>the sky</u>   .

2. The sun's rays were as hot as <u>a barbecue grill</u>   .

3. My pillow is as soft as <u>a kitten</u>   .

4. My car is as reliable as <u>the days on a calendar</u>   .

5. Jeremy's room is as messy as <u>a rat's nest</u>   .

Metaphors

Metaphors state the comparison between two things directly using a state-of-being verb. So, instead of saying "Life is *like* mashed potatoes," a metaphor would state "Life *is* mashed potatoes." For example, someone might say, "Life is not a bed of roses for Maya" in reference to a friend who is struggling to simultaneously work, get through school, and bring up a family. That person is comparing a "bed of roses," a vision of peace and beauty, with the hectic pace and financial struggles of Maya's life in order to highlight the difficulties she is having.

Exercise 3: Metaphors

Directions: Fill in the blanks below with a noun for the words in parentheses to create metaphors. Answers will vary. Sample answers are given.
Example: Her food is <u>garbage</u>. (something distasteful)

1. The football player is a/an <u>giant</u> of a man. (something large and solid)

2. The way she can recall information is amazing. Her mind is a/an <u>computer</u>. (something neat or orderly)

3. When he wakes up in the morning his face is a/an <u>a sheet of sandpaper</u> to the touch. (something rough or scratchy)

4. Tina's worried about her baby. She's so light she's just a/an <u>feather</u>. (something that weighs very little)

5. Gloria was a/an <u>a mule</u>; nobody could get her to change her mind. (something stubborn or unyielding)

Personification

Personification is a special type of metaphor in which nonhuman or inanimate objects are given human traits or attributes. If you were to say, "The ocean stretched lazily, caressing the shore with gentle waves," you would be using personification. The ocean is not a person, but in the sentence it is being described as acting like one.

Exercise 4: Personification

Directions: Replace the italicized word in each sentence with one of your own. Make sure the sentence still makes sense. Answers will vary. Sample answers are given.
Example: The alarm clock *told* the time. shrieked

1. The front door *squealed* when she entered. ___squeaked___

2. The car *sputtered* when I turned on the engine. ___coughed___

3. His hair *stands up* after using that gel. ___salutes___

4. The flood *swallowed* the whole village. ___gobbled___

5. The moon *walks* across the sky. ___skates___

Poetry

Can you find the figurative language in the following cartoon?

4-21

© 2007 Bil Keane, Inc.
Dist. by King Features Synd.
www.familycircus.com

JEFF
and
Bil KEANE

**"Our car's engine can imitate
Kittycat! Daddy said it's
purring like a kitten!"**

Exercise 5: Poetry

Directions: Read this poem by Billy Collins, the U.S. poet laureate for 2002–2003, and answer the questions that follow.

"The essentials of poetry are rhythm, dance, and the human voice."

—Earle Birney

Introduction to Poetry

I ask them to take a poem
and hold it up to the light
like a color slide

or press an ear against its hive.
I say drop a mouse into a poem
and watch him probe his way out,

or walk inside the poem's room
and feel the walls for a light switch.

I want them to water ski
across the surface of a poem
waving at the author's name on the shore.
But all they want to do
is tie the poem to a chair with a rope
and torture a confession out of it.

They begin beating it with a hose
to find out what it really means.

—Billy Collins

From *The Apple That Astonished Paris*, 1996, University of Arkansas Press, Fayetteville, Arkansas Copyright 1988

1. Who is the speaker referring to when he says "they" and "them"?

   students; people who overanalyze poetry

2. According to the first four stanzas, which of the five senses (sight, hearing, touch, taste, smell) are necessary to read a poem?

   sight, hearing, touch

3. What does the speaker mean when he says, "I want them to water ski across the surface of a poem waving at the author's name on the shore"? Don't worry about who wrote the poem just enjoy it.

4. According to the speaker, those looking at a poem "tie the poem to a chair with a rope," "torture a confession out of it," and "begin beating it with a hose." What do these images suggest to you? How do they contrast to the other images the speaker has already described?

   They suggest "torturing" a poem. They contrast with the idea of

   experiencing it.

5. How does the speaker feel a poem should be read? Read the poem to find

   your own meaning.

6. How do you think a poem should be read? Answers will vary.

7. What is the main idea of the poem? What is the author's purpose in

   writing the poem? Poetry is meant to be enjoyed not overanalyzed. His

   purpose is to persuade.

Exercise 6: Practice Identifying Similes and Metaphors

Directions: Indicate whether the comparison being made in each of these sentences is expressed through a simile (**S**) or a metaphor (**M**).

____M____ 1. Truth is a shadow. (Stephen Crane)

____S____ 2. My heart is like a singing bird. (Christina Rossetti)

____M____ 3. Morning is a new sheet of paper for you to write on. (Eve Merriam)

____M____ 4. All the world's a stage. (William Shakespeare)

____S____ 5. The snow was like a blanket covering the earth.

____S____ 6. The sun's glare was like a flashlight shining in her face.

____S____ 7. The Mississippi River looked like molten chocolate.

_____S_____ 8. I sat folded like a lawn chair in the backseat of the tiny car.

_____M_____ 9. Her eyes were question marks.

_____S_____ 10. He was as quiet as a cat stalking a bird.

_____S_____ 11. His eyes were as big as saucers.

_____M_____ 12. She is the sun to me.

_____S_____ 13. He slipped away like a shadow.

_____S_____ 14. His body lay as stiff as a candle in the coffin.

_____M_____ 15. She was a ray of sunshine.

Exercise 7: Recognizing Personification

Directions: Choose the answer that best explains the meaning of the italicized word or phrase.

Example: The chair _groaned_ when Derek sat down.

Meaning: A chair can't groan. The author is implying that the chair is weak or that Derek is too heavy for it.

_____c_____ 1. The alarm clock _screamed_ at me to wake up. This means that
     a. the alarm was too quiet.
     b. the clock was ticking.
     c. the alarm was loud.
     d. I was ready to get up.

_____c_____ 2. The darkness in the cave _imprisoned_ Marla. This means Marla felt
     a. surrounded by bats.
     b. free to come and go as she pleased.
     c. as though she couldn't escape.
     d. all of the above.

_____a_____ 3. The leaves on the tree _danced_ in the wind. This means the leaves
     a. moved about in different directions.
     b. turned red and yellow.
     c. didn't move.
     d. were ready to fall from the tree.

c 4. The city *woke up and stretched*. This means that the city
   a. remained dark and quiet.
   b. shut down for the day.
   c. was becoming more active at the start of the day.
   d. was a large urban area.

b 5. The hours waiting in the hospital *crawled* by. This means that time
   a. passed by rapidly.
   b. seemed to drag.
   c. sped up as the hours went by.
   d. was being spent wisely.

c 6. His sunburned skin looked *angry*. This means that his skin looked
   a. smooth and soft.
   b. wrinkled.
   c. painfully red.
   d. covered with freckles.

b 7. The book *begs* to be read. This means that the book
   a. is hard to find in the library.
   b. looks like a really good book.
   c. looks all right.
   d. costs a lot of money.

d 8. Time *marches* on means that time
   a. comes to a halt.
   b. stops and starts.
   c. has become tired.
   d. keeps moving forward.

Exercise 8: Comparisons in Literature

Directions: For each sentence, identify the two things being compared and name one trait that the two things have in common. Then give the meaning of the comparison.

Example:

My love is like a red, red rose
That's newly sprung in June.

—Robert Burns

Real subject: my love

Compared to: red rose

Trait in common: fresh and beautiful

Meaning: His love is beautiful to him.

1. There came a wind like a bugle.
    —Emily Dickinson

    Real subject: ___wind___

    Compared to: ___bugle___

    Trait in common: ___loud___

    Meaning: ___The wind was roaring.___

2. The fog comes on little cat feet.
    —Carl Sandburg

    Real subject: ___fog___

    Compared to: ___little cat feet___

    Trait in common: ___soft; stealthy, quietly___

    Meaning: ___Fog comes in quietly.___

3. Thin as a scythe he stood there.
    —Donald Justice

    Real subject: ___he___

    Compared to: ___scythe___

    Trait in common: ___thin___

    Meaning: ___He is a thin man.___

4. The night is a big black cat.
    —G. Orr Clark

    Real subject: ___night___

    Compared to: ___black cat___

    Trait in common: ___dark___

    Meaning: ___Night is very dark.___

5. His cheeks were like roses, his nose like a cherry.
   —Clement C. Moore

   Real subject: him – Santa's cheeks and nose

   Compared to: roses and a cherry

   Trait in common: red color

   Meaning: His cheeks and nose are very red.

6. She stood in front of the altar shaking like a freshly caught fish.
   —Maya Angelou

   Real subject: she – bride shaking

   Compared to: freshly caught fish

   Trait in common: shaking

   Meaning: She was very nervous.

7. What dreams we have and how they fly. Like rosy clouds across the sky.
   —Paul Laurence Dunbar

   Real subject: dreams

   Compared to: clouds

   Trait in common: fast moving, floating

   Meaning: We move in and out of dreams.

8. In the morning the city spreads its wings.
   —Langston Hughes

   Real subject: city

   Compared to: bird's wings

   Trait in common: opening up

   Meaning: The coming day prompts activity in the city.

Extended Metaphor

When they use an **extended metaphor,** authors draw out a comparison between two unlike things beyond a single word or phrase. Instead, they carry the comparison through a paragraph, a whole poem, or even an entire essay or article. In doing so, they often use multiple comparisons between dissimilar ideas or things. Using a lengthy comparison like this can help the reader to visualize an event much more clearly.

Exercise 9: Extended Metaphor in an Article

Directions: As you read the following article, note the extended metaphor and then answer the questions that follow. As you are reading this article, think about your own experience buying a new or used car.

TACKLING VOCABULARY

quarry   an animal that is being hunted down, prey; anything being hunted or pursued

query   to question, to ask about

stalk   to pursue game or an enemy

jargon   special words and phrases used by people in the same line of work

CAR BUYING TURNS MEN INTO BIG GAME HUNTERS

Karen Peterson

Men hunt a new car for up to three months before buying; they sneak up on their quarry, peer into dealership windows after-hours and bring their prey home like a trophy, studies indicate.

"Men hunt for cars the way an experienced tracker hunts for wild game," says Mike Lafavore, of *Men's Health* magazine."They spend a lot of time planning their attack, arming themselves with the necessary weapons and stalking their prey when hopefully it can't see them."

Nearly half (48%) of men spend between three weeks and three months thinking about buying a new car before they buy it, says a survey of 2,153 men done for the magazine by J.D. Power and Associates. The average span is 14 weeks.

Thirty-two percent deliberately stalk cars at closed dealerships, checking them out when no other hunters are around. "They want to sneak up, kick the tires on the lot, peer into car windows when they are alone," he says.

Almost 30% of hunters were irritated with dealers whenever they bought. Reasons: Dealers withheld a better price, 34%; were dishonest, 27%; too pushy, 22%; charged extra fees, 21%; used jargon, 10%; didn't provide a test drive, 5%; smoked, 5%; and criticized other dealers 4%.

The men's magazine did not query women. But if men are hunters of cars, women are the gatherers of truly useful information: "Women tend to be much more practical than men," says Lafavore, whose father was a car salesman. "His car is a trophy; hers is transportation."

From "Car Buying Turns Men into Big Game Hunters" by Karen Peterson, *USA Today,* September 20, 1995

1. Peterson uses an extended metaphor to describe the car-buying habits of men. Specifically, she compares a man hunting for a new car to a big game hunter tracking wild game. List the similarities between the two activities.

    Both spend time getting ready to make a move (plan). They both sneak a look

    when no one is watching (stalk). They both bring home trophies.

2. In the last paragraph, the writer compares the attitudes of men and women toward the acquisition of a car. In the author's view, what do men want from a new car? What do women want from a new car?

    Women think of a car in terms of transportation. Men want their car to be a

    trophy that they can show off.

Exercise 10: Extended Metaphor in a Cartoon

Directions: Study the Cathy cartoon below and then answer the questions that follow.

CATHY © 1995 Cathy Guisewite. Reprinted with permission of Universal Press Syndicate. All rights reserved.

1. How does the Cathy cartoon illustrate the difference between male and female attitudes toward the acquisition of a new car?

    Men want to know every detail and to be sure they come out on top. Women

    want to avoid being cheated too badly, buy it, and go home.

2. In the last panel of the cartoon, Cathy is using figurative language to describe her feelings. What does she mean when she says, "They splattered self-doubt particles all over my nice new windshield"?

They made Cathy doubt the wisdom of her new purchase. She was no longer

so sure that she had gotten a good deal.

3. Write an appropriate caption or main idea sentence for the cartoon.

Answers will vary.

Exercise 11: Extended Metaphor in a Poem

Directions: The following poem, is an extended metaphor in which the figurative comparison is carried through the entire poem. Read the poem and answer the questions that follow.

Metaphor

Morning is
a new sheet of paper
for you to write on.

Whatever you want to say,
all day,
until night
folds it up
and files it away.

The bright words and the dark words
are gone
until dawn
and a new day
to write on.

—Eve Merriam

1. What two things are being compared in the first two lines? morning

and a new sheet of paper

2. What happens at night? the day is over and words end

3. What does dawn bring? a new day and a new sheet of paper

4. What does the poem say about controlling your own life? You have

control. Go day by day.

5. Is the tone of this poem positive or negative? Explain your answer.

    <u>Positive. Each day gives a new beginning.</u>

6. Is the phrase "night folds it up" an example of a simile, metaphor, or

    personification? <u>personification</u>

7. What does the author mean by "bright words"? What does the author

    mean by "dark words"? <u>positive words versus negative words</u>

8. How do you feel at the start of a new day? <u>Answers will vary.</u>

Exercise 12: Extended Metaphor in Song Lyrics

Directions: Read the song "The River" by country singer Garth Brooks and then answer the questions that follow.

The River

You know a dream is like a river
Ever changing as it flows.
And the dreamer's just a vessel
That must follow where it goes.

Trying to learn from what's behind you
And never knowing what's in store
Makes each day a constant battle
Just to stay between the shore.

(Chorus)
And I will sail my vessel
Till the river runs dry
Like a bird upon the wind
These waters are my sky.
I'll never reach my destination if I never try
So I will sail my vessel
Till the river runs dry.

Too many times we stand aside
And let the water slip away
Till what we put off till tomorrow
Has now become today.

So don't you sit upon the shoreline
And say you're satisfied
Choose to chance the rapids
And dare to dance the tide.

"Those who aim at great deeds, must also suffer greatly."
—Plutarch

(Chorus)
Yes, I will sail my vessel . . .

There's bound to be rough waters
And I know I'll take some falls
But with the good Lord as my captain
I can make it through them all.

(Chorus)
Yes I will sail my vessel . . .
Till the river runs dry
Till the river runs dry.

—Garth Brooks

1. In the first stanza, how are a dream and a river similar? both change

   _____

2. "A dream is like a river" is an example of what type of figurative

   language? simile

3. "And the dreamer's just a vessel" is an example of what type of figurative

   language? metaphor

4. In the second stanza, explain the difficulties that a dreamer faces.

   One must learn from the past, but go ahead into the unknown future.

5. What viewpoint about life is expressed in the chorus? Identify and label

   the figurative language. Keep going – don't stop trying. "River runs"

   – personification, "like a bird" – simile, "waters are my sky" – metaphor.

   _____

6. Write a main idea sentence expressing the meaning of the third stanza.

   We let our chances go by when we procrastinate.

7. "And let the water slip away" is an example of what type of figurative

   language? personification

8. What course of action is being expressed in the fourth stanza?

   Take chances – don't sit on the sidelines.

9. What is meant by "rough waters" in the fifth stanza? What main idea is

   being expressed in this stanza? <u>Hard times. There will be hard times, but</u>

   <u>faith can get you through them.</u>

10. The main idea of the song is that <u>If you have a dream, there will be hard</u>

    <u>times trying to accomplish it, but persevere</u>   .

11. Explain how the entire song can be regarded as an extended metaphor.

    <u>Both a dream and a river have calm spots and places of turbulence.</u>

    _____

Optional:

12. On a separate sheet of paper, combine the main idea of each stanza into
    a summary of the song.

Working with Symbols

A **symbol** is something that stands for something larger than itself. It represents more than its literal meaning. For example, a cupid symbolizes love, a scale symbolizes justice, a red cross symbolizes first aid, Uncle Sam symbolizes the U.S.A., and for New Year's Eve an old man symbolizes the passing of the old year and a baby symbolizes the beginning of the new one.

Exercise 13: Practice with Symbols

Directions: The poem "Sympathy" by Paul Laurence Dunbar, a son of former slaves, makes a bird cage a symbol for a lack of freedom. Read the poem and answer the questions that follow.

Sympathy

I know what the caged bird feels, alas!
When the sun is bright on the upland slopes;
When the wind stirs soft through the springing grass,
And the river flows like a stream of glass;
When the first bird sings and the first bud opes,
And the faint perfume from its chalice steals—
I know what the caged bird feels!

I know why the caged bird beats his wing
Till its blood is red on the cruel bars;
For he must fly back to his perch and cling
When he fain would be on the bough a-swing;

> And a pain still throbs in the old, old scars
> And they pulse again with a keener sting—
> I know why he beats his wing!
>
> I know why the caged bird sings, ah me,
> When his wing is bruised and his bosom sore,—
> When he beats his bars and he would be free;
> It is not a carol of joy or glee,
> But a prayer that he sends from his heart's deep core,
> But a plea, that upward to Heaven he flings—
> I know why the caged bird sings!
>
> —Paul Laurence Dunbar

1. What does the bird symbolically represent?

    The bird represents all human beings who are being held against their will.

2. What is the significance of the title? Does the title tell us anything about the author's feelings?

    The word "sympathy" means having common feelings, emotions, or

    experiences. The poet feels the distress of the caged bird.

3. In the last stanza, what is the bird expressing when it sings? How might the bird's plight relate to slavery? Can you think of other circumstances when human beings are trapped against their will?

    The bird's song is meant to express the desire to be free. Slaves are like the

    bruised bird in that they are desperate for freedom.

4. What is the purpose of the five situations described in the first stanza? Would the caged bird be happier if it didn't know about the beauty of nature beyond its cage?

    The scenes represent the beauty of nature and the five senses that we

    experience these scenes with. The bird's plight is worse because of what it can

    see just outside the cage.

Imagery

In addition to similes, metaphors, and personification, writers use **imagery** to create word pictures. They describe a person, setting, or object using sensory

© ZITS partnership, King Features Syndicate.

images. The words or phrases they use may emphasize any one, or all, of our five senses (sight, sound, taste, touch, and smell). The Zits cartoon gives an example of such vivid imagery.

In the following excerpt, the author uses vivid sensory descriptions and figurative language to describe an old woman. The author's purpose in using such language is to create in the reader's mind a vivid mental picture of her and to convey a specific tone or mood.

Exercise 14: Imagery

Directions: As your read the passage, look for details that you could see, touch, hear, smell, or taste. Then write the phrases that contain these sensory images on the lines provided. Finally, write a short paragraph describing the overall mood created by the images and what feelings the excerpt aroused in you, the reader.

She was horrible. Her face was the color of a dirty pillowcase, and the corners of her mouth glistened with wet, which inched like a glacier down the deep grooves enclosing her chin. Old-age liver spots dotted her cheeks, and her pale eyes had black pinpoint pupils. Her hands were knobby, and the cuticles were grown up over her fingernails. Her bottom plate was not in, and her upper lip protruded; from time to time she would draw her nether lip to her upper plate and carry her chin with it. This made the wet move faster.

Something had happened to her. She lay on her back, with the quilts up to her chin. Only her head and shoulders were visible. Her head moved slowly from side to side. From time to time she would open her mouth wide, and I could see her tongue undulate faintly. Cords of saliva would collect on her lips; she would draw them in, then open her mouth again. Her mouth seemed to have a private existence of its own. It worked separate and apart from the rest of her, out and in, like a clam hole at low tide. Occasionally it would say, "Pt," like some viscous substance coming to a boil.

Harper Lee, *To Kill a Mockingbird*, pp. 115–116

Sensory Images

1. face the color of a dirty pillowcase

2. wet inched like a glacier down deep grooves

3. old age liver spots dotted cheeks

4. pale eyes with black pinpoint pupils

5. knobby hands

6. upper lip protruded

7. tongue undulating

8. cords of saliva

9. mouth like a clam at low tide

10. saying "pt" like a viscous substance coming to a boil

Your Paragraph

Answers will vary.

Exercise 15: Imagery/Group Activity

Directions: Choose one of these photographs of the Grand Canyon and write a description of it using sensory images and figurative language. Your description can be in either poem or prose format. Try to have all five senses represented. Brainstorm with your classmates by talking about the size of the canyon, the changing colors, the mule ride to the bottom, the Colorado River, and so on.

READING

"There is never, really, any release from the consequences of adversity until you decide to do something about them."

GETTING FOCUSED

In his book *The Winner Within*, Pat Riley shares his techniques for creating a winning attitude. He also shows how adversity can open the door to new opportunities. Although this excerpt describes catastrophic events in the past, notice how similar these "thunderbolts" are to events that have occurred recently.

BIO-SKETCH

Pat Riley is generally considered one of America's greatest coaches and is known for using psychological techniques to inspire his players to work as a team. Riley, a former player and broadcaster, coached the 1980s Los Angeles Lakers to four championship titles in nine years. From 1991 to 1995, he was coach of the New York Knicks and led them to the NBA finals. Riley is currently the coach and president of the Miami Heat. In 2006, under Coach Riley, the Heat won their first NBA championship. Riley is the only coach in NBA history to be coach of the year with three different teams.

TACKLING VOCABULARY

adversity   a state of wretchedness or misfortune; trouble

divestiture   a stripping or taking away of possessions

THUNDERBOLTS

Pat Riley

"Sweet are the uses of adversity." William Shakespeare

"Now you're looking at a man that's gettin' kinda mad; I've had lots of luck, but it's all been bad. No matter how I struggle and strive I'll never get out of this world alive." Hank Williams

"Success in life comes not from holding a good hand, but in playing a poor hand well." Denis Waitley and Rem L. Witt

August 30, 1992, Florida City: A young couple walked through rubble where their house used to stand, the same house where the young man had been a boy, where his father had lived for fifteen years. Looking around, they saw ripped-up hunks of aluminum siding from destroyed trailer houses, pink tufts of fiber-glass insulation scattered, cracked two-by-fours and wet, shiny-looking spots in the grass which turned out to be shards of broken glass.

2   Two framed photographs were the only family possessions they could find. The man looked across all the adjacent home sites, each one as demolished as his own.

3   "It doesn't look like a town," he said. "The trees are all naked or gone. It's a whole other world."

4   Because of a natural phenomenon called Hurricane Andrew, the husband and wife who searched their home wreckage for belongings were among more than a quarter of a million people who were left homeless overnight across a two-hundred-mile-wide swath of South Florida. Their houses, as well as the shops and businesses where they used to work, were equally swept away.

5   "People want to know what's going to happen to them," the mayor of Florida City said. "But there is no quick fix." A woman with three children told a reporter, "It hurts to think about the future."

6   Still, human beings are a lot more resilient than they realize. With the phone lines down, storm survivors communicated by painting messages on the sides of buildings. A spray-can telegram on the side of one house told friends, GRANDMA NEWTON IS OK.

7   Andrew was a disaster greater than most of us will ever experience. The scars it left will be slow to heal. But the people of Florida will build again. They will be back. That's what a Thunderbolt experience should teach you to do: take on adversity and come back, better than before.

8   A Thunderbolt is something beyond your control, a phenomenon that one day strikes you, your team, your business, your city, even your nation. It rocks you, it blows you into a crater. You have no choice except to take the hit. But you do have a lot of choice about what to do next. That much is in your power. In the coming years, expect the sky to blaze with Thunderbolts. They're part of the game of constant change.

9   Our whole planet seems to be a collection of flash points. In Africa, in Eastern Europe, everywhere—governments and borderlines are changing at accelerating speed. More often than not, those changes are introduced through coups, strife, and bloodletting.

10   The *Winner Within* must know how to field the stress-filled change of Thunderbolts—and that includes winners of every sort, because Thunderbolts can strike businesses as easily as they do governments, communities, or individuals. In fact, business columns and magazines are chock full of Thunderbolt reports every day.

11   Some Thunderbolts are sheer shots out of the blue. Others spring out of partly cloudy skies, where vigilant attention to weather reports could have provided advance warning. That means monitoring trends, public policy issues, and regulatory agencies.

12   Thunderbolts are a prime factor in upsetting the competitive applecart. Whether it is a powerful competitor drastically lowering its pricing or a quality inspector dramatically increasing standards, a Thunderbolt spells immediate adversity for someone. But that adversity also carries a positive charge: it strips away all the nonessentials and forces you back to your basic strengths. Adversity shoves you down to your core values and beliefs, to the things that matter most. Back on bedrock, you find the reasons and the strength to carry on and carry through.

13   Sometimes when adversity strikes, we rail against fate. We brutally and unfairly punish ourselves or we lash out at the people around us. We blame others. We stop and wait for someone else to show us the way, to open the door. Or we play the victim. "That's the way it goes. There's nothing I could do. It was meant to be."

"What does not destroy me makes me strong."
—Friedrich Nietzsche

14 Rocked by adversity, people often get so much empathy and caring poured on them that their own misfortune actually starts to feel good . . . sort of special: "What a tough break," everybody tells them. "You don't deserve it." What soothing consolation this is!

15 But sympathy is like junk food. It has no real nourishment. The emptiness comes back very quickly. And nothing gets accomplished in the meantime. There is never, really, any release from the consequences of adversity until you decide to do something about them.

16 Forget about sympathy. Strengthen your state of mind instead. Even if the odds have shifted against you, go after your goal with the same effort, the same belief and the same faith. If you hear yourself starting sentences with "If only" or "I could've" or "We should've," you've heard thoughts that are going in the wrong direction. "Shoulda, coulda and woulda won't get it done."

✔ COMPREHENSION CHECKUP

Multiple Choice

Directions: Write the letter of the correct answer on the blank provided.

_____b_____ 1. Coach Riley thinks that Florida
  a. is unlikely to experience another devastating hurricane.
  b. will be able to rebuild.
  c. will not be able to rebuild.
  d. none of the above.

_____d_____ 2. Which of the following would be considered a "Thunderbolt" as defined and described by Coach Riley?
  a. a tornado in Kansas
  b. a terrorist attack on New York City
  c. civil war in Sudan
  d. all of the above

_____c_____ 3. According to Riley, "Thunderbolts" can strike
  a. businesses.
  b. individuals.
  c. both of the above.
  d. neither of the above.

_____b_____ 4. According to Riley, "Thunderbolts" can cause all of the following *except*
  a. physical destruction.
  b. gradual change.
  c. immediate adversity.
  d. a return to basic values.

True or False

Directions: Indicate whether the statement is true or false by writing **T** or **F** on the blank provided.

___F___ 1. Pat Riley was the coach of the Miami Heat when Hurricane Andrew struck.

___T___ 2. Coach Riley believes that obsessing about the past is not going to get people anywhere.

___F___ 3. Most of us will face disasters as great as Hurricane Andrew.

___F___ 4. There are usually quick and easy solutions to Thunderbolts.

___T___ 5. Paying attention to trends might help us avoid Thunderbolt situations in the future.

___T___ 6. Coach Riley believes that people faced with disaster are a lot stronger than they think they are.

Short-Answer Questions

Directions: Answer the questions below using complete sentences.

1. What is Riley's main idea? What is his purpose? Riley wants us to reach inside ourselves to find the strength to deal with difficult situations with a positive attitude. His purpose is to help us realize that bad things happen to everyone.

2. Explain Riley's definition of a "Thunderbolt." What does a thunderbolt symbolize? A thunderbolt is something beyond your control that one day strikes you. It is "a bolt from the blue" that is symbolic of all of life's special challenges.

3. In paragraph 8, what does Riley mean when he says, "It rocks you, it blows you into a crater"? It has a devastating impact on you.

4. Why is Riley expecting the sky "to blaze with Thunderbolts" in the future? <u>The world is now changing very rapidly thereby creating new tensions</u> <u>and thunderbolts.</u>

_____

5. What does Riley mean when he says we should pay attention to "weather reports"? Does he mean this literally or figuratively? <u>Some situations can</u> <u>be prevented if we pay attention to the warning signs. He is using the term</u> <u>figuratively.</u>

6. Give an example of a "positive charge" when you are "back on bedrock." <u>A positive charge occurs when you rid yourself of the superflous things and go</u> <u>back to your basic strengths. Examples will vary.</u>

_____

7. What does it mean to "drink in solace"? <u>It means to give up and listen to the</u> <u>outpouring of sympathy from everyone.</u>

_____

8. In what way is sympathy like "junk food"? Think of another simile for sympathy and write it below. <u>It is like junk food in that it is temporarily</u> <u>filling, but it is not good for you in the long run. It doesn't provide the</u> <u>necessary sustenance to live and grow. Examples will vary.</u>

Vocabulary in Context

Directions: Define the italicized words by looking at their context in the excerpt, and then use each word to write a sentence of your own.

1. *shards* (paragraph 1) Definition: <u>fragments</u>

   Sentence:_____

2. *resilient* (paragraph 6) Definition: <u>capable of bouncing back</u>

   Sentence:_____

3. *rail* (paragraph 13) Definition: <u>utter bitter complaints</u>

   Sentence:_____

Directions: Match the following expressions to their definitions.

1. __d__ upset the applecart   a. hastily contrived remedy

2. __f__ out of the blue   b. at the foundation; the lowest point

3. __a__ quick fix   c. jam-packed; filled to overflowing

4. __g__ take the hit   d. spoil carefully laid plans

5. __e__ flash point   e. a critical state; combustible

6. __c__ chock full   f. without warning; suddenly

7. __b__ back on bedrock   g. suffer the consequences

Directions: Choose the correct definition of each word according to how it is used in the sentence.

__c__ 1. If you are *vigilant*, you are
        a. neglectful.
        b. destructive.
        c. watchful.

__c__ 2. If a building is *demolished*, it is
        a. constructed.
        b. decorated.
        c. destroyed.

__a__ 3. If a car is *accelerating*, it is going
        a. faster.
        b. slower.
        c. in reverse.

_____b_____ 4. If a friend shows you *empathy*, he is being

  a. obnoxious.

  b. sympathetic.

  c. critical.

_____c_____ 5. If your friend is sitting *adjacent* to you, she is sitting

  a. far away from you.

  b. two seats away.

  c. next to you.

_____b_____ 6. If your day was filled with *strife*, it was

  a. peaceful.

  b. filled with conflict.

  c. a really good day.

In Your Own Words

1. What large-scale Thunderbolt situations have occurred recently? How have the communities involved handled them?

2. In October 2006, an Amish community was the scene of a devastating incident in which young schoolgirls were brutally murdered by a man who then committed suicide. The incident took place in a local schoolhouse, which the community then razed. The grieving Amish families rallied around their own people and also made a special effort to comfort the widow and young children of the murderer. How does their behavior illustrate Pat Riley's philosophy?

Written Assignment

1. Create your own metaphor to explain how to handle adversity.

2. Write a paragraph explaining how you successfully coped with some difficulty in your life.

Internet Activity

1. The official Miami Heat website at www.nba.com/heat provides information on players, coaches, and statistics. Click on "history," choose any year, and summarize the information provided.

2. Use the net to gather information about Hurricane Katrina. How does the damage caused by Andrew compare to the damage caused by Katrina?

7 Fact and Opinion

HOW GOOD ARE YOUR POWERS OF OBSERVATION?

Do you notice things or are you unobservant? Are you a Sherlock Holmes? Or do you look but not see?

Find out how observant you really are by taking this little quiz. It concerns things you see almost every day. If you answer five to seven questions correctly, you will have earned an average score. Anything over that, and you have a sharp eye for details.

1. You probably know it's red with white letters, but what is the shape of the stop sign?
2. Which way does Abe Lincoln face on the penny?
3. In which hand does the Statue of Liberty hold her torch?
4. How many tines are on a standard dinner fork?
5. On which side of their uniforms do police officers wear their badges?
6. Is page one of a book on the left or on the right?
7. How many sides does a common pencil have?
8. Does it say "Coke" or "Coca-Cola" on the can of the soft drink?
9. Which way do you flip a wall switch to turn it on—up or down?
10. What color is the top light on a traffic light?
11. In the kitchen or bathroom sink, which side of the faucet is the hot water knob on?
12. When you clasp your hands together, which thumb is on top?

FACT AND OPINION

A **fact** is a statement that can be proved to be true or false in some objective way. You can prove it yourself, or you can turn to a reliable authority such as records, tests, or historical or scientific documents. Statements of fact often rely on concrete data or measurements.

Answers to the Observation Quiz

In the observation quiz, *all* of the answers to the questions are factual because the information can be verified by reference materials or your own personal observations.

1. The shape is an octagon.
2. Lincoln is facing to the right.
3. She holds the torch in her right hand.
4. There are four.
5. The badge is worn on the left.
6. It is on the right.
7. It has six sides.
8. It says Coca-Cola.
9. You flip the switch up.
10. Red is on the top.
11. The hot water is on the left.
12. For most people, the right thumb is on top.

"When I want your opinion, I will give it to you."
—Laurence J. Peter

An **opinion** expresses a personal preference or value judgment. Statements of opinion can't be proved to be true or false. Statements predicting the future are ordinarily opinions no matter how likely or reasonable they seem. Here are some examples of opinions:

He is going to win the Senate election in November.

It is going to rain tomorrow.

He was an outstanding president.

I work a lot harder than he does.

Clues to Identifying an Opinion

Any word that indicates a value judgment on someone's part signals that the person is probably expressing an opinion. People can almost always disagree, for example, about whether it is better or worse to perform a particular action, like telling a white lie. Sentences that contain the following words are likely to express a value judgment and, therefore, to also contain an author's opinion about a topic.

attractive/beautiful	bad/good	best/worst
effective	greatest	highest/lowest
interesting	most/least	necessary
nice	successful	

Similarly, the following words or phrases may signal an opinion is being given.

apparently	many experts agree
I believe	one interpretation is
in my opinion	one possibility is
in my view	perhaps
it seems likely	this suggests

Keep in mind that not all opinions carry equal weight. Some opinions are more sound than others. Poorly reasoned opinions or opinions that are not supported by facts are of little value. On the other hand, opinions from someone knowledgeable in the field, an expert opinion, can be very reliable.

Most of what we read and hear is a combination of fact and opinion. In order to be a critical reader, you must be able to tell the difference between a factual statement and an opinion. Writers sometimes present opinions as though they were facts. You need to be able to recognize when this is happening.

Exercise 1: Crime Scene Facts

Directions: Study the crime scene picture on the next page carefully for three minutes, cover it up and then answer as many of the following questions as you can. The questions all call for a factual response.

At the Scene of the Crime

1. What time is it by the bank clock? <u>5:45</u>

2. What day of the week is it? <u>Saturday</u>

3. What is the name of the outdoor café? <u>Jane's</u>

4. What are the names of the two streets? <u>Myrtle St.</u>   and <u>Bates Ave.</u>

5. How many guns are visible? <u>one</u>

6. How many bags of money are visible? <u>three</u>

7. How many fire hydrants are at the crime scene? <u>one</u>

8. What store is next door to the café? <u>Crawfordtown Produce</u>

9. What is the license number of the car parked in front of the store?

    <u>F 472</u>

10. Between what times is the car allowed to legally park at that

    intersection? <u>any time other than 4–6 P.M.</u>

11. What part of the car is being vandalized? <u>tire</u>

12. How many people are wearing hats? <u>one</u>

13. Besides the bank robbery, what crimes are being committed?

    <u>stealing a purse, stealing grapes</u>

14. What endangers the man with the glasses? <u>a falling flower pot</u>

15. How many people are in the picture? <u>10</u>

16. Identify the holdup men from this lineup and put a check mark beside the letters under their pictures.

<u>A</u>   <u>B</u> ✔   <u>C</u>   <u>D</u>   <u>E</u> ✔

Exercise 2: Facts and Opinions

Directions: Indicate whether the following statements are facts or opinions by writing **F** or **O** in the blanks provided.

_F_ 1. According to the U.S. Bureau of the Census, about 4 million heterosexual couples are currently living together.

_F_ 2. There are more people under the age of 30 than over that age who are living together without being married.

_F_ 3. Approximately 22 million singles have tried online dating.

_O_ 4. The Internet is a really good place to locate people who share your interests.

_O_ 5. The Internet will definitely increase a person's chance of finding a good match.

_O_ 6. Online relationships are dangerous or deadly.

_F_ 7. Studies have found higher divorce rates among couples who have lived together prior to marriage.

_____F_____ 8. The U.S. Bureau of the Census reports that the median age for marriage is now 26.8 years for men and 25.1 years for women.

_____O_____ 9. People who have experienced divorce in their families have negative views about marriage.

_____O_____ 10. Single people are pressured to get married and have children.

_____F_____ 11. About 95 percent of all Americans get married at some time in their life.

_____F_____ 12. Research by Linda Waite (at NYU) shows that married people report being happier than unmarried people.

_____F_____ 13. Over 50 percent of married women are in the labor force.

_____F_____ 14. As of 2002, the percentage of married population in the United States is lower than it was in 1970.

_____O_____ 15. Being a parent is an overwhelming responsibility.

Exercise 3: Facts and Opinions

Directions: Indicate whether the following statements are facts or opinions by writing **F** or **O** in the blanks provided.

_____F_____ 1. According to the research of Carducci and Stein, 50 percent of college students consider themselves shy.

_____O_____ 2. It seems like opportunities for face-to-face interactions are decreasing because of ATM machines, video games, voice mail, and faxes.

_____O_____ 3. E-mail is a wonderful way for shy people to communicate.

_____F_____ 4. A recent study found that greater use of the Internet was associated with a decline in communication among family members.

_____O_____ 5. It is predicted that greater reliance on media technology will cause higher rates of shyness in the future.

_____O_____ 6. There are worse things in life than being shy.

_____O_____ 7. Shy people are probably very good listeners.

_____O_____ 8. Shy people are needed in group situations because not everybody can be a leader.

_____O_____ 9. Shy people should just avoid situations that make them anxious.

_____O_____ 10. Shyness is a big nuisance.

_____F_____ 11. A study by Schmidt and Fox found extreme shyness associated with depression and loneliness.

_____O_____ 12. Unfamiliar people and situations always trigger attacks of shyness.

_____F_____ 13. When giving a speech in front of a large group, 73 percent of college students said they felt shy.

_____F_____ 14. The Shyness Institute is directed by psychologist Philip Zimbardo.

_____O_____ 15. Shy people feel lonely in the middle of a party.

_____O_____ 16. Shyness should not interfere with achieving personal and professional success.

Exercise 4: Facts and Opinions

Directions: Read the following article, then indicate whether each of the following statements are facts or opinions by writing **F** in **O** on the blanks provided.

IS AMERICA TOO RUDE?

Matt Crenson

People say you're rude.
You walk around bleating into that cell phone as if you're the only person for blocks. You curse like Madonna on Letterman, your kids think the world is their personal playground, and you drive like a maniac.

That's what respondents to a national survey had to say about American manners.

A full 79% of the 2,013 adults surveyed by telephone by research group Public Agenda said a lack of respect and courtesy in American society is a serious problem. Sixty-one percent believe things have gotten worse in recent years.

"You really see the majority of Americans pretty anxious about these issues," said Jean Johnson, director of programs at Public Agenda, a New York–based non-profit organization. "People do think this is an area of society that they would like to see some improvement on."

Poor customer service has become so rampant that nearly half of those surveyed said that they have walked out of a store in the past year because of it.

Half said they often see people talking on cellular telephones in a loud or annoying manner. And six drivers in 10 said they regularly see other people driving aggressively or recklessly.

Many people admitted to rude behavior themselves. More than a third said they use foul language in public. About the same percentage confessed to occasional bad driving.

The results were remarkably consistent geographically, with little difference in rudeness awareness between the heartland and the coasts. Opinion on only one issue, the use of foul language, split significantly among regions of the country. While three out of four Southerners said it is always wrong to take God's name in vain, half of those surveyed from the Northeast said that there is nothing wrong with it or that it falls somewhere between right and wrong.

The researchers followed up their telephone survey with focus groups. In those discussions, some people blamed overcrowding in malls, stadiums, and other public places. Others said Americans' increasingly busy lives are making them ruder. And one woman in Texas blamed The King.

"It was shocking when Elvis was shaking his hips up there, but now we see whole naked bodies," she said. "It started with Elvis, and that was a little overboard, but that was the beginning of what we have today."

Matt Crenson, *Arizona Republic,* Wednesday, April 3, 2002, p. A6

____F____ 1. A full 79% of the 2,013 adults surveyed by telephone by research group Public Agenda said a lack of respect and courtesy in American society is a serious problem.

____O____ 2. People do think this is an area of society that they would like to see some improvement on.

____F____ 3. And six drivers in 10 said they regularly see other people driving aggressively or recklessly.

____F____ 4. More than a third said they use foul language in public.

____F____ 5. The researchers followed up their telephone survey with focus groups.

____F____ 6. While three out of four Southerners said it is always wrong to take God's name in vain . . .

____F____ 7. And one woman in Texas blamed The King.

____O____ 8. "It started with Elvis, and that was a little overboard, but that was the beginning of what we have today."

Do you think the selection is primarily based on fact or opinion?

fact _____

Exercise 5: Facts and Opinions

Directions: Locate three facts and three opinions in the following reading and write them on the lines below.

"ALL SHOOK UP"

Two Elvis skydiving groups try to "chute" each other down.

First there was Elvis. He was the King, and he is, most likely, no longer with us. Then came the Elvis impersonators. There appear to be thousands of them all over the world, and their number increases daily.

Then came the skydiving Elvis impersonators. There are two groups of skydiving Elvis impersonators in Las Vegas alone. And they're suing each other.

The competing jumpers had their genesis in the 1992 movie *Honeymoon in Vegas,* starring Nicolas Cage and Sarah Jessica Parker, which featured a troupe of skydiving Elvises. Life must imitate art, because the movie spawned a new career track for guys with pompadours and spangled jumpsuits who also happen to be Airborne-qualified.

Las Vegas impresario Richard Feeney and his partner Joe Speck promptly put together the 10-man Flying Elvi, who began appearing at casino openings and amusement parks. But in January 1993, Mark Miscevic, one of the Elvi, bounced off a parked Oldsmobile Delta 88 during an Elvi jump and knocked himself into a coma for six weeks. After several months of recuperation, Miscevic, who coordinated skydiving for *Honeymoon,* decided to branch out on his own.

With the blessing of the King's estate, he started the Flying Elvises and eventually was joined by four other renegade Elvi. "Using 'Elvi' was disrespectful," says Miscevic, 47, a Vegas real-estate executive Monday through Friday. Feeney, who calls his group the Elvi because he likes to think it's the Latin plural of Elvis, sued in federal court, claiming service-mark infringement, unfair competition, deceptive trade practices, and interference with business opportunity. He is suing to blow the Elvises out of the sky, claiming his group alone owns the right to jump from planes while dressed as Elvis. Miscevic is countersuing on behalf, he says, of anyone who wants to hit the silk in the name of the King. "Let's compete in the free market," he says.

If the two sides can't hammer out a settlement, they'll face off in federal court. That way, a judge can settle the whole mess—suit, countersuit and jumpsuit.

2/27/95 People

"There is no such thing as justice—in or out of court."

—Clarence Darrow

Facts

1. There are two groups of skydiving Elvis impersonators in Las Vegas alone.

2. But in January 1993, Mark Miscevic, one of the Elvi, bounced . . .

3. The competing jumpers had their genesis in the 1992 . . .

Opinions

1. He was the King, and he is, most likely, no longer with us. _____

2. Life must imitate art, because the movie spawned . . . _____

3. "Using 'Elvi' was disrespectful," . . . _____

READING

*"Not only can innocent people appear guilty, but guilty
people can also learn to beat the polygraph."*

GETTING FOCUSED

Do you think lie detectors are capable of reliably telling whether someone is
lying? Consider the case of Floyd Fay. To prove himself innocent of the murder
of his friend Fred, Fay volunteered to take a lie detector test. Unfortunately, he
failed and then spent two years in prison before the real killer confessed.

Did you know that even the best "deception detectors," Secret Service
agents, are successful only 70 percent of the time?

BIO-SKETCH

Michael Passer is the coordinator of introductory psychology classes at the
University of Washington. He has taught introductory psychology for over 20
years. In addition to teaching, Passer has published more than 20 scientific
articles.

TACKLING VOCABULARY

autonomic involuntary The autonomic nervous system is concerned with
the parts of the body that function involuntarily without our awareness,
such as the heart, lungs, blood, and glands

THE LIE DETECTOR CONTROVERSY

Michael W. Passer and Ronald E. Smith

Do you think emotional arousal can tell us whether someone is telling the truth
or lying? A scientific instrument known as a polygraph measures physiological responses, such as respiration, heart rate, blood pressure, and skin conductance (which increases in the presence of emotion due to sweat gland activity).
Because we have less control over physiological responses than over numerous
other behaviors, many people regard the polygraph as a nearly infallible means

FIGURE 1

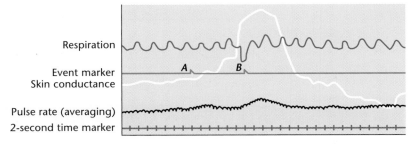

Respiration

Event marker
Skin conductance

Pulse rate (averaging)
2-second time marker

of establishing whether someone is telling the truth. However, this approach to detecting lying by increases in emotional arousal is highly controversial.

2   Figure 1 shows a portion of a polygraph record. Polygraph examiners compare physiological responses to critical questions (e.g., "Were you present at Jesse James National Bank when it was robbed the night of August 4, 2003?") with responses to control questions that make no reference to the crime or crime scene. In this case, note the changes that occurred on the autonomic measures after an emotionally loaded question was asked (point A to point B in the Figure 1).

3   The issue, however, is whether this emotional response to a critical question means that the person was lying. Herein lies one major problem with polygraph tests. Innocent people may appear guilty when doubt, fear, or lack of confidence increases their autonomic activity. Even a thought like, "What if my answer makes me look guilty, even though I'm not?" in response to a critical question could send the polygraph pens into spasms that might suggest a lie. As David Lykken, a leading critic of the lie detector, has noted, "polygraph pens do no special dance when we are lying."

4   Not only can innocent people appear guilty, but guilty people can also learn to beat the polygraph. For example, by biting their tongue or curling their toes when control questions are asked, people can produce an arousal response to those questions that looks similar to the arousal that occurs when they actually lie on critical questions. William Casey, former director of the U.S. Central Intelligence Agency, used to delight in his ability to fool the lie detector. Fred Fay, a prison convict who had been falsely convicted of a murder partly on the basis of a polygraph test, also became an expert at defeating polygraph tests. On one occasion, Fay coached 27 fellow inmates who were scheduled for polygraph tests. All of the inmates told Fay they were guilty of the relevant crimes. Yet after only 20 minutes of instruction, 23 of the 27 inmates managed to beat the polygraph. Such results sharply contradict the notion of an infallible lie detector.

5   Misgivings about the validity of polygraph tests are supported by studies in which experienced polygraph examiners were given the polygraph records of suspects known to be either innocent or guilty on the basis of other evidence. The experts were asked to judge the guilt or innocence of the suspects. They usually did quite well in identifying the guilty, attaining accuracy rates of 80 to 98 percent. However, they were less accurate in identifying the innocent, judging as many as 55 percent of the truly innocent suspects to be guilty in some

"The lie is a condition of life."

—Friedrich Nietzsche

studies. These error rates call into question the adage that an innocent person has nothing to fear from a polygraph test.

6   Largely because of an unacceptably high likelihood that an innocent person might be judged guilty, the American Psychological Association has supported legal challenges to polygraph testing. Congressional testimony by psychologists strongly influenced passage of the Employee Polygraph Protection Act in 1988, which prohibits most nongovernmental polygraph testing. Moreover, polygraph results alone cannot be used to convict people of crimes in most jurisdictions. Nonetheless, local and federal governments continue to use polygraph tests in internal criminal investigations and in police officer and national security screening despite the weight of research evidence against their validity for these purposes.

> Passer, Michael W., and Smith, Ronald E., *Psychology*, 3rd edition, New York: McGraw-Hill, 2007, pp. 380–381

▼ COMPREHENSION CHECKUP

Multiple Choice

Directions: Write the letter for the correct answer to each question on the lines provided.

___b___ 1. The authors' of this selection probably believe that
  a. polygraph evidence should be admissible in court cases.
  b. people should be cautious about polygraph testing.
  c. polygraph machines can definitely determine whether a person is guilty or innocent.
  d. both the government and business should make more use of the polygraph machine.

___b___ 2. The authors' purpose in writing this selection is to
  a. entertain.
  b. inform.
  c. persuade.
  d. amuse.

___a___ 3. The tone of this selection is
  a. objective.
  b. optimistic.
  c. outraged.
  d. gloomy.

___a___ 4. "On one occasion, Fay coached 27 fellow inmates who were scheduled for polygraph tests." This sentence makes a statement of
  a. fact.
  b. opinion.

_____c_____　　5. The main idea expressed in paragraph 3 is

　　a. The issue, however, is whether this emotional response to a critical question means that the person was lying.

　　b. Herein lies one major problem with polygraph tests.

　　c. Innocent people may appear guilty when doubt, fear, or lack of confidence increases their autonomic activity.

　　d. As David Lykken, a leading critic of the lie detector, has noted, "polygraph pens do no special dance when we are lying."

_____a_____　　6. In paragraph 1, what does the transition word *because* signal?

　　a. cause and effect

　　b. compare and contrast

　　c. definition

　　d. steps in a process

_____d_____　　7. In paragraph 5, what does the transition word *however* signal?

　　a. addition

　　b. conclusion

　　c. comparison

　　d. contrast

_____b_____　　8. The transition word *moreover* in paragraph 6 indicates

　　a. contrast.

　　b. addition.

　　c. reversal.

　　d. conclusion.

_____b_____　　9. The authors' of the selection would probably agree that

　　a. polygraphs are reasonably accurate in detecting deception.

　　b. the error rate for polygraph testing is too high to be acceptable.

　　c. the polygraph just needs some minor improvements to make it more reliable.

　　d. giving polygraph tests should be prohibited.

_____a_____　　10. According to the selection, the polygraph test is more likely to

　　a. label an innocent person guilty.

　　b. label a guilty person innocent.

True or False

Directions: Indicate whether the statement is true or false by writing **T** or **F** on the blank provided.

_____T_____ 1. There are ways to fool polygraph machines.

_____T_____ 2. A subject's emotional reaction can affect the results of polygraph testing.

_____T_____ 3. A polygraph can be inaccurate.

_____F_____ 4. Human beings have more control over physiological responses than over other behaviors.

_____T_____ 5. A polygraph examiner asks both critical and control questions of a subject.

_____T_____ 6. The polygraph examiner compares the subject's reactions to critical questions with those for control questions.

_____F_____ 7. The American Psychological Association is strongly in favor of polygraph testing.

_____T_____ 8. The polygraph measures emotional arousal.

Vocabulary in Context

Directions: Choose one of the words in the following list to complete each of the sentences below. Use each word only once.

adage	infallible	prohibit
coached	misgivings	relevant
contradicted	numerous	spasms
controversial	physiologically	validity

1. The report that cigarettes do not cause lung cancer has no _____validity_____ .

2. It is important to keep yourself healthy both psychologically and _____physiologically_____ .

3. The issue of cloning has become increasingly _____controversial_____ with many scientists supporting further research and other groups opposing the idea on moral or religious grounds.

4. When deciding what college to attend, cost is a highly _____relevant_____ consideration.

5. Laws _____prohibit_____ minors from smoking cigarettes or drinking alcohol.

6. There is no foolproof means of assessing when a person is telling a lie; therefore polygraph machines are not _____infallible_____ .

7. Many people suspect that quiz show winners are often secretly _____coached_____ by someone associated with the show.

8. An old __adage__ is "when the cat's away, the mice will play."

9. When Erin left her teenage son alone for the weekend, he got into trouble; so she had __misgivings__ about leaving him alone over the Fourth of July.

10. I rarely get to see her because she has __numerous__ friends.

11. The suspect in the robbery stuck to his story, but every witness called by the prosecutor __contradicted__ him.

12. The movie was so funny that she went into __spasms__ of laughter.

In Your Own Words

1. Do you consider lie detector tests to be an invasion of privacy? Why or why not? Are there times when you think polygraph testing is a good idea? If so, when?

2. Do you think employers should be allowed to give lie detector tests to job applicants? Why or why not?

3. If a prospective employer asked you to take a lie detector test, would you agree to do it?

4. Do you think that the results of polygraph examinations should be admissible as evidence in criminal trials?

Written Assignment

1. According to research by Bella DePaulo (1996), during an average week, people lie to about one-third of those with whom they interact. On average, people tell about ten lies per week, with the greatest lying committed by those who are most sociable and concerned about creating favorable impressions. Lying to spare another person's feelings is usually reserved for those for whom we care a great deal.

   How can we tell when someone is lying? Psychologists think we should focus less attention on the face and instead look at actions. Some sample body movements that might indicate deception are fidgeting of the hands and feet and shifting of body posture. Also, we might want to pay attention to changes in a person's speech patterns. For instance, when people lie they tend to give shorter answers, the pitch in their voice rises slightly, and their speech is slower and filled with more pauses ("ahs" and "uhms"). What do you think? Based on your own experience, when people are being deceitful, do their faces or body language give them away? Write a paragraph giving your opinion.

2. Do you think it is easier to detect the lies of people you know better or those you know less well? Give reasons.

3. Write a paragraph in which you reflect on the meaning of the following quotation from your own experience. "Always tell the truth. Then you don't have to remember anything."—Mark Twain

4. The FBI has launched a program to give lie detector tests to hundreds of state and local police officers assigned to terrorist task forces. The purpose is to help prevent espionage and to fight against information leaks. However, the head of the largest police union, the Fraternal Order of Police, has serious concerns about the program. What do you think? Is this a good use of polygraph testing? Write a paragraph discussing this issue.

Internet Activity

Check out the following U.S. Department of Labor websites for a good discussion of employee rights as protected by the Employee Polygraph Protection Act of 1988 (EPPA):

www.dol.gov/compliance

Enter "Employee Polygraph Protection Act" into a search engine. Briefly summarize your findings.

READING

"Robinson especially became the object of hate mail, death threats, and racial slurs."

"Ethnic prejudice has no place in sports, and baseball must recognize that truth if it is to maintain stature as a national game."

—Branch Rickey

GETTING FOCUSED

Branch Rickey, general manager of the Brooklyn Dodgers, took the most significant action of his career when he hired Jackie Robinson to be the first African American to play in the major leagues. Until that point, whites and blacks played in separate leagues. While the white big leagues got most of the attention, there were several Negro leagues. Some of the star players in those leagues were Satchel Page, Josh Gibson, Buck Leonard, and Monte Irvin, all of whom ultimately became members of the national Baseball Hall of Fame.

Shortly before his death in 1965 at age 83, Rickey sent a telegram to Jackie Robinson, who by that time was retired from baseball and involved in the civil rights movement with Martin Luther King, Jr.

Wheelchair bound, Rickey apologized to Robinson for not joining him at the march on Selma, Alabama. Robinson responded with a letter that read: "Mr. Rickey, things have been very rewarding for me. But had it not been for you, nothing would be possible. Even though I don't write to you much, you are always on my mind. We feel so very close to you, and I am sure you know our love and admiration is sincere and dedicated. Please take care of yourself. We know where your heart is. We will take care of the Selma, Alabamas, and do the job."

(continued)

BIO-SKETCH

James Kirby Martin is a distinguished professor of history at the University of Houston. His areas of special interest include early American history and social and cultural issues in America.

TACKLING VOCABULARY

fidgeted   moved about in a nervous or restless way

prohibited   forbidden

barnstormed   played in small towns

balk   an illegal motion by a pitcher

virtuoso   showing special knowledge or skill in a field

INTEGRATION IN SPORTS

James Kirby Martin

On April 18, 1946, the sports world focused on a baseball field in Jersey City, an industrial wasteland on the banks of the Passaic River. It was the opening day for the Jersey City Giants of the International League. Their opponents were the Montreal Royals, the Brooklyn Dodgers' farm team. Playing second base for the Royals was Jackie Roosevelt Robinson, a pigeon-toed, highly competitive, marvelously talented African-American athlete. The stadium was filled with curious and excited spectators, and in the press box sportswriters from New York, Philadelphia, Baltimore, and cities further west fidgeted with their typewriters. It was not just another season-opening game. Professional baseball, America's national game, was about to be integrated.

2   Since the late nineteenth century, professional baseball, and most other professional team sports, had prohibited interracial competition. White athletes played for the highest salaries, in the best stadiums, before the most spectators. During the same years, black teams barnstormed the country, playing where they could and accepting what was offered. For them, the pay was low, the stadiums rickety, and the playing conditions varied between bad and dangerous.

3   Jackie Robinson came to bat in the first inning. His very presence had ended segregation in "organized baseball." Nervous, he later recalled that his palms seemed "too moist to grip the bat." He didn't even swing at the first five pitches. On the sixth pitch, he hit a bouncing ball to the shortstop who easily threw him out.

4   In the third inning, Robinson took his second turn at bat. With runners on first and second, he swung at the first pitch and hit it over the left-field fence 330 feet away. In the press box sat Wendell Smith and Joe Bostic, two African American reporters for the *Amsterdam News*. They later wrote, "Our hearts beat just a little faster and the thrill ran through us like champagne bubbles."

5   Robinson wasn't through for the day. In the fifth inning, he had a bunt single, stole second, advanced to third on a ground ball, and faking an attempt to steal home, forced a balk and scored. It was a virtuoso performance. During the remainder of the game, he had two more hits, another stolen base, and forced a second balk. In the field he was tough, intense, and smart. It was a fine day for Robinson and his supporters.

6   The success of Jackie Robinson in baseball led to the integration of the other major professional sports. In 1946, the Cleveland Rams moved their football franchise to Los Angeles, and to boost ticket sales they signed African Americans Kenny Washington and Woody Strode, both of whom had played football with Robinson at UCLA. Professional football then became the next to be integrated. In 1950, the Boston Celtics of the National Basketball Association signed Chuck Cooper of Duquesne to a professional contract. The same year, the United States Lawn Tennis Association allowed African Americans to compete at Forest Hills. In a relatively short time, integration came to American professional sports.

7   The process was not without individual pain. Robinson especially became the object of hate mail, death threats, and racial slurs. Opposition runners spiked him and pitchers threw at him. Off the field, he faced a life of segregated restaurants, clubs, theaters, and neighborhoods. Patient, witty, and quick to forgive, he endured extraordinary humiliation. He became an American hero, but he paid dearly. Throughout the 1946 and 1947 seasons, Robinson was plagued by headaches, bouts of depression, nausea, and nightmares. Talking about the pressures on her husband, Rachel Robinson recalled, "There were the stresses of just knowing that you were pulling a big weight of a whole lot of people on your back . . . I think Jackie felt that there would be serious consequences if he didn't succeed and that one of them would be that nobody would try again for a long time." Of course, other African-American players also confronted trials on and off the field, but as Robinson's teammate Roy Campanella said, "nothing compared to what Jackie was going through."

8   Integration in sports preceded integration in society at large. But in both sports and the civil rights movement, racial gains were paid for by individuals willing to risk serious hardships. Change seldom came easily and the struggle never ended quickly.

> Excerpts from *America and Its Peoples*, Vol. 2, 5th ed. by James Kirby Martin et al. Copyright © 2004 by James Kirby Martin, Randy Roberts, Steven Mintz, Linda O. McMurry and James H. Jones. Reprinted by permission of Pearson Education, Inc.

✔ COMPREHENSION CHECKUP

Fact and Opinion

Directions: Identify statements of fact with an **F** and statements of opinion with an **O**.

    F   1. Their opponents were the Montreal Royals, the Brooklyn Dodgers' farm team.

    O   2. It was not just another season-opening game.

    F   3. Jackie Robinson came to bat in the first inning.

    F   4. He didn't even swing at the first five pitches.

    F   5. Professional football then became the next to be integrated.

    F   6. In 1950 the Boston Celtics of the National Basketball Association signed Chuck Cooper of Duquesne to a professional contract.

    F   7. Opposition runners spiked him, and pitchers threw at him.

    O   8. Patient, witty, and quick to forgive, he endured extraordinary humiliation.

    F   9. Robinson's teammate Roy Campanella said, "nothing compared to what Jackie was going through."

    O   10. Change seldom came easily, and the struggle never ended quickly.

Directions: Identify each numbered sentence in the following paragraphs as either a fact **(F)** or an opinion **(O).**

(1) In the third inning, Robinson took his second turn at bat. (2) With runners on first and second, he swung at the first pitch and hit it over the left-field fence 330 feet away. (3) In the press box sat Wendell Smith and Joe

Bostic, two African-American reporters for the *Amsterdam News*. (4) They later wrote, "Our hearts beat just a little faster and the thrill ran through us like champagne bubbles."

Sentence 1 _____F_____

Sentence 2 _____F_____

Sentence 3 _____F_____

Sentence 4 _____F_____

(1) Robinson wasn't through for the day. (2) In the fifth inning, he had a bunt single, stole second, advanced to third on a ground ball, and faking an attempt to steal home, forced a balk and scored. (3) It was a virtuoso performance. (4) During the remainder of the game, he had two more hits, another stolen base, and forced a second balk. (5) In the field he was tough, intense, and smart. (6) It was a fine day for Robinson and his supporters.

Sentence 1 _____O_____

Sentence 2 _____F_____

Sentence 3 _____O_____

Sentence 4 _____F_____

Sentence 5 _____O_____

Sentence 6 _____O_____

Directions: In the following sentences, underline the words that indicate an opinion.

1. Playing second base for the Royals was Jackie Roosevelt Robinson, a pigeon-toed, <u>highly competitive, marvelously talented</u> African-American athlete.

2. The stadium was filled with <u>curious</u> and <u>excited</u> spectators, and in the press box sportswriters from New York, Philadelphia, Baltimore, and cities further west <u>fidgeted</u> with their typewriters.

True or False

Directions: Indicate whether each statement is true or false by writing **T** or **F** in the blank provided.

_____F_____   1. Jackie Robinson played football at USC.

_____T_____   2. The Montreal Royals were the Brooklyn Dodgers' farm team.

_____F_____   3. Jackie Robinson played third base.

_____T_____   4. Professional baseball was integrated in 1946.

_____F_____   5. Professional football was integrated before professional baseball.

Matching

Directions: Match each of the people listed below with his description. Write the letter of the description on the appropriate blank.

_____c_____   1. Kenny Washington   a. played with the Brooklyn Dodgers

_____d_____   2. Branch Rickey   b. reporter for *Amsterdam News*

_____f_____   3. Josh Gibson   c. played with the Los Angeles Rams

_____e_____   4. Chuck Cooper   d. person who hired Robinson

_____b_____   5. Joe Bostic   e. played with Boston Celtics

_____g_____   6. Rachel Robinson   f. played in the Negro leagues

_____a_____   7. Roy Campanella   g. wife of Jackie Robinson

In Your Own Words

1. Even though the players on teams in professional sports are ethnically diverse today, management and ownership in professional sports lags behind. Do you think that ethnic prejudice is still being felt in professional sports? What could be done to improve ethnic balance at all levels of professional sports?

2. Only Jackie Robinson has had the distinction of having his jersey, No. 42, retired from all baseball teams. Most recently Latino groups have lobbied to have Roberto Clemente's No. 21 jersey similarly retired. What do you think? Should this honor be reserved for the man who originally broke the color barrier?

Written Assignment

What sorts of personal characteristics may lead a person to break barriers? Many people who have broken barriers have been quiet, unassuming types like the late Rosa Parks. How would you handle the intense scrutiny and pressure that comes from being the very first? Choose an occupation and write a short essay describing how you would handle being a role model.

Internet Activity

Jackie Robinson is well known for being the first African American to play professional baseball in the National League. For a bit of trivia, type "Larry Dolby" into any search engine and find out what he did.

8 Bias

Doug Marlette cartoon copyright © Tribune Media Services, Inc. All Rights Reserved. Reprinted with permission.

1. What bias is being expressed in the cartoon?

    _____

    _____

2. What clues led you to your answer?

    _____

    _____

In this cartoon, the Native Americans are expressing a desire to close the borders and keep the new immigrants, the Pilgrims, out. The author's point of view is that we should probably be more tolerant of immigration. An author's point of view can be favorable, unfavorable, or neutral. In this case, the author is biased in favor of immigration.

The word **bias** is defined as "leaning in favor of or against something or someone" and "partiality or prejudice." The Smothers Brothers (a popular music-and-comedy team of the sixties) had a routine in which the final line was "Mom always liked you best!" In other words, the sons were claiming that their mom played favorites, thus demonstrating partiality or bias.

Some writers are like the Smothers brothers' mom in that they make no attempt to conceal their biases. Their goal is to convince the reader to agree with their particular **point of view,** or perspective, on any given issue. Other writers try to convey their information as objectively as possible. These writers rely primarily on factual material that can be proven to be either true or false. They usually include both sides of an issue in order to present a balanced or fair view. The material included in encyclopedias is an example of material that is less likely to be biased.

Denotation and Connotation

Authors can demonstrate their biases by the words they choose to express their ideas. Authors can use the **denotative** meaning of a word, which is simply its dictionary definition. Or they can favor **connotative** words that indicate strong emotion and express partiality. We refer to these words as "loaded" because they carry an extra emotional "charge." Not all words have emotional or connotative meanings. Some words are neutral. Look at the following sentences:

Luz just bought *furniture* for her apartment.

Luz just bought *antiques* for her apartment.

Luz just bought *junk* for her apartment.

Each of these sentences describes Luz's actions. The first sentence is neutral or objective because no judgment is being expressed. The second sentence expresses a bias in favor of Luz because antiques are considered to be valuable. The third sentence demonstrates a bias against Luz's actions because junk is considered to be undesirable. Notice how just one word can help the author convey a particular point of view.

Now look at the italicized words in the following example to determine which statement seems more biased.

Matt's mother *demanded* that he be home by midnight.

Matt's mother *advised* that he be home by midnight.

The denotative, or dictionary meaning, of *demanded* indicates that a person who "demands" has the right or the authority to do so. A synonym for *demand* is *order*. On the other hand, to *advise* means to "recommend" or "inform." You can see that *demand* carries more emotion than *advise*.

In the following example, which sentence seems more neutral?

The *crowd* gathered at the gate of the king's palace.

The *mob* gathered at the gate of the king's palace.

In this example, *crowd* implies a large group of people gathered together. It is a more neutral term than *mob*, which implies a crowd that is unruly and threatening.

Exercise 1: Positive or Negative Connotations

Directions: The following words are from the selections in this chapter. Indicate whether they are positive (**P**) or negative (**N**) in tone.

N	perverse		N	burden
N	tragedy		N	cringe
P	precious		N	smashed
P	valued		P	gentle
N	encumbrance		N	frivolous
N	stubborn		N	wasteful
P	opportunity		N	grisly
N	inefficiency		N	slaughtered
N	corruption		N	gruesome
N	dilapidated		N	unethical
P	clean		N	parsimonious
P	delight		P	prosperous
P	beautiful		N	cheap

Exercise 2: Negative Connotations

Directions: The following word pairs have similar denotative (dictionary) meanings, but dissimilar connotative (emotional) meanings. Underline the word in each pair with the more negative connotation.

1. sound　　　　　　noise

2. home　　　　　　shack

3. inexpensive   cheap

4. picky   careful

5. good-natured   silly

6. gaudy   colorful

7. inappropriate   tasteless

8. foolish   unwise

9. declined   collapsed

10. curious   nosy

11. cautious   fearful

12. firm   obstinate

Exercise 3: Using Positive, Negative, and Neutral Words

Directions: Describe a sporting event (a basketball game, soccer tournament, baseball game) by first using positive words, then negative words, and then neutral words.

Description Using Positive Words

Answers will vary.

_____

_____

_____

_____

Description Using Negative Words

Answers will vary.

_____

_____

_____

_____

Description Using Neutral Words
Answers will vary.

_____

_____

_____

_____

Exercise 4: Bias Practice

Directions: In each of the following sentences, two words are given in parentheses. Choose the word that adds the most bias to the sentence and then explain its meaning.

Example: The public has recently learned that in the past prisoners have been subjected to (horrific, medical) testing.

In this example the most biased word is *horrific* because it implies something that shocks or disgusts.

1. In a (bizarre, unusual) series of events, three college students became involved in setting fires to churches.

Biased word <u>bizarre</u>   Meaning <u>strange or grotesque</u>

2. When the doctor examined the young man's knee, he found (extensive, disfiguring) damage.

Biased word <u>disfiguring</u>   Meaning <u>defacing; spoiling the looks of</u>

3. The Mayans maintained a (flourishing, successful) civilization from before the birth of Jesus until around 1600.

Biased word <u>flourishing</u>   Meaning <u>growing strongly; prospering</u>

4. Scientists are excited by the (astonishing, interesting) discovery of ice crystals on Enceladus, Saturn's fourth-largest moon.

Biased word <u>astonishing</u>   Meaning <u>amazing</u>

Directions: Each of the following sentences contains three words in parentheses. Write the most neutral word on the line provided. Then write the most biased word along with an explanation of why it is the most biased.

5. After the long drought, the residents of Phoenix face the (challenge, task, obstacle) of discovering new ways to conserve water.

Neutral word <u>task</u>   Most biased word <u>obstacle</u>

<u>It's something in the way; an obstruction.</u>

6. Climbers on Mt. Everest made a (recent, grisly, frightening) discovery of the frozen bodies of two men.

   Neutral word <u>recent</u>   Most biased word <u>grisly</u>

   <u>It's something very horrible; gruesome.</u>

7. Is drug use (common, pervasive, rampant) among professional athletes?

   Neutral word <u>common</u>   Most biased word <u>rampant</u>

   <u>It's something that spread wildly without control.</u>

8. The Roman Empire (survived, triumphed, existed) for several centuries.

   Neutral word <u>existed</u>   Most biased word <u>triumphed</u>

   <u>It implies great victory or success.</u>

9. The (obsolete, ancient, dated) plane skidded off the runway, but none of the passengers were harmed.

   Neutral word <u>dated</u>   Most biased word <u>obsolete</u>

   <u>It's completely out of fashion.</u>

Directions: Underline the biased words in each of the following sentences.

10. At the Academy Awards, Keira Knightley wore a <u>stunningly</u> beautiful gown.

11. The drowning of three kittens in the neighborhood pool was <u>disgusting</u>.

12. Many people consider the congressman an <u>idiot</u> because he keeps changing his positions on the issues.

13. Parental involvement is <u>sadly lacking</u> in many children's lives.

14. Is it a good idea to dress small children in <u>outrageously</u> expensive outfits?

15. The new parents are sure their newborn baby girl is the <u>most adorable</u> baby in the hospital.

Directions: Underline the most biased sentence in each of the following paragraphs. Look for descriptive language and words with connotative meanings (very positive or very negative).

16.   The stands are packed with 125,000 enthusiastic fans wearing caps and jackets touting their favorite sports superhero. Many have driven hundreds of miles for the chance to be part of this sport they love so dearly. Welcome to the world of NASCAR (National Association of Stock Car Auto Racing). If you are not already a fan, take a chance and watch a NASCAR event on TV or visit a track in your area. It's a lot of fun watching the drivers maneuver for position on the track. You'll soon learn what a grueling sport it is as nerves and skills are tested for hours at a time. <u>NASCAR is a thrilling, absorbing, highly entertaining sport—and death may be only a turn away.</u> Maybe you'll become a fan too.

Nickels, William G., *Understanding Business*, 7th edition, New York: McGraw-Hill, 2005, p. 427

17.   <u>On December 16, 1937, the second escape attempt from Alcatraz ended in the death of two inmates at the merciless hands of the swift, icy, menacing waters of the bay.</u> Theodore Cole was serving fifty years for kidnapping, and Ralph Roe ninety-nine years for bank robbery. On a cold and foggy day, with a strong eight mph outgoing tide, Cole and Roe engaged in what they had considered their well-planned escape. After the guard had left at 1:00 P.M., Roe and Cole wrenched loose the cut bars, dropped to the ground below, and proceeded to a locked gate in the fence. Here, they used a wrench to break the gate lock, after which they climbed down to a ledge twenty feet below. They were now at the water's edge. Each inmate carried a sealed five gallon can with straps attached to act as a life preserver, and a knife. Shortly after entering the water, the two men were grabbed by the swift current and swept outward toward the ocean where they were torn loose from their supportive cans. They both disappeared beneath the surface of the water never to be seen again.

Adler, Freda, *Criminal Justice*, 4th edition, New York: McGraw-Hill, 2006, p. 355

Directions: Read each of the following paragraphs. For each one, write the letter for the group of words that suggest the writer's bias on the line provided.

18.   As media violence becomes more realistic, kids can experience more gore in a day than most people would experience in a lifetime, even during military combat. For example, in one popular video game you can kill an entire marching band with a flame-thrower. Some of your victims won't die right away. They will just writhe in pain, begging you to finish them off. What effects do such experiences have on people who play violent video games? Reviews of a large number of studies lead to the unmistakable conclusion that violent video games increase aggressive behavior in children and young adults. It's little wonder that medical and psychological experts recently concluded that violent video games are an extremely serious threat to public health.

Coon, Dennis, *Psychology*, 10th edition, Belmont, CA: Wadsworth, 2006, p. 291

_____b_____   a. realistic, public health, marching band
              b. gore, writhe in pain, serious threat
              c. video games, psychological experts, military combat

19. There is much to be worried about in our global environment. Evidence is growing relentlessly that we are degrading our environment and consuming resources at unsustainable rates. Biodiversity is disappearing at a pace unequaled since the end of the age of dinosaurs 65 million years ago. Irreplaceable topsoil erodes from farm fields, threatening global food supplies. Ancient forests are being destroyed to make newsprint and toilet paper. Rivers and lakes are polluted with untreated sewage, while soot and smoke obscure our skies. Even our global climate seems to be changing to a new regime that could have catastrophic consequences.

Cunningham, William P., *Environmental Science,* 9th edition, New York: McGraw-Hill, 2007, p. 3

_____c_____ a. global environment, evidence, sewage
b. food supplies, dinosaurs, climate
c. catastrophic, degrading, irreplaceable

20. The mall is one of America's most socially and economically important phenomena. They are self-contained imitations of cities—but in a setting from which many of the more troubling and annoying features of downtowns have been carefully and systematically eliminated. Malls are insulated from the elements. They are policed by private security forces who (unlike real police) can and usually do keep "undesirable" customers off the premises. They are purged of bars, pornography shops, and unsavory businesses. They are off limits to beggars, vagrants, the homeless, and anyone else the managers consider unattractive to their customers. Malls are designed with women, the principal consumers in most families, mainly in mind. Malls also are important to teenagers, who flock to them in the way that earlier generations had flocked to street-corners and squares in traditional downtowns. The malls are places for teenagers to meet friends, go to movies, avoid parents, and hang out. They are places to buy records, clothes, or personal items. And they are places to work. Low paying retail jobs, plentiful in malls, are typical first working experiences for many teens.

Brinkley, Alan, *American History,* 12th edition, New York: McGraw-Hill, 2007, p. 890

_____a_____ a. troubling and annoying, undesirable, unsavory
b. phenomena, self-contained, plentiful
c. imitations, eliminated, insulated

POINT OF VIEW

The author's **point of view** is his or her way of looking at a subject. An author's point of view is important because it can indicate the author's purpose for writing. An author can present a balanced point of view if more than one side of an issue is presented and a biased point of view if one specific position or side of an argument is favored.

Exercise 5: Point of View in an Ad

Directions: Look at the ad and answer the questions that follow.

1. What does the ad favor?

   humane treatment of animals

2. What does the ad oppose?

   wearing animal fur

3. What point of view is being expressed in the advertisement?

   The ad is opposed to killing animals for their fur.

4. What word in the ad best indicates the ad's point of view?

   compassion

Exercise 6: Identifying an Author's Point of View in Textbook Material

Directions: Read each of the following textbook excerpts and indicate the author's point of view using your own words.

Example

The immigrants before 1880 were largely from Great Britain, Ireland, Germany, and the Scandinavian countries. They were desirable people. Most of the Germans went to the farms in Michigan, Illinois, and Wisconsin. Most of the Scandinavian-Danes, Swedes, and Norwegians settled in Wisconsin, Minnesota, and the Dakotas. The prosperous country in those regions is a monument to-day to their thrift, industry, and intelligence.

Kyle Ward, *History in the Making*, New York: New Press, 2006, p. 228

Authors' point of view: The author has a favorable point of view toward

these particular immigrants. The words he chooses have positive connota-

tions. He refers to the immigrants as "desirable" people. The land they cul-

tivated is "prosperous." He uses the word "monument." The character traits

he includes are all favorable ones—"thrift, industry, and intelligence."

"What do we live for if not to make life less difficult for each other."

—George Eliot

1. Just how might helping others benefit the health of the helper? By helping others, we focus on things other than our own problems. Helping others can be effective at banishing a bad mood or a case of the blues. Helping may block physical pain because we can pay attention to only a limited number of things at a given time. Helping others can also expand our perspective and enhance our appreciation for our own lives. Helping may benefit physical health by providing a temporary boost to the immune system and by combating stress and hostile feelings linked to the development of chronic diseases. You can experience "helpers high" and the other personal rewards of volunteering as soon as you begin helping others. (p. 587)

Authors' point of view: By helping others, you also help yourself.

"Death—the last voyage, the longest, the best."

—Thomas Wolfe

2. People often feel uncomfortable in the presence of a person who is close to dying. What can we say? How should we act? It may seem that any attempt to be comforting could result only in words that are empty and meaningless. Yet we want to express concern and establish meaningful contact with the person who is facing death. In such circumstances, the most important gift we can bring is that of listening. Offering the dying person opportunities to speak openly and honestly about his or her experience can be crucial, even when such conversation is initially painful. Dying people need to know

that they are valued, that they are not alone, that they are not being unfairly judged, and that those closest to them are also striving to come to terms with a difficult situation. As with any relationship, there are opportunities for growth on both sides. (p. 619)

Authors' point of view: Even though it's difficult, we need to make time to listen

to the dying person.

3.   The typical American diet has changed significantly in recent decades—and not for the better. Americans now consume too many calories, often in the form of added sugars and fats, but too few vitamins and minerals. What can be done? Several different strategies have been proposed. First, change the price structure of food. Add small taxes on soft drinks, fast food, and other nutrient-poor foods. Second, prominently print or post basic nutrition information for meals ordered in restaurants and for convenience foods or fast foods. Third, restrict food advertising aimed at children. Finally, consumers need to speak with their dollars. Make it a priority to only purchase healthy foods. (p. 367)

Authors' point of view: We need to take a proactive approach to change the

American diet for the better.

4.   We hold the world in trust for future generations and for other forms of life. Our responsibility is to pass on to the next generation an environment no worse, and preferably better, than the one we enjoy today. Although many environmental problems are complex and seem beyond the control of the individual, there are ways that people can make a difference to the future of the planet. It may seem like a hassle to consider the environmental impact of the things you buy, but a few simple choices can make a big difference without ruining your lifestyle. Remember the four Rs of green consumerism:

Reduce the amount of trash and pollution you generate by consuming and throwing away less.

Reuse as many products as possible—either yourself or by selling them or donating them to charity.

Recycle all appropriate materials and buy recycled products whenever possible.

Respond by educating others about reducing waste and recycling.

Keep in mind that doing something is better than doing nothing. Even if you can't be a perfectly green consumer, doing your best on any purchase *will* make a difference. (pp. 694, 698)

Authors' point of view: It's a big problem, but people can start doing things to

help preserve the planet.

5.   It is important to recognize that large corporations and manufacturers are the ones primarily responsible for destruction of the environment. Many of them have jumped on the environmental bandwagon with public relations and advertising campaigns designed to make them look good, but they haven't changed their practices nearly enough to make a difference. To influence them, people have to become educated, demand changes in production methods, and elect people to office who consider environmental concerns along with sound business incentives. (p. 714)

Authors' point of view: Large corporations and manufacturers need to be held

accountable for destroying the environment.

6.   Unintentional injuries (those injuries that occur without harm being intended) are the leading cause of death in the United States for people under age 35. Motor vehicle crashes, falls, and fires often result in unintentional injuries. There are many steps that can be taken to reduce the risk of injuries. Safety belts can help lower injury rates, as can public education campaigns about risky behaviors such as driving under the influence of alcohol or smoking in bed. Ultimately, though, it is up to each individual to take responsibility for his or her own actions and make wise choices about safety behaviors. Changing your unsafe behaviors before they lead to injuries is the best way of improving your chances of leading a safe lifestyle. (p. 662)

Authors' point of view: People can save themselves from injuries or death by

changing unsafe behaviors.

> All information from Insel, Paul, and Roth, Walton T., *Core Concepts in Health*, 10th ed., New York: McGraw-Hill, 2006

Exercise 7: Andrea Yates—the Yates Tragedy

In the summer of 2001, Andrea Yates, a Houston, Texas, stay-at-home mother, drowned her five children, ages 6 months to 7 years, in a bathtub in their home. Afterward, she called her husband at work, where he was a computer engineer, and told him he needed to come home.

While infanticide dates back to ancient times, these murders were the subject of a lot of media scrutiny because the mother was apparently suffering from a severe form of postpartum psychosis. Postpartum psychosis is rare, occurring in 1–2 out of every 1,000 births, and usually starts about six weeks after delivery. Symptoms may include delusions, hallucinations, sleep disturbances, and obsessive thoughts about the baby.

In 2005, Yates's conviction was overturned, and she was retried in the summer of 2006 and found not guilty by reason of insanity. Readers of various periodicals that featured her story responded by writing letters to the editor giving their opinions about the crime.

Directions: Read the following letters and answer the multiple-choice questions that follow them.

LETTER 1

(1) In 1978, I too went through the hell of postpartum depression. (2) As a nurse, I knew this was no ordinary "baby blues." (3) After proper medication and a two-week hospital stay, I recovered. (4) I was also advised by my psychiatrist not to have any more children. (5) Unlike Andrea and Rusty Yates, I listened. (6) The real heartbreak here is not only the deaths of the Yates' beautiful children, but that this meek and easygoing woman went along with this demanding, self-centered man and had a fifth child when she was clearly not mentally capable. (7) Rusty Yates should be the one to stand trial. (8) As for Andrea, I pray she receives the love, care, and support she has been denied for too long.

from Nancy Hayden, Danville, Virginia, *People Magazine*, July 3, 2001, p. 4

b _____ 1. The tone of the writer toward Andrea Yates is
   a. resentful and unforgiving.
   b. concerned and sympathetic.
   c. skeptical and suspicious.
   d. indifferent and neutral.

b _____ 2. A key point the writer makes is
   a. Andrea Yates alone is fully responsible for the murder of her children.
   b. Rusty Yates bears a lot of responsibility for the murder of their children.
   c. postpartum depression should not be taken seriously as an illness.
   d. overly controlling husbands can expect their wives to harm their children.

a _____ 3. To support her message, the writer uses
   a. personal experience as an example.
   b. statistics.
   c. figurative language.
   d. synonyms and antonyms.

b _____ 4. Which of the following statements best reveals the writer's attitude toward Rusty Yates?
   a. He was sensitive to the needs of his wife.
   b. He was dictatorial and self-absorbed.
   c. He was too easygoing.
   d. He needed more support from his wife.

_d___ 5. The sentence containing the most emotionally loaded language is

    a. Sentence 3.

    b. Sentence 4.

    c. Sentence 5.

    d. Sentence 6.

LETTER 2

(1) I attended the memorial service for the Yates children. (2) I watched their father move from casket to casket looking at each of the children and whispering to them. (3) Clearly he was conflicted between the sight of his five murdered children and his wife who sat in Harris County jail. (4) With all the warning signs, including depression and suicide attempts, I wonder how an intelligent husband could have allowed this woman to be alone with these children.

from Gary Goodfriend, Houston, Texas, *People Magazine*, July 3, 2001, p. 4

_c___ 1. The writer would probably agree with which of the following statements?

    a. As a former nurse, Andrea Yates was more than qualified to raise her children.

    b. Rusty Yates wanted nothing further to do with his wife.

    c. Andrea Yates's should not have been left alone to care for her children.

    d. Rusty Yates's life was stressful enough without having to worry about his wife's mental state.

_c___ 2. The third sentence means

    a. Rusty Yates was certain he should blame his wife.

    b. Rusty Yates was certain he should support his wife.

    c. Rusty Yates wanted to blame his wife and at the same time he wanted to support her.

    d. Rusty Yates did not care about either his wife or his children.

_d___ 3. All of the following are statements of fact *except*

    a. Andrea Yates was in the Harris County jail at the time of the funeral.

    b. the writer attended the memorial service for the slain children.

    c. five Yates children were murdered.

    d. Rusty Yates was clearly conflicted.

_d___ 4. Which of the following is a value judgment that the writer
          seems to have made?

      a. The father had lost his right to grieve for his slain children.

      b. A suicidal and depressed mother is an inappropriate
          caregiver for young children.

      c. An intelligent and aware husband would not have left his
          children alone with their mother under those circumstances.

      d. Both b and c.

LETTER 3

(1) Any sympathy I felt for Russell Yates turned to anger at about his third press conference. (2) The underlying theme of this tragic story is that he has a dinosaur attitude, keeping his wife barefoot and pregnant at any cost. (3) He had her give up her nursing career, spend 24 hours a day, seven days a week with her kids, and continually impregnated her irrespective of her mental illness. (4) As for Andrea, she chose to turn her rage to systematically murdering her own children. (5) I notice she didn't hurt herself at all. (6) Maybe they should both be prosecuted.

from Betty Arenson, Santa Clarita, California, *People Magazine*, July 3, 2001, p. 4

_d___ 1. Which of the following phrases from the letter demonstrates the
          writer's negative feelings toward Russell Yates?

      a. keeping his wife barefoot and pregnant

      b. had her give up her nursing career

      c. continually impregnated her

      d. all of the above

_b___ 2. Which of the following best describes the writer's attitude
          toward Andrea Yates?

      a. ambivalent

      b. outraged

      c. objective

      d. compassionate

_c___ 3. Which of the following statements is a fact?

      a. Russell Yates has held many interesting press conferences.

      b. Both Andrea and Rusty Yates deserve to be prosecuted.

      c. Andrea Yates was previously a nurse.

      d. Andrea Yates had too many children.

_____b_____ 4. The expression "dinosaur attitude" implies

      a. being considerate of others.

      b. holding outdated values.

      c. being slow-witted.

      d. being large and awkward.

LETTER 4

(1) Imagine holding your struggling child underwater until he stops moving. (2) Andrea Yates did this not once, not twice, but five times. (3) Postpartum or not, this woman is a murderer. (4) We don't tolerate someone insane killing other people's children. (5) Why should we tolerate someone killing her own?

from Debbie Thompkins, Plano, Texas, *People Magazine*, July 3, 2001, p. 4

_____a_____ 1. Which of the following would the writer agree with?

      a. Insanity should not give someone a license to murder.

      b. Insane people are not responsible for their actions.

      c. Andrea Yates is not responsible for her actions because she was suffering from postpartum depression.

      d. None of the above.

_____d_____ 2. A reasonable inference that can be made from the writer's letter is

      a. the writer feels sympathy for Andrea Yates.

      b. the writer finds Andrea Yates's crime reprehensible.

      c. the writer believes that the deaths of so many young children make the crime even more horrific.

      d. both b and c.

_____a_____ 3. The writer would likely agree with which of the following?

      a. Society should not allow a mother to kill her own children and then get away without punishment.

      b. It is permissible to take the life of one's own child if one has a good reason.

      c. Some murders should go unpunished.

      d. Andrea Yates has suffered enough punishment already.

_____c_____ 4. Which of the following best describes the writer's main purpose?

      a. She wants to show compassion to Andrea Yates.

      b. She thinks Andrea Yates is being treated unfairly.

      c. She wants to condemn Andrea Yates's actions.

      d. She does not feel people should pass judgment on what other people do with their children.

"(Children are) spoken of as a responsibility, a legal liability, or an encumbrance."

GETTING FOCUSED

The following excerpt is taken from the essay "Somebody's Baby," which appears in the book *High Tides in Tucson* by Barbara Kingsolver. Carefully read the excerpt to determine the author's bias. As you read, think about your own opinion on how we treat children in the United States. Also think about how your opinion might affect your interpretation of this reading selection.

BIO-SKETCH

Barbara Kingsolver, a full-time writer since 1987, was born in Annapolis, Maryland, in 1955, and received her B.A. from Depauw University and her M.S. from the University of Arizona. Her first novel, *Bean Trees*, published in 1988, was a highly acclaimed book discussing relationships among women. She has received numerous awards for her books, articles, and poetry. In 2000, she was awarded the National Humanities Medal, honoring her for her service to the arts.

TACKLING VOCABULARY

foot the bill   pay the bill; settle the accounts

SOMEBODY'S BABY

Barbara Kingsolver

In the U.S.A., where it's said that anyone can grow up to be President, we parents are left pretty much on our own when it comes to the Presidents-in-training. Our social programs for children are the hands-down worst in the industrialized world, but apparently that is just what we want as a nation. It took a move to another country (Spain) to make me realize how thoroughly I had accepted my nation's creed of every family for itself. Whenever my daughter crash-landed in the playground, I was startled at first to see a sanguine, Spanish-speaking stranger pick her up and dust her off. And if a shrieking bundle landed at *my* feet, I'd furtively look around for the next of kin. But I quickly came to see this detachment as perverse when applied to children, and am wondering how it ever caught on in the first place.

2   My grandfathers on both sides lived in households that were called upon, after tragedy struck close to home, to take in orphaned children and raise them without a thought. In an era of shortage, this was commonplace. But one generation later that kind of semi-permeable household had vanished, at least among the white middle class. It's a horrifying thought, but predictable enough, that the

worth of children in America is tied to their dollar value. Children used to be field hands, household help, even miners and factory workers—extensions of a family's productive potential and so in a sense, the property of an extended family. But *precious* property, valued and coveted. Since the advent of child-labor laws, children have come to hold an increasingly negative position in the economy. They're spoken of as a responsibility, a legal liability, or an encumbrance. The political shuffle seems to be about making sure they cost as little as possible, and that their own parents foot the bill. Virtually every program that benefits children in this country, from *Sesame Street* to free school lunches, has been cut back in the last decade—in many cases, cut to nothing. If it takes a village to raise a child, our kids are knocking on a lot of doors where nobody seems to be home. . . .

3   If we intend to cleave like stubborn barnacles to our great American ethic of every nuclear family for itself, then each of us had better raise and educate offspring enough to give us each day, in our old age, our daily bread. If we don't wish to live by bread alone, we'll need not only a farmer and a cook in the family, but also a home repair specialist, an auto mechanic, an accountant, an import-export broker, a forest ranger, a therapist, an engineer, a musician, a poet, a tailor, a doctor, and at least three shifts of nurses. If that seems impractical, then we can accept other people's kids into our lives, starting now.

"Somebody's Baby" from *High Tides in Tucson: Essays From Now or Never* by Barbara Kingsolver. Copyright © 1995 by Barbara Kingsolver. Reprinted by permission of HarperCollins Publishers.

COMPREHENSION CHECKUP

1. What is Kingsolver's main idea? The United States is doing a poor job helping families raise their children.

2. What is Kingsolver's bias (or point of view) about the way the United States treats children? Our social programs are the worst in the industrialized world. She thinks people believe it's every family for itself.

3. To what extent does Kingsolver rely on facts to support her opinions? She presents an emotional argument that is primarily opinion.

4. Give some examples of Kingsolver's use of connotative language to support her arguments. horrifying thought, precious property, valued and coveted, responsibility, liability, encumbrance, stubborn

Vocabulary in Context

Directions: Find the words in paragraph 1 that mean:

1.   sanguine   cheerful; confident

2.   detachment   a state of being aloof; disinterested

3.   industrialized   characterized by machine production

4.   furtively   done in a stealthy manner; sneaky

5.   creed   statement of beliefs; principles

6.   perverse   deviating from what is considered right or good

Find the words in paragraph 2 that mean:

1.   coveted   wanted ardently

2.   commonplace   ordinary

3.   encumbrance   an obstruction; a burden

4.   advent   arrival; coming

5.   decade   a period of ten years

Find the words in paragraph 3 that mean:

1.   ethic   a system of moral standards

2.   import   to bring in goods from another country to sell

3.   nuclear   a basic social unit consisting of parents and their children living in one household

4.   cleave   to adhere; cling to

5.   export   to send goods to another country for sale

6.   barnacles   a saltwater shellfish that attaches itself to rocks, ship bottoms, and so on

In Your Own Words

Considering that Kingsolver's purpose is to persuade the reader to accept her point of view, did she change your opinion on this issue?

Written Assignment

1. What further information would you like to have to be able to better evaluate Kingsolver's thesis?

2. Create a slogan or bumper sticker that expresses Kingsolver's point of view. Example: "Kids are people too."

Internet Activity

Did you know that Kingsolver wrote her first novel in a closet? Consult her official website to find out more about her writing career. To read about her early years, click on "About Barbara: Biography." Then write a short biographical sketch or profile about her.

http://www.kingsolver.com

EUPHEMISMS

Euphemisms are pleasant-sounding words or expressions that are substituted for ones that could be offensive. Euphemisms can be used to deliberately mislead, or to simply be polite or inoffensive. Sometimes people use euphemisms to make their occupations seem more important. In the cartoon here, the "babysitter" would rather be referred to as a "child management and control technician.

DENNIS THE MENACE

"SHE DOESN'T WANT TO BE CALLED A BABY SITTER ANYMORE. NOW IT'S 'CHILD MANAGEMENT AND CONTROL TECHNICIAN.'"

Euphemisms are often used by politicians and government agencies seeking to put a favorable spin on things. For instance, if the government wants to promote the ability of agencies to listen in on citizens' private conversations, it probably won't use the term *eaves-dropping*, which has negative connotations. Instead, it will use the euphemistic expression *electronic intercepts*. Because the phrase "raising taxes" has a negative connotation, members of Congress who want to do that may instead talk about "enhancing revenue." Using euphemisms to show events in a more positive light contributes to a biased presentation of information.

Exercise 8: Euphemisms

Directions: Match each of the euphemistic words and phrases with the letter of their correct definition.

c	1. behavior modification	a.	old person
m	2. cemetery	b.	gossip
h	3. pavement deficiencies	c.	rewards and punishment
g	4. correctional facilities	d.	broken; not working
l	5. conversationally selective	e.	alcoholic
j	6. inner city	f.	concentration camps
i	7. ethnic cleansing	g.	prisons
o	8. constructive dismissal	h.	potholes
a	9. senior citizen	i.	people getting rid of a group of people they hate
b	10. speedy transmission of near factual material	j.	poor section of town; ghetto
n	11. vertically challenged	k.	late
k	12. rescheduled arrival time	l.	shy
d	13. inoperative	m.	graveyard
f	14. relocation centers	n.	short
e	15. social drinker	o.	fired

READING

"In August 1892, strange things started to happen in the Borden home."

GETTING FOCUSED

However little one might know about Lizzie Borden, she is forever immortalized in the following playground verse:

Lizzie Borden took an axe
And gave her mother forty whacks.

READING *continued*

And when she saw what she had done,
She gave her father forty-one.

BIO-SKETCH

James Kirby Martin is a distinguished professor of history at the University of Houston. He is the author, co-author, or editor of 11 books.

TACKLING VOCABULARY

parsimonious   too careful in spending; thrifty; miserly

preponderance   superior in amount, weight, power, or importance

preconceived   to form an opinion in advance from previously held prejudice

LIZZIE BORDEN: VICTORIAN WOMAN AND MURDERER

James Kirby Martin

Andrew Borden had, as the old Scotch saying goes, short arms and long pockets. He was cheap not because he had to be frugal but because he hated to spend money. He had dedicated his entire life to making and saving money, and tales of his unethical and parsimonious business behavior were legendary in his hometown of Fall River, Massachusetts. Local gossips maintained that as an undertaker he cut off the feet of corpses so that he could fit them into undersized coffins that he had purchased at a very good price. Andrew, however, was not interested in rumors or the opinions of other people; he was more concerned with his own rising fortunes. By 1892 he had amassed over half a million dollars. He controlled the Fall River Union Savings Bank, and he served as a director of the Globe Yard Mill Company, the First National Bank, the Troy Cotton and Manufacturing Company, and the Merchants Manufacturing Company.

2   Andrew was rich, but he did not live like a wealthy man. Instead of living alongside the other prosperous Fall River citizens in the elite neighborhood known as the Hill, Andrew resided in an area near the business district called the Flats. He liked to save time as well as money, and from the Flats he could conveniently walk to work. For his daughters Lizzie and Emma, whose eyes and dreams focused on the Hill, life in the Flats was an intolerable embarrassment. Their house was a grim, boxlike structure lacking both comfort and privacy. Since Andrew believed that running water on each floor was a wasteful luxury, the only washing facilities were a cold-water faucet in the kitchen and a laundry room water tap in the cellar. Also in the cellar was the only toilet in the house. To make matters worse, the house was not connected to the Fall River gas main. Andrew preferred to use kerosene to light his house. Although it did not provide as good light or burn as cleanly as gas, it was less expensive. To save even more money, he and his family frequently sat in the dark.

3   The Borden home was far from happy. Lizzie and Emma, ages 32 and 42 in 1892, strongly disliked their stepmother Abby and resented Andrew's penny-pinching ways. Lizzie especially felt alienated from the world around her. Although Fall River was the largest cotton-manufacturing town in America, it offered few opportunities for the unmarried daughter of a prosperous man. Society expected a woman of Lizzie's social position to marry, and while she waited for a proper suitor, her only respectable social outlets were church and community service. So Lizzie taught a Sunday School class and was active in the Woman's Christian Temperance Union, the Ladies' Fruit and Flower Mission, and other organizations. She kept herself busy, but she was not happy.

4   In August 1892, strange things started to happen in the Borden home—after Lizzie and Emma learned that Andrew had secretly changed his will. Abby became violently ill. In time, so did the Borden maid Bridget Sullivan and Andrew himself. Abby told a neighborhood doctor that she had been poisoned, but Andrew refused to listen to her wild ideas. Shortly thereafter, Lizzie went shopping for prussic acid, a deadly poison, that she said she needed to clean her seal-skin cape. When a Fall River druggist refused her request, she left the store in an agitated state. Later in the day, she told a friend that she feared an unknown enemy of her father's was after him. "I'm afraid somebody will do something," she said.

5   On August 4, 1892, Bridget awoke early and ill, but she still managed to prepare a large breakfast of johnnycakes, fresh-baked bread, ginger and oatmeal cookies with raisins, and some three-day-old mutton and hot mutton soup. After eating a hearty meal, Andrew left for work. Bridget also left to do some work outside. This left Abby and Lizzie in the house alone. Then somebody did something very grisly. As Abby was bent over making the bed in the guest room, someone moved into the room unobserved and killed her with an ax.

6   Andrew came home from lunch earlier than usual. He asked Lizzie where Abby was, and she said she did not know. Unconcerned, Andrew, who was not feeling well, lay down on the parlor sofa for a nap. He never awoke. Like Abby, he was slaughtered by someone with an ax. Lizzie "discovered" his body, still lying on the sofa. She called Bridget, who had taken the back stairs to her attic room: "Come down quick; father's dead; somebody came in and killed him."

7   Experts have examined and reexamined the crime, and most have reached the same conclusion: Lizzie killed her father and stepmother. In fact, Lizzie was tried for the gruesome murders. Despite a preponderance of evidence, however, an all-male jury found her not guilty, a verdict arrived at without debate or disagreement. A woman of Lizzie's social position, they affirmed, simply could not have committed such a terrible crime.

8   Even before the trial began, newspaper and magazine writers had judged Lizzie innocent for the same reason. As historian Kathryn Allamong Jacob, an expert on the case, noted, "Americans were certain that well-brought-up daughters could not commit murder with a hatchet on sunny summery mornings." Criminal women, they believed, originated in the lower classes and even looked evil. A criminologist writing in the *North American Review* commented, "[The female criminal] has coarse black hair and a good deal of it. . . . She has often a long face, a receding forehead, overjutting brows, prominent cheek bones, an exaggerated frontal angle, and nearly always square jaws." They did not look like round-faced Lizzie and did not belong to the Ladies' Fruit and Flower Mission.

9   Jurors and editorialists alike judged Lizzie Borden according to their preconceived notions of Victorian womanhood. They believed that such a woman was

gentle, docile, and physically frail, short on analytical ability but long on nurturing instincts. "Women," wrote an editorialist for *Scribner's*, "are merely large babies. They are shortsighted, frivolous, and occupy an intermediate stage between children and men." Too uncoordinated and weak to accurately swing an ax and too gentle and unintelligent to coldly plan a double murder, a woman of Lizzie's background simply had to be innocent because of her basic innocence.

"Lizzie Bordon: Victorian Woman and Murderer" from *America and Its Peoples,* Vol. 2, 5th ed. by James Kirby Martin et al. Copyright © 2004 by James Kirby Martin, Randy Roberts, Steven Mintz, Linda O. McMurry and James H. Jones. Reprinted by permission of Pearson Education, Inc.

COMPREHENSION CHECKUP

Directions: Write the letter of the correct answer on the blank provided.

___a___ 1. In paragraph 1, the author's use of the saying "short arms and long pockets" is meant to demonstrate that Andrew Borden was

    a. stingy with money.

    b. generous with money.

    c. unconcerned about money.

    d. kind to his daughter Lizzie.

___a___ 2. In paragraph 1, the words *cheap* and *frugal* are

    a. synonyms.

    b. homonyms.

    c. antonyms.

    d. rhymes.

___d___ 3. Andrew Borden was associated with all of the following businesses *except*

    a. the funeral industry.

    b. the banking and savings industry.

    c. cotton and manufacturing.

    d. the legal profession.

___c___ 4. Paragraph 1 tells us that Andrew Borden

    a. was acutely interested in what people had to say about him.

    b. practiced good and honest business tactics.

    c. was intent on amassing a fortune.

    d. dedicated his life to helping others.

___b___ 5. In paragraph 1, the writer's point of view toward Andrew Borden is

    a. favorable.

    b. unfavorable.

_____b_____ 6. In paragraph 2, the transition words *but* and *instead* indicate
   a. addition.
   b. contrast.
   c. cause and effect.
   d. definition.

_____c_____ 7. The transition words in paragraphs 4, 5, and 6 indicate the following pattern of organization:
   a. cause and effect.
   b. compare and contrast.
   c. chronological order.
   d. example.

_____c_____ 8. The writer encloses the word *discovered* in quotes in paragraph 6 to indicate that
   a. Lizzie found her father's body unassisted.
   b. Lizzie was the first person to locate her father's body.
   c. Lizzie knew right where her father's body was because she had killed him.
   d. Lizzie and Bridget were working together to commit the murders.

_____d_____ 9. The author thinks that Lizzie was judged to be innocent by both the jury and journalists because
   a. it was assumed that she was too genteel for such a hideous crime.
   b. it was assumed that she was physically unable to wield the ax.
   c. it was assumed that a church-going individual could not have committed such a crime.
   d. all of the above.

_____a_____ 10. As used in paragraph 8, the words *coarse, receding, overjutting,* and *exaggerated* have a
   a. negative connotation.
   b. positive connotation.

_____a_____ 11. The author's purpose in writing this selection was to
   a. discuss two murders in relation to feelings about women in the late 19th century.
   b. persuade the reader to join a modern-day women's rights organization.
   c. have the Lizzie Borden murder case retried.
   d. discuss the special problems of wealthy people.

True or False

Directions: Indicate whether the statement is true or false by writing **T** or **F** on the blank provided.

_____T_____ 1. Andrew Borden did not pay much attention to Abby's claims that she had been poisoned.

_____T_____ 2. Lizzie Borden was active in both church and community projects.

_____T_____ 3. The reader can infer from paragraph 4 that Andrew's will was no longer favorable to Lizzie.

_____F_____ 4. Experts who examined the crime scene believed that Lizzie was innocent of the murders.

_____F_____ 5. Living in the Flats was not the least bit embarrassing to Lizzie and Emma.

_____T_____ 6. Andrew Borden was not above suffering hardships to save money.

_____T_____ 7. The verdict to acquit Lizzie Borden was unanimous.

_____T_____ 8. The preconceived notions of the jurors about women led to Lizzie's acquittal.

_____F_____ 9. Four people in the Borden household became violently ill after Andrew Borden's will was changed.

_____T_____ 10. The title of the selection indicates the author's opinion about whether Lizzie Borden committed the murders.

Vocabulary in Context

Directions: Choose words from the following list to complete each of the sentences below. Use each word only once.

agitated	docile	frugal	prosperous
alienated	frail	intolerable	receding
amassed	frivolous	legendary	unethical

1. Susie _amassed_ a great deal of information about her topic prior to writing her research paper.

2. He is such a _frugal_ person he doesn't even throw away a pencil or paper clip.

3. Today __unethical__ business practices are likely to be prosecuted.

4. The __legendary__ country singer Johnny Cash, immortalized in the movie *Walk the Line*, died in 2003.

5. Microsoft Corporation, with revenues of $39 billion in 2005, continues to be a very __prosperous__ business.

6. When the pain from his broken leg became __intolerable__, the skier passed out.

7. Don's thoughtless remarks about Brenda's family forever __alienated__ her.

8. The families of the miners became __agitated__ when they first heard the news of a possible mine disaster.

9. The __frail__ 10-year-old weighing only 40 pounds needed to be hospitalized.

10. With money being tight, Karen's __frivolous__ purchases annoyed her father.

11. Ten days after the storm, the flood waters are finally __receding__.

12. The __docile__ labrador retriever is a good choice for an active family with small children.

Directions: Write your own definition for each italicized word after studying its context in the sentence. Then check your definition in the dictionary.

1. There's no need to be a *penny-pincher* now that you've finally got

   a full-time job. __stingy__

2. People of a high social class are members of a social *elite*.

   __special group__

In Your Own Words

1. What was the author's purpose in including the story about Andrew Borden cutting off the feet of corpses?

2. In the Victorian era, women were perceived as innocent and gentle or as "large babies." How are women viewed today?

3. At the time of the murders, it was thought that women of a certain background were incapable of committing a crime of this magnitude. Crime was thought to originate in the lower classes. How are things different today? Is a woman more likely to be convicted of a serious crime if she is from a higher or a lower class?

Written Assignment

At the time of the murders, few opportunities existed for single women. In contrast, many opportunities are available today. Do women today still face discrimination in pursuing careers? If so, what obstacles stand in the way?

Internet Activity

Do a Google search by typing in "women in the Victorian era." Write a paragraph describing your findings about how women were treated during this period.

READING

"Had I remained in India, I would probably live my entire existence within a five mile radius of where I was born."

GETTING FOCUSED

What do you think is so special about the United States that people from all around the world make sacrifices to come here?

BIO-SKETCH

Dinesh D'Souza is the Robert and Karen Rishwain Fellow at Stanford University. In 1987–88, he served as senior policy analyst at the Reagan White House. D'Souza's books have all been best-sellers. They include *Letters to a Young Conservative*, *Illiberal Education*, and *What's So Great About America?*, from which this excerpt is taken.

TACKLING VOCABULARY

Rotary Club   a worldwide organization devoted to serving the community and fostering world peace

conventional wisdom   a widely held belief, attitude, or opinion

Horatio Alger   (1832–1898) wrote over 130 "dime" novels all having the same rags-to-riches theme Each book featured a poor hero who achieved success and wealth through honesty, determination, and hard work.

to boot   besides, in addition

WHAT'S SO GREAT ABOUT AMERICA?

Dinesh D'Souza

I came to the United States as a Rotary Club exchange student from Mumbai (formerly Bombay), India, in 1978. During my first year in America, I lived with host families in Patagonia, Arizona, and attended Patagonia Union High School, where I graduated in a senior class of 32 students. What a change it was for me to come from one of the world's biggest cities to this tiny place on the road between Tucson and Mexico.

2   Yet my experience in this provincial Arizona town helped launch my adult life in a way that cosmopolitan Mumbai could not have done. How did America change my life? The conventional wisdom is that immigrants come to America for one reason: to make money. This notion is conveyed endlessly in the "rags to riches" literature on immigrants, and it is reinforced by America's critics, who like to think of America as buying the affection of immigrants through the promise of making them filthy rich.

3   But this Horatio Alger narrative is woefully incomplete; indeed, it misses the real attraction of America to immigrants, and to people around the world.

4   There is enough truth in the conventional account to give it a surface plausibility.

5   Certainly America offers a degree of mobility and opportunity unavailable elsewhere, not even in Europe. Only in America could Pierre Omidyar, whose ancestry is Iranian and who grew up in France, have started a company like eBay. Only in America could Vinod Khosla, the son of an Indian army officer, become a shaper of the technology industry and a billionaire to boot as founder of Sun Microsystems.

6   In addition to providing unprecedented social mobility and opportunity, America gives a better life to the ordinary guy than does any other country. Let's be honest: Rich people live well everywhere. America's greatness is that it has extended the benefits of affluence, traditionally available to the very few, to a large segment in society.

7   We live in a nation where construction workers spend $4 on a cappuccino, where maids drive rather nice cars, where plumbers take their families on vacation to the Caribbean. Recently I asked an Indian acquaintance why he has been trying so hard to relocate to America. He replied, "I really want to move to a country where the poor people are fat."

8   The typical immigrant, who is used to the dilapidated infrastructure, mind-numbing inefficiency, and multilayered corruption of Third World countries, arrives in America to discover, to his wonder and delight, that everything works: The roads are clean and paper-smooth, the highway signs are clear and accurate, the public toilets function properly, when you pick up the telephone you get a dial tone, you can even buy things from the store and then take them back.

9   As I discovered when I first arrived in this country, the American supermarket is a thing to behold: endless aisles of *every* imaginable product, many different types of cereal, 50 flavors of ice cream. Today's supermarkets are full of unappreciated inventions: quilted toilet paper, fabric softener, cordless phones, disposable diapers, roll-on luggage.

10   So, yes, in material terms America offers the newcomer a better life. Still, the material allure of America does not capture the deepest source of its

appeal. How, I ask myself, would my life have been different had I never come to America? I was raised in a middle-class family in India. I didn't have luxuries, but I didn't lack necessities.

11 Materially, my life is better in the United States, but it is not a fundamental difference. My life has changed far more dramatically in other ways.

12 Had I remained in India, I would probably live my entire existence within a five mile radius of where I was born. I would undoubtedly have married a woman of my identical religious and socioeconomic background, possibly someone selected by my parents. I would face relentless pressure to become an engineer or a doctor.

13 My socialization would have been entirely within my own ethnic community. I would have had a whole set of opinions that could be predicted in advance. In sum, my destiny would to a large degree have been given to me.

14 By coming to America, I have seen my life break free of these traditional confines. The counselor at Patagonia Union High School took me under his tutelage and vowed to help me get into an Ivy League college. Without him, I probably would not have been admitted to Dartmouth College, where I became interested in literature, and switched my major to the humanities.

15 Soon I developed a fascination with politics, and resolved to become a writer, which is something you can do in America, and which is not easy to do in India. I married a woman of English, Scotch-Irish, French and German ancestry. Eventually I found myself working in the White House, even though I was not an American citizen. I cannot imagine any other country allowing a non-citizen to work in its inner citadel of government.

16 In most of the world, even today, your identity and your fate are largely handed to you. This is not to say that you have no choice, but it is a choice within given parameters. In America, you get to write the script of your own life. What to be, where to live, whom to love, whom to marry, what to believe, what religion to practice—these are all decisions that, in America, we make for ourselves. Here we are the architects of our own destiny.

17 "Self-determination" is the incredibly powerful idea that is behind the worldwide appeal of the United States. Young people throughout the world find irresistible the prospect of being in the driver's seat of their own lives. So, too, the immigrant discovers that America permits him to break free of the constraints that have held him captive, so that the future becomes a landscape of his own choosing.

18 In a sense, the day that I arrived in the United States in early September 1978 was my own Independence Day.

"What's So Great About America?" by Dinesh D'Souza from *The Arizona Republic*, July 21, 2002. Reprinted by permission of the author.

 COMPREHENSION CHECKUP

1. What examples does D'Souza provide to illustrate America's "mobility and opportunity"?

himself, Pierre Omidyar of eBay, Vinod Khosla of Sun Microsystems

2. List the points of contrast D'Souza makes between America and Third World countries.

    Here even the ordinary guy leads a good life. Everything works here and

    material goods are plentiful.

3. According to D'Souza, aside from material things, what is the *real* attraction of America to immigrants? How would D'Souza's life have been different if he had remained in India?

    In America, you can break free from tradition. There is self-determination

    here. In India, D'Souza's life would have been entirely predictable.

4. What does it mean to "write the script of your own life"? What other phrases does D'Souza use to express the same concept?

    architect of our own destiny, self-determination, driver's seat of their own

    lives, landscape of own choosing, means – determine your future

5. Identify the words in paragraph 8 that have a negative connotation.

    dilapidated, mind-numbing inefficiency, corruption

    Identify the words in the same paragraph that have a positive connotation.

    delight, wonder, clean, paper-smooth, clear, accurate

6. Does the author have a positive or a negative point of view toward the United States?

    positive

7. Does D'Souza have a bias about India? If so, what is his bias?

    Yes, in India one has to conform to social restrictions.

Vocabulary in Context

Directions: Use the vocabulary words to complete the crossword puzzle.

affluence	cosmopolitan	parameters	segment
behold	dilapidated	plausibility	unprecedented
constraints	launch	provincial	woefully
conveyed	material	reinforced	

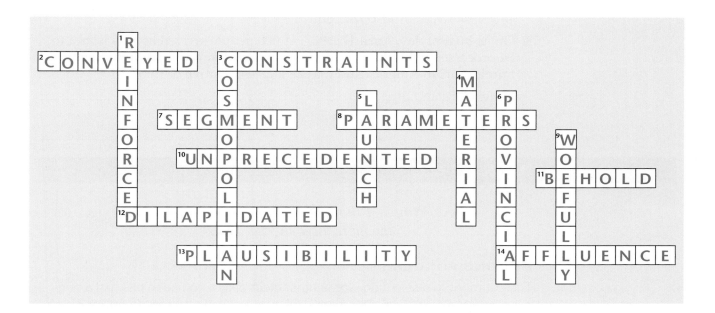

ACROSS CLUES

2. communicated
3. limitations, restrictions
7. section, part
8. boundaries
10. unparalleled
11. observe

12. run-down
13. credibility, believability
14. wealth

DOWN CLUES

1. strengthened, supported
3. worldly, sophisticated

4. wealth, possessions
5. start
6. unsophisticated
9. distressingly, sadly

In Your Own Words

1. What kind of person do you think you have to be to leave your native country behind and settle in a new land?

2. What do you appreciate about the United States? How is America different from other countries?

3. How do you feel about legal requirements that pressure immigrants to learn English?

Written Assignment

If you are new to this country, write about what attracted you to the United States. If your family has been here for a while, try to talk to someone who knows the family history. When did the first family member arrive in your state? What kind of hardships did they face? How did they overcome them?

Internet Activity

1. Check out the following website to learn more about D'Souza. Write a short paragraph giving your impressions of his accomplishments.

   http://www.dineshdsouza.com

2. On its busiest day, April 17, 1907, 11,000 people arrived at Ellis Island to be processed. Visit the website to discover what it was like for recent immigrants to America and maybe locate a relative or two.

   www.ellisisland.org

READING

"Why is it that the more connected we get, the more disconnected I feel?"

GETTING FOCUSED

The author of this selection worries that electronic automation has had a negative impact on our lives. The prefix *auto* means "self," and so if something is automated, it runs by itself with little or no human intervention. As you read this selection, think about your own personal experiences with electronic and other types of automation.

BIO-SKETCH

Michael Alvear is a freelance writer, a syndicated columnist, a commentator for National Public Radio, and the author of several books. One of his most recent books is *Alexander the Great: The Man Who Brought the World to Its Knees*.

TACKLING VOCABULARY

untethered   not held or fastened, as by a line, rope, or chain

shushed   ordered or urged to be quiet

intimacy   relating in a close, familiar, affectionate way

alienation   the act of being made to feel alone and cut off from other people

Luddite   The original Luddites were workers in England who in the early part of the nineteenth century destroyed machinery because they thought its use would decrease employment. Today this term is used to describe anyone who is opposed to new technologies or technological change

FOR CONVERSATION, PRESS 1

Michael Alvear

A funny thing happened on the way to the communications revolution: we stopped talking to one another.

2   I was walking in the park with a friend recently, and his cell phone rang, interrupting our conversation. There we were, walking and talking on a beautiful sunny day and—poof!—I became invisible, absent from the conversation.

3   The park was filled with people talking on their cell phones. They were passing other people without looking at them, saying hello, noticing their babies, or stopping to pet their puppies. Evidently, the untethered electronic voice is preferable to human contact.

4   The telephone used to connect you to the absent. Now it makes people sitting next to you feel absent. Recently I was in a car with three friends. The driver shushed the rest of us because he could not hear the person on the other end of his cell phone. There we were, four friends zooming down the highway, unable to talk to one another because of a gadget designed to make communication easier.

5   Why is it that the more connected we get, the more disconnected I feel? Every advance in communications technology is a setback to the intimacy of human interaction. With e-mail and instant messaging, we can now communicate without talking to each other. With voice mail, you can conduct entire conversations without ever reaching anyone. If my mom has a question, I just leave the answer on her machine.

6   As almost every conceivable contact between human beings gets automated, the alienation index goes up. You can't even call a person to get the phone number of another person anymore. Directory assistance is almost always fully automated.

7   Pumping gas at the station? Why say good-morning to the attendant when you can swipe your credit card at the pump and save yourself the bother of human contact?

8   Making a deposit at the bank? Why talk to a clerk who might live in the neighborhood when you can just insert your card into the ATM?

9   Pretty soon you won't have the burden of making eye contact at the grocery store. Some supermarket chains are using a self-scanner so you can check yourself out, avoiding those annoying clerks who look at you and ask how you are doing.

10   I am no Luddite. I own a cell phone, an ATM card, a voice-mail system, an e-mail account. Giving them up isn't an option—they're great for what they're intended to do. It's their unintended consequences that make me cringe.

11   More and more, I find myself hiding behind e-mail to do a job meant for conversation. Or being relieved that voice mail picked up because I didn't really have time to talk. The industry devoted to helping me keep in touch is making me lonelier—or at least facilitating my antisocial instincts.

12   So I've put myself on technology restriction: no instant messaging with people who live near me, no cell-phoning in the presence of friends, no letting the voice mail pick up when I'm home.

13   What good is all this gee-whiz technology if there's no one in the room to hear you exclaim, "Gee whiz"?

"For Conversation, Press 1" by Michael Alvear. Reprinted by permission of the author.

◥COMPREHENSION CHECKUP

Multiple Choice

Directions: Write the letter of the correct answer on the blank provided.

_____b_____ 1. The topic of this selection could best be described as
  a. cell phones.
  b. automated communications.
  c. problems with e-mail.
  d. conversation.

_____d_____ 2. We can infer from this selection that the author
  a. prefers automated communication over face-to-face communication.
  b. believes that automated communication improves the quality of person-to-person communication.
  c. believes that there should be government control of automated communication.
  d. none of the above.

_____d_____ 3. All of the following automated communication devices are mentioned in the selection *except*
  a. the cell phone.
  b. the telephone answering machine.
  c. the ATM machine.
  d. the FAX machine.

_____a_____ 4. The main idea of this selection is
  a. people should put limits on their use of automated technology.
  b. for the sake of politeness, people should avoid automated technology.
  c. people should make greater use of automated technology.
  d. people should avoid ATM cards.

_____d_____ 5. In paragraph 5, the prefix *dis* in the word *disconnected* means
  a. always.
  b. more.
  c. toward.
  d. not.

_____b_____ 6. An *anti-social* person would likely
  a. host a birthday party for a friend.
  b. stay at home in his room by himself.
  c. go out with others after a football game.
  d. have visitors over frequently.

_____d____ 7. The author expresses a positive bias in favor of
  a. talking on a cell phone to one friend while in the company of another friend.
  b. ignoring people in parks in order to talk on the cell phone.
  c. instant messaging people who live close by.
  d. saying hello to people one meets throughout the day.

_____a____ 8. The author's point of view is that
  a. advances in communications technology can reduce the quality of human contact.
  b. electronic communication is preferable to human contact because it's more efficient.
  c. electronic communication is good because it reduces the need for human interaction.
  d. none of the above.

True or False

Directions: Indicate whether the statement is true or false by writing **T** or **F** on the blank provided.

_____F____ 1. The author is abandoning his cell phone and e-mail account.

_____T____ 2. The author would likely be upset if a friend began to talk on a cell phone while they were eating dinner together.

Vocabulary in Context

As discussed in the Getting Focused section at the beginning of this selection, the prefix *auto* means "self." Think of two other words that contain the prefix *auto* and explain their meaning. Answers will vary.

Your Word _____ Meaning _____

Your Word _____ Meaning _____

In Your Own Words

1. Excluding the automated devices discussed in this selection, give an example of an automated device that has made your life both easier and harder at the same time. Explain your answer.

2. Supermarkets are now experimenting with shopping carts that will automatically scan your purchases as you put your groceries in them. Would the author of the reading selection agree or disagree that this new automated device is a step in the right direction? Explain your answer.

3. The author has placed some limits on himself: no instant messaging with people who live near him, no cell-phoning in the presence of friends, no letting the voice mail pick up when he's home. Do you think these restrictions are likely to improve the author's quality of life? Why or why not?

4. Explain what the author means by the following statements: "The telephone used to connect you to the absent. Now it makes people sitting next to you feel absent."

5. The author gives many examples of ironic events. List a few and explain why they are ironic.

Written Assignment

Many authors of etiquette books are appalled by what they consider the poor manners of those who receive gifts for various occasions and send thank-you notes by means of e-mail. In some cases, individuals even respond with a generic e-mail as in "Dear Friends, Thank you for the wedding gifts." Do you think e-mail thank-you notes are acceptable? Or are they rude? And is any thank you better than no thank you at all? Write a few paragraphs giving your opinion.

Internet Activity

You might find it interesting to research either the history of the telephone or the history of the cell phone. Alexander Graham Bell and Elisha Gray are credited with inventing the telephone and Martin Cooper with inventing the cell phone. As you access these websites, be sure to note the sizes of the original telephone and cell phone. While cell phones were a rarity 15 years ago, they are now a $30 billion a year industry.

http://inventors.about.com/library/inventors/bltelephone.htm

http://inventors.about.com/cs/inventorsalphabet/a/martin_cooper.htm

READING

"On the basis of experiments like these, Loftus and Palmer concluded that eyewitness testimony is unreliable."

GETTING FOCUSED

In August 2005, Luis Diaz was released from prison after serving 25 years for rapes he apparently did not commit. One of his convictions was vacated because of DNA evidence. Barry Scheck, co-founder of the Innocence Project, said that Mr. Diaz's case "is the best evidence yet that witnesses can make devastating mistakes, and that such testimony, however earnest and convincing, cannot be trusted." Eight victims identified Mr. Diaz in lineups as their rapist. Scheck said that 120 of 160 exonerations since the advent of DNA testing in 1989 have been based on mistaken witness identification. The selection that follows provides a timely discussion of eyewitness testimony and offers reasons for mistaken identification.

READING *continued*

BIO-SKETCH

Charles G. Morris is professor emeritus in psychology at the University of Michigan.

TACKLING VOCABULARY

exonerated   cleared from accusation, guilt, or blame

EYEWITNESS TESTIMONY: CAN WE TRUST IT?

"Steven Avery Exonerated after 18 Years in Prison"

Charles G. Morris

Based almost entirely on the eyewitness identification testimony of a single individual, Steven Avery was convicted of brutally attacking, raping and nearly killing a woman in 1985 and was sentenced to 32 years in prison. Although Avery offered alibis from 14 witnesses and documentation showing he wasn't at the scene of the crime, it took repeated legal challenges and new advances in DNA testing for him to overcome the conviction. Finally on September 11, 2003, Mr. Avery was exonerated of all charges and released from prison.

2   *I know what I saw!* When an eyewitness to a crime gives evidence in court, that testimony often overwhelms evidence to the contrary. Faced with conflicting or ambiguous testimony, jurors tend to put their faith in people who saw an event with their own eyes. However, there is now compelling evidence that their faith in eyewitnesses is often misplaced. Whereas eyewitness accounts are essential to courtroom testimony, studies clearly show that people who say, "I know what I saw," often don't know.

3   For more than 20 years, Elizabeth Loftus has been the most influential researcher into eyewitness memory. In a classic study, Loftus and Palmer showed experimental participants a film depicting a traffic accident. Some of the participants were asked, "About how fast were the cars going when they hit each other?" Other participants were asked the same question but with the words *smashed into*, *collided with*, *bumped into*, or *contacted* in place of *hit*. The researchers discovered that people's reports of the cars' speed depended on which word was inserted in the question. Those asked about cars that "smashed into" each other reported that the cars were going faster than those who were asked about cars that "contacted" each other. In another experiment, the participants were also shown a film of a collision and then were asked either "How fast were the cars going when they hit each other?" or "How fast were the cars going when they smashed into each other?" One week later, they were asked some additional questions about the accident that they had seen on film the week before. One of the questions was "Did you see any broken glass?" More of the participants who had been asked about cars that had "smashed into" each other reported that they had seen broken glass than did participants who had been asked the speed of cars that "hit" each other. These findings illustrate

how police, lawyers, and other investigators may, often unconsciously, sway witnesses and influence subsequent eyewitness accounts. On the basis of experiments like these, Loftus and Palmer concluded that eyewitness testimony is unreliable.

4   Why do eyewitnesses make mistakes? Some research suggests that the problem may be *source error:* People are sometimes unable to tell the difference between what they witnessed and what they merely heard about or imagined. This is especially true for young children. We all know what it is like to imagine an event in a particularly vivid way and then later to have difficulty remembering whether the event really happened or we simply imagined it. Indeed, studies have shown that imagining an event sometimes makes people believe it actually happened. Similarly, if you hear information about an event you witnessed, you might later confuse your memory of that information with your memory of the original event. For instance, studies have shown that if an eyewitness receives confirming feedback after picking a suspect out of a police lineup, the feedback often increases the reported *certainty* of their recognition. Other studies have shown that simply describing the perpetrator shortly after the incident occurs actually interferes with memories of what the person actually looked like, thus making it more difficult for the eyewitness to pick the correct person out of a lineup at a later date.

5   Even more disturbing, positive feedback following a lineup has been shown to change subsequent statements by witnesses with regard to "how good their view was" or "how much attention they paid to the crime." The impact of subsequent information seems to be particularly strong when it is repeated several times as is often the case with extensive media coverage, or when it comes from an authority figure such as a police officer. On the basis of this research, many psychologists contend that if people paid more attention to the source of their memories, eyewitness accounts would be more reliable.

6   Whatever the reason for eyewitness errors, there is good evidence that such mistakes can send innocent people, such as Steven Avery, to jail. Increasingly, courts are recognizing the limits of eyewitness testimony. For example, judges instruct juries to be skeptical about eyewitness testimony and to evaluate it critically. But we still have a long way to go: A study of over 1,000 cases in which innocent people were convicted of crimes concludes that errors made by eyewitnesses were the single most persuasive element leading to false conviction.

Excerpts from *Understanding Psychology,* 7th ed., by Charles G. Morris and Albert A. Maisto. Copyright © 2006. Reprinted by permission of Pearson Education, Inc.

◢ COMPREHENSION CHECKUP

1. What is the main idea of the second paragraph?

   The main idea is <u>a juror's faith in eyewitness testimony is often misplaced</u>.

2. In the second paragraph, what does the transition word *however* signal?

   However signals <u>contrast</u>   .

3. Write the main idea of paragraph 3.

   On the basis of experiments, Loftus and Palmer concluded that eyewitness

   testimony is unreliable   .

4. According to paragraph 4, what are some of the factors that can affect the ability to identify someone?

   Source error—they confuse what they saw with what they hear or imagine   .

5. In paragraph 4, what does the transition word *similarly* signal?

   Similarly signals comparison   .

6. Write the main idea of paragraph 6.

   Eyewitness testimony can lead to false convictions   .

Vocabulary in Context

1. According to the context clues given, what does the word *ambiguous* mean?

   "Faced with conflicting or *ambiguous* testimony . . ." (paragraph 2)

   Ambiguous means not clear; not definite   .

___a___ 2. In paragraph 4, the word *perpetrator* most likely means
      a. criminal.
      b. continual.
      c. privileged.
      d. person.

3. Use your dictionary to supply a synonym for the following underlined words.

   a. ". . . Mr. Avery was underlined{exonerated} of all charges . . ." (paragraph 1)

      synonym: cleared

   b. ". . . a film underlined{depicting} a traffic accident." (paragraph 3)

      synonym: portraying

   c. ". . . an event in a particularly underlined{vivid} way" (paragraph 4)

      synonym: striking

d. "... the case with <u>extensive</u> media coverage ..." (paragraph 5)

synonym: widespread; vast

4. Determine the meaning of the word *skeptical* from the context of this sentence.

"... judges instruct juries to be *skeptical* about eyewitness testimony and to evaluate it critically."

Skeptical means questioning; doubtful   .

5. After evaluating the title of the reading and the incidents and experiments described by the author, do you think he has a positive, negative, or neutral point of view toward eyewitness testimony? negative

Explain your answer. The title expresses a bias as does the first example of

Steven Avery. Only one side is presented.

6. In what paragraph does the author talk about how connotative words in

questions can influence the answers witnesses give? three

In Your Own Words

1. Do you think that expert witnesses should be allowed to explain to juries the problems with eyewitness testimony? Why or why not?

2. After reading this selection, how reliable do you think eyewitness testimony is?

3. What do you think the criminal justice system should do to prevent tragedies such as that described in the reading from happening in the future?

4. Have you ever had an experience where you made a mistake in identifying someone?

Written Assignment

1. Can you think of any safeguards that could make eyewitness testimony more reliable? Write a short paragraph discussing this issue.

2. Study the box entitled "Factors Affecting the Accuracy of Eyewitness Perceptions." What results surprise you? Can you think of any additional factors that might affect eyewitness testimony? Write a paragraph giving your opinion.

Factors Affecting the Accuracy of Eyewitness Perceptions

SOURCES OF ERROR	SUMMARY OF FINDINGS
Stress	Very high levels of stress impair the accuracy of eyewitness perceptions.
Weapon focus	The presence of a weapon impairs an eyewitness' ability to accurately identify the culprit's face.
Exposure time	The less time an eyewitness has to observe an event, the less accurately he or she will perceive and remember it.
Accuracy-confidence	An eyewitness' confidence is not a good predictor of his or her accuracy.
Cross-racial perceptions	Eyewitnesses are better at identifying members of their own race than they are at identifying people of other races.
Post-event information	Eyewitness testimony about an event often reflects not only what was actually seen but also information obtained later on.
Color perception	Judgments of color made under monochromatic light (such as orange street light) are highly unreliable.
Wording of questions	An eyewitness' testimony about an event can be affected by how the questions put to that witness are worded.
Unconscious transference	Eyewitnesses sometimes identify as a culprit someone they have seen in another situation or context.
Trained observers	Police officers and other trained observers are no more accurate as eyewitnesses than the average person.
Time estimation	Eyewitnesses tend to overestimate the duration of events.
Attitudes, expectations	An eyewitness' perception and memory for an event may be affected by his or her attitudes and expectations.

Kassin, Ellsworth, & Smith, 1989, in Coon, Dennis, *Introduction to Psychology*, 8th ed., 1998, p. 228

3. Study the cartoon by Gary Trudeau. In what ways does the cartoon illustrate the key points made in the reading selection?

DOONESBURY. Universal Press Syndicate © 2000 Garry Trudeau.

Internet Activity

Conduct a search using the phrase "eyewitness testimony." Are there any recent accounts of a miscarriage of justice caused by eyewitness testimony?

Understanding Textbook Material

*"If you think too long,
you think wrong."*

—Jim Kaat

CHAPTERS IN PART 4

FIGURE 9.1 Shark jaws have several triangular teeth. Individual teeth often have even small serrations, or denticles, along the edges. A tiger shark *(Galeocerdo cuvier)* may grow and discard 24,000 teeth in a 10-year period! These are the jaws of a sandtiger shark *(Carharias taurus).*

From Peter, Castro, and Michael E. Huber, *Marine Biology*, 5th ed., New York: McGraw-Hill, 2005, p. 148. Originally from JeffRottman/Stone/Getty Images.

It has been said that a picture is worth a thousand words, and such is the case with the photo here. The textbook from which Figure 9-1 is taken discusses characteristics of sharks, but the picture brings the authors' verbal description to life.

HOW TO USE AND INTERPRET VARIOUS TYPES OF VISUAL AIDS

Visual aids, such as the one from the marine biology textbook, are often used in textbooks, journals, and newspapers to help the reader better understand the written material. Visual aids can be as simple as a photo or as complicated as a statistical table. In this chapter we will introduce you to bar graphs, tables, pie charts, maps, drawings or diagrams, line graphs, flow charts, photos, and cartoons. Each of the exercises is tied into a reading selection in this book. The title of the reading is provided for each exercise.

What to Look For In a Visual Aid

Before plunging into a visual aid, here are some things to look at first:

1. **Read the title and subtitle** because these will tell you what the visual aid is about.

2. **Look at any keys or legends** because they will help you interpret the data.

3. **Look at how the visuals are organized,** for example, note what information is being shown on the horizontal and vertical axes of a line graph.

4. **Look at what units of measurement** are being used and note, for example, the titles of the columns in a bar graph.

5. **Look at what kinds of comparisons** are being made between different kinds of information.

6. **Think about why the visual is being included** and what point it is being used to make.

7. **Determine the source and date of the information** in the visual so you can tell how objective and how up-to-date the data are. This is important because visual aids need to be accurate, unbiased, and current.

8. **If included, read the caption below the visual aid.**

9. **Read the text that accompanies the visual** for additional information and to better understand the point it is making.

Now look at the simple bar graph in Figure 9.2. (p. 402) Notice that the title is "Top U.S. States by Domestic Traveler Spending." The bars are horizontal with the names of the states on the left-hand side and the dollar amounts spent by domestic travelers listed across the top. According to the information below the title, all the dollar amounts are given in billions of dollars. The specific amount of dollars spent in each state is listed at the end of each bar. The purpose of this graph is to give the reader a visual way of seeing which states benefit most from domestic traveler spending. One immediately notices that California and Florida have the largest amount of traveler spending. The source, the Travel Industry Association

FIGURE 9.2 **Top U.S. States by Domestic Traveler Spending**

Source: Travel Industry Association of America (billions of dollars; in 2004) (Found in *The World Almanac and Book of Facts:* 2007, New York: World Almanac Books, 2007, p. 89.)

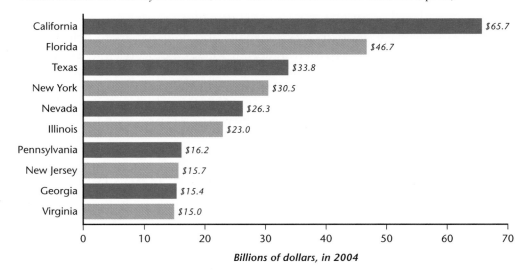

Billions of dollars, in 2004

of America, a widely respected business organization, should provide un-biased factual data. The date, 2004, is fairly current, thus giving up-to-date information.

The photo and bar graph that you have been studying are typical of the kinds of visual aids you will see in your textbooks.

BAR GRAPHS

Bar graphs are one of the most common types of visual aids. They can provide information using vertical (up and down) or horizontal (left to right) bars or columns. Bar graphs are an easy way to visualize statistical information.

Vertical Bar Graphs

In **vertical bar graphs** units of measure are usually found on the left-hand or vertical axis, while items to be compared and contrasted are listed along the bottom or horizontal axis.

Exercise 1: Vertical Bar Graphs

Life is not a Fairy Tale, by Fantasia Barrino, Warm-up 3

The vertical bar graph in Figure 9.3 provides information related to illiteracy rates in various parts of the world and gives separate bars for women and men. As with any graph, first note the title, source, and date of the information. Then look at the units of measure on the left-hand vertical axis and the areas of the world that are named along the bottom or horizontal axis.

Directions: After looking at the graph and becoming familiar with its information, answer the questions that follow.

1. Over what years was the information collected? 2000–2004

2. What organization put the information in this graph together? UNESCO Those letters stand for the United Nations Education, Social, and Cultural Organization, a major part of the United Nations.

3. The percentage numbers for illiteracy rates on the left-hand vertical axis give percentages in _____ 20 _____ percent intervals.

4. What region has the lowest illiteracy rates for both men and women?

   Central Asia

5. What region has the highest illiteracy rates for women? South and

   West Asia

6. In the Arab states and in South and West Asia, the percentage of illiteracy for women is roughly _____ 20 _____ percent higher than for men.

FIGURE 9.3 **World Illiteracy Rates by Region and Sex, 2000–2004.** From UNESCO website: www.uis.unesco.org/ev.php?ID=5020_201&ID2=DO_TOPIC - 25k

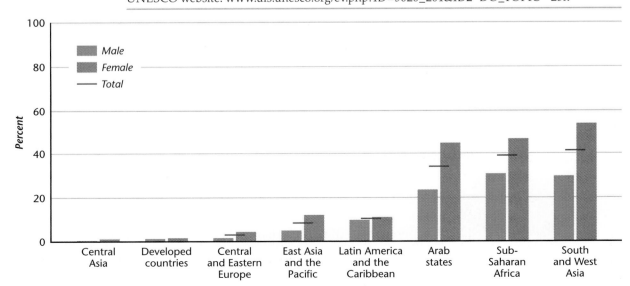

7. Does the graph give any information as to what countries fall into

   what regions? <u>no</u> Would this be a problem in inter-

   preting this graph? <u>yes</u> If so, how might the lack of

   this information lead to difficulties in interpreting the graph? <u>You would</u>

   <u>not know in what region a specific country would be included.</u>

Horizontal Bar Graphs

Horizontal bar graphs are similar to vertical bar graphs, but the bars go horizontally across the page from left to right instead of up and down. The vertical axis on the left-hand side usually indicates different types of categories while the horizontal axis indicates the amount, number, or size of each category.

Exercise 2: Horizontal Bar Graphs

Moving Beyond Your Computer: The Internet and the Web, by Robert S. Feldman, Warm-up 4

The graph in Figure 9.4 is based on information from the Pew Internet and American Life Project, which is sponsored by Pew Charitable Trusts, a nonprofit organization that gives cash donations to other nonprofit groups in much the same manner as does the Bill and Melinda Gates Foundation. According to surveys made by the Pew Internet and American Life Project, as of 2006, 73 percent of American adults use the Internet. That currently represents about 147 million people.

Directions: After looking at the graph and becoming familiar with the information it contains, answer the questions that follow.

1. The numbers across the bottom indicate the <u>percent</u> of Internet users.

2. The bar titles on the left side of the graph indicate the <u>type</u> of Internet activity.

3. What are the two most popular uses of the Internet? <u>search engines,</u>

   <u>e-mail</u>

4. What percentage of people using the Internet use it to check the weather?

   <u>78%</u>

FIGURE 9.4 **15 Most Popular Uses of the Internet by Percent of Users**

Based on surveys conducted by the Pew Internet and American Life Project conducted in 2004–2005. Information is from the organization's website, http://www.pewinternet.org.

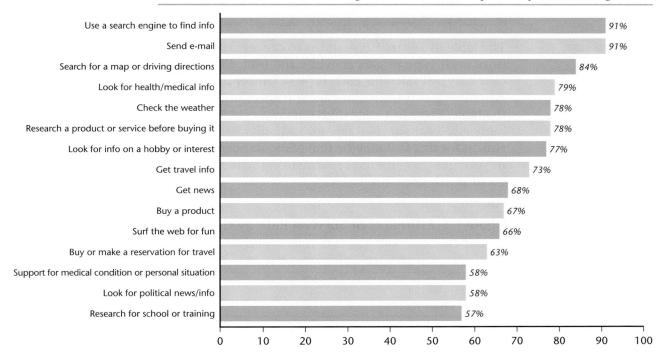

5. Does this graph tell you the percentage of different groups of people that have access to a computer or how many people in the United States own a home computer? <u>no</u>

<u> d </u> 6. According to the article "Moving Beyond Your Computer," what might you use to gain information to answer question 5?

    a. the World Wide Web

    b. web links

    c. a search engine

    d. all of the above

7. If you have used the Internet, what have you primarily used it for?

<u>Answers will vary.</u>

TABLES

Another type of visual aid is a table. **Tables** organize information, often numbers or statistics, in rows and columns that allow the reader to compare statistical data. Usually the left-hand column will identify the categories of the information while the columns to the right will give numerical values for each of these categories.

Exercise 3: Tables

It's Not About the Bike, by Lance Armstrong, Chapter 4

The table in Figure 9.5 pertains to cancer deaths. The left-hand column identifies each type of cancer while the four columns to the right give the percent survival rates for each type of cancer after 5, 10, 15, and 20 years. Lance Armstrong had testicular cancer (cancer of the testis), but as you will find in the table, there is a very high survival rate for this type of cancer. Notice the higher 20-year survival rate for testicular cancer than for prostate cancer. The reason for this fact may be that testicular cancer is much more likely to occur in younger people such as Armstrong while prostate cancer is more likely to occur much later in life.

Figure 9.5 Estimates of Survival Rate by Cancer Type Data from Hermann Brenner, *The Lancet*, 2002, 360, 1131–1135; original data from SEER of the US National Cancer Institute and was derived from 1973–1998 data.

% Survival Rates

	5 year	10 year	15 year	20 year
Prostate	98.8	95.2	87.1	81.1
Thyroid	96.0	95.8	94.0	*
Testis	94.7	94.0	91.1	88.2
Melanomas	89.0	86.7	83.5	82.8
Breast	86.4	78.3	71.3	65.0
Hodgkin's disease	85.1	79.8	73.8	67.1
Corpus uteri, uterus	84.3	83.2	80.8	79.2
Urinary, bladder	82.1	76.2	70.3	67.9
Cervix, uteri	70.5	64.1	62.8	60.0
Larynx	68.8	56.7	45.8	37.8
Rectum	62.6	55.2	51.8	49.2
Kidney, renal pelvis	61.8	54.4	49.8	47.3
Colon	61.7	55.4	53.9	52.3
Non-Hodgkin's	57.8	46.3	38.3	34.3

Oral cavity, pharynx	56.7	44.2	37.5	33.0
Ovary	55.0	49.3	49.9	49.6
Leukemia	42.5	32.4	29.7	26.2
Brain, nervous system	32.0	29.2	27.6	26.1
Multiple myeloma	29.5	12.7	7.0	4.8
Stomach	23.8	19.4	19.0	14.9
Lung and bronchus	15.0	10.6	8.1	6.5
Esophagus	14.2	7.9	7.7	5.4
Liver, bile duct	7.5	5.8	*	*
Pancreas	4.0	3.0	2.7	2.7

*Data incorrect as found in *The Lancet*.

Directions: Look at the table and then answer the questions that follow.

1. The vertical categories are listed by <u>percentage</u> survival rates for 5, 10, 15, and 20 years.

2. The survival rate for testicular cancer for 5 years is <u>94.7</u> percent.

3. What two types of cancer have the highest survival rates for 5 years?

   <u>prostate, thyroid</u>

4. Which cancer has the lowest survival rate in all categories?

   <u>pancreas</u>

5. What might be reasons that the survival rate for lung cancer is very

   low? <u>Answers will vary.</u>

6. Look up "myeloma" in the dictionary. After finding out about what type of cancer myeloma is, why do you think that survival rates for multiple myeloma are so low, especially after 20 years?

   <u>It occurs in multiple sites and is in the bone marrow.</u>

PIE CHARTS

Pie charts represent percentages or proportions of a whole as pie-shaped sections of a circle. The whole of the circle represents 100 percent, and each pie-shaped piece represents a percentage of that total.

Exercise 4: Pie Charts

Car Buying Turns
Men into Big Game
Hunters,
by Karen Peterson,
Chapter 6

The two pie charts in Figure 9.6 help us understand how American car-buying habits have changed in the decade from 1993 to 2003.

FIGURE 9.6 **Period Sales for Motor Vehicles for 1993 and 2003 by Percentage** Information from *National Transportation Statistics: 2006;* Bureau of Transportation Statistics, U.S. Department of Transportation.

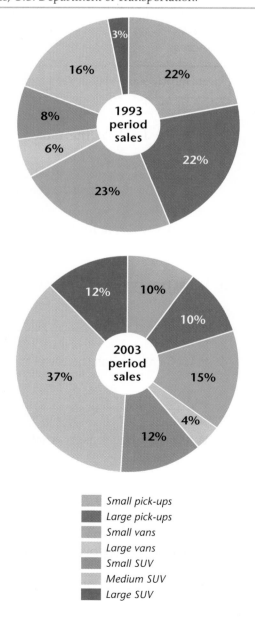

Directions: After looking at the two pie charts, answer the questions that follow.

1. What two years are being contrasted? <u>1993 and 2003</u>

2. What type of vehicle was the most popular in 1993? <u>small vans</u>

   In 2003? <u>medium SUV</u>

3. What was the percentage increase in sales of medium SUVs between 1993 and 2003? <u>21%</u>

4. Do these pie charts tell you the total number of sales for these different types of vehicles for 1993 and 2003? <u>no</u>

5. What was the percentage decrease in sales for all pickups from 1993 to 2003? <u>12%</u>

6. What do you think the pie charts will look like in 2013 and why?

   <u>Answers will vary.</u>

MAPS

Maps can be used for a variety of purposes. **Maps** are most commonly used to show the locations of countries, states, cities, roads, rivers, streets, and so on. Maps can also show similarities or differences between countries, states, and cities. They are used in all sorts of textbooks (geography, history, biology, ecology, sociology) and are used to show all types of information (geology of an area, animal populations, climate variations, and so forth.)

Exercise 5: Maps

Thunderbolts, by Pat Riley, Chapter 6

The two maps in Figure 9.7 show the routes and intensity of two very deadly hurricanes, Hurricane Andrew in 1992 and Hurricane Katrina in 2005.

Directions: Look at the maps and then answer the questions that follow.

1. In which ocean did each of the hurricanes begin? <u>Atlantic</u>

2. What state did each hurricane hit first? <u>Florida</u>

FIGURE 9.7 **Paths of Hurricanes Andrew and Katrina** From "Hurricane Preparedness," National Hurricane Center (NHC) and National Oceanic and Atmospheric Administration (NOAA) website, July 11, 2006.

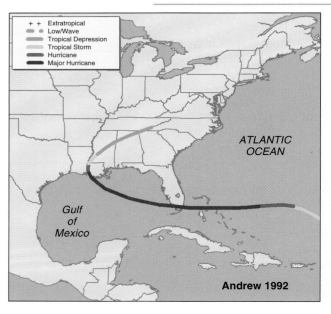 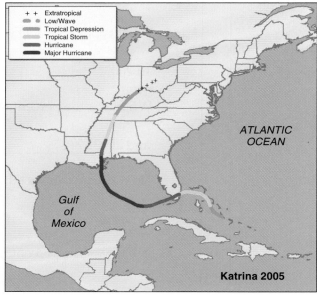

3. After hitting that state, what body of water did they both pass over?

Gulf of Mexico

4. Name another state that both hurricanes hit. Louisiana

5. Both hurricanes circled in a (clockwise/counterclockwise)

clockwise   pattern.

6. Has your state been hit by major hurricanes? If so, when? _____

Describe what happened. Answers will vary.

7. What natural disasters are common in your state? Answers will vary.

DIAGRAMS

Another type of visual aid is the diagram. **Diagrams** are artists' drawings of particular concepts or complex processes. Diagrams are used when a textbook writer has written about a particular subject but realizes that a visual

FIGURE 9.8 **Strong onshore winds in a hurricane pile water against the shore, forming a storm surge (high sea level) that may cause severe flooding on a low-lying coast. Damage is worse at high tide.** From Diane Carlson, et. al., *Earth Revealed*, 6th ed., New York: McGraw-Hill, 2006, p. 521.

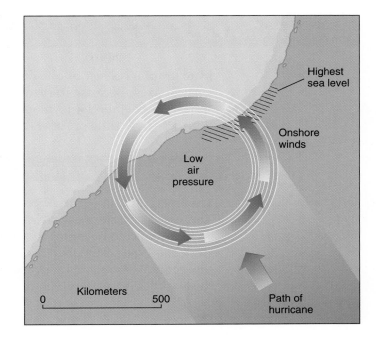

aid would help students better understand the concept or process. Diagrams are especially useful in science textbooks. A biology textbook might have a diagram of the muscles of the arm, an astronomy textbook a diagram of the solar system, and a chemistry textbook a diagram showing how atoms interconnect to form molecules.

Exercise 6: Diagrams

Thunderbolts, by Pat Riley, Chapter 6

Figure 9.8 is a diagram of a hurricane. The author of the geology textbook from which this diagram is taken has given the reader an explanation of the causes and processes of a hurricane but also wants the reader to see what she has been discussing.

Directions: Look at the diagram, read the caption beside it, and then answer the questions that follow.

1. The circular air movement moves in a (clockwise/counterclockwise) <u>counterclockwise</u> pattern.

2. The winds of a hurricane form around an area of <u>low</u> air pressure.

3. The measurement scale for this diagram is in <u>kilometers</u> .

4. The highest sea levels are where the winds turn into the <u>shore</u> . (shore/sea)

5. According to the caption, damage is worse at <u>high</u> tide.

LINE GRAPHS

Line graphs consist of one or more lines that join points along horizontal or vertical axes. Because information can be plotted in this way, it is possible to show more detailed information than in bar graphs. Line graphs can plot relationships over time or show differences in variables.

Exercise 7: Line Graphs

Integration in Sports, by James Kirby Martin, Chapter 7

The line graph in Figure 9.9 represents students in de facto minority schools. The word *de facto* means "in fact" or "actually." Even though white schools were ordered to desegregate in the 1954 *Brown v. Board of Education* decision, since the 1980s, schools have been resegregating. In fact, since the 1990s, the segregation of students of every racial group has increased. White students are the least likely to attend multiracial schools and are the most isolated group.

Directions: Look at the graph and then answer the questions that follow.

1. Between 1968 and 1980, was the percentage of blacks in de facto minority

   schools rising or falling? falling

2. Over the past 25 years, which group—blacks or Latinos—has had a higher percentage of students in de facto minority schools?

   Latinos

FIGURE 9.9 **Students in De Facto Minority Schools** Gary Orfield and Chungmel Lee, "Racial Transformation and the Changing Nature of Segregation," Civil Rights Project, Harvard University, January 2006. From David Sadker, et al., *Teachers, Schools, and Society,* 8th ed., New York: McGraw-Hill, 2008, p. 83.

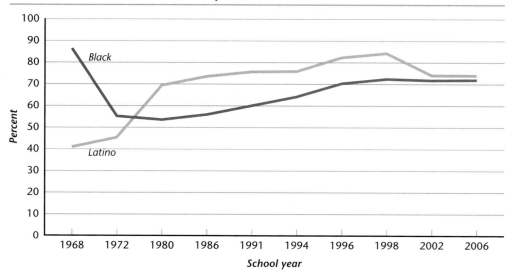

3. Over the past 25 years, has the percentage of blacks and Latinos in de

facto minority schools increased or decreased? increased

_____c_____ 4. Over the past 5 years, how would you describe the relationship
between the rates for blacks and Latinos in *de Facto* minority
schools?
a. Blacks have a higher rate.
b. Latinos have a much higher rater.
c. The rates for the two groups have been about the same.

5. Would you expect the heavily segregated schools to be high-poverty or

low-poverty schools? high-poverty

6. Do you believe that desegregation of America's schools will ever be

possible? Explain your answer. Answers will vary.

FLOW CHARTS

Often textbook authors use **flow charts** to visually explain the steps in a complex process. Authors will usually highlight each step in a box with arrows between the boxes. A biology textbook might have a flow chart showing the steps in the photosynthesis process. A criminal justice or American government textbook might use a flow chart to explain how criminal cases proceed through the state and federal court systems. A health textbook might include a flow chart to demonstrate how food is digested and processed.

Exercise 8: Flow Charts

The Psychology
of Personality,
by Dennis Coon,
Chapter 10

Figure 9.10 is a flow chart that explains how a cycle of low self-esteem establishes itself. Not only look at the flow chart but read the caption below it.

Directions: After looking at the chart and reading the caption below it, answer the questions that follow.

1. What are the two conditions that follow low performance expectation?

   reduced effort and high anxiety

2. What does actual failure produce? low self-esteem

FIGURE 9.10 **The cycle of low self-esteem begins with an individual's already having low self-esteem. As a consequence, the person will have low performance expectations and expect to fail a test, thereby producing anxiety and reduced effort. As a result, the person will actually fail, and failure in turn reinforces low self-esteem.** Flow chart from Robert S. Feldman, *Understanding Psychology*, 8th ed., New York: McGraw-Hill, 2005, p. 468.

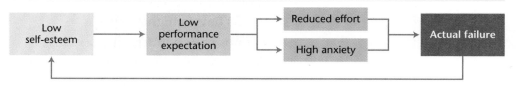

3. Does this chart explain how to get out of the low self-esteem cycle?

   no

4. Without giving a specific name, do you know anyone personally who has

   fallen into this vicious cycle?

   If so, explain. Answers will vary.

PHOTOS

Photos are used in various types of print media such as newspapers, magazines, and of course, textbooks. Photos can be used to highlight points being made in the text or simply used to make the written material more visually appealing. For example, photos in the sports section of a newspaper may highlight a key play in a game or simply be a great action photo taken during a game.

Exercise 9: Photos

Bats' New Image, by Anastasia Toufexis, Warm-up 4

Figure 9.11 is an example of a photo used in a biology textbook to illustrate how a bat plays a role in the pollination process.

Directions: After looking at the photo and reading its caption, answer the questions that follow.

1. Do you have a positive or negative attitude toward bats?

   Answers will vary.

2. Does this photo help to give a more positive image to the bat?

   Probably more positive. It looks like a hummingbird feeding.

FIGURE 9.11 **Bat-pollinated flowers are large, sturdy flowers that can take rough treatment. Here the head of the bat is positioned so that its bristly tongue can lap up nectar.** In Sylvia S. Mader, *Biology*, 8th ed., New York: McGraw-Hill, 2004, p. 499); Original source: © Merlin D. Tuttle, Bat Conservation International.

3. Does the caption tell the reader what specific type of flower the bat is pollinating? No, it doesn't.

4. How strong must the flower be so that the bat can stick its tongue into it?

   sturdy

5. What was the original source of this photo? Melvin D. Tuttle, Bat Conservation International

CARTOONS

Cartoons are drawings that show a funny situation and often have captions that emphasize the point they are making. Cartoons are wonderful visual aids in textbooks. Readers are attracted to them because they know they will make them laugh. But cartoons, like the ones in this textbook, can also be used to illustrate particular points being discussed in the text.

There are several types of cartoons. The most common type is the strip cartoon. Examples of strip cartoons would be "Frank and Ernest," "Blondie," "Dennis the Menace," and "Zits." A second type of cartoon is the political cartoon. These are usually found on the editorial page of a newspaper and often deal with recent national or local political issues. A third type of cartoon is found in specific magazines such as *Time, Sports Illustrated,* or *Newsweek* and is used to illustrate a particular story.

Exercise 10: Cartoons

Uses and Misuses of Credit, by Jack Kapoor, Chapter 9

The cartoon in Figure 9.12 was originally created for *The New Yorker* magazine. It is used here to illustrate the reading at the end of this chapter on the use and misuse of credit.

Directions: Look at the cartoon and then answer the questions that follow.

1. What ceremony is being celebrated in the cartoon? graduation from

   college

2. The cartoonist is making the point that college graduates not only get

   degrees but also accumulate large amounts of debt   .

Now read the following article related to the use and misuse of credit.

"Graduates, faculty, parents, creditors . . ."

FIGURE 9.12   Arnie Levin cartoon copyright © The New Yorker Collection 1993 Arnie Levin from cartoonbank.com. All Rights Reserved.

READING

"By her senior year, Wendy had amassed $9,000 in credit card debt and couldn't make the monthly payments of nearly $200."

GETTING FOCUSED

In this chapter you have learned how to read a variety of types of visual aids. This reading discusses the advantages and disadvantages of using credit cards. In addition to the regular questions following the article, you will be asked to answer some questions related to two graphs which pertain to the reading.

BIO-SKETCH

Jack Kapoor, the lead author of this reading, has taught business and economics at the College of DuPage, Glen Ellyn, Illinois, since 1969. In addition to the book from which this reading is taken, he is a co-author of several textbooks, including *Business: A Practical Approach; Business; Business and Personal Finance;* and *Focus on Personal Finance.*

TACKLING VOCABULARY

credit   receiving cash, goods, or services and paying for them in the future

vulnerable   susceptible to temptation

USES AND MISUSES OF CREDIT

Jack Kapoor

Using credit to purchase goods and services may allow consumers to be more efficient or more productive or to lead more satisfying lives. There are many valid reasons for using credit. A medical emergency may leave a person strapped for funds. A homemaker returning to the workforce may need a car. It may be possible to buy an item now for less money than it will cost later. Borrowing for a college education is another valid reason. But it probably is not reasonable to borrow for everyday living expenses or finance a Corvette on credit when a Ford Focus is all your budget allows.

2   "Shopaholics" and young adults are most vulnerable to misusing credit. College students are a prime target for credit card issuers, and issuers make it very easy for students to get credit cards. Wendy Leright, a 25-year-old teacher in Detroit, knows this all too well. As a college freshman, she applied for and got seven credit cards, all bearing at least an 18.9 percent interest rate and a $20 annual fee. Although unemployed, she used the cards freely, buying expensive clothes for herself, extravagant Christmas presents for friends and family, and even a one-week vacation in the Bahamas. "It got to a point where I didn't even look at the price tag," she said. By her senior year, Wendy had amassed

$9,000 in credit card debt and couldn't make the monthly payments of nearly $200. She eventually turned to her parents to bail her out. "Until my mother sat me down and showed me how much interest I had to pay, I hadn't even given it a thought. I was shocked," Wendy said. "I would have had to pay it off for years."

3   Using credit cards increases the amount of money a person can spend to purchase goods and services now. But the trade-off is that it decreases the amount of money that will be available to spend in the future. However, many people expect their incomes to increase and therefore expect to be able to make payments on past credit purchases and still make new purchases.

4   Here are some questions you should consider before you decide how and when to make a major purchase, for example, a car:

- Do I have the cash I need for the down payment?

- Do I want to use my savings for this purchase?

- Does the purchase fit my budget?

- Could I use the credit I need for this purchase in some better way?

- Could I postpone the purchase?

- What are the opportunity costs of postponing the purchase (alternative transportation costs, a possible increase in the price of the car)?

- What are the dollar costs and the psychological costs of using credit (interest, other finance charges, being in debt and responsible for making a monthly payment)?

5   If you decide to use credit, make sure the benefits of making your purchase now (increased efficiency or productivity, a more satisfying life, etc.) outweigh the costs (financial and psychological) of using credit. Thus, credit when effectively used, can help you have more and enjoy more. When misused, credit can result in default, bankruptcy, and loss of creditworthiness.

Advantages of Credit

6 Consumer credit enables people to enjoy goods and services now—a car, a home, an education, help in emergencies—and pay for them through payment plans based on future income.

7   Credit cards permit the purchase of goods even when funds are low. Customers with previously approved credit may receive other extras, such as advance notice of sales and the right to order by phone or to buy on approval. In addition, many shoppers believe it is easier to return merchandise they have purchased on account. Credit cards also provide shopping convenience and the efficiency of paying for several purchases with one monthly payment.

8   Credit is more than a substitute for cash. Many of the services it provides are taken for granted. Every time you turn on the water tap, flick the light switch, or telephone a friend, you are using credit.

9   It is safer to use credit, since charge accounts and credit cards let you shop and travel without carrying a large amount of cash. You need a credit card to

make a hotel reservation, rent a car, and shop by phone. You may also use credit cards for identification when cashing checks, and the use of credit provides you with a record of expenses.

10 Finally, credit indicates stability. The fact that lenders consider you a good risk usually means you are a responsible individual. However, if you do not repay your debts in a timely manner, you will find that credit has many disadvantages.

Disadvantages of Credit

11 Perhaps the greatest disadvantage of using credit is the temptation to overspend. It seems easy to buy today and pay tomorrow. But continual overspending can lead to serious trouble. Failure to repay a loan may result in loss of income, valuable property, and your good reputation. It can even lead to court action and bankruptcy. Misuse of credit can create serious long-term financial problems, damage to family relationships, and a slowing of progress toward financial goals. Therefore, you should approach credit with caution and avoid using it more extensively than your budget permits.

12 Remember, credit costs money. It is a service for which you must pay. Paying for purchases over a period of time is more costly than paying for them with cash. Purchasing with credit rather than cash involves one very obvious trade-off: the fact that it will cost more due to monthly finance charges and the compounding effect of interest on interest.

"A man is rich in proportion to the things he can afford to let alone."

—Henry David Thoreau

Summary: Advantages and Disadvantages of Credit

13 The use of credit provides immediate access to goods and services, flexibility in money management, safety and convenience, a cushion in emergencies, a means of increasing resources, and a good credit rating if you pay your debts back in a timely manner. But remember, the use of credit is a two-sided coin. An intelligent decision as to its use demands careful evaluation of your current debt, your future income, the added cost, and the consequences of overspending.

Excerpts from *Personal Finance*, 8th ed., Jack Kapoor et al. Copyright © 2007 The McGraw-Hill Companies, Inc. Reprinted by permission of The McGraw-Hill Companies, Inc.

✔ COMPREHENSION CHECKUP

Multiple Choice

Directions: Write the letter for the correct answer to each question on the lines provided.

  b 1. The author's purpose in writing this selection is
    a. to persuade the reader not to use credit cards.
    b. to present information on the advantages and disadvantages of credit cards.
    c. to encourage the use of credit cards in most circumstances.
    d. to give several examples of when credit cards have been misused.

___a___ 2. The main method of paragraph organization in many paragraphs such as paragraphs 1, 3, 10, and 13 is
   a. comparison and contrast.
   b. chronological order.
   c. steps in a process.
   d. classification.

___d___ 3. The author would agree with which of the following statements?
   a. We should use our credit cards whenever possible.
   b. We should have several credit cards so our total credit limit can be higher.
   c. We should never use credit cards.
   d. We should use credit cards when appropriate such as for traveling, shopping by phone, and making hotel reservations.

___d___ 4. The word *interest* in paragraph 2 means
   a. state of curiosity or concern about something.
   b. a right claim or legal share.
   c. involvement with or participation in something.
   d. a charge for a loan.

___a___ 5. All of the following are credit situations *except*
   a. paying rent at the beginning of the month.
   b. paying your electric bill.
   c. charging a restaurant meal on a credit card.
   d. buying a car over time.

True or False

Directions: Indicate whether the statement is true or false by writing **T** or **F** in the space provided.

___T___ 1. Proper use of credit cards can indicate financial stability.

___F___ 2. College students find it difficult to obtain credit cards because of their lack of credit.

___T___ 3. The author would probably agree that using a credit card for needed purchases over the Internet would be appropriate.

___T___ 4. It's usually best to pay off your credit card bills when they come to you each month.

___F___ 5. This reading discusses the differences between debit cards and credit cards.

Vocabulary in Context

Directions: In the paragraphs indicated in parentheses, find the words that correctly match the definitions given, and write them in the spaces provided.

1. well grounded; just (paragraph 1)   valid

2. lavish or imprudent expenditure (paragraph 2)   extravagant

3. something that saves work (paragraph 7)   convenience

4. reliability; dependability (paragraph 10)   stability

5. a general estimation in which a person is held (paragraph 11)   reputation

In Your Own Words

1. One of the authors of this textbook once stated to his father, an accountant, that if he used all his credit cards to their maximum limits he would not be able to afford to pay them off. His father replied by saying that credit card companies don't want people to pay off their credit cards. Do you think that credit card companies should advise people about the use and misuse of credit cards?

2. A new type of credit agency that has been popping up on almost every street corner is the payday loan office. These companies typically give short-term loans at very high interest rates. Do you think these companies serve a purpose? Should their interest rates be regulated?

Written Assignment

Write a paragraph about a credit or loan situation that hurt you financially.

Internet Activity

Go to www.creditcards.com. Click on one of the types of credit cards that is listed in the left-hand side of the screen. Write a few sentences about what you found out about these credit cards.

Visual Aids

Visual Aid 1

Directions: Look at the table on page 422 and answer the questions below.

1. What is the title of the table? Consumer Credit Spending 2000, 2003, and 2008 (Projected)

CONSUMER CREDIT SPENDING 2000, 2003, AND 2008 (PROJECTED) (numbers in billions of dollars)

U.S. Census Bureau, *Statistical Abstract of the United States 2006*, Table 1175, p. 766.
Source: HSN Consultants Inc., Carpinteria, CA, *The Nilson Report*, twice monthly.

Type of credit	2000	2003	2008 (proj.)
Total[1]	1,458	1,735	2,604
Bank[2]	938	1,164	1,744
Phone	21	19	16
Store	120	133	146
Oil Company	50	48	64
Other[3]	329	371	634

[1]Cardholders may hold more than one card.

[2]Visa and MasterCard credit cards.

[3]Miscellaneous cards such as Discover, American Express, Diners Club, automobile rental, and Universal Air Travel Plan (UATP).

2. What agency published the information in the table? _____

   U.S. Census Bureau _____

3. What was the original source of this information? HSN Consultants _____

4. The amounts are in billions _____ of dollars.

5. Which type of credit card is projected to be used less by 2008?

   phone _____ What do you think would be the reason for the decrease

   in use of these cards? increased use of cell phones _____

6. Give two examples of store credit cards. Target, Macy's _____

Internet Activity

One reason for the 70 percent projected increase from 2003 to 2008 in "Other" types of cards may be the projected increase in the Universal Air Travel Plan. In any search engine type in "Universal Air Travel Plan" and find out what they are. Find out who would use them and why they would be used.

Directions: Look at the bar graph on page 423 and then answer the questions below.

Credit Card Holders and Credit Cards Held From U.S. Census Bureau, *Statistical Abstract of the United States 2004–2005,* Table 1185, p. 747. Found in Jack Kapoor, *Personal Finance,* p. 175. * Estimated.

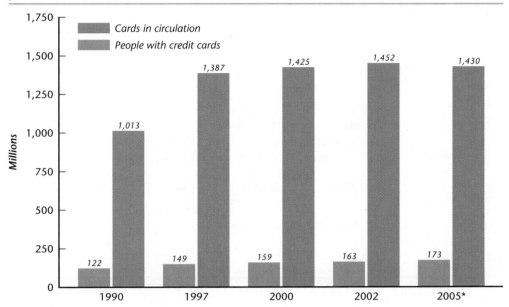

1. Who publishes the annual *Statistical Abstract of the United States*?

   U.S. Census Bureau

2. The left-hand axis of the graph indicates that the numbers are in

   millions

3. How many people had credit cards in 1990? 122 million

   In 2005? 173 million

4. How many cards were in circulation in 1990? 1,013 million

   In 2005? 1,430 million

5. Did the number of credit cards increase or decrease per person between 1990 and 2005? decreased   (Divide the total number of credit cards for those two years by the number of people with credit cards.)

6. Does this graph indicate how much money was actually being loaned per

   person or per card? no

10 Textbook Selections

In this chapter of *Racing,* you will have an opportunity to practice the study skills you have already been introduced to and learn new techniques such as annotating, outlining, and mapping.

Included in this chapter are two partial chapters from college textbooks. First there is a selection on memory from a psychology textbook by Robert Feldman. Next is a selection on personality from an introductory psychology textbook by Dennis Coon. Both authors are well-known and respected in their fields.

ANNOTATING, OUTLINING, MAPPING, AND SUMMARIZING

Annotating, outlining, mapping, and summarizing are four useful techniques you can use when studying for classes. Each technique requires you to digest information and transform it into a more abbreviated format you can use to effectively study and learn the material. Before using any of these techniques, you should skim and read the material first and begin implementing the SQ3R method discussed in Warm-Up 4.

Underlining and Highlighting

Underlining with a pen or pencil or **highlighting** with a magic marker is the first step in transforming text into something more meaningful. You can use underlining and highlighting to identify the main points made by an author. You should underline or highlight only the most important points or key words. Underlining or highlighting a whole paragraph requires no thought on your part and makes it difficult to find the most important information later when you are studying. Look at the underlining that has been done to the reading about the three types of memory on page 425.

Annotating

Annotating is the second step in the transformation process. **Annotating** requires you to think about the text and write notes in the margin as you read. These annotations provide an explanation of the material by identifying the main points made by the author and indicate where important examples are given, steps in a process are listed, or important examples are provided. Annotations can also consist of your comments on the material and any questions you might have about it. Now look at the reading on pages 425–426 and note the annotations in the margin of the text.

The following is a list of techniques you can use for making annotations. They are suggestions: You can adapt them and add your own abbreviations and symbols to make your own system of annotation.

- Underline important terms and concepts.

- Write MI next to main ideas.

- Circle definitions and meanings or write Def. (definition) in the margin.

- Write key words and definitions in the margin or write KV (key vocabulary) beside important words.

- Use EX to indicate an example.

- Signal where important information can be found with (IMP) or a symbol like an asterisk (*) in the margin.

- Signal summaries with SUM or write your own short summaries in the margin.

- Use a question mark (?) in the margin to indicate a point that needs further explanation.

- Indicate where the answers to particular questions in the text can be found by writing ANS (answer).

Exercise 1: Underlining, Highlighting, and Annotating

Directions: The following excerpt titled "Three Types of Memory" has been underlined and annotated for you. Use this as a model to annotate paragraphs 1–14 of the reading titled "Memorization" on page 487.

THREE TYPES OF MEMORY

MI There are three different memory storage systems or stages through which information must travel if it is to be remembered: sensory, short-term, and long-term. The first stage, **sensory memory**, refers to the initial, momentary

DEF storage of information, lasting only an instant. A momentary flash of lightning, the sound of a twig snapping, and the sting of a pinprick all represent stimulation of exceedingly brief duration. Such stimuli are initially—and briefly—stored in sensory memory, the first repository of the information the world presents to us. Sensory memory in general is able to store information for only a very short time. If information does not pass to short-term memory it is lost for good. Sensory memory employs a "file or forget it" approach to its job. It operates as a kind of snapshot that stores information for a brief moment in time. But it is as if each snapshot, immediately after being taken, is destroyed and replaced with a new one. Unless the information in the snapshot is transferred to some other type of memory, it is lost.

Stage I Sensory— initial memory stage

Useless to us unless DEF transferred

EX Reason for 7-digit phone numbers

<u>Stage 2</u> *Short-term memory*

<u>Stage 3</u> *Long-term memory*

Elaborative rehearsal

DEF Link to other memory or transform it

EX
EX

2. Because the information that is stored briefly in <u>sensory memory</u> consists of representations of raw <u>sensory stimuli, it is not meaningful to us</u>. For us to make sense of it, the <u>information must be transferred to the next stage of memory: short term memory</u>. **Short-term memory** is the memory store in which information first has meaning, although the maximum length of retention is relatively short. The specific amount of information that can be held in short-term memory has been identified as <u>seven items or "chunks" of information</u>. For instance, we can hold a seven-digit phone number (like 236-4610) in our short-term memory. Just how brief is short-term memory? Anyone who has looked up a telephone number and forgotten the number at the sound of the dial tone knows that information in short-term memory does not remain there for long. Most psychologists believe that information in short-term memory is lost after fifteen to twenty-five seconds—unless it is transferred to long-term memory.

3. The third type of memory is **long term memory.** Information is stored in long term memory on a relatively permanent basis although it may be difficult to retrieve. The transfer of material <u>from short-term to long-term memory</u> proceeds largely on the basis of rehearsal, the repetition of information that has entered short-term memory. <u>Rehearsal</u> accomplishes two things. First, as long as the information is repeated, it is maintained in short-term memory. More important, however, rehearsal allows us to transfer the information into long-term memory. Whether the transfer is made from short-term to long-term memory seems to depend largely on the <u>kind of rehearsal that is carried out</u>. If the information is simply repeated over and over again—as we might do with a telephone number while we rush from the phone book to the phone—it is kept current in short-term memory, but it will not necessarily be placed in long-term memory. Instead, as soon as we stop punching in the phone numbers, the number is likely to be replaced by other information and will be completely forgotten.

4. In contrast, if the information in short-term memory is rehearsed, using a process called **elaborative rehearsal,** <u>it is much more likely to be transferred into long-term memory</u>. Elaborative rehearsal occurs when the <u>information is considered and organized in some fashion</u>. The organization might include <u>expanding the information</u> to fit into a <u>logical framework</u>, <u>linking it to another memory</u>, turning it into an image, or <u>transforming it in some other way</u>. For example, a list of vegetables to be purchased at a store could be woven together in memory as items being used to prepare an elaborate salad, could be <u>linked to the items bought on an earlier shopping trip</u>, or could be thought of <u>in terms of the image of a farm with rows of each item</u>.

5. <u>Material</u> that makes its way from short-term memory to <u>long-term memory</u> enters a storehouse of <u>almost unlimited capacity</u>. Like a new file we save on a hard drive, the information in long-term memory is filed and coded so that we can retrieve it when we need it.

Feldman, Robert S., *Essentials of Understanding Psychology*, 6th ed., New York: McGraw-Hill, 2005, pp. 218–222

Outlining

Outlining is a formal method of organizing material. If you create a complete outline of what you have read, you can actually study from it and not have to refer back to the textbook. An outline should reflect an orderly arrangement of ideas going from the most general to the most specific. Often you can use the headings in a textbook selection as the main topics in an outline and the subheadings as main ideas. Each division in an outline is more specific than the division that precedes it.

Main headings (topics) are represented by Roman numerals (I, II, III, IV, V, etc.). The next level of headings (main ideas) are represented by capital letters (A, B, C, etc.), the next level (major supporting details) by Arabic numbers (1, 2, 3, 4, etc.), and the next level (minor supporting details) by lowercase letters (a, b, c, d, etc.).

In an outline, you cannot have just one subtopic; there must always be two or more. For example, if there is a subtopic A, there must be a subtopic B. If there is a subtopic 1, there must be a subtopic 2. Remember when you are putting in subtopics, you are actually dividing the topic into two parts like a pie. If you cut a pie, you will have at least two pieces.

Here is a sample outline for the "Three Types of Memory" passage.

Main Idea: There are three different memory storage systems.

    I. Sensory memory
      A. Momentary
        1. Flash of lightning
        2. Sound of twig snapping
        3. Sting of pinprick
      B. First repository
      C. File or forget it
   II. Short-term memory
      A. Meaningful information
        1. Short—lost after 15–25 seconds unless transferred
        2. Seven items—like a 7-digit phone number
        3. Held if just repeated over and over
      B. Can proceed to long-term
  III. Long-term memory
      A. Requires elaborative rehearsal
        1. Information considered
        2. Information organized
          a. expanding information
          b. linking to another memory
          c. turning it into an image
      B. Unlimited capacity
      C. Can be retrieved when needed

Exercise 2: Outlining

Directions: Make an outline of paragraphs 1–14 of "Memorization" on page 430. (These are the same paragraphs you just underlined—or highlighted—and annotated.)

Mapping

Mapping is like outlining but less formal and more visual. Although there are no formal rules for mapping, you will see that you have topics, main ideas, details, and so on, just as you have in an outline. A sample map of the "Three Types of Memory" passage appears on page 429. Notice that with this map, you can actually see how each step in the memory process flows into the next, something it is more difficult to see in an outline.

Exercise 3: Mapping

Directions: Using paragraphs 1–14 of "Memorization," make a map of the main points in the reading.

Now that you have made both an outline and a map of the same reading material, you can begin to see the advantages and disadvantages of both. The advantage of outlining is its formal structure, but its disadvantage is that you cannot always place points in chronological order. Maps allow you to use chronological order, for example, to see the steps in a process or the flow of events, but may be more difficult to follow. In deciding which format to use, first consider the material itself—which format would be better for organizing the material? Second, consider yourself—which method is easier for you to use to create a tool to study from?

Summarizing

Summarizing involves condensing what you read to only the most important information and writing it down using your own words. Generally speaking, a summary should be about one-third the length of the original information. It should include only what is written about in an article and should not include any of your own opinions about the ideas expressed by the author. You need to learn how to write summaries because you will be required to write summaries of journal articles in other classes. Summaries can also be used to study from, just as you would study from an outline or map. Here are some guidelines for writing a summary:

- Identify the main ideas and major supporting details in the article and underline them, list them on a piece of paper, or make an outline of them as described above. This will serve as a guide as you write your summary.

- Start with a sentence that states the topic of the article and the main point the author is making about it.

- Be sure to include the name of the author and the title of the selection.

- List each of the main ideas and details in the order they appear in the article.

- If the author expresses an opinion on the topic of the article, you should include it in your summary.

- Remember to use your own words, not the author's.

- Remember not to include your opinions about the material you are summarizing.

Here is a sample summary of the "Three Types of Memory."

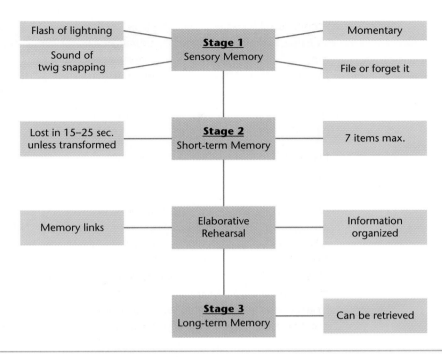

Map of "Three Types of Memory"

There are three types of memory—sensory, short-term, and long-term memory. Sensory memory is very brief and is lost for good if not transferred into short-term memory. Examples of sensory memory might be a flash of lightning, a twig snapping, or the sting of a pinprick. Sensory memory is our first repository of information.

Short-term memory is the second stage in the memory process. In short-term memory we begin to add meaning to the information, but the length of retention is quite short. An example of short-term memory would be a telephone number. You may even forget the phone number by the time you begin to dial it. Our maximum amount of information in this stage is seven items or "chunks."

Long-term memory is the third and permanent stage of holding memory. In order for memory to transfer from short-term memory to long-term memory, it must go through an elaborative rehearsal process. This process takes the information through a transformation or linking process. The information is expanded into a logical framework, linked to another memory, or in some way is transformed. Long-term memory has an almost unlimited capacity. It is filed and coded so that we can retrieve information later.

Exercise 4: Summarizing

Directions: Write your own summary of paragraphs 1–14 of "Memorization" on page 430. After underlining, annotating, outlining, and mapping these paragraphs, summarizing the reading should be fairly easy.

READING

"Memory researchers have found that people actually remember things better in the place where they first studied and learned them."

GETTING FOCUSED

What is the name of the third president of the United States? What states joined the Union in 1959? What is the name of your fifth-grade teacher? Most of us worry about memory lapses and are constantly trying to find ways to remember information more quickly and easily. This selection is chock full of tips and strategies to improve memory.

BIO-SKETCH

Robert Feldman, a professor of psychology at the University of Massachusetts, is well known as an author of textbooks on psychology and study skills.

TACKLING VOCABULARY

visualizing   forming a picture of something in the mind

abstract   theoretical; separate from concrete reality

litmus   a substance that turns red in an acid and blue in a base

tactile   pertaining to the sense of touch

MEMORIZATION

Robert S. Feldman

Don't think of memorization as pumping gasoline (new information) into an almost-empty gas tank (your brain). You're not filling something that is empty. On the contrary, you are filling a container that already has a lot of things in it, that is infinitely expandable, and that never empties out.

2   If you approach each memorization task as something entirely new and unrelated to your previous knowledge, you'll have enormous difficulty recalling it. On the other hand, if you connect it to what you already know, you'll be able to recall it far better. The way to get your brain to do this organizational work for you is by thinking about the associations the new material has with the old.

3   Say, for example, you need to remember information about the consequences of global warming, such as the fact that the level of the oceans is predicted to rise. You might think about the rising level of the ocean as it relates to your personal memories of visits to the beach. You might think what a visit to the beach would be like with dramatically higher water levels, visualizing a shrunken shoreline with no room for sunbathing. Then whenever you think about global warming in the future, your mind is likely to associate this fairly abstract concept with its concrete consequences for beaches. The association you made makes the information personal, long-lasting, and useful.

4   As critical thinking expert Diane Halpern points out, having an organized memory is like having a neat bedroom: it's value is that you know you'll be able to find something when you need it. To prove the point, try this exercise she devised.

5   Read the following 15 words at the rate of approximately one per second:

girl	flute	green
heart	blue	lung
robin	organ	eagle
purple	man	child
finger	hawk	piano

6   Now, cover the list, and write down as many of the words as you can on a separate sheet of paper. How many words are there on your list? _____

7   After you've done this, read the following list:

green	child	lung
blue	piano	finger
purple	flute	eagle
man	organ	hawk
girl	heart	robin

8   Now cover this second list and write down as many of the words as you can on the other side of the separate sheet of paper.

9   How many words did you remember this time? Did you notice that the words on both lists are identical? Did you remember more the second time? (Most people do.) Why do you think most people remember more when the words are organized as they are in the second list?

10   Memories can also be organized by place. *Where* you learn something makes a difference in how well you can recall it. Memory researchers have found that people actually remember things better in the place where they first studied and learned them. Consequently, one of the best ways to jog your memory is to try to re-create the situation in which you first learned what you're trying to remember. If you memorized the colors that litmus paper turns when it is placed in acids and bases while you were lying in bed, it might be helpful during a test to recall the correct colors by imagining yourself lying on your bed thinking about the colors.

11   Another effective place-related strategy is to introduce new data into your mind in the place that you know you're going to need to recall it at some future moment.

12   For instance, suppose you know that you're going to be tested on certain material in the room in which your class is held. Try to do at least some of your studying in that room.

13   One of the good things about the work of memorization is that you have your choice of literally dozens of techniques. Depending on the kind of material you need to recall and how much you already know about the subject, you can turn to any number of methods.

14   As we sort through the various options, keep in mind that no one strategy works by itself. (And some strategies don't work at all: for example, forget about drugs like ginko biloba—there's no scientific evidence that they are effective.) Instead, try the following proven strategies and find those that work best for you.

Rehearsal

15 Think it again: rehearsal. Say it aloud: rehearsal. Think of it in terms of the three syllables that make up the word: re—hear—sal. OK, one more time—say the word "rehearsal."

16 If you're scratching your head over the last paragraph, it's to illustrate the point of rehearsal: to transfer material that you encounter into memory. If you don't rehearse information in some way, it will end up like most of the information to which we're exposed: on the garbage heap of lost memory.

17 To test if you've succeeded in transferring the word "rehearsal" into your memory, put down this book and go off for a few minutes. Do something entirely unrelated to reading this book. Have a snack, catch up on the latest sports scores on ESPN, or read the front page of the newspaper.

18 Are you back? If the word "rehearsal" popped into your head when you picked up this book again, you've passed your first memory test. You can be assured that the word "rehearsal" has been transferred into your memory.

19 Rehearsal is the key strategy in remembering information. If you don't rehearse material, it will never make it into memory. Repeating the information, summarizing it, associating it with other memories, and above all thinking about it when you first come across it will ensure that rehearsal will be effective in pushing the material into memory.

Mnemonics

20 This odd word (pronounced in an equally odd fashion, with the "m" silent— "neh MON ix") describes formal techniques used to make material more readily remembered. Mnemonics are the tricks-of-the-trade that professional memory experts use, and you too can use them to nail down the sort of information you will often need to recall for tests.

21 Among the most common mnemonics are the following:

- **Acronyms**
  FACE
  Roy G. Biv

22 You're already well acquainted with acronyms, words or phrases formed by the first letters of a series of terms. For instance, FACE spells out the names of the notes that appear in the spaces on the treble clef music staff ("F," "A," "C," and "E," starting at the bottom of the staff.) Roy G. Biv is a favorite of physics students who must remember the colors of the spectrum (red, orange, yellow, green, blue, indigo, and violet).

23 The benefit of acronyms is that they help us to recall a complete list of steps or items. The drawback, though, is that the acronym itself has to be remembered, and sometimes we may not recall it when we need it. For instance, Roy G. Biv is not exactly the sort of name that readily comes to mind. And if we're unable to remember an acronym, it won't be of much use to us. Even if we do remember Roy G. Biv, we might get stuck trying to recall what a particular letter stands for. (For example, we'd probably prefer not to spend a lot of time during a test trying to remember if the "B" stands for brown, or beige, or blue.)

- **Acrostics**

24 After learning to use the acronym "FACE" to remember the notes on the spaces of the music staff, many beginning musicians learn that the names on

the lines of the staff form the acrostic, "Every Good Boy Deserves Fudge." Acrostics are sentences in which the first letters spell out something that needs to be recalled. The benefits—as well as the drawbacks—of acrostics are similar to those of acronyms. As an example of the usefulness of acronyms try the following exercise:

1. Figure out an acronym to remind you of the names of the five Great Lakes, using the first letters of their names (which are Erie, Huron, Michigan, Ontario, Superior).

2. Devise an acrostic for the nine planets in order of their average distance from the sun. Their names, in order, are Mercury, Venus, Earth, Mars, Jupiter, Saturn, Uranus, Neptune, Pluto.

25 How successful were you in devising effective acronyms and acrostics? Is the act of creating them an important component of helping to remember what they represent, or would having them created by someone else be as helpful in recalling them? For your information, a common acronym for the Great Lakes is HOMES (**H**uron, **O**ntario, **M**ichigan, **E**rie, **S**uperior), and a popular acrostic for the order of the planets is **M**y **V**ery **E**ducated **M**other **J**ust **S**erved **U**s **N**ine **P**izzas.

● Rhymes and Jingles

26 "Thirty days hath September, April, June, and November . . ." If you know the rest of the rhyme, you're familiar with one of the most commonly used mnemonic jingles in the English language. You may have also heard of the English spelling rule, "I before E, except after C." (The spelling rule will serve you well only when you want to make the sound of EE as in "Receive" and "Deceive.")

27 Although mnemonics are helpful, keep in mind that they have a number of significant shortcomings. First, they don't focus on the meaning of the items being remembered. Because information that is learned in terms of its surface characteristics—such as first letters that form a word—is less likely to be retained than information that is learned in terms of its meaning, mnemonic devices are an imperfect route to memorization.

28 There's another problem with mnemonics. Sometimes it takes as much effort to create a mnemonic device as it would to memorize the material in the first place. And because the mnemonic itself has no meaning, it can be forgotten.

29 Despite these drawbacks, mnemonics can be useful. They are particularly helpful when the material being memorized includes a list of items or a series of steps.

The Method of Loci and the Peg Method: Special Help for Recalling Sequences and Lists

30 The ancient Greeks had a way with words. Their orators could deliver speeches that went on for hours, without notes. How did they remember what they wanted to say?

31 They used a procedure called the method of loci. *Loci* is the Latin word for "places," and it helps describe a procedure in which items in a sequence you wish to remember—such as the sections of a speech or a series of events—are thought of as "located" in a different place in a building.

32 Consider, for example, a speech that has three major sections: an introduction, a main body, and a conclusion. Each of the three sections has various points that you need to recall also.

33 To use the method of loci, you'd first visualize the living room, kitchen, and bedroom of a house with which you were familiar. Next, you'd mentally "place" the introduction of the speech into the living room of the house. You would mentally place each of the *parts* of the introduction on a different piece of furniture, following the way the furniture was laid out in the room (for example, you might proceed clockwise from the door). The easy chair might contain the first point of the introduction, the sofa the next point, and an end table the last point. Then you'd move into the kitchen and do the same thing with the body of the paper, laying out your arguments on different pieces of kitchen furniture or appliances. Finally, you'd end up in the bedroom, where you'd "place" the conclusion.

Involve Multiple Senses

34 ● **When you learn something, use your body.** Don't sit passively at your desk. Instead, move around. Stand up; sit down. Touch the page. Trace figures with your fingers. Talk to yourself. Think out loud. It may seem strange, but doing this increases the number of ways in which the information is stored. By involving every part of your body, you've increased the number of potential ways to trigger a relevant memory later, when you need to recall it.

35 ● **Draw and diagram the material.** In a concept map, each key idea is placed in a different part of the map, and related ideas are placed near it—above, below, or beside it. A "finished" concept map looks something like a map of the solar system, with the largest and most central idea in the center (the "sun" position), and related ideas surrounding it at various distances. It has also been compared to a large tree, with numerous branches and sub-branches radiating out from a central trunk. When we create a concept map, one of the things we're doing is expanding the modalities in which information can be stored in our minds.

36 Other types of drawing can be useful in aiding later recall. Creating drawings, sketches, and even cartoons can help us remember better. Your creations don't have to be great art, or detailed, involved illustrations. Even rough sketches are effective, because creating them gets both the visual and tactile senses involved. For practice see Exercise #1: "Harry and Bill."

37 ● **Visualize.** Visualization is a technique by which images are formed to ensure that material is recalled. Visualization serves several purposes: it helps make abstract ideas concrete; it engages multiple senses; it permits us to link different bits of information together; it provides us with a context for storing information.

38 What kind of visualization works best? There's a simple rule: weird is good. The more extreme, outlandish, and eccentric image you create, the more notable it will be and so the easier it will be to remember. And if you can remember the image, you'll probably remember the information that's attached to it.

Exercise #1: Harry and Bill

Practice in Remembering What You Read: Involving Multiple Senses

I. Below are two people's names with a list of 10 descriptive details for each. Give yourself a second or two to look at each detail. Then cover the list with a sheet of paper and see how many details you can recall.

First Person: Harry

1. bald
2. red-faced
3. thin
4. laughing
5. short-sleeved shirt
6. shorts
7. small eyes
8. large ears
9. sandals
10. heart tattoo

Second Person: Bill

1. glasses
2. short hair
3. necktie
4. sad
5. suit
6. wristwatch
7. cuffs on pants
8. pipe in hand
9. shoes that tie
10. belt

First Person's Name

1. _____
2. _____
3. _____
4. _____
5. _____
6. _____
7. _____
8. _____
9. _____
10. _____

Second Person's Name

1. _____
2. _____
3. _____
4. _____
5. _____
6. _____
7. _____
8. _____
9. _____
10. _____

(Most people are able to recall fewer than eight of the details.)

II. Go back to the original lists and work through the following activities.

1. Think of two people you have known or whose pictures you have seen who remind you of Harry and Bill. Associate Harry's and Bill's special features with their features.

2. Mentally visualize Harry and Bill and then draw pictures of each of them. Label the ten details in each picture.

3. Look away from the pictures you have drawn and see if you can recall the ten features of Harry and Bill without looking. If you can't recall the information, look back at the pictures and try again. Now cover up everything and reproduce the details in the original lists.

First Person's Name	**Second Person's Name**
1. _____	1. _____
2. _____	2. _____
3. _____	3. _____
4. _____	4. _____
5. _____	5. _____
6. _____	6. _____
7. _____	7. _____
8. _____	8. _____
9. _____	9. _____
10. _____	10. _____

How did you do? Try tomorrow and a week from now to visualize Harry and Bill. (Based on information in *Improving Reading* by Nancy V. Wood, New York: Holt, Rinehart and Winston, 1984, pages 214–215)

Excerpts from *Power Learning*, 3rd ed., by Robert S. Feldman. Copyright © 2007 The McGraw-Hill Companies, Inc. Reprinted by permission of The McGraw-Hill Companies, Inc.

COMPREHENSION CHECKUP

Multiple Choice

Directions: Write the letter for the correct answer to each question on the lines provided.

____d____ 1. The author thinks that a brain
   a. is usually empty.
   b. already contains a lot of information.
   c. always has the capacity to learn even more.
   d. both b and c.

____d____ 2. Mnemonics are
   a. acronyms.
   b. acrostics.
   c. rhymes and jingles.
   d. all of the above.

_____a_____ 3. If the author were reading this selection orally, he would probably sound

   a. matter-of-fact.
   b. disapproving.
   c. emotional.
   d. humorous.

_____c_____ 4. A word that means the same as *predicted* in paragraph 3 is

   a. increased.
   b. begged.
   c. forecast.
   d. willed.

_____c_____ 5. The author would agree with all of the following *except*

   a. people remember things better in the place where they first learned them.
   b. it might be wise to study in the room where a future test will be held.
   c. rehearsing information you want to remember is a complete waste of time.
   d. associating new material with other memories is a good way to recall it in the future.

_____b_____ 6. When the author states that "having an organized memory is like having a neat bedroom," he means that

   a. a bedroom is a place to rest and relax.
   b. you'll be able to find something when you need it.
   c. people forget things easily.
   d. none of the above.

_____c_____ 7. The sentence "And because the mnemonic itself has no meaning, it can be forgotten" in paragraph 28 indicates

   a. there are problems with mnemonics.
   b. mnemonics are sometimes more trouble than they're worth.
   c. both a and b.
   d. none of the above.

_____d_____ 8. What would be the best dictionary definition for the word *bases* in paragraph 10?

   a. bottom supports on which things rest
   b. parts of bodies or surfaces
   c. the four corners of a baseball diamond
   d. chemical compounds that react with acids to form salts

_____b_____   9. The author has probably written this selection to
   a. entertain the reader with interesting stories about memorization.
   b. explain how memory works.
   c. persuade the reader to buy books on improving memory.
   d. both b and c.

_____c_____ 10. The word *place* as used in paragraph 33 means
   a. a particular portion of space.
   b. any part of a body or surface.
   c. to put or set in a particular location.
   d. to finish among the first three competitors of a race.

True or False

Directions: Indicate whether the statement is true or false by writing **T** or **F** in the blank provided.

_____T_____   1. According to the author, it is easier to visualize unusual images.

_____T_____   2. Drawing and diagramming material is related to creating a concept map.

_____F_____   3. According to the author, memorization is likened to filling an empty container.

_____F_____   4. People remember things best when they lie on their beds.

_____F_____   5. Research has demonstrated that ginko biloba improves memory.

Vocabulary in Context

Directions: Write a definition for each of the following words consistent with how the word is used in the paragraph indicated in parentheses. You can refer to your dictionary if necessary.

1. consequences (paragraph 3) effects or results

2. researchers (paragraph 10) people who make an extensive investigation into something

3. strategy (paragraph 11) a plan or method; technique

4. material (paragraph 12) key elements; ideas or facts

5. options (paragraph 14) choices

6. staff (paragraph 22) a set of horizontal lines on which music is written

7. spectrum (paragraph 22) a band or series of colors

▼ COMPREHENSION CHECKUP

Multiple Choice

Directions: Write the letter for the correct answer to each question on the lines provided.

_____d_____ 1. Which of the following titles best sums up the material covered?
- a. "Personality Characteristics in Different Cultures"
- b. "Characteristics"
- c. "The Importance of Developing a Good Self-Concept"
- d. "Understanding Personality"

_____c_____ 2. The most important point the author is making in the selection is
- a. the term *personality* is misunderstood.
- b. most people have strong personalities.
- c. each person has a unique pattern of thinking, behaving, and expressing feelings.
- d. there are a number of ways and terms to describe personality.

_____d_____ 3. The author defines the term *personality* as
- a. charm.
- b. charisma.
- c. style.
- d. none of the above.

_____d_____ 4. The author of this selection probably feels that
- a. self-concept is the mental picture you have of your personality.
- b. self-concept is constructed out of daily experiences.
- c. our self-concept can affect our behavior.
- d. all of the above.

_____a_____ 5. The author suggests that
- a. a capable person who is respected is likely to have high self-esteem.
- b. a person with high self-esteem is likely to lack confidence.
- c. a person with low self-esteem is likely to be proud and self-respecting.
- d. self-esteem is unlikely to vary from culture to culture.

_____c_____ 6. Our personality is shaped by
- a. heredity.
- b. environment.
- c. both of the above.
- d. neither of the above.

<u>   c   </u>   7. In paragraph 10, the author suggests that

        a. an extrovert is outgoing in all situations.

        b. *inward* and *outward* mean the same thing.

        c. in some situations an introverted person may be outgoing.

        d. one category can capture personality differences in people.

<u>   b   </u>   8. According to the author, from which of the following countries would a person be most interested in helping the group rather than the individual?

        a. Russia

        b. Japan

        c. Canada

        d. United States

<u>   d   </u>   9. Paragraphs 15–18 suggest that

        a. ideas about self-esteem are the same from culture to culture.

        b. self-esteem in the United States is based on personal success.

        c. in Asian cultures self-esteem is based on the well-being of the group.

        d. both b and c.

<u>   d   </u>   10. Identical twins who are raised apart would still probably have which of the following similar traits?

        a. appearance

        b. voice quality

        c. nervous tics

        d. all of the above

True or False

Directions: Indicate whether the statement is true or false by writing **T** or **F** in the blank provided.

<u>   T   </u>   1. Personality traits are usually quite stable.

<u>   T   </u>   2. It is likely that an extrovert does not behave in an outgoing manner all of the time.

<u>   F   </u>   3. The basis of self-esteem is quite similar in all cultures.

<u>   T   </u>   4. Twins who have been raised apart from each other often have very similar characteristics and traits.

<u>   F   </u>   5. The author uses the terms *personality* and *character* as synonyms.

Vocabulary in Context

Directions: Choose one of the following words to complete the sentences below. Use each word only once.

conscientious	deduce	downplay	optimistic	revise
consistency	distinct	identical	reputations	stable

1. The fans could _____deduce_____ that the pitcher was really mad at himself when he came into the dugout and punched the water cooler.

2. There was a _____distinct_____ smell of fresh paint in the room.

3. Now that you are finishing this class, you should feel _____optimistic_____ that you can be successful in college and earn a college diploma.

4. Although Molly was in the intensive care unit with a gunshot wound to the chest, the doctors categorized her condition as being _____stable_____.

5. The _____reputations_____ of several professional bike riders fell after they were implicated in the use of illegal substances.

6. Don't _____downplay_____ your ability to succeed in life. You can be all that you want to be.

7. After writing a rough draft, Antonio began to _____revise_____ his paper.

8. What made Monica a good student was her _____consistency_____ in doing good work.

9. Bill was _____conscientious_____ in sticking with his new exercise routine.

10. No two people have _____identical_____ fingerprints or DNA.

Knowledge of Word Parts
(Note to Instructor: exercise best used after completion of Warm-Up 2.)

Directions: Match the word part definition in the second column with the underlined word part in the first column.

____i____   1. use<u>ful</u>   a. write

____g____   2. <u>uni</u>que   b. able to

____o____   3. <u>mis</u>used   c. like something

____a____   4. de<u>scribe</u>d   d. quality of

___f___	5. adjust<u>ment</u>	e. before
___e___	6. <u>pre</u>dict	f. state of being
___j___	7. <u>super</u>market	g. one
_m or l_	8. <u>un</u>founded	h. ten
___d___	9. competitive<u>ness</u>	i. full of
___k___	10. worth<u>less</u>	j. above or beyond
_l or m_	11. <u>in</u>accurate	k. without
___n___	12. <u>inter</u>dependence	l. not
___h___	13. <u>dec</u>ades	m. not
___b___	14. agree<u>able</u>	n. between or among
___c___	15. friend<u>ly</u>	o. badly

In Your Own Words

1. If you have been out of high school for a few years and have been to a high school reunion, how similar were the personalities of people at the reunion to what they were like in high school?

2. Do you think animals have personalities?

3. Can you think of someone who has good character? What traits does that person possess?

4. How would you describe a healthy personality?

5. What influence do you think siblings have on each other's personalities?

6. Do you think personality tests have much validity? Can you give some specific examples?

7. Do you think certain personalities are better suited for particular jobs?

8. Do you read your daily horoscope in the newspaper? Do you think the information given accurately describes your personality?

Written Assignment

1. Write a paragraph describing how your personality is similar to and different from the personalities of your brothers and sisters.

2. How has your cultural background played a role in developing your personality? In a paragraph, describe specific aspects of your culture that influenced key traits in your personality.

3. Personality assessments help you understand how you respond to the world around you—including information, thoughts, feelings, people, and events. Assess your personality using the following Personality Spectrum I, which was developed by Dr. Joyce Bishop. Then write a short essay summarizing what you discovered about yourself.

Personality Spectrum I

Step 1 Rank-order the four responses to each question from most like you (4) to least like you (1) so that for each question you use the numbers 1, 2, 3, and 4 one time each. Place the numbers on the lines next to the responses.

1. **I like instructors who**

    _____ a. tell me exactly what is expected of me

    _____ b. make learning active and exciting

    _____ c. maintain a safe and supportive classroom

    _____ d. challenge me to think at higher levels

2. **I learn best when the material is**

    _____ a. well organized

    _____ b. something I can do hands-on

    _____ c. about understanding and improving the human condition

    _____ d. intellectually challenging

3. **A high priority in my life is to**

    _____ a. keep my commitments

    _____ b. experience as much of life as possible

    _____ c. make a difference in the lives of others

    _____ d. understand how things work

4. **Other people think of me as**

    _____ a. dependable and loyal

    _____ b. dynamic and creative

    _____ c. caring and honest

    _____ d. intelligent and inventive

5. **When I experience stress I would most likely**

    _____ a. do something to help me feel more in control of my life

    _____ b. do something physical and daring

    _____ c. talk with a friend

    _____ d. go off by myself and think about my situation

6. **I would probably not be close friends with someone who is**

    _____ a. irresponsible

    _____ b. unwilling to try new things

    _____ c. selfish and unkind to others

    _____ d. an illogical thinker

continued

Personality Spectrum I *continued*

7. **My vacations could be described as**

   _____ a. traditional

   _____ b. adventuresome

   _____ c. pleasing to others

   _____ d. a new learning experience

8. **One word that best describes me is**

   _____ a. sensible

   _____ b. spontaneous

   _____ c. giving

   _____ d. analytical

Step 2 Add up the total points for each letter.

Total for a. _____ Organizer

Total for b. _____ Adventurer

Total for c. _____ Giver

Total for d. _____ Thinker

Carol Carter, Joyce Bishop, Sarah Lyman Kravits, *Keys to Success*, 5th ed., New Jersey, Pearson/Prentice Hall, 2006, p. 72

Internet Activity

1. Recently, some psychologists and medical doctors have begun to speculate that some personalities are more likely to get cancer than others. Do you think there is such a thing as a cancer-prone personality? Research this area, and summarize your conclusions.

2. Do you think there is such a thing as a Type A personality? Research the characteristics of this personality.

Supplementary Readings

"Becoming number one is easier than remaining number one."

—Bill Bradley

CHAPTER IN PART 5

451

CHAPTER 11

Readings on the World of Work and Relationships and Behavior

THE WORLD OF WORK

READING

"Prepare for a crop, and make the crop, and you go to work for the best money wages . . . that you can get."

GETTING FOCUSED

In the following letter, Abraham Lincoln, our sixteenth president, is trying to persuade his stepbrother, John D. Johnston, to change his attitude toward work.

BIO-SKETCH

Lincoln was president of the United States during the bloody Civil War. Though largely self-taught, Lincoln managed to read the classics such as the Bible and Shakespeare, which helped him develop his distinctive speaking and writing style. His two most famous speeches are the Gettysburg Address and the Second Inaugural Address, both noted for their brevity and the beauty and clarity of their language. Lincoln was assassinated by John Wilkes Booth while attending a play at Ford's Theater, plunging the nation into mourning. Today we remember him when we celebrate President's Day in February.

TACKLING VOCABULARY

comply   to do what is asked or demanded; yield; submit to

ABRAHAM LINCOLN DENIES A LOAN

Abraham Lincoln

December 24, 1848

Dear Johnston:

Your request for eighty dollars, I do not think it best to comply with now. At the various times when I have helped you a little, you have said to me, "We can get along very well now," but in a very short time I find you in the same difficulty again. Now this can only happen by some defect in your conduct. What

452

that defect is, I think I know. You are not *lazy*, and still you are an *idler*. I doubt whether since I saw you, you have done a good whole day's work, in any one day. You do not very much dislike to work, and still you do not work much, merely because it does not seem to you that you could get much for it.

2   This habit of uselessly wasting time, is the whole difficulty; it is vastly important to you, and still more so to your children, that you should break this habit. It is more important to them, because they have longer to live, and can keep out of an idle habit before they are in it, easier than they can get out after they are in.

3   You are now in need of some ready money; and what I propose is, that you shall go to work, "tooth and nail," for somebody who will give you money for it.

4   Let father and your boys take charge of your things at home—prepare for a crop, and make the crop, and you go to work for the best money wages, or in discharge of any debt you owe, that you can get. And to secure you a fair reward for your labor, I now promise you that for every dollar you will, between this and the first of May, get for your own labor either in money or your own indebtedness, I will then give you one other dollar.

5   By this, if you hire yourself at ten dollars a month, from me you will get ten more, making twenty dollars a month for your own work. In this, I do not mean you shall go off to St. Louis, or the lead mines, or the gold mines in California, but I mean for you to go at it for the best wages you can get close to home—in Coles County.

6   Now if you will do this, you will soon be out of debt, and what is better, you will have a habit that will keep you from getting in debt again. But if I should now clear you out, next year you will be just as deep in as ever. You say you would almost give your place in Heaven for $70 or $80. Then you value your place in Heaven very cheaply, for I am sure you can with the offer I make you get the seventy or eighty dollars for four or five months' work. You say if I furnish you the money you will deed me the land, and if you don't pay the money back, you will deliver possession—

7   Nonsense! If you can't now live *with* the land, how will you then live without it? You have always been kind to me, and I do not now mean to be unkind to you. On the contrary, if you will but follow my advice, you will find it worth more than eight times eighty dollars to you.

Affectionately

Your brother
A. Lincoln

William J. Bennett, *The Book of Virtues*, Simon & Schuster, 1993, pp. 403–404.

✓ COMPREHENSION CHECKUP

1. What distinction does Lincoln make between being a lazy person and being an idler? An idler is a person who wastes time. A lazy person is someone not willing to work or exert himself or herself.

2. What does this letter reveal to you about Lincoln's attitude toward work?

   Lincoln upholds the principle of working hard — putting in a good day's work.

   Work is an honorable endeavor.

3. What point is Lincoln making when he refers to Johnston's children?

Johnston is a role model to his children. He must display good work habits so

that his children will imitate them.

4. Why does Lincoln want Johnston to stay close to home? He doesn't want

to destroy the family bond. Also, Johnston will be less likely to develop new

vices, and there will be no additional lodging expense.

5. Why does Lincoln tell Johnston that he must value his place in Heaven

very cheaply? Johnston is willing to give up his place in Heaven for the paltry

sum of $70 or $80.

Vocabulary in Context

Directions: Write the letter for the correct answer to each question on the lines provided.

　　b　　1. The expression "tooth and nail" means
　　　　　a. elderly or old.
　　　　　b. with all one's strength or resources.
　　　　　c. a very small pointed stick for getting bits of food free from between the teeth.
　　　　　d. pleasing to the taste.

　　a　　2. As used in the selection, the expression "clear you out" means
　　　　　a. settle your debts.
　　　　　b. prove you innocent.
　　　　　c. move you out.
　　　　　d. harvest your crop.

　　b　　3. A synonym for *fair* as in "a *fair* reward" is
　　　　　a. heavenly.
　　　　　b. just.
　　　　　c. clear.
　　　　　d. excessive.

Directions: Match the vocabulary words in column A with their definitions in column B. Place the correct letter in the space provided.

Column A		Column B
c	1. defect	a. behavior
e	2. vastly	b. supply
a	3. conduct	c. flaw
f	4. propose	d. agree to
b	5. furnish	e. greatly
d	6. comply with	f. suggest

In Your Own Words

1. Do you think that Lincoln's offer made sense? Is it what Johnston expected? Why or why not?

2. Do you think Johnston will accept Lincoln's offer?

3. Give a short description of Johnston's character based on Lincoln's comments about him.

Written Assignment

Choose one of the following statements by Abraham Lincoln and explain its meaning in a paragraph. How does the statement relate to the selection?

"Always bear in mind that your own resolution to succeed is more important than any other."

"I'm a slow walker but I never walk back."

"You cannot build character and courage by taking away a man's initiative and independence."

"You cannot escape the responsibility of tomorrow by evading it today."

"You cannot help men permanently by doing for them what they could and should do for themselves."

Internet Activity

The issue of *Time* magazine for July 4, 2005, features Abraham Lincoln. Some topics covered in the issue include the following: "the secrets of Lincoln's political genius," "his private struggle with depression," "his complicated views on race," and "the strange saga of his wife." The article also mentions the following website: www.time.com/time/covers/20050704, which contains additional information about Lincoln, including the origins of the Lincoln bedroom. Visit the site and write a short paragraph discussing something you didn't previously know about Lincoln.

READING

*"Now we could let it go like this / And take the easy route /
But doin' things the easy way / Ain't what it's all about."*

GETTING FOCUSED

The following poem is taken from Red Steagall's second book, *The Fence That Me and Shorty Built*, published in 2001.

BIO-SKETCH

Red Steagall, an internationally known cowboy poet and recording artist, is the 2006 Poet Laureate of Texas. In April 2003, he was inducted into the Hall of Great Westerners at the National Cowboy and Western Heritage Museum.

TACKLING VOCABULARY

"bob" wire   barbed wire fencing made from strands of wire twisted together with small pieces of sharply pointed wire at short intervals

auger   a tool for boring holes in the ground

maul   a heavy hammer with a wooden head used for driving stakes

buckaroo   a cowboy

bluff   an attempt to deceive someone into believing that one can or is going to do something

THE FENCE THAT ME AND SHORTY BUILT

Red Steagall

We'd picked up all the fencing tools
And staples off the road.
An extra roll of "bob" wire
Was the last thing left to load.

I drew a sleeve across my face
To wipe away the dirt.
The young man who was helping me
Was tuckin' in his shirt.

I turned around to him and said,
"This fence is finally done,
With five new strands of 'bob' wire
Shinin' proudly in the sun.
The wire is runnin' straight and tight
With every post in line.
The kinda job you're proud of,
One that stands the test of time."

The kid was not impressed at all,
He stared off into space.
Reminded me of years ago,
Another time and place.
I called myself a cowboy,
I was full of buck and brawl,
I didn't think my hands would fit
Post augers and a maul.

They sent me out with Shorty
And the ranch fence building crew.
Well, I was quite insulted
And before the day was through,

I let him know that I'm a cowboy.
"This ain't what I do.
I ain't no dadgummed nester,
I hired out to buckaroo."

He said, "We'll talk about that son,
When we get in tonight.
Right now you pick them augers up.
It's either that or fight."
Boy, I was diggin' post holes
Faster than a Georgia mole.
But if a rock got in my way
I simply moved the hole.

So when the cowboys set the posts,
The line went in and out.
Old Shorty's face got fiery red
And I can hear him shout,

"Nobody but a fool would build
A fence that isn't straight.
I got no use for someone who ain't
Pullin' his own weight.

I thought for sure he'd hit me;
Glad he didn't have a gun.
I looked around to find a place
Where I could duck and run.

But Shorty walked up to me
Just as calm as he could be.
Said, "Son I need to talk to you,
Let's find ourselves a tree."

He rolled a Bull Durham cigarette
As we sat on the ground.
He took himself a puff or two
Then slowly looked around.

"Son, I ain't much on schoolin',
Didn't get too far with that.
But there's a lot of learnin'
Hidden underneath this hat.

I got it all the hard way,
Every bump and bruise and fall.
Now some of it was easy,
But then most weren't fun a'tall.

But one thing that I always got
From every job I've done,
Is do the best I can each day
And try to make it fun.

I know that bustin' through them rocks
Ain't what you like to do.
By gettin' mad you've made it tough
On me and all the crew.

Now you hired on to cowboy
And you think you've got the stuff.
You told him you're a good hand
And the boss has called your bluff.

So how's that gonna make you look
When he comes ridin' through,
And he asks me who dug the holes
And I say it was you.
Now we could let it go like this
And take the easy route.
But doin' things the easy way
Ain't what it's all about.

The boss expects a job well done
From every man he's hired.
He'll let you slide by once or twice,
Then one day you'll get fired.

If you're not proud of what you do,
You won't amount to much.

You'll bounce around from job to job
Just slightly out of touch.

Come mornin' let's re-dig those holes
And get that fence in line.
And you and I will save two jobs,
Those bein' yours and mine.

And someday you'll come ridin' through
And know you had a hand

"Success is dependent
on effort."
   —Sophocles

In something that's withstood the years.
Then proud and free from guilt,
You'll smile and say "Boy that's the fence
That me and Shorty built."

"The Fence That Me and Shorty Built" by Red Steagall. Reprinted with permission by the author, Red Steagall.

 COMPREHENSION CHECKUP

1. What is Shorty's attitude toward work? What kind of work brings satisfaction?

He believes in working hard and doing his best.

2. What kind of picture do you get of Shorty? Of the author as a young man? Of the young man who built a fence with the author at the start of the poem? Give a brief description of all three.

The young man thinks digging a fence is beneath him. The author was initially

like the young man but became like Shorty. Shorty takes pride in his work.

Vocabulary in Context

1. What do you think the expression "buck and brawl" means?

like riding a wild horse – orneriness; feistiness

2. What is a "nester"?

a homesteader; someone who stays in one place and cultivates the land

In Your Own Words

In Your Own Words

1. In what ways are Abraham Lincoln's advice and Shorty's advice similar?

2. How do the quotations below support the main idea of the selection?

"Blessed is he who has found his work." —Thomas Carlyle

"A job doesn't get done when it's started with a promise and finished with an alibi." —R. Lewis Bowman

Written Assignment

Directions: Choose one of the following:

1. Write a few paragraphs giving advice to a friend about how to behave at work.

2. Write a few paragraphs describing the kind of work that makes you feel proud and gives you satisfaction.

3. Write a paragraph describing your previous job history. Explain why you liked or disliked each previous job. What did each of your previous jobs teach you about yourself and the sort of career you would like to have?

4. What kind of work do you want to do? Interview some people already active in this field. How do these people feel about their work? Write a paragraph discussing your findings.

Internet Activity

Log on to Red Steagall's website at http://www.redsteagall.com. What do you find interesting about his background? Steagall currently hosts a week-end radio show featuring poems, songs, and stories about the American cowboy. For more information about the program, visit http://www.cowboy corner.com.

READING

"These days scores of young workers are seeking answers to the age-old question: What do I wear to work?"

GETTING FOCUSED

William G. Nickels, author of the popular college textbook *Understanding Business*, says that in the working world a good presentation is everything. How you look and dress is important because you never get a *second* chance to make a good *first* impression. Nickels says that in dress "consistency is essential." You can't wear nice clothing a few days a week and then show up to work looking like you're off to mow the lawn. Today, many businesses don't require employees to wear suits. Instead, they have adopted a policy of "business casual." Unfortunately, this type of clothing means different things to different people. But experts are agreed that what it doesn't mean is "sloppy or sleazy." The selection below gives some guidelines on making a good impression.

BIO-SKETCH

Maria Puente is a staff writer for *USA Today*.

READING *continued*

TACKLING VOCABULARY

pizzazz   style; energy; vitality

take-no-prisoners   Behaving in an excessively aggressive or ardent manner. The phrase has a military origin and means that all enemy soldiers should be killed and none taken prisoner.

pendulum   something that changes its direction or position regularly, often alternating between two extremes

HOW *NOT* TO DRESS FOR WORK

Maria Puente

She was young and ambitious, and she wanted to make an impression on her first day as an administrative staffer at a Los Angeles architecture firm. And she did: She showed up wearing a slinky black cocktail dress.

2   The guys at the firm noticed.

3   "It did seem sort of strange," says Anthony Poon, principal architect and founder of Poon Design Group, one of those hip firms where creativity and pizzazz are admired.

4   But not *too* much pizzazz.

5   "We have a bunch of creative people here, and they're not wearing navy suits and white shirts," Poon says. "But we do have clients we can't alienate. So there's a balance of expressing creative flair and also being professional."

6   Ah, yes, finding that balance. These days, scores of young workers are seeking answers to the age-old question: What do I wear to work? So many workers and workplaces are in such a muddle over this that a growing band of consultants has appeared to help them clean up.

7   "It has gotten so crazy, a major pharmaceutical company called up and said, 'Help! People are wearing *spandex* to work!'" says Gail Madison, a Philadelphia-area etiquette and protocol consultant who regularly advises students at prestigious colleges that it won't kill them to take out their nose rings before a job interview.

8   "They say, 'I'm not going to be someone I'm not,'" Madison says. "They're clueless about how the world works. I tell them if you want to play basketball you can't run on court without a uniform or without knowing the rules."

9   It's fair to say it was ever thus: Cranky oldsters have always harrumphed about "those kids" who show up for work dressed like slobs or sluts. Yet these days it really does seem to many—young, old and not all cranky—that a lot of newcomers to the workforce are either completely unaware or outright defiant about what is appropriate attire for the office.

10   Listen to some of the voices from workplaces around the USA:

11   "A woman, and not a young one, wore yoga-type pants, a baggy T-shirt and terry-cloth-type scuff slippers to my office," says Dana Marsh, 35, a software company employee outside Washington, D.C.

12   "Our receptionist comes to work dressed for a night on the town, in tight pants, low-cut tops, short, short skirts," says Taresa Mikle, 29, a university business manager in Houston.

13   "A young woman arrived for her job interview "wearing a short, short sundress, looked completely sunburned and windblown, had on a backpack and Birkenstock sandals. And this was for an interview. "When I interviewed, I wore a suit and tie and I combed my hair," says Chris Massey, 24, who works at an advertising agency in Jacksonville.

14   Yikes. All of this leads to another age-old question: What were these people thinking?

15   Actually, experts say, the problem may be just that: They weren't thinking. Many have spent the previous four or five years in college happily dressing like slobs. Once they graduate, they don't have professional wardrobes, or the money to assemble one quickly, even if they know what to buy.

16   "Look at guys in college—they've got pierced ears, gel-spiked hair, goatees, flashy clothes, baggy jeans, big boots, unironed shirts, lint, stains, nothing matches," says Jared Shapiro, co-author of *Going Corporate: Moving Up Without Screwing Up*, a survival manual for the young and clueless. "In the corporate world, you have to dress like your boss, or the people above your boss."

17   "We have a lot of students who don't understand either business casual or business formal," says Stacey Harris, a university orientation official. Even for a formal event on campus, they'll show up in a skirt but a really, *really* short skirt. It's ridiculous."

18   For some young people, it's not ridiculous, it's who they are. For their baby-boomer parents, "being themselves" probably meant wearing their hair long; for this generation, it might be shaved heads and lots of tattoos.

19   "There is this attitude of, 'This is how I am, take it or leave it,'" says Jennifer Bosk, director of alumni relations at the joint campus of Indiana and Purdue Universities in Fort Wayne, Indiana.

20   "I wish there was a college course on how getting ahead doesn't depend just on how smart or good you are—it's partly playing the game and looking the part. But it doesn't seem to matter to this group."

21   That attitude won't do in the current take-no-prisoners economy. "Today's world is very competitive. "Getting and keeping a job is tough," says Kim Johnson Gross, co-author of several *Dress Smart* books. "It's not about you and your rights, it's about you representing a company and the brand culture of that company. It's about your clothes getting in the way of your message."

22   Of course, no one wants to return to the silly old days when women could be chastised—or even banned from the U.S. Senate floor—for wearing a pantsuit. But many people say the pendulum has swung too far.

23   Mary Lou Andre, an image consultant, helps her corporate clients understand the effect of wardrobes on their ability to communicate. She always says, "the more skin, the less power."

24   Once she saw a young woman in a Boston office lobby wearing an Ann Taylor suit and hot-pink flip-flops. "People can't help connecting the dots. Why would anyone trust that woman with their investments or their project if she doesn't have enough common sense to understand that's not OK?"

25 Young people who treasure their Goth look are just going to have to suck it up and go unGoth—or work in a record store, because the rest of the American working world is, as the current saying goes, "just not that into you" anymore.

"How NOT To Dress For Work," by Maria Puente from *USA Today,* December 1, 2004. Reprinted with permission.

COMPREHENSION CHECKUP

___c___ 1. The main idea of the selection is that
   a. in the world of work, the more skin that shows, the less power a person has.
   b. getting and keeping a job is very difficult.
   c. many newcomers to the workforce need to pay more attention to wearing appropriate business attire.
   d. there should be a college course on what to wear to work.

2. What does Anthony Poon mean when he talks about a balance between expressing creative flair and being professional? (paragraph 5)

   It's OK to be yourself, but look and be as professional as you can.

3. In paragraph 9, what two reasons does the author give to explain why young people show up at the office in inappropriate attire?

   a. They are unaware.

   b. They are outright defiant.

4. Paragraph 15 gives reasons to explain the behavior of the people cited as examples in paragraphs 11–13. List two of these reasons.

   a. They weren't thinking.

   b. They don't have professional wardrobes.

5. Explain how clothes can "get in the way of your message."

   You won't be taken seriously or considered to be responsible.

6. Explain the following expressions from the selection:

   a. "clueless about how the world works" no idea; unaware

   b. "looking the part" looking like you belong there

   c. "connecting the dots" figuring out the whole picture

d. "suck it up"   <u>just do it and don't complain</u>

e. "just not that into you"   <u>you're nothing special</u>

True or False

Directions: Indicate whether the statement is true or false by writing **T** or **F** in the blank provided.

<u>T</u>   1. The author suggests that many newcomers to the workforce do not understand how to dress appropriately for work.

<u>T</u>   2. According to Stacey Harris, the concept of business casual or business formal is confusing to a lot of students.

<u>T</u>   3. A take-no-prisoners economy is a cut-throat economy.

<u>T</u>   4. If the pendulum has swung too far, it means that things have gone to an extreme in one direction.

<u>F</u>   5. A person with pizzazz is likely to be dull and passive.

<u>F</u>   6. The author would likely consider flip-flops to be appropriate attire for a job interview.

<u>F</u>   7. The expression "scores of young workers" implies very few.

<u>T</u>   8. Age-old questions are likely to have been asked many times before.

Vocabulary in Context

Directions: For each question, look in the paragraph listed in parentheses and find the word that matches the definition.

1. <u>slinky</u>   (paragraph 1) made of soft, clinging material that follows the body closely

2. <u>alienate</u>   (paragraph 5) estrange; make indifferent or hostile

3. <u>flair</u>   (paragraph 5) knack; talent; ability

4. <u>muddle</u>   (paragraph 6) confused state of affairs; mess

5. <u>prestigious</u>   (paragraph 7) having a high reputation; esteemed

6. _____cranky_____ (paragraph 9) ill-tempered; grouchy

7. _____defiant_____ (paragraph 9) show open disregard; be contemptuous

8. _____chastised_____ (paragraph 22) criticized severely

9. _____banned_____ (paragraph 22) prohibited; barred

10. _____treasure_____ (paragraph 25) greatly value; prize

In Your Own Words

1. Many psychologists believe that people evaluate each other within a few minutes of meeting for the first time. And we tend to make an immediate judgment about the other person based on what we see. In your experience, do you think first impressions matter? Why or why not?

2. Do you think casual Fridays at the office are a good idea? Does informal clothing lead to informal behavior at work?

3. Many etiquette books say that the best advice about what to wear to the office is to dress each day as if you were going to an interview. Do you agree? Why or why not?

4. Do you think what employees wear to work can affect the success of their business? For instance, if an employee dresses sloppily, do you think a customer might assume that the business is poorly organized?

Written Assignment

It is said that what you wear on the outside is a reflection of who you are on the inside. What do you think your clothing says about who you are? Do you think your school clothing indicates that you are a capable person? Does the clothing you wear to job interviews say "Hire Me, I'm the best person for the job"? Write a paragraph giving your answers to these questions.

Internet Activity

Additional pointers on dressing appropriately can be found by conducting the following Internet searches: "tips on dressing for interviews" and "tips on appropriate business dress." Consult one of the sites below and list some of the tips you find there. To find more tips, you might want to visit *The Etiquette Ladies* (Lowena Bayer and Karen Mallett) at their website:

http://www.etiquetteladies.com

Or take their "Dress for Success Test" at

http://www.canoe.ca/LifewiseWorkEtiquette/eti-work6.html

"Milton Hershey was both a dreamer and a builder."

GETTING FOCUSED

The only place where success comes before work is in the dictionary. Milton Hershey is an example of a person who worked hard at the candy-making business and eventually found success.

BIO-SKETCH

William Nickels is an associate professor of business at the University of Maryland. Jim McHugh is an associate professor of business at St. Louis Community College. And Susan McHugh is a learning specialist with extensive training and experience in adult education and curriculum development.

TACKLING VOCABULARY

apprenticeship   a process of on-the-job training by which a person learns a trade from someone with skill and experience

trolley   Trolley cars, which were common in the first half of the twentieth century, are the forerunner of modern light-rail systems now being built in many metropolitan areas. As with modern light rail, trolley cars usually ran on tracks and were connected to overhead electrical power lines.

renowned   celebrated or famous

endowments   large amounts of money given to support institutions such as universities

HERSHEY'S CHOCOLATE

William G. Nickels, Jim McHugh, and Susan McHugh

Every kid deserves a hug and a kiss. At least that's what Milton Hershey, founder of the Hershey Chocolate Company (now Hershey Foods Corporation), thought. Way back in 1907, when Hershey first introduced Hershey's Kisses, each little chocolate was hand-wrapped. Today's wrapping machines can wrap up to 33 million Kisses a day—that's more than 12 billion a year! As sweet as a Hershey's Kiss is, it is only one of dozens of types of candy produced and distributed by Hershey Foods today.

2   Milton Hershey's love for candy-making started early in his life. After a brief apprenticeship with a candy-maker, Hershey opened his own candy shop in Philadelphia when he was only 18. That shop failed after six years. Hershey knew he needed to learn a lot more about candy-making and quality in order to succeed. He traveled to Denver, Colorado, to work in a caramel factory where he learned about the benefits of using fresh milk in the candy-making process.

"You always pass failure on the way to success."

—Mickey Rooney

3   Soon Hershey thought he was ready to try it on his own again. He first set up shop in Chicago, then New Orleans, and then New York City. Eventually he ended up in Lancaster, Pennsylvania, where he was finally successful in forming the Lancaster Caramel Company. Hershey designed some equipment to cover the caramel with chocolate and, as they say, the rest is history. Hershey sold the caramel company but kept the chocolate-making equipment and the rights to make chocolate. Hershey returned to his birthplace, Derry Church, Pennsylvania, and built a chocolate manufacturing plant near the heart of dairy country, where he could get the fresh milk he needed to make the finest milk chocolate.

4   Hershey built a new community, Hershey, Pennsylvania, around his chocolate plant. Soon the town sported a bank, a department store, a school, a park, several churches, a golf course, a zoo, and a trolley system (to bring in workers from nearby towns). The town remains very much a company town. The streets have names such as Chocolate and Cocoa. The bank gives its customers Hershey's Kisses. The street lamps are shaped like kisses.

5   Hershey was renowned for supporting his workers during the Great Depression of the 1930s. Hershey kept people at work building a grand hotel, a community building, a sports arena, and a new office building for the factory. During World War II, when Hershey had to stop production of Kisses because the foil wrappers were needed for the war effort, Hershey used his chocolate-molding department to make over 3 billion chocolate rations for the military troops.

6   Milton Hershey and his wife, Catherine, believed that people are morally obligated to share the fruits of their success. They established the Hershey Industrial School, now called the Milton Hershey School. The school houses, feeds, clothes, and educates some 1,300 disadvantaged children. The school still owns a substantial share of Hershey's Foods. In fact, the school's endowment fund, now valued at over $5.4 billion, is larger than the endowments of most Ivy League colleges.

7   Milton Hershey was both a dreamer and a builder. He had the genius to develop his chocolate business in the right place at the right time. His personal convictions about the obligations of wealth and the quality of life in the town he founded have made the company, the community, and the school his living legacy.

Excerpts from *Understanding Business*, 7th ed., William Nickels et al. Copyright © 2005 The McGraw-Hill Companies, Inc. Reprinted by permission of The McGraw-Hill Companies, Inc.

 COMPREHENSION CHECKUP

Multiple Choice

Directions: Write the letter for the correct answer to each question on the lines provided.

_____b_____ 1. The city of Hershey, Pennsylvania, was
     a. originally called Lancaster.
     b. a new city built around the Hershey factory in Derry Church.
     c. an old community that began in the 1700s.
     d. none of the above.

_a_ 2. Hershey set up his own chocolate shops or plants in all of the following cities *except*

    a. Denver.

    b. New Orleans.

    c. Chicago.

    d. Derry Church.

_d_ 3. You can infer from this article that Hershey

    a. was more interested in making money than the welfare of his workers.

    b. succeeded with his first candy shop.

    c. today produces about 12 different types of candy.

    d. gave some of his earnings back to the community.

_b_ 4. The Milton Hershey School

    a. is mainly for children from wealthy families.

    b. has students from families without much money.

    c. is poorly funded.

    d. is not interested in educating children.

_d_ 5. Hershey was born in

    a. New York City.

    b. Chicago.

    c. Denver.

    d. none of the above.

True or False

Directions: Indicate whether the statement is true or false by writing **T** or **F** in the blank provided.

_T_ 1. Hershey was 24 years old when his first shop failed.

_F_ 2. Hershey had to fire most of his workers during the Great Depression.

_F_ 3. Hershey chocolates are still hand-wrapped.

_T_ 4. Troops who fought in World War II ate chocolate made by Hershey.

_T_ 5. Hershey sold a caramel company.

Vocabulary in Context

Directions: Read each statement and select the appropriate word from the list to fill in the blank. Then write each word in the puzzle.

apprenticeship	distributed	molding	renowned
benefits	endowments	obligated	sported
convictions	legacy	plants	

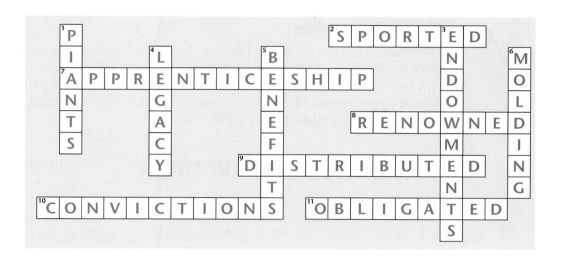

ACROSS CLUES

2. Most cities that have hosted the Olympic games have ___sported___ new stadiums and arenas.

7. Plumbers and electricians often go through formal ___apprenticeship___ programs.

8. Orlando, Florida, is ___renowned___ as the home of Disney World.

9. The Red Cross ___distributed___ various necessities to the people of New Orleans after Hurricane Katrina.

10. Many people have strong ___convictions___ in relation to abortion.

11. All of us are ___obligated___ to pay our taxes.

DOWN CLUES

1. General Motors and Ford have closed several of their automobile manufacturing ___plants___.

3. Bill and Melinda Gates have given ___endowments___ to universities and nonprofit programs.

4. The ___legacy___ of Martin Luther King was his desire to have racial equality.

5. We are learning more about the health ___benefits___ of eating chocolate.

6. ___Molding___ machines are used to form molten steel into pipes.

In Your Own Words

1. On some farms, cacao trees are grown with native plants and pesticides are not used. Are you willing to pay more for chocolate that is labeled organic?

2. Dutch researchers say that dark chocolate contains large amounts of catechin antioxidants, which may have a protective effect against heart disease and possibly cancer. Antioxidants are said to improve health by removing free radicals. Given this information, do you think chocolate can be part of a healthful diet? How often do you eat dark chocolate?

3. Based on your own experience, do you think eating chocolate helps relieve stress?

4. Do you think that people should consume only so much chocolate? How much is too much?

Written Assignment

Directions: Chocolate that is labeled "fair trade" guarantees farmers a fair price for their cocoa beans and is not produced by child or slave labor. Are you willing to pay a higher price for chocolate to ensure better living conditions for workers on cacao plantations? Read the following excerpt and then write a few paragraphs giving your opinion.

THE HIGH PRICE OF CHOCOLATE

In the spring of 2001, news media around the world reported a shameful tale that lies hidden behind the delicious taste of chocolate. Slave trading was revealed when a slave ship loaded with children was discovered off the coast of Benin in West Africa headed for cacao plantations in the Ivory Coast. Almost half of the world's cocoa is grown in West Africa, especially in the Ivory Coast. On some Ivory Coast plantations, cocoa beans are harvested by young boys, typically 12 to 16 years old. Many of them were lured from their homes and sold to plantation owners. The United Nations Children's Fund (UNICEF) indicates that as many as 200,000 children (both boys and girls) from West and Central Africa are taken from their families each year with the promise of a better life. Parents in Mali, Benin, and Burkina Faso are assured that their children will get an education and jobs in the Ivory Coast and Gabon. Parents often agree, believing that their children will also be sending money home in the future. Families are frequently given a token "advance" payment that may be as little as $15; this is usually the last time they see their children, and it may be the last time they receive any money. The children are passed along by middlemen and eventually sold to cocoa plantations, where they work as field hands, domestic workers, and even prostitutes. Children who have escaped from some of the plantations describe the deplorable living conditions, lack of food, hard work, and beatings. Consumers have no way of knowing whether the chocolate they are eating came from slave plantations because by the time the cocoa beans arrive at large chocolate companies in the United States and Europe, those harvested by slaves have been mixed in with those harvested by paid workers. Antislavery activists estimate that as much as 40% of the chocolate we eat might be produced with the help of child slaves. Human rights organizations are recommending that consumers ask chocolate companies for assurances that the chocolate they sell did not involve slave labor.

Levetin, Estelle, and McMahon, Karen, *Plants and Society*, 3rd edition, New York: McGraw-Hill, 2003, p. 266

2. **Directions:** What is your opinion of the following information? Do you accept the author's reasoning and conclusions? What is the author's tone of voice? Is the author trying to be funny or serious or some of each? Write a short paragraph discussing your conclusions.

IS CHOCOLATE A VEGETABLE?

- Chocolate is derived from cacao beans. Bean = vegetable. Sugar is derived from either sugar CANE or sugar BEETS. Both are plants, which places them in the vegetable category. Thus, chocolate is a vegetable.

- To go one step further, chocolate candy bars also contain milk, which is a dairy product. So candy bars are a health food.

- Chocolate-covered raisins, cherries, orange slices, strawberries, and cranberries all count as fruit; so eat as many as you want.

Diet tip: Eat a chocolate bar before each meal. It'll take the edge off your appetite, and you'll eat less.

- If calories are an issue, store your chocolate on top of the fridge. Calories are afraid of heights, and they will jump out of the chocolate to protect themselves. (We're testing this with other snack foods as well.)

NEWS FLASH: "Stressed" spelled backward is "desserts." So, to reverse being "stressed" . . . CHOCOLATE!!!

Author Unknown—from Thomas S. Ellsworth—Ed:anon.

Internet Activity

1. Go to the Hershey's website, www.hersheys.com, and find a Hershey's product you are not familiar with. Write a description of the product and three things you learned about it. The website is obviously written to get you to buy Hershey's products. What information might have been left out in the description of this product that could discourage you from buying it?

2. Do some chocolate research. Who gave chocolate its name and what does *theobroma cacao* mean? What did the Olmec, Mayan, and Aztec civilizations have to do with chocolate? What dishes are popular in Mexico that combine chocolate and chili?

RELATIONSHIPS AND BEHAVIOR

READING

"But the other person is obviously in pain. What should you do? Should you keep giving shocks or should you stop?"

GETTING FOCUSED

After World War II, the major excuse that Nazi officers gave for their participation in atrocities during the war was that they were "only following orders."

(continued)

As a result, psychologist Stanley Milgram became intrigued with the concept of obedience and conducted the classic experiment described below. Could Milgram's research also apply to the 2003 Abu Ghraib prison scandal?

BIO-SKETCH

The primary author of this textbook, Karen Huffman, is an associate professor at Palomar College in California.

TACKLING VOCABULARY

conformity   following of rules, order, customs, or accepted ideas

obedience   compliance with a command

SOCIAL INFLUENCE: CONFORMITY AND OBEDIENCE

Karen Huffman

Pretend for the moment that you are one of the people responding to this ad on the next page. As you arrive at the Yale University laboratory, you are introduced to the experimenter and to another participant in the experiment. The experimenter explains that he is studying the effects of punishment on learning and memory, and that one of you will play the role of the learner and the other will play the role of the teacher. You draw lots, and on your paper is written "teacher." The experimenter leads you into a room where he straps the other participant—the "learner"—into an "electric chair" apparatus that looks escape-proof. The experimenter then applies some electrode paste to the learner's wrist "to avoid blisters and burns" and attaches an electrode that is connected to a shock generator.

2   You are then shown into an adjacent room and asked to sit in front of the shock generator, which is wired through the wall to the chair of the learner. As you can see in the picture [p. 474], the shock machine consists of 30 switches that represent increasingly higher levels of shock in 15-volt increments. In addition, labels appear below each group of levers, ranging from "slight shock," to "danger: severe shock," all the way to "XXX."

3   The experimenter explains that it is your job to teach the learner a list of word pairs and to punish any errors by administering a shock. With each wrong answer, you are to give a shock one level higher on the shock generator—for example, at the first wrong response, you give a shock of 15 volts; at the second wrong response, 30 volts; and so on.

4   As the experiment begins, the learner seems to be having problems with the task because the responses are often wrong. Thus, you find that before long you are inflicting shocks that must be extremely painful. Indeed, after you administer 150 volts, the learner begins to protest and demands, "Get me out of here . . . I refuse to go on."

"All cruelty springs from weakness."

—Seneca

Public Announcement

WE WILL PAY YOU $4.00 FOR ONE HOUR OF YOUR TIME

Persons Needed for a Study of Memory

*We will pay five hundred New Haven men to help us complete a scientific study of memory and learning. The study is being done at Yale University.

*Each person who participates will be paid $4.00 (plus 50¢ carfare) for approximately 1 hour's time. We need you for only one hour; there are no further obligations. You may choose the time you would like to come (evenings, weekdays, or weekends).

*No special training, education, or experience is needed. We want:

Factory workers	Businessmen	Construction Workers
City employees	Clerks	Salespeople
Laborers	Professional people	White-collar workers
Barbers	Telephone workers	Others

All persons must be between the ages of 20 and 50. High school and college students cannot be used.

*If you meet these qualifications, fill out the coupon below and mail it now to Professor Stanley Milgram, Department of Psychology, Yale University, New Haven. You will be notified later of the specific time and place of the study. We reserve the right to decline any application.

*You will be paid $4.00 (plus 50¢ carfare) as soon as you arrive at the laboratory.

---

5   You hesitate and wonder what you should do. The experimenter urges you to continue and insists that even if the learner makes no response, you must keep increasing the shock levels. But the other person is obviously in pain. What should you do? Should you keep giving the shocks or should you stop?

6   Actual participants in this series of experiments suffered real conflict when confronted with this problem. The following dialogue took place between the experimenter and one of the teachers:

Teacher: I can't stand it. I'm not going to kill that man in there. You hear him hollering?

Experimenter: As I told you before, the shocks may be painful, but [there is no permanent tissue damage].

Learner (screaming): Let me out of here, you have no right to keep me here. Let me out of here, let me out, my heart's bothering me, let me out! (*Teacher shakes head, pats the table nervously.*)

Teacher: You see, he's hollering. Hear that? Gee, I don't know.

Experimenter: The experiment requires . . . .

Teacher (interrupting): I know it does, sir, but I mean—hunh! He doesn't know what he's getting in for. He's up to 195 volts!
(*Experiment continues through 210 volts, 225 volts, 240 volts, 255 volts, 270 volts, at which point the teacher, with evident relief, runs out of word-pair questions.*)

Experimenter: You'll have to go back to the beginning of that page and go through them again until he's learned them all correctly.

Teacher: Aw, no, I'm not going to kill that man. You mean I've got to keep going up with the scale? No sir. He's hollering in there. I'm not going to give him 450 volts.

"Just knowing what is right is not enough; we must do what is right."

—Anonymous

7   What do you think happened? Did the man continue? It may surprise you that this particular teacher continued to give shocks in spite of the learner's strong protests and even continued to the highest level when the learner refused to give any more answers.

8   As you may have guessed, the purpose of this experiment was not really to study the effects of punishment on learning. The psychologist who designed the experiment, Stanley Milgram, was investigating the question of obedience to authority. In fact, no shocks were administered at all—the "learner" was an accomplice of the experimenter and simply pretended to be shocked.

9   How obedient do you think you would have been? Milgram conducted a survey to determine how people expected they would perform in such an experiment. No one predicted that they would go past the 300-volt level, and less than 25 percent predicted that they would go beyond 150 volts. Even Milgram

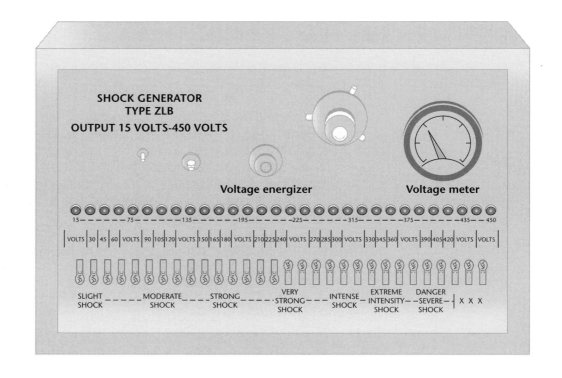

was surprised when a full 65 percent of the participants actually administered the maximum shock intensity.

"Social Influence: Conformity and Obedience" from *Psychology in Action,* 4th ed., by Karen Huffman et al. Copyright © 1997. Reprinted by permission of John Wiley & Sons, Inc.

Conformist or Nonconformist?

Now it's your turn. How do you think you would behave in the following situation? Would you be a conformist or a nonconformist? The following information is taken from *Psychology* by Dennis Coon.

QUACK LIKE A DUCK

Dennis Coon

Imagine your response to the following events. On the first day of class, your instructor begins to establish the basic rules of behavior for the course. Draw a line under the first instruction you think you would refuse to carry out.

1. Seats are assigned and you are told to move to a new location.
2. You are told not to talk during class.
3. Your instructor tells you that you must have permission to leave early.
4. You are told to bring your textbook to class at all times.
5. Your instructor tells you to use only a pencil for taking notes.
6. You are directed to take off your watch.
7. The instructor tells you to keep both hands on your desktop at all times.
8. You are instructed to keep both of your feet flat on the floor.
9. You are told to stand up and clap your hands three times.
10. Your instructor says, "Stick two fingers up your nose and quack like a duck."

At what point would you stop obeying such orders? In reality, you might find yourself obeying a legitimate authority long after that person's demands had become unreasonable. What would happen, though, if a few students resisted orders early in the sequence? Would that help free others to disobey?

Milgram discovered that group support can greatly reduce destructive obedience. When real subjects saw two other "teachers" (both actors) resist orders and walk out of the experiment, only 10 percent continued to obey. Thus, a personal act of courage or moral fortitude by one or two members of a group may free others to disobey misguided or unjust authority.

Excerpts from *Psychology: A Modular Approach to Mind and Behavior,* 10th ed., by Dennis Coon, 2006. Reprinted with permission of Wadsworth, a division of Thomson Learning: www.thomsonrights.com. Fax: 800-730-2215.

✔ COMPREHENSION CHECKUP

Multiple Choice

Directions: Write the letter for the correct answer to each question on the lines provided.

___b___ 1. The author's purpose in writing this selection about Milgram's experiment was to
  a. persuade the reader that his experiment was unethical.
  b. describe the experiment to introductory psychology students.
  c. entertain the reader with the experiment.
  d. explain how to administer shock treatments to encourage learning.

___c___ 2. The suffix *ful* in the word *painful* in paragraph 4 means
  a. above.
  b. under.
  c. full of.
  d. after.

___a___ 3. All of the following statements are true *except*
  a. there was an actual electric chair.
  b. the teacher continued with the shocks against his better judgment.
  c. the experimenter kept pushing the teacher to administer higher shocks.
  d. the study was conducted at Yale University.

___d___ 4. The main pattern of organization for this selection is
  a. compare and contrast.
  b. listing.
  c. classification.
  d. chronological order

___a___ 5. The prefix *mis* in *misguided* means
  a. badly.
  b. over.
  c. not.
  d. none of the above.

True or False

Directions: On the line in front of each statement, write **T** if the statement is true or **F** if the statement is false.

_____F_____ 1. This experiment shows that people in authority do not have much ability to elicit obedience.

_____T_____ 2. Milgram's experiment demonstrates that people can be coerced into actions that go against their values.

_____F_____ 3. The purpose of Milgram's experiment was to show a person how to teach through the giving of electric shocks.

_____T_____ 4. Milgram found that if one or two people in a group speak up, other group members may speak up as well.

_____T_____ 5. Many people are willing to obey an authority figure, even if doing so violates their own principles.

Vocabulary in Context

Directions: Using the context clues provided in the selection, match each word in column A with its correct definition from column B. Write the letter of the definition in the blank provided.

Column A		**Column B**
_____g_____	1. role	a. misled; mistaken
_____j_____	2. draw lots	b. proper; lawful
_____i_____	3. apparatus	c. encountered as something to be dealt with
_____m_____	4. adjacent	d. recommends earnestly; compels
_____h_____	5. increments	e. a person who knowingly helps another in wrongdoing
_____l_____	6. inflicting	f. the highest amount or degree
_____d_____	7. urges	g. a part or character
_____c_____	8. confronted	h. regular additions; an increase
_____n_____	9. evident	i. complex instrument for a particular purpose
_____e_____	10. accomplice	j. to choose by chance

f	11.	maximum	k.	strength or courage
b	12.	legitimate	l.	imposing something unwelcome
k	13.	fortitude	m.	near; adjoining
a	14.	misguided	n.	plain or clear

Sequencing

Directions: Place the events in the order in which they occurred in the selection, numbering the steps in order from first (1) to last (7).

<u> 4 </u>   You sit in front of a shock generator.

<u> 5 </u>   You administer a shock of 150 volts.

<u> 7 </u>   The word pairs are repeated, and the teacher continues to the highest level.

<u> 2 </u>   You draw lots.

<u> 3 </u>   The learner is strapped into an "electric chair."

<u> 1 </u>   You answer an ad at Yale University Laboratory.

<u> 6 </u>   At 270 volts, there are no more word pairs.

In Your Own Words

1. When is it good to obey authority? To disobey?

2. Who do you think is most obedient to authority—men or women? Why?

3. What do you think is the significance of Stanley Milgram's studies?

4. How much do you conform to others' expectations?

5. How does Milgram's experiment help to explain binge drinking in fraternity initiation rites?

6. How can people be taught to be less like sheep and to critically evaluate situations? How would you go about raising children to think for themselves?

Written Assignment

1. What does the following quotation mean to you?

   "If a man does not keep pace with his companions, perhaps it is because he hears a different drummer. Let him step to the music which he hears, however measured or far away." —Henry David Thoreau

   Give a brief explanation with concrete examples from your own life.

2. Milgram's research determined that "disobedient models can have a tremendous impact." For example, in one variation of his classic experiment, two "teachers" were instructed to refuse to shock the learner. The other teachers who watched the disobedient models were significantly less likely to be obedient.

   Do some research on the effects of important role models who defied authority. Some possible examples are Rosa Parks, who in 1955 stood up against discrimination in the Alabama bus system; employees of Rockwell International who in 1986 notified NASA officials that the *Challenger* space shuttle wasn't safe; and activist Karen Silkwood, who in 1974 campaigned against unsafe practices in the nuclear plant where she worked. Or go to the Internet to discover more recent whistleblowers. Write a few paragraphs discussing your findings.

3. Write a couple of paragraphs describing what your reaction would be in the following situation.

   You have just transferred to a new college and are attending your first class. When the instructor enters, your fellow classmates instantly rise, bow to the instructor, and then stand quietly, with their hands behind their backs. You've never encountered such behavior, and it makes no sense to you. Is it more likely that you will (1) jump up to join the rest of the class or (2) remain seated? Do you think experiments like this one and the one described by Milgram are ethical? Should experiments like this be allowed to take place on campus facilities?

   Robert S. Feldman *Understanding Psychology,* 7th ed., p. 213

Internet Activity

1. What happens when you put good people in an evil place? Read about the 1971 Stanford Prison experiment at the websites below. Try to answer the following question: Do you think the findings of Professor Zimbardo's study apply to the behavior of actual inmates and correctional officers in real prisons and jails?

   http://www.prisonexp.org/index.html

   http://www.zimbardo.com

2. Go to the website below to read parts of the "Charter of the International Military Tribunal," a document written for the Nuremberg trials that laid out the rules by which the Nazi officials were going to be tried. In

particular, read Article 6 of that document. How does it make the Nazi leaders responsible for their own actions?

http://www.law.umkc.edu/faculty/projects/ftrials/nuremberg/ NurembergIndictments.html

READING

"The emperor stood in front of the mirror admiring the clothes he couldn't see."

GETTING FOCUSED

Have there ever been occasions in your life when you were afraid to tell someone the truth because you thought you might be ridiculed or made to seem less intelligent than you really are? The story that follows illustrates what can happen when people fail to think for themselves.

BIO-SKETCH

Hans Christian Andersen was born in Odense, Denmark, in 1805. The son of a shoemaker, he grew up in poverty. It was his talent as a poet that first brought Andersen to the attention of Denmark's king, Frederick VI, who then became a patron. Andersen published his first collection of fairy tales in 1835. His goal in many of these tales was to point out the faults and weaknesses of human beings. Many of his best stories, including "The Little Mermaid" and "The Emperor's New Clothes," have a deeper meaning that only an adult can understand.

TACKLING VOCABULARY

attire   splendid garments

intricate   complex

crimson   deep, purplish red

canopy   a covering, usually of fabric, often supported by poles. It is suggestive of an occasion of splendor

THE EMPEROR'S NEW CLOTHES

Hans Christian Andersen

Many, many years ago there was an emperor who was so terribly fond of beautiful new clothes that he spent all his money on his attire. He did not care about his soldiers, or attending the theater, or even going for a drive in the

"We are never deceived; we deceive ourselves."

—Goethe

park, unless it was to show off his new clothes. He had an outfit for every hour of the day. And just as we say "The king is in his council chamber," his subjects used to say, "The emperor is in his clothes closet."

2   In the large town where the emperor's palace was, life was pleasant and happy; and every day new visitors arrived. One day two swindlers came. They told everybody that they were weavers and that they could weave the most marvelous cloth. Not only were the colors and patterns of their material extraordinarily beautiful, but the cloth had the strange quality of being invisible to anyone who was unfit for office, or unforgivably stupid.

3   "This is truly marvelous," thought the emperor. "Now if I had robes cut from that material, I should know which of my counselors were unfit for his office, and I would be able to pick out my clever subjects myself. They must weave some material for me!" And he gave the swindlers a lot of money so they could start working at once.

4   They set up a loom and acted as if they were weaving, but the loom was empty. The fine silk and gold threads they demanded from the emperor they never used, but hid them in their own knapsacks. Late into the night they would sit before their empty looms, pretending to weave.

5   "I would like to know how they are getting along," thought the emperor; but his heart beat strangely when he remembered that those who were stupid or unfit for their office would not be able to see the material. Not that he was really worried that this would happen to him. Still, it might be better to send someone else the first time and see how he fared. Everybody in town had heard about the cloth's magic quality and most of them could hardly wait to find out how stupid or unworthy their neighbors were.

6   "I shall send my faithful prime minister over to see how the weavers are getting along," thought the emperor. "He will know how to judge the material, for he is both clever and fit for his office, if any man is."

7   The good-natured old man stepped into the room where the weavers were working and saw the empty loom. He closed his eyes and opened them again. "God preserve me!" he thought. "I cannot see a thing!" But he didn't say it out loud.

8   The swindlers asked him to step a little closer to the loom so that he could admire the intricate patterns and marvelous colors of the material they were weaving. They both pointed to the empty loom, and the poor old prime minister opened his eyes as wide as he could; but it didn't help, he still couldn't see anything.

9   "Am I stupid?" he thought. "I can't believe it, but if it is so, it is best no one finds out about it. But maybe I am not fit for my office. No, that is worse, I'd better not admit that I can't see what they're weaving."

10   "Tell us what you think of it," demanded one of the swindlers.

11   "It is beautiful. It is lovely," mumbled the old prime minister, adjusting his glasses. "What patterns! What colors! I shall tell the emperor that it pleases me ever so much."

12   "That is a compliment," both the weavers said; and now they described the patterns and told which shades of color they had used. The prime minister listened attentively, so that he could repeat their words to the emperor; and that is exactly what he did.

13   The two swindlers demanded more money, and more silk and gold thread. They said they had to use it for their weaving, but their loom remained as empty as ever.

14   Soon the emperor sent another of his trusted counselors to see how the work was progressing. He looked and looked just as the prime minister had, but since there was nothing to be seen, he didn't see anything.

15   "Isn't it a marvelous piece of material?" asked one of the swindlers; and they both began to describe the beauty of their cloth again.

16   "I am not stupid," thought the emperor's co-counselor. "I must be unfit for my office. That is strange; but I'd better not admit it to anyone." And he started to praise the material, which he could not see, for the loveliness of its patterns and colors.

17   "I think it is the most charming piece of material I have ever seen," declared the counselor to the emperor.

18   Everyone in town was talking about the marvelous cloth that the swindlers were weaving.

19   At last the emperor himself decided to see it before it was removed from the loom. Attended by the most important people in the empire, among them the prime minister and the counselor who had been there before, the emperor entered the room where the weavers were weaving furiously on their empty loom.

20   "Isn't it magnificent?" asked the prime minister.

21   "Your Majesty, look at the colors and the patterns," said the counselor.

22   And the two old gentlemen pointed to the empty loom, believing that all the rest of the company could see the cloth.

23   "What!" thought the emperor. "I can't see a thing! Why, this is a disaster! Am I stupid? Am I unfit to be emperor? Oh, it is too horrible!" Aloud, he said, "It is very lovely. It has my approval," while he nodded his head and looked at the empty loom.

24   All the counselors, ministers, and men of great importance who had come with him stared, and stared; but they saw no more than the emperor had seen, and they said the same thing that he had said, "It is lovely." And they advised him to have clothes cut and sewn, so that he could wear them in the procession at the next great celebration.

25   "It is magnificent! Beautiful! Excellent!" All of their mouths agreed, though none of their eyes had seen anything. The two swindlers were decorated and each given the title "Royal Knight of the Loom."

26   The night before the procession, the two swindlers didn't sleep at all. They had sixteen candles lighting up the room where they worked. Everyone could see how busy they were, getting their emperor's new clothes finished. They pretended to take the cloth from the loom; they cut the air with their big scissors, and sewed with needles without thread. At last they announced: "The emperor's clothes are ready!"

27   Together with his courtiers, the emperor came. The swindlers lifted their arms as if they were holding something in their hands, and said, "These are the trousers. This is the robe, and there is the train. They are all as light as if they were made of spider webs! It will be as if Your Majesty had almost nothing on, but that is their special virtue."

28   "Oh, yes," breathed all the courtiers; but they saw nothing for there was nothing to be seen.

29   "Will your Imperial Majesty be so gracious as to take off your clothes?" asked the swindlers. "Over there by the big mirror, we shall help you put your new ones on."

30   The emperor did as he was told; and the swindlers acted as if they were dressing him in the clothes they should have made. Finally they tied around his waist the long train which two of his most noble courtiers were to carry.

31 The emperor stood in front of the mirror admiring the clothes he couldn't see.

32 "Oh, how they suit you! A perfect fit!" everyone exclaimed. "What colors! What patterns! The new clothes are magnificent!"

33 "The crimson canopy, under which Your Imperial Majesty is to walk, is waiting outside," said the imperial master of court ceremony.

34 "Well I am dressed. Aren't my clothes becoming?" the emperor turned around once more in front of the mirror, pretending to study his finery.

35 The two gentlemen of the imperial bedchamber fumbled on the floor, trying to find the train which they were supposed to carry. They didn't dare admit that they didn't see anything, so they pretended to pick up the train and held their hands as if they were carrying it.

36 The emperor walked in the procession under his crimson canopy. And all the people of the town, who had lined the streets or were looking down from the windows, said that the emperor's clothes were beautiful. "What a magnificent robe! And the train! How well the emperor's clothes suit him!"

37 None of them were willing to admit that they hadn't seen a thing; for if anyone did, then he was either stupid or unfit for the job he held. Never before had the emperor's clothes been such a success.

38 "But he doesn't have anything on!" cried a little child.

39 "Listen to the innocent one," said the proud father, and the people whispered among each other and repeated what the child had said.

40 "He doesn't have anything on. There's a little child who says that he has nothing on."

41 "He has nothing on!" shouted all the people at last.

42 The emperor shivered, for he was certain that they were right; but he thought, "I must bear it until the procession is over." And he walked even more proudly, and the two gentlemen of the imperial bedchamber went on carrying the train that wasn't there.

> "The Emperor's New Clothes" by Hans Christian Andersen from *A Treasury of Hans Christian Andersen,* translated by Erik Christian Haugaard.

COMPREHENSION CHECKUP

Multiple Choice

Directions: Write the letter of the best answer for each question in the space provided without looking back at the story.

_____a_____ 1. The swindlers in the story take advantage of the emperor's

    a. vanity.

    b. wisdom.

    c. compassion.

    d. generosity.

_____b_____ 2. The swindlers in the story claim that their fabric is invisible to all those who are

    a. successful.

    b. incompetent.

    c. intelligent.

    d. lazy.

_____c_____   3. The cloth is supposed to have properties that are
     a. glamorous.
     b. evil.
     c. magical.
     d. majestic.

_____c_____   4. The new clothes were said to be
     a. shabby.
     b. disgraceful.
     c. magnificent.
     d. disappointing.

_____b_____   5. When the emperor sent his counselors to see how the work was progressing, he was indicating his belief that the counselors were
     a. inefficient.
     b. trustworthy.
     c. ignorant.
     d. predictable.

_____b_____   6. When the cloth was finished, the two swindlers were
     a. reprimanded.
     b. commended.
     c. forgiven.
     d. arrested.

_____d_____   7. The king was made aware of his folly by a comment from
     a. the prime minister.
     b. the co-counselor.
     c. the courtiers.
     d. a young child.

_____c_____   8. Refusing to admit his mistake, the king continued to walk through the street with great
     a. shame.
     b. remorse.
     c. dignity.
     d. happiness.

_____b_____   9. The king's train was difficult to carry because
     a. it was very heavy.
     b. it was invisible.
     c. it was encrusted with jewels.
     d. it was as light as spiderwebs.

_____c_____ 10. The emperor's primary interest in life was
        a. taking care of his subjects.
        b. getting exercise.
        c. accumulating fine clothing.
        d. building his military.

Vocabulary in Context

Directions: Choose one of the following words to complete each of the sentences below. Use each word only once. Be sure to pay close attention to the context clues provided.

attentive	finery	fumbled	intricate	mumble
fared	fond	furiously	loom	procession

1. Even though Chad ____fared____ poorly on his driver's exam, he is not discouraged and will try to pass the test again in a couple of months.

2. Sara is so ____fond____ of her new car that she won't let anyone else drive it for even a minute.

3. Ingrid worked ____furiously____ to get her term paper completed before the professor's deadline.

4. The quarterback ____fumbled____ the ball in the last two minutes of the game, but luckily for him the other team failed to capitalize on his mistake.

5. At the Heard Museum Indian Fair, in Phoenix, Arizona, large crowds were gathered around the ____loom____ of Betty Bia, a master weaver.

6. Matt was so overly ____attentive____ to his date that she began to feel suffocated by his concern.

7. Because his mouth was full of food, Steve was only able to ____mumble____ when I asked him how he liked dinner.

8. Wilma's ____intricate____ bracelet features a small cameo inlaid with mother-of-pearl.

9. The presenters at the Grammy Awards are always dressed in showy ____finery____ from the collections of the leading American and European designers.

10. The Rose Bowl Parade, which is held in Pasadena, California, is a magnificent ____procession____ featuring bands and floats from around the country.

In Your Own Words

1. Why was it easy for the swindlers to deceive the emperor? To deceive the counselors? What does this story illustrate about human nature?

2. What enabled the young child to speak the truth so readily? What caused the adults to say what was convenient and socially acceptable rather than the real truth?

3. What kind of ruler do you think the king was? What does his consuming interest in his finery say about his character?

4. In what way did the king display his vanity? In what way did he display his pride?

5. Montaigne said, "There is nothing that poisons princes so much as flattery, and nothing by which the wicked more easily gain credit with them." What role does flattery play in the story?

Written Assignment

Write a modern-day version of "The Emperor's New Clothes." You might want to write your version of the story in today's slang (the clean variety!).

Internet Activity

The following website has 168 of Hans Christian Andersen's fairy tales. Read one of the tales and then briefly summarize it. Include your opinion of whether the story would be suitable for a child.

http://hca.gilead.org.il

READING

> "'It isn't fair, it isn't right,' Mrs. Hutchinson
> screamed and then they were upon her."

GETTING FOCUSED

An allegory is a narrative that has more than one level of meaning—a literal one and a symbolic one. In an allegory, the setting and each of the characters in the story symbolically represent particular ideas or qualities.

    One of the most famous allegories from the realm of popular culture is the film *Star Wars* and its sequels, *The Empire Strikes Back* and *Return of the Jedi*. Each of these stories, created by George Lucas, is based on the conflict between good (Luke Skywalker) and evil (Darth Vader). The other characters are also symbolic representations. Obi Wan Kenobi and Yoda represent wisdom and tradition. Han Solo represents the conflict between greed and virtue, and Princess Leia represents purity and goodness. In the final film, Luke and Darth battle for supremacy, and in the end Luke successfully defeats the "dark side," bringing peace and harmony to the galaxy.

READING *continued*

The Lottery, Shirley Jackson's best-known work, is also an allegory. By choosing to tell this story in an allegorical fashion, Jackson is able to go beyond its literal meaning by condemning those people who do not think for themselves. As you are reading this story, try to determine what each of the characters in the story is meant to symbolically represent.

BIO-SKETCH

Shirley Jackson was born in 1916 in California. A graduate of Syracuse University, she married literary critic Stanley Edgar Hyman in 1940 and settled in Bennington, Vermont. While raising her four children, she began to write the horror stories for which she achieved lasting fame. Her novel, *The Haunting of Hill House,* was made into a 1999 movie starring Liam Neeson, Owen Wilson, and Catherine Zeta-Jones. However, Jackson's most famous work is the short story *The Lottery,* which is featured below. In 1965, Jackson died in her sleep of apparent heart failure.

TACKLING VOCABULARY

lottery   a drawing of lots; any happening or process that is or appears to be determined by chance

THE LOTTERY

Shirley Jackson

The morning of June 27th was clear and sunny, with the fresh warmth of a full summer day; the flowers were blossoming profusely and the grass was richly green. The people of the village began to gather in the square, between the post office and the bank, around ten o'clock; in some towns there were so many people that the lottery took two days and had to be started on June 26th, but in this village, where there were only about three hundred people, the whole lottery took less than two hours, so it could begin at ten o'clock in the morning and still be through in time to allow the villagers to get home for noon dinner.

2   The children assembled first, of course. School was recently over for the summer, and the feeling of liberty sat uneasily on most of them; they tended to gather together quietly for a while before they broke into boisterous play, and their talk was still of the classroom and teacher, of books and reprimands. Bobby Martin had already stuffed his pockets full of stones, and the other boys soon followed his example, selecting the smoothest and roundest stones; Bobby and Harry Jones and Dickie Delacroix—the villagers pronounced this name "Dellacroy"—eventually made a great pile of stones in one corner of the square and guarded it against the raids of the other boys. The girls stood aside, talking among themselves, looking over their shoulders at the boys, and the very

small children rolled in the dust or clung to the hands of their older brothers or sisters.

3   Soon the men began to gather, surveying their own children, speaking of planting and rain, tractors and taxes. They stood together, away from the pile of stones in the corner, and their jokes were quiet and they smiled rather than laughed. The women, wearing faded house dresses and sweaters, came shortly after their menfolk. They greeted one another and exchanged bits of gossip as they went to join their husbands. Soon the women, standing by their husbands, began to call to their children, and the children came reluctantly, having to be called four or five times. Bobby Martin ducked under his mother's grasping hand and ran, laughing, back to the pile of stones. His father spoke up sharply, and Bobby came quickly and took his place between his father and his oldest brother.

4   The lottery was conducted—as were the square dances, the teenage club, the Halloween program—by Mr. Summers, who had time and energy to devote to civic activities. He was a round-faced, jovial man and he ran the coal business, and people were sorry for him, because he had no children and his wife was a scold. When he arrived in the square, carrying the black wooden box, there was a murmur of conversation among the villagers, and he waved and called, "Little late today, folks." The postmaster, Mr. Graves, followed him, carrying a three-legged stool, and the stool was put in the center of the square and Mr. Summers set the black box down on it. The villagers kept their distance, leaving a space between themselves and the stool, and when Mr. Summers said, "Some of you fellows want to give me a hand?" there was a hesitation before two men, Mr. Martin and his oldest son, Baxter, came forward to hold the box steady on the stool while Mr. Summers stirred up the papers inside it.

5   The original paraphernalia for the lottery had been lost long ago, and the black box now resting on the stool had been put into use even before Old Man Warner, the oldest man in town, was born. Mr. Summers spoke frequently to the villagers about making a new box, but no one liked to upset even as much tradition as was represented by the black box. There was a story that the present box had been made with some pieces of the box that had preceded it, the one that had been constructed when the first people settled down to make a village here. Every year, after the lottery, Mr. Summers began talking again about a new box, but every year the subject was allowed to fade off without anything being done. The black box grew shabbier each year; by now it was no longer completely black but splintered badly along one side to show the original wood color, and in some places faded or stained.

6   Mr. Martin and his oldest son, Baxter, held the black box securely on the stool until Mr. Summers had stirred the papers thoroughly with his hand. Because so much of the ritual had been forgotten or discarded, Mr. Summers had been successful in having slips of paper substituted for the chips of wood that had been used for generations. Chips of wood, Mr. Summers had argued, had been all very well when the village was tiny, but now that the population was more than three hundred and likely to keep on growing, it was necessary to use something that would fit more easily into the black box. The night before the lottery, Mr. Summers and Mr. Graves made up the slips of paper and put them in the box, and it was then taken to the safe of Mr. Summers' coal company and locked up until Mr. Summers was ready to take it to the square next morning. The rest of the year, the box was put away, sometimes one place, sometimes another; it had spent one year in Mr. Graves' barn and another year underfoot

in the post office, and sometimes it was set on a shelf in the Martin grocery and left there.

7   There was a great deal of fussing to be done before Mr. Summers declared the lottery open. There were the lists to make up—of heads of families, heads of households in each family, members of each household in each family. There was no proper swearing-in of Mr. Summers by the postmaster, as the official of the lottery; at one time, some people remembered, there had been a recital of some sort, performed by the official of the lottery, a perfunctory, tuneless chant that had been rattled off duly each year; some people believed that the official of the lottery used to stand just so when he said or sang it, others believed that he was supposed to walk among the people, but years and years ago this part of the ritual had been allowed to lapse. There had been, also, a ritual salute, which the official of the lottery had had to use in addressing each person who came up to draw from the box, but this also had changed with time, until now it was felt necessary only for the official to speak to each person approaching. Mr. Summers was very good at all this; in his clean white shirt and blue jeans, with one hand resting carelessly on the black box, he seemed very proper and important as he talked interminably to Mr. Graves and the Martins.

8   Just as Mr. Summers finally left off talking and turned to the assembled villagers, Mrs. Hutchinson came hurriedly along the path to the square, her sweater thrown over her shoulders, and slid into place in the back of the crowd. "Clean forgot what day it was," she said to Mrs. Delacroix, who stood next to her, and they both laughed softly. "Thought my old man was out back stacking wood," Mrs. Hutchinson went on, "and then I looked out the window and the kids was gone, and then I remembered it was the twenty-seventh and came a-running." She dried her hands on her apron, and Mrs. Delacroix said, "You're in time though. They're still talking away up there."

9   Mrs. Hutchinson craned her neck to see through the crowd and found her husband and children standing near the front. She tapped Mrs. Delacroix on the arm as a farewell and began to make her way through the crowd. The people separated good-humoredly to let her through; two or three people said, in voices just loud enough to be heard across the crowd, "Here comes your Missus, Hutchinson," and "Bill, she made it after all." Mrs. Hutchinson reached her husband, and Mr. Summers, who had been waiting, said cheerfully, "Thought we were going to have to get on without you, Tessie." Mrs. Hutchinson said, grinning, "Wouldn't have me leave m'dishes in the sink, now, would you, Joe?" and soft laughter ran through the crowd as the people stirred back into position after Mrs. Hutchinson's arrival.

10   "Well, now," Mr. Summers said soberly, "guess we better get started, get this over with, so's we can go back to work. Anybody ain't here?"

11   "Dunbar," several people said. "Dunbar, Dunbar."

12   Mr. Summers consulted his list. "Clyde Dunbar," he said. "That's right. He's broke his leg, hasn't he? Who's drawing for him?"

13   "Me, I guess," a woman said, and Mr. Summers turned to look at her. "Wife draws for her husband," Mr. Summers said. "Don't you have a grown boy to do it for you, Janey?" Although Mr. Summers and everyone else in the village knew the answer perfectly well, it was the business of the official of the lottery to ask such questions formally. Mr. Summers waited with an expression of polite interest while Mrs. Dunbar answered.

14   "Horace's not but sixteen yet," Mrs. Dunbar said regretfully. "Guess I gotta fill in for the old man this year."

15   Right," Mr. Summers said. He made a note on the list he was holding. Then he asked, "Watson boy drawing this year?"

16   A tall boy in the crowd raised his hand. "Here," he said. "I'm drawing for m'mother and me." He blinked his eyes nervously and ducked his head as several voices in the crowd said things like "Good fellow, Jack," and "Glad to see your mother's got a man to do it."

17   Well," Mr. Summers said, "guess that's everyone. Old Man Warner make it?"

18   "Here," a voice said, and Mr. Summers nodded.

19   A sudden hush fell on the crowd as Mr. Summers cleared his throat and looked at the list. "All ready?" he called. "Now I'll read the names—heads of families first—and the men come up and take a paper out of the box. Keep the paper folded in your hand without looking at it until everyone has had a turn. Everything clear?"

20   The people had done it so many times that they only half listened to the directions; most of them were quiet, wetting their lips, not looking around. Then Mr. Summers raised one hand high and said, "Adams." A man disengaged himself from the crowd and came forward. "Hi, Steve," Mr. Summers said, and Mr. Adams said, "Hi, Joe." They grinned at one another humorlessly and nervously. Then Mr. Adams reached into the black box and took out a folded paper. He held it firmly by one corner as he turned and went hastily back to his place in the crowd, where he stood a little apart from his family, not looking down at his hand.

21   "Allen," Mr. Summers said, "Anderson . . . . Bentham."

22   "Seems like there's no time at all between lotteries any more," Mrs. Delacroix said to Mrs. Graves in the back row. "Seems like we got through with the last one only last week."

23   "Time sure goes fast," Mrs. Graves said.

24   "Clark . . . . Delacroix."

25   "There goes my old man," Mrs. Delacroix said. She held her breath while her husband went forward.

26   "Dunbar," Mr. Summers said, and Mrs. Dunbar went steadily to the box while one of the women said, "Go on Janey," and another said, "There she goes."

27   "We're next," Mrs. Graves said. She watched while Mr. Graves came around from the side of the box, greeted Mr. Summers gravely, and selected a slip of paper from the box. By now, all through the crowd there were men holding the small folded papers in their large hands, turning them over and over nervously. Mrs. Dunbar and her two sons stood together, Mrs. Dunbar holding the slip of paper.

28   "Harburt . . . . Hutchinson."

29   "Get up there, Bill," Mrs. Hutchinson said, and the people near her laughed.

30   "Jones."

31   "They do say," Mr. Adams said to Old Man Warner, who stood next to him, "that over in the north village they're talking of giving up the lottery."

32   Old Man Warner snorted. "Pack of crazy fools," he said "Listening to the young folks, nothings good enough for *them.* Next thing you know, they'll be wanting to go back to living in caves, nobody work any more, live *that way* for a while. Used to be a saying about 'Lottery in June, corn be heavy soon.' First thing you know, we'd all be eating stewed chickweed and acorns. There's *always* been a lottery," he added petulantly. "Bad enough to see young Joe Summers joking with everybody."

33   "Some places have already quit lotteries," Mrs. Adams said.

34   "Nothing but trouble in *that,*" Old Man Warner said stoutly. "Pack of young fools."

35 "Martin." And Bobby Martin watched his father go forward. "Overdyke . . . . Percy."

36 "I wish they'd hurry," Mrs. Dunbar said to her older son. "I wish they'd hurry."

37 "They're almost through," her son said.

38 "You get ready to run tell Dad," Mrs. Dunbar said.

39 Mr. Summers called his own name and then stepped forward precisely and selected a slip from the box. Then he called, "Warner."

40 "Seventy-seventh year I been in the lottery," Old Man Warner said as he went through the crowd. "Seventy-seventh time."

41 "Watson." The tall boy came awkwardly through the crowd. Someone said, "Don't be nervous, Jack," and Mr. Summers said, "Take your time, son."

42 "Zanini."

43 After that, there was a long pause, a breathless pause, until Mr. Summers holding his slip of paper in the air, said, "All right, fellows." For a minute, no one moved, and then all the slips of paper were opened. Suddenly, all the women began to speak at once, saying, "Who is it?" "Who's got it?" "Is it the Dunbars?" "Is it the Watsons?" Then the voices began to say, "It's Hutchinson. It's Bill," "Bill Hutchinson's got it."

44 "Go tell your father," Mrs. Dunbar said to her older son.

45 People began to look around to see the Hutchinsons. Bill Hutchinson was standing quiet, staring down at the paper in his hand. Suddenly, Tessie Hutchinson shouted to Mr. Summers, "You didn't give him time enough to take any paper he wanted. I saw you. It wasn't fair!"

46 "Be a good sport, Tessie," Mrs. Delacroix called, and Ms. Graves said, "All of us took the same chance."

47 "Shut up, Tessie," Bill Hutchinson said.

48 "Well, everyone," Mr. Summers said, "that was done pretty fast, and now we've got to be hurrying a little more to get done in time." He consulted his next list. "Bill," he said, "you draw for the Hutchinson family. You got any other households in the Hutchinsons?"

49 "There's Don and Eva," Mrs. Hutchinson yelled. "Make *them* take their chance!"

50 "Daughters draw with their husbands' families, Tessie," Mr. Summers said gently. "You know that as well as anyone else."

51 "It wasn't *fair*," Tessie said.

52 "I guess not, Joe," Bill Hutchinson said regretfully. "My daughter draws with her husband's family, that's only fair. And I've got no other family except the kids."

53 "Then, as far as drawing for families is concerned, it's you," Mr. Summers said in explanation, "and as far as drawing for households is concerned, that's you, too. Right?"

54 "Right," Bill Hutchinson said.

55 "How many kids, Bill?" Mr. Summers asked formally.

56 "Three," Bill Hutchinson said. There's Bill Jr., and Nancy, and little Dave. And Tessie and me."

57 "All right, then," Mr. Summers said. "Harry, you got their tickets back?"

58 Mr. Graves nodded and held up the slips of paper. "Put them in the box, then," Mr. Summers directed. "Take Bill's and put it in."

59 "I think we ought to start over," Mrs. Hutchinson said, as quietly as she could. "I tell you it wasn't *fair*. You didn't give him enough time to choose. *Everybody* saw that."

60   Mr. Graves had selected the five slips and put them in the box, and he dropped all the papers but those onto the ground, where the breeze caught them and lifted them off.

61   "Listen, everybody," Mrs. Hutchinson was saying to the people around her.

62   "Ready, Bill?" Mr. Summers asked, and Bill Hutchinson, with one quick glance around at his wife and children, nodded.

63   "Remember," Mr. Summers said, "take the slips and keep them folded until each person has taken one. Harry, you help little Dave." Mr. Graves took the hand of the little boy, who came willingly with him up to the box. "Take a paper out of the box, Davy," Mr. Summers said. Davy put his hand into the box and laughed.

64   "Take just *one* paper," Mr. Summers said. "Harry, you hold it for him." Mr. Graves took the child's hand and removed the folded paper from the tight fist and held it while little Dave stood next to him and looked up at him wonderingly.

65   "Nancy next," Mr. Summers said. Nancy was twelve, and her school friends breathed heavily as she went forward, switching her skirt, and took a slip daintily from the box. "Bill Jr.," Mr. Summers said, and Billy, his face red and his feet overlarge, nearly knocked the box over as he got a paper out. "Tessie," Mr. Summers said. She hesitated for a minute, looking around defiantly, and then set her lips and went up to the box. She snatched a paper out and held it behind her.

66   "Bill," Mr. Summers said, and Bill Hutchinson reached into the box and felt around, bringing his hand out at last with the slip of paper in it.

67   The crowd was quiet. A girl whispered, "I hope it's not Nancy," and the sound of the whisper reached the edges of the crowd.

68   "It's not the way it used to be," Old Man Warner said clearly. "People ain't the way they used to be."

69   "All right," Mr. Summers said. "Open the papers. Harry, you open little Davy's." Mr. Graves opened the slip of paper and there was a general sigh through the crowd as he held it up and everyone could see that it was blank. Nancy and Bill Jr. opened theirs at the same time, and both beamed and laughed, turning around to the crowd and holding their slips of paper above their heads.

70   "Tessie," Mr. Summers said. There was a pause, and then Mr. Summers looked at Bill Hutchinson, and Bill unfolded his paper and showed it. It was blank.

71   "It's Tessie," Mr. Summers said, and his voice was hushed. "Show us her paper, Bill."

72   Bill Hutchinson went over to his wife and forced the slip of paper out of her hand. It had a black spot on it, the black spot Mr. Summers had made the night before with the heavy pencil in the coal-company office. Bill Hutchinson held it up and there was a stir in the crowd.

73   "All right, folks," Mr. Summers said. "Let's finish quickly." Although the villagers had forgotten the ritual and lost the original black box, they still remembered to use stones. The pile of stones the boys had made earlier was ready; there were stones on the ground with the blowing scraps of paper that had come out of the box. Mrs. Delacroix selected a stone so large she had to pick it up with both hands and turned to Mrs. Dunbar. "Come on," she said. "Hurry up."

74   Mrs. Dunbar had small stones in both hands, and she said, gasping for breath, "I can't run at all. You'll have to go ahead and I'll catch up with you."

75   The children had stones already, and someone gave little Davy Hutchinson a few pebbles.

76   Tessie Hutchinson was in the center of a cleared space by now, and she held her hands out desperately as the villagers moved in on her. "It isn't fair," she said. A stone hit her on the side of the head.

"With luck on your side, you can do without brains."

—Giordano Bruno

77 Old Man Warner was saying, "Come on, come on, everyone." Steve Adams was in the front of the crowd of villagers, with Mrs. Graves beside him.

78 "It isn't fair, it isn't right," Mrs. Hutchinson screamed and then they were upon her. [1948]

POSTSCRIPT

After the story's initial publication in *The New Yorker* on June 28, 1948, Jackson received a lot of verbal and written abuse. She said that "millions of people, and my mother, had taken a pronounced dislike to me." Three main themes dominated the letters she received that first summer. These themes might be identified as "bewilderment, speculation, and plain old-fashioned abuse." Ironically, in the beginning, people were not as concerned with the meaning of the story, but rather "where these lotteries were held, and whether they could go there and watch."

✓ COMPREHENSION CHECKUP

Multiple Choice

Directions: Write the letter of the correct answer to each question on the lines provided.

_____c_____ 1. What was the original reason for having the lottery?
   a. to make use of the black box
   b. to gather for a joyous celebration
   c. to ensure a good harvest
   d. to give the children something to do during their summer vacation

_____d_____ 2. Why do the villagers continue to participate in the lottery every year?
   a. The black box is still in good condition.
   b. Mr. Summers and Mr. Graves are in favor of continuing.
   c. They would disappoint Old Man Warner.
   d. They don't want to break with tradition.

_____b_____ 3. Who appears to be in charge in the story?
   a. Mr. Graves
   b. Mr. Summers
   c. Old Man Warner
   d. Mr. Hutchinson

_____a_____ 4. Why did Tessie Hutchinson arrive late?
   a. She forgot what day it was.
   b. She stopped to gather rocks.
   c. She was gossiping with Mrs. Delacroix.
   d. She wanted Mr. Summers to start without her.

_____b_____ 5. What does Tessie say is wrong with the lottery?

    a. The lotteries are held too frequently.

    b. Her husband didn't have enough time to select the paper he wanted.

    c. Other towns have given the lottery up.

    d. The lottery is not modern enough.

_____d_____ 6. Tessie wants another family member to "draw" with the Hutchinson's. Who is it?

    a. her son Davy

    b. Harry Graves

    c. Bobby Martin

    d. her married daughter Eva

Vocabulary in Context

Directions: Using the vocabulary words below fill in the crossword puzzle.

beamed	hush	lapse	petulantly	underfoot
boisterous	interminably	paraphernalia	profusely	
gravely	jovial	perfunctory	reprimands	

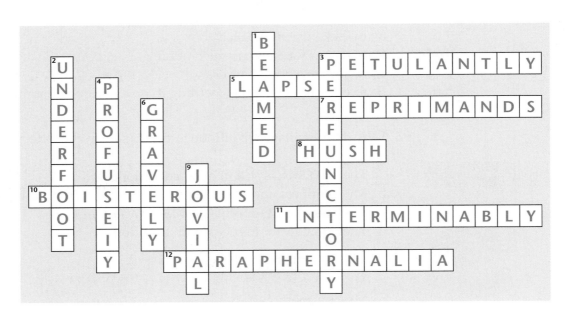

ACROSS CLUES

3. peevishly; showing sudden irritation over a trivial matter

5. fall into disuse

7. rebukes

8. silence

10. rough and noisy

11. unendingly

12. equipment; apparatus

DOWN CLUES

1. smiled brightly

2. in the way

3. unenthusiastic; apathetic

4. abundantly; in great amount

6. solemnly

9. jolly; good-natured

In Your Own Words

1. What new idea do Mr. Adams and Mrs. Adams mention? What do you think the two of them symbolically represent?

2. How does Old Man Warner respond to their suggestion? What do you think he symbolically represents?

3. What does Tessie's husband, Bill, symbolize?

4. Is Tessie's behavior typical of a mother? Why or why not?

5. What is the significance of the black box? In what way is it symbolic?

6. In what ways do some villagers demonstrate their reluctance and anxiety to participate in the proceedings?

7. What does the setting symbolically represent?

8. What does Mr. Summers symbolize?

Written Assignment

1. Make a profile sketch of Tessie by listing her key character traits. Some traits are directly stated in the story, and others must be inferred from the evidence presented. Be able to justify each of your descriptions by citing specific passages.

2. Write a few paragraphs discussing the many ironic elements in the story. You might want to start with the title.

Internet Activity

Jackson wrote about scary things. For fun, research the origin of Halloween. Share your findings with classmates.

READING

"But 2morrow I change. / A chance 2 build anew."

GETTING FOCUSED

How does the poem "And 2Morrow" address the issues of growing up around violence, poverty, and racism in the ghettoes?

BIO-SKETCH

Tupac Shakur—rapper, activist, and poet—attended the prestigious Baltimore School for Performing Arts as a youth, and then moved to Oakland, California, where he "hung with the wrong crowd." By age 20, he had already been

(continued)

arrested eight times and served eight months in prison. In 1994, he was shot five times, but survived. He was later killed in Las Vegas in 1996 in what is still an unsolved crime.

The name *Tupac* means "shining serpent" in Inca. The name *Shakur* means "thankful to god" in Arabic. Tupac is listed in the *Guinness Book of World Records* as the best-selling rap/hip-hop artist ever, having sold some 73 million albums worldwide. His music continues to be both popular and controversial.

TACKLING VOCABULARY

fueled   encouraged or stimulated by

gnawing   trouble or torment; erode

AND 2MORROW

Tupac Shakur

Today is filled with anger
Fueled with hidden hate
Scared of being outcast
Afraid of common fate
Today is built on tragedies
which no one wants 2 face
Nightmares 2 humanities
and morally disgraced
Tonight is filled with rage
Violence in the air
Children bred with ruthlessness
Because no one at home cares
Tonight I lay my head down
But the pressure never stops
gnawing at my sanity
content when I am dropped
But 2morrow I change
A chance 2 build anew
Built on spirit, intent of heart
And ideals based on truth
And 2morrow I wake with second wind
And strong because of pride
2 know I fought with all my heart
2 keep my dream alive

"The future belongs to those who believe in the beauty of their dreams."
—Eleanor Roosevelt

"And 2Morrow" from *The Rose That Grew from Concrete* by Tupac Shakur. Copyright © 1999 by The Estate of Tupac Shakur. Reprinted with permission.

COMPREHENSION CHECKUP

1. What two things are being contrasted in the poem? today and tomorrow

   _____

2. What does the author see as the difference between the two? Today is full

   of anger and hate. Tomorrow is full of promise.

3. Why do you think the author uses the numeral "2" in the poem? to reflect

   the "2" in the name Tupac

4. Does the poem end on a positive or negative note? Give reasons for your

   choice. positive – He's going to fight to fulfill his dreams.

5. What is the poet's attitude toward how children are raised? They are

   neglected and become ruthless.

6. What makes the poet feel strong and capable? His pride in knowing that he

   has fought hard to keep his dream alive makes him feel strong.

7. What makes the poet feel helpless and afraid? He's afraid of the violence

   and tragedy prevalent in the inner city.

8. What does "second wind" mean? overcoming tiredness and finding new

   energy and enthusiasm

9. What view of the world does the poet have? probably realistic given the

   circumstances of his life

Vocabulary in Context

Directions: If the italic vocabulary word is used correctly, write **T** on the line. If it is used incorrectly, write **F** on the line.

_____F_____ 1. An *outcast* is readily accepted by other members of the group.

_____T_____ 2. It was Romeo and Juliet's *fate* to fall in love.

_____T_____   3. There is no *disgrace* in losing if you do your best.

_____T_____   4. Her wish to make a better life for her family *fueled* her desire to get a good education.

_____F_____   5. It is one of life's *tragedies* to enjoy a picnic in the park.

_____T_____   6. Living through the devastating earthquake was a *nightmare*.

_____F_____   7. To be *ruthless* is to be compassionate and considerate.

_____T_____   8. Jealousy was *gnawing* at her heart.

_____T_____   9. She is a *morally* admirable person.

_____F_____   10. In her *rage* over having been elected president of the senior class, she thanked everyone within sight.

In Your Own Words

Do you think setting this poem to music would add to or detract from its message?

Written Assignment

Is there something you feel strongly about? Express your thoughts and feelings about this subject in a lyrical way. The poet Robert Frost wrote, "A poem begins in delight but ends in wisdom." Conclude your poem with some insight about your chosen subject.

Internet Activity

Do some research into the history of rap. Try to discover what elements it is composed of and who is credited with being the first rapper. Write a short paragraph giving your conclusions. .

Appendix: Answer Key for Warm-Up 2

Exercise 7: As cyanide "kills instantaneously and the muscles go limp," Maxim couldn't possibly have held the bottle clutched in his hand. It had to have been put there after death!

Exercise 8: No legal will could be dated November 31. November contains only 30 days.

Exercise 9: Rall could not have found the will between pages 157 and 158 as he claimed. Try putting a piece of paper between those pages in the book nearest you!

Exercise 10: Princess Minerva said she had not heard the thief enter her trailer. That ruled out Willie in his clanking and clattering knight's rig. When confronted with this inconsistency, Kathy confessed to the robbery.**"Success is dependent on effort."**

Credits

Text Credits

Introduction: pp. 4–6, From *Environmental Science: A Global Concern,* 9th ed., by William P. Cunningham et al. Copyright © 2007 The McGraw-Hill Companies, Inc. Reprinted by permission of The McGraw-Hill Companies, Inc.; **Pp. 12–14,** Reprinted with the permission of Scribner, an imprint of Simon & Schuster Adult Publishing Group, from *Best Seat in the House* by Christine Brennan. Copyright © 2006 by Christine Brennan. All rights reserved.

Warm-Up 1: p. 25 (Frank & Ernest) Copyright © 2003 Thaves. Reprinted by permission of Tom Thaves; **pp. 35–36,** "How a Prince Learned to Read" by James Baldwin is from The Baldwin Online Children's Literature Project at 222.mainlesson.com. Reprinted with permission.

Warm-Up 2: p. 50 (Wizard of ID) Reprinted by permission of John L. Hart FLP and Creators Syndicate, Inc.; **pp. 58–60,** Excerpts about Ancient Egyptian Writing are from *The Mystery of the Hieroglyphs: The Story of the Rosetta Stone and the Race to Decipher Egyptian Hieroglyphs* by Carol Donoughue. Illustrations by Claire Thorne. Copyright © 1999 by Carol Donoughue. Reprinted by permission of Oxford University Press.

Warm-Up 3: p. 66 (Frank & Ernest) Copyright © 2004 Thaves. Used by permission of Tom Thaves; **p. 68,** Family Circus © Bil Keane, Inc. King Features Syndicate; **pp. 85–86,** Excerpt reprinted with permission of Simon & Schuster Adult Publishing Group from *Life Is Not a Fairy Tale* by Fantasia. Copyright © 2005 19 Merchandising Ltd.; **p. 90,** Copyright © 1993 Gary Brookins, Richmond Times-Dispatch; **pp. 91–93,** "Doing What Comes Naturally" by Joe Kita from *Parents* magazine, December 1999. Reprinted by permission of the author.

Warm-Up 4: pp. 100–101, Excerpts from *Understanding Your Health,* 9th ed., by Wayne A. Payne et al. Copyright © 2007 The McGraw-Hill Publishing Companies, Inc. Reprinted by permission of The McGraw-Hill Companies, Inc.; **p. 108,** Copyright © The New Yorker Collection 2000 John Caldwell from cartoonbank.com. All Rights Reserved; **p. 108** Levin cartoon copyright ©

The New Yorker Collection 1998 Arnie Levin from cartoonbank.com. All Rights Reserved; **pp. 106–110,** Excerpts from *Power Learning,* 3rd ed., by Robert S. Feldman. Copyright © 2007 The McGraw-Hill Companies, Inc. Reprinted by permission of The McGraw-Hill Companies, Inc.; **pp. 116–119,** "Bat's New Image" by Anastasia Toufexis from *Time* magazine, August 20, 1995. Reprinted with permission of *Time,* via RightsLink and The Copyright Clearance Center.

Chapter 1: p. 124, © ZITS Partnership, King Features Syndicate; **p. 136,** Marmaduke © United Feature Syndicate; **p. 140,** "2 Shot Dead at Wal-Mart" by Pat Flannery, David Madrid and Christine Romero. Copyright © *Arizona Republic,* August 24, 2005. Used with permission. Permission does not imply endorsement; **p. 149,** Family Circus © Bill Keane, Inc. King Features Syndicate; **pp. 154–155,** Excerpts from *Psychology,* 7th ed., by John Santrock. Copyright © 2003 The McGraw-Hill Companies, Inc. Reprinted by permission of The McGraw-Hill Companies, Inc.

Chapter 2: p. 158, Copyright © The New Yorker Collection 1963 James Stevenson from cartoonbank.com. All Rights Reserved; **pp. 174–176,** "Fishin' Superstition: Its more than just luck" is reprinted by permission of ESPN Internet Ventures; **pp. 179–181,** "Hope Diamond" by Russell Smith is reprinted by permission of Russell Smith; **pp. 186–187,** "Stadium Nights" by Bob Greene. Copyright © 1992 by Bob Greene. Reprinted by permission of the author.

Chapter 3: p. 206, GARFIELD © Paws, Inc. Reprinted with permission of Universal Press Syndicate. All rights reserved; **pp. 209–210,** "Heroes" by Erma Bombeck is reprinted with permission from the Aaron M. Priest Literary Agency; **p. 216,** (Frank & Ernest) Copyright © 1999 Thaves. Used by permission of Tom Thaves; **pp. 225–226,** "The Survivor" by Thomas Fields-Meyer et al. from *People* magazine, May 26, 2003; **pp. 230–232,** "Stand up for Yourself" by Bruce Baldwin as published in *PACE* magazine, Piedmont Airlines, February 1987. Reprinted by permission of the author.

Chapter 4: p. 243 (B.C.) Copyright © Creators Syndicate, Inc.; **pp. 245–246,** "Water Water

Everywhere and Not a Drop for Free" by Dave Barry. Copyright © 2000 Dave Barry. Reprinted by permission of the author, and not to be duplicated without the author's permission; **pp. 256–257,** "Love and the Cabbie" by Art Buchwald. Reprinted by permission of the Estate of Art Buchwald; **pp. 260–262,** Excerpt from *Every Second Counts* by Lance Armstrong and Sally Jenkins. Copyright © 2003 by Lance Armstrong. Used by permission of Broadway Books, a division of Random House, Inc.; **pp. 266–267,** "The Big Hero of Littleton" by Rick Reilly from *The Life of Reilly: The Best of Sports Illustrated's Rick Reilly.* Copyright © 2000. Originally published in *Sports Illustrated,* May 3, 1999.

Chapter 5: p. 276, George B. Abbott cartoon is reprinted by permission of the artist; **p. 276,** Art Bouthillier cartoon is reprinted by permission of the artist. Art Bouthillier is an Editorial Cartoonist for *The South Whidbey Record* and can be reached at art@whidbey.com.; **p. 277,** Copyright © The New Yorker Collection 1990 Peter Steiner from cartoonbank.com. All Rights Reserved; **p. 278,** Copyright © Martha F. Campbell. Reprinted by permission of the artist; **pp. 294–303,** "Beware the Dog" from *Over To You: Ten Stories of Flyers and Flying* by Roald Dahl. Reprinted by permission of the Estate of Roald Dahl and the Watkins/Loomis Agency.

Chapter 6: p. 306, © ZITS Partnership. King Features Syndicate; **p. 308,** Dennis the Menace © North American Syndicate; **p. 310,** Family Circus © Bill Keane, Inc. King Features Syndicate; **p. 318,** CATHY © 1995 Cathy Guisewite. Reprinted with permission of Universal Press Syndicate. All rights reserved; **p. 324,** © ZITS partnership, King Features Syndicate; **pp. 327–329,** "Thunderbolts" from *The Winner Within* by Pat Riley. Copyright © 1993 by Riley & Company, Inc. Used by permission of G.P. Putnam's Sons, a division of Penguin Group (USA) Inc.

Chapter 7: pp. 350–352, Excerpts from *America and Its Peoples,* Vol. 2, 5th ed. by James Kirby Martin et al. Copyright © 2004 by James Kirby Martin, Randy Roberts, Steven Mintz, Linda O. McMurry and James H. Jones. Reprinted by permission of Pearson Education, Inc.

Chapter 8: p. 356, Doug Marlette cartoon copyright © Tribune Media Services, Inc. All Rights Reserved. Reprinted with permission; **pp. 372–373,** "Somebody's Baby" from *High Tides in Tucson: Essays From Now or Never* by Barbara Kingsolver. Copyright © 1995 by Barbara Kingsolver. Reprinted

by permission of HarperCollins Publishers; **p. 375,** Dennis the Menace © North America Syndicate; **pp. 377–379,** "Lizzie Bordon: Victorian Woman and Murderer" from *America and Its Peoples,* Vol. 2, 5th ed. by James Kirby Martin et al. Copyright © 2004 by James Kirby Martin, Randy Roberts, Steven Mintz, Linda O. McMurry and James H. Jones. Reprinted by permission of Pearson Education, Inc.; **pp. 384–385,** "What's So Great About America?" by Dinesh D'Souza from *The Arizona Republic,* July 21, 2002. Reprinted by permission of the author; **p. 389,** "For Conversation, Press 1" by Michael Alvear. Reprinted by permission of the author; **p. 393,** Excerpts from *Understanding Psychology,* 7th ed., by Charles G. Morris and Albert A. Maisto. Copyright © 2006. Reprinted by permission of Pearson Education, Inc.; **p. 398,** DOONESBURY. Universal Press Syndicate © 2000 Garry Trudeau.

Chapter 9: p. 416, Fig. 9.12 Arnie Levin cartoon copyright © The New Yorker Collection 1993 Arnie Levin from cartoonbank.com. All Rights Reserved; **pp. 417–419,** Excerpts from *Personal Finance,* 8th ed., Jack Kapoor et al. Copyright © 2007 The McGraw-Hill Companies, Inc. Reprinted by permission of The McGraw-Hill Companies, Inc.

Chapter 10: pp. 430–436, Excerpts from *Power Learning,* 3rd ed., by Robert S. Feldman. Copyright © 2007 The McGraw-Hill Companies, Inc. Reprinted by permission of The McGraw-Hill Companies, Inc.; **pp. 440–444,** Excerpts from *Psychology: A Modular Approach to Mind and Behavior,* 10th ed., by Dennis Coon, 2006. Reprinted with permission of Wadsworth, a division of Thomson Learning: www.thomsonrights.com. Fax: 800-730-2215.

Chapter 11: pp. 456–459, "The Fence That Me and Shorty Built" by Red Steagall. Reprinted with permission by the author, Red Steagall; **pp. 461–462,** "How NOT To Dress For Work," by Maria Puente from *USA Today,* December 1, 2004. Reprinted with permission; **pp. 466–467,** Excerpts from *Understanding Business,* 7th ed., William Nickels et al. Copyright © 2005 The McGraw-Hill Companies, Inc. Reprinted by permission of The McGraw-Hill Companies, Inc.; **pp. 472–475,** "Social Influence: Conformity and Obedience" from *Psychology in Action,* 4th ed., by Karen Huffman et al. Copyright © 1997. Reprinted by permission of John Wiley & Sons, Inc.; **pp. 475,** Excerpts from *Psychology: A Modular Approach to Mind and Behavior,* 10th ed., by Dennis Coon, 2006. Reprinted with permission of Wadsworth, a division of Thomson Learning: www.thomsonrights.com. Fax: 800-730-2215;

pp. 480–483, "The Emperors New Clothes" by Hans Christian Andersen from *A Treasury of Hans Christian Andersen*, translated by Erik Christian Haugaard; **pp. 487–493,** "The Lottery" from *The Lottery* by Shirley Jackson. Copyright © 1948, 1949 by Shirley Jackson. Copyright renewed 1976, 1977 by Laurence Hyman, Barry Hyman, Mrs. Sarah Webster and Mrs. Joanne Schnurer. Reprinted by permission of Farrar, Straus and Giroux, LLC; **p. 496,** "And2Morrow" from *The Rose That Grew from Concrete* by Tupac Shakur. Copyright © 1999 by The Estate of Tupac Shakur. Reprinted with permission.

Photo Credits

Page 1: AP Images/Jack Smith; **36:** Archivo Iconografico, SA/Corbis; **61:** © Burke/Triolo/Brand X Pictures/Jupiterimages; **84:** Robert Galbraith/Reuters/Corbis; **115:** Courtesy of Mel Clayton Ford; **117:** Reprinted with permission of the copyright owner, Dex Media, Inc.; **123:** AP Images/Petros Giannakouris; **180:** Smithsonian Institution/Corbis; **185:** Reuters/Corbis; **196:** © Comstock Images/Alamy; **208:** AP Images/Mark Inglis; **254:** (left) Jacket Cover from The Wall Street Journal Guide to Understanding Money and Investing by Kenneth M. Morris and Virginia M. Morris. Used by permission of Fireside, a division of Simon & Schuster, Inc., (right) Jacket Cover from All Your Worth by Elizabeth Warren and Amelia Warren Tyagi. Used by permission of Free Press, a division of Simon & Schuster, Inc.; **255:** (left) "Book cover", copyright 2006, from Dave Barry's Money Secrets by Dave Barry. Used by permission of Crown Publishers, a division of Random House, Inc., (right) Jacket Cover from Strapped Why America's 20- and 30-Somethings Can't Get Ahead by Tamara Draut. Used by permission of Doubleday, a division of Random House, Inc.; **259:** © Wolfgang Rattay/Reuters/Corbis; **265:** AP Images; **271:** © Gregory Shamus/Getty Images; **272:** Bonnie McCarthy; **294:** Skyscan/Corbis; **326:** (top) Digital Vision/PunchStock, (bottom) John Wang/Getty Images; **344:** © Spencer Grant/PhotoEdit, Inc.; **350:** AP Images/Jack Harris; **364:** Courtesy of The Humane Society of the United States; **399:** AP Images/Aynsley Floyd; **400:** © Jeffrey Rotman/Getty Images; **415:** © Dr. Merlin D. Tuttle/Photo Researchers, Inc.; **451:** AP Images/EPA/Oliver Multhaup

Index